The Christian Story

The Christian Story

Authority: Scripture in the Church for the World

A Pastoral Systematics
VOLUME II

by
Gabriel Fackre

GRAND RAPIDS, MICHIGAN
WILLIAM B. EERDMANS PUBLISHING COMPANY

255 Jefferson Ave. S.E., Grand Rapids, Mich. 49503

Printed in the United States of America

Library of Congress Cataloging-in-Publication Data
(Revised for volume 2)

Fackre, Gabriel J.
The Christian story.

Includes indexes.
Contents: [v. 1]. A narrative interpretation of basic Christian doctrine—v. 2. Authority, scripture in the church for the world.

1. Theology, Doctrinal. I. Title.
BT75.2.F33 1984 230 85-205691

ISBN 0-8028-1989-3 (v. 1. : pbk.)
ISBN 0-8028-0276-1 (v. 2. : pbk.)

The publisher gratefully acknowledges the following for permission to quote from their publications:

John Knox Press; Orbis Books; Scholars Press; Westminster Press

From *Womenguides: Readings toward a Feminist Theology*, by Rosemary Radford Ruether, copyright 1985. Used by permission of Beacon Press.

From *In Memory of Her*, by Elisabeth Schussler Fiorenza, copyright 1983 by Elisabeth Schussler Fiorenza. Reprinted by permission of the Crossroad Publishing Company.

From *Models of Revelation*, by Avery Dulles, copyright 1983 by Avery Dulles. Used by permission of Doubleday and Co.

From *Challenges to Inerrancy: A Theological Response*, by Gordon Lewis and Bruce Demarest, Moody Bible Institute of Chicago, Moody Press. Used by permission.

From *The Battle for the Trinity*, © 1985 by Donald G. Bloesch. Published by Servant Publications, P.O. Box 8617, Ann Arbor, MI 48107. Used by permission.

From *Validity in Interpretation*, by E. D. Hirsch, Jr., copyright 1967 by Yale University Press. Used by permission.

Contents

To Dorothy
Life Partner on the Way to the Truth

Acknowledgments

This work is the second in the systematic series, *The Christian Story,* and the first of the volumes on individual topics. Originally the subject was "authority and revelation"; yet the longer it grew the clearer became the need to divide it into two volumes. Thus, Volume 2 is on the *concept* of authority and Volume 3 will treat the *doctrine* of revelation. Together they constitute an introduction to a narrative interpretation of Christian belief, preparing the way for subsequent individual volumes on other chapters in the Story—from the doctrine of creation to the doctrine of consummation.

First, some background. The research and writing for this volume have taken six years. The way I have gone about developing the material reflects my argument throughout for a truly catholic theological method. Both hermeneutics and systematics entail a running conversation within the whole people of God. Authenticity of result is related, I believe, to catholicity of perspective. Some of what this means is discussed in the autobiographical introduction to the entire series that is in this volume. Here I want to mention a few of the diverse partners in conversation who have made me think more deeply or differently about the authority of Scripture.

Evangelicals have pressed the authority of Scripture in our time. As an "evangelical ecumenical," I have listened hard and also questioned insistently. Exchanges with Carl Henry, Donald Bloesch, Clark Pinnock, Robert Johnston, David Wells, Mark Branson, Roger Nicole, Royce Gruenler, Mark Noll, Richard Peace, Gerald Sanders, Martin Duffy, William Boylan, and Lawrence Wood have been helpful to me. Evangelical meetings at the American Academy of Religion, a Wheaton College conference, visits to Gordon-Conwell Theological Seminary, dialogue with the Biblical Witness Fellowship in the United Church of Christ—all are settings that further sensitized me to evangelical concerns.

Feminists have raised serious questions about both the authority and interpretation of Scripture. Again, I have listened hard and questioned insistently. Within our Andover Newton faculty Ellie McLaughlin, Carole Fontaine, Jane Cary Peck, and earlier Phyllis Trible have made it impossible to avoid the soul-searching required by a "hermeneutics of suspicion." The Craigville Colloquies brought into existence a feminist dialogue group that caused much self-examination, with Lois Happe, Dee Crabtree, Barbara Gerlach, Valerie Russell, and Sharon Ringe posing critical questions. Others, with strong commitments to both the classical Christian tradition and critical awareness, were also influential, including Virginia Child, Elsabeth Hilke, Carole Baker, and Llewellyn Smith. Personal conversation over time in the American Theological Society, mission ventures, the ecumenical research center at St. John's Abbey, Collegeville, Minnesota, UCC theological projects, etc., with Letty Russell, Elisabeth Schüssler Fiorenza, Rosemary Radford Ruether, Susan Thistlethwaite, and Peggy Way have had their impact.

Roman Catholic thinking on authority and revelation cannot be far from one's mind when linked with Boston College in a joint graduate program. In these sixteen years, former colleagues Franz Joseph Van Beeck and Richard McBrien, and present colleagues Robert Daly, Pheme Perkins, Fred Lawrence, Ernest Fortin, and Matthew Lamb have broadened my outlook. On issues of authority and revelation, Avery Dulles has done most to instruct me, during his year of research at Boston College while writing *Models of Revelation,* and in association with him in the American Theological Society.

Our own Andover Newton faculty has been a very important testing place for some of these theses, both in theological give-and-take and in a particular faculty forum in which the last chapter of this book was scrutinized. Max Stackhouse and I have talked about these things for a very long time; so too George Peck, colleague in the systematics department as well as president of our school. Earlier, Roger Hazelton, and now my present and promising systematics colleague Mark Heim, have gone up one side and down the other. Charles Carlston has been especially helpful in New Testament matters, and William Robinson has asked tough questions in the same area. William Holladay in Old Testament has kept Jeremiah ever before me. Elsie McKee has provided Reformation perspective. Long-time friend and mission colleague Dean Orlando

Costas never lets me forget the Two-Thirds World in relation to which theology today must be done. On the same matter and related Hispanic perspectives Bob Pazmiño, Felix Carrion, and Mortimer Arias have reinforced that. Eddie O'Neal, who teaches black theology and powerfully represents it in its pastoral and preaching mode, regularly brings my abstractions down to earth. Black theological issues have also been clarified for me by Percel Alston and J. Deotis Roberts. As the genius of Andover Newton is its being a "school of the church," theology cannot be done outside the context of the practice of ministry. George Sinclair and Meredith Handspicker in the Church and Ministry Department, Joseph O'Donnell, Maria Harris, Julieanne Hallman, and Daniel Novotny, too, and Henry Brooks and Earl Thompson in pastoral psychology have left their mark on this venture. So also did deceased friend John Billinsky.

Teaching in the Boston area brings with it the advantage of relationships with eight other theological schools in the Boston Theological Institute. That means, among other things, membership in its systematics section, the Boston Theological Society. The society took time to react to some of the theses in this book and also has put up with my comments over the years on this and related subjects. I am grateful to Owen Thomas for his thoughtful response to the specifics. In this group Gordon Kaufman, Paul Van Buren, Francis Schüssler Fiorenza, Leroy Rouner, and John Connelly have also probed where things needed to be probed. James Luther Adams's notes, counsel, and comradeship over forty years, as well as associations with him in Boston academia, have meant much to my wife, Dot, as well as to me. Correspondence or conversation with other theological colleagues on hermeneutical matters, especially Bernard Anderson, Carl Braaten, and Paul Knitter have helped. Theological writings that have left their mark can be seen from the contents and endnotes themselves.

Theological collegiality with students has had a formative role in this work. This is especially true of the several hundred members in the year-long systematic theology sequences in the mid-eighties who forced me daily to defend my theses, and puzzled over and improved my diagrams. Many conversations with Natan Setiabudi about this text and his doctoral work gave me a needed Asian perspective. A seminar in "The Use of the Bible in Theology" in 1986 worked with me while on its own hermeneutical journey. From that latter group Phil Jamieson, Mary DeSocio, Patricia Anderson, Mark New, and David Atwell tracked down a number of footnotes for Chapter 2. In that same group and also in the systematics class I am deeply indebted to Betsy Horner, whose skill in both biblical studies and computers enabled the transfer of this manuscript to the word processor. Faculty secretary Kay Coughlin was a big assist in production as well.

Teaching at Andover Newton means relationship to The Center for the Ministry of the Laity. The stress on "the whole people of God" throughout this work reflects some of its eight-year influence on me. I pay tribute in particular to Richard Broholm, who conceived the center, and to the laity in it who made me say more clearly what I mean. In particular, I thank Ned Bennett and Fred Rozelle, whose witness in the workplace has meant "the cost of discipleship." Also important have been laity in the science task force at Eliot Church who have engaged me in dialogue about these things, especially Arnold Reif and Philip Sharp, scientists who take their theology seriously.

I speak in the Introduction about the influence of pastors in the forming of a systematics that is written for them. In these acknowledgments, however, I want to thank some of the people who especially left their mark: Herbert Davis, friend and ally in mission for twenty-five years—from Mississippi voter registration campaigns in the sixties to leadership in the Craigville Colloquies in the eighties; Monday morning Theological Tabletalkers James Crawford, Joseph Bassett, Norman De Puy, John O'Donnell, Pat Green, Kenneth Williams, James Demarais-Morse, Gary Jenkins, Jean Curtis, Thomas Boates, Paul Sangree, Lori Buehler, Diane Kessler, Patrick Downey, and Jonathan Mills; holding his own in this group of preachers is *Atlantic Monthly* senior editor Michael Curtis; Boston Ministers Club members Horace Allen, Harry and Judith Hoehler, Peter Conley, Stanley Harakas, Mary Hennessy, George Williams, Amos Wilder, James Nash; other stalwarts in the United Church of Christ mission and theological renewal movements, George Geisler, Francis X. Pirazzini, Steven Wayles, Daniel Johnson, Allen Happe, Howard Paine, Harry Royer, Frederick Trost, Theodore Trost, Donald Overlock, Alfred Williams, William McKinney, Richard Floyd, George Nye, Alan McLean, Robert Davis, David Yohn, and Craig Millett; theologically concerned people within the structures of the United Church of Christ including Thomas Dipko, Robert Witham, Reuben Sheares, and Avery Post; William Baran, friend and pastor of South Church, Centerville, Massachusetts; Wallace Fisher, Lutheran pastor and comrade in mission.

Real occasions as well as real people have been important to the birth of this book. Some of them are mentioned in its autobiographical section. Here I want especially to thank the creators and participants of the Craigville Colloquies. Craigville Center director and lay theologian Richard Eggers made it possible for them to happen. Craigville's resident biblical theologian, Willis Elliott, has not only been crucial to that process but also a valued regular partner in conversation on theological basics. Several national gatherings of "ecumenicals, evangelicals, and charismatics" brought to be by Albert Outler provided proof to me that improbable convergences were not impossible. A Buddhist-Christian dialogue arranged by friend John Cobb opened up a new horizon. Local congregational exchanges, especially in Eliot Church, Newton, and South Church, Centerville, were important. Lively theological interchange at the advisory council meetings of *Interpretation*—continuing a twenty-five-year running conversation with Paul and Elizabeth Achtemeier—has been intellectually catalytic. Andover Newton and Theological Tabletalk, already mentioned, were also theologically fertile settings. While protest actions may seem unlikely places for theology, they have been important environments in which "reflection in the context of involvement" has become more than a slogan.

Authors' dedications say a lot about their debts. Ten of my books have been dedicated to members of my family, and this systematics series is no exception. The difference in their roles then and now is the degree of active theological give and take. Gabrielle, ten years into pastoral ministry, tested some of these theses with clergy groups, gave me clarifying feedback, and took on the arduous task of preparing the subject index. Skye, with her theological cum legal vitalities, helped me to see this venture as a continuation of "A Catechism for Skye" (see Introduction). Judy's courageous journey through personal crises brought home quandaries and learnings from her in theodicy. Kirk's theological and literary probes never let me forget the questions of the "baby boomers." Bonnie's prison ministry kept me in touch with too easily ignored realities. And our children's spouses have also become important interlocutors: Gary as Iowa pastor, Chris as California attorney-to-be, Warren as Boston prison theologian, Alice as Boston computer specialist.

My greatest debt is to my spouse. "To Dorothy: who taught me the meaning of I and Thou"; this dedication of an early volume about our Pittsburgh mission ministry is as apt in 1987 as it was in 1958. What I know about theology as partnership and conversation I have, finally, learned from her.

To have the theological will is one thing. To have the way is another. William B. Eerdmans, Jr., made the way for this series. It began with a visit from him to our Cambridge sabbatical location in 1975. Now, twelve years later, we are two volumes along that way. I am deeply grateful for his support of this pastoral systematics. Let Providence decide if our vision of the way ahead was clear.

Gabriel Fackre
Epiphany 1987

Introduction

A desk lamp goes on, a book is opened, pad and pencil are near at hand. Before the day's encounters with the living and the dying the pastor remembers the week's central hour when a community waits to be fed, and prepares for it. Prayer is offered, Scripture read, books are taken down from the shelf and studied, hard thinking is done. This is how the writer pictures those for whom this series is written.

Dreamer! Who has time to spend in such disciplines? What busy pastor can pore over tomes of theology? Clergy are out among the people where the caring for persons and the confronting of powers must be done. Besides, who reads books these days anyway?

We are in trouble if the skeptic is right. The nurture of congregations in the solidities of faith will go undone. Already the signs of theological anemia are everywhere to be seen. However, I disagree with doubters. These volumes on basic Christian doctrine are undertaken because I believe the teachers and preachers of the Christian faith have not forgotten their ordination vows. In the midst of crowded schedules and impossible demands they want to be faithful to their call to feed the hungry soul as well as body (John 21:6).

The Christian Story, Volume 2, is an affirmation of pastors. While the overview volume was written for a more general readership, these subsequent studies are designed to assist the "steward of identity" in fulfilling his or her call.[1] Each will represent a more inten-

1. A description of the pastoral office is developed in vol. 1, *The Christian Story: A Narrative Interpretation of Basic Christian Doctrine* (rev. ed.; Grand Rapids: Eerdmans, 1984), 175-84. Hereafter referred to as *CS*.

sive and extensive investigation of a basic doctrine, the "chapters" in the Christian Story. The central custodianship of this lore of identity is given to the ordained clergy. That number includes those in paraparochial and supraparochial ministries—the chaplain in hospital, college, military, or industrial setting, the missionary or missioner, the bishop or executive, the teacher, the retired parson. However, as Peter Berger put it in a day when it was being dismissed as an obsolete institution, the local congregation is the principal place where the Story is regularly told.[2] There those trained in schools of theology and charged in solemn ceremonies most often tell and celebrate the Good News. The ministry of the laity, finally getting the attention it deserves, cannot be prepared adequately for its work in the world without the service rendered to the Body by pastors and teachers. The ministries of vitality need the ministries of identity.[3] These volumes, then, are written primarily for those charged with "the equipment of the saints" (Eph. 4:12).

As befits a learned pastoral ministry with a will and a way to think hard about ultimate matters, no apology is made for employing the specialist language of Christian theology. References to important literature and significant debates in each subject appear throughout. "Academic" is not a term of abuse by this reckoning. But a generalized academia is not the primary audience. Specific commitment is assumed in the reader; the conversation is "from faith to faith."[4] But the citation of literature is done with an awareness of the pressures of time and circumstance on those who read while they sit, but also run after they read.[5] Furthermore, use is made of methods of organizing complex data familiar to pastors in preaching and pedagogy, including "ideal types," models, and similar modes of large-scale classification (recognizing the mobility within and among types as well as their ideality). Methodology here also does not scorn mnemonic devices so necessary in pastoral

2. Peter Berger, "Letter on the Parish Ministry," *The Christian Century* (April 29, 1964): 547-50.

3. And the ministers of identity need the ministers of vitality. On the interrelationship see *CS*, 175-81.

4. The title of a work by B. Davie Napier, *From Faith to Faith* (New York: Harper, 1955).

5. A second tier of discussion that goes on in the notes parallels the analysis in the main text. It consists of citations of literature on the subject that I believe might be of interest to the pastor, and as English documentation would be accessible to the pastor.

work, from the alliterative categories to the theological circle and line drawings interspersed throughout.

As a narrative systematics, we begin in a different way. While striving to avoid the pitfalls of faddish storytelling theologies of the seventies and eighties, some important things can be learned from their experiments. The call by the narratologists to attend to affect and experience challenges the exclusive emphasis on abstract and discursive modes of communication that customarily mark theological work. The biography of God does not ignore our autobiographies. Augustine and Luther did not, nor should we. This is especially so when we become sufficiently self-critical about our theologies to recognize that what we say about the divine pilgrimage is influenced by our own journey. Thus this Introduction tries to mate life and doctrine by looking at threads of formative experience in the writer's life from different angles: mission, Christology, Scripture, ecclesiology. Then an examination of a theological laboratory, Craigville, prepares the way for engagement with the specifics of authority and revelation.

A PERSONAL JOURNEY

Theological Text in Mission Context

The people to whom these pages are addressed are the kind of people with whom I have lived and worked. Their commitment to mission took early form in me at the University of Chicago Divinity School in the mid-1940s with the partner to whom this volume is dedicated. For both of us the mentorship of James Luther Adams and study in the Federated Faculties was "reflection in the context of involvement," or "doing theology," and "critical reflection on praxis," as it has been described more recently. It meant reading Reinhold Niebuhr, Karl Barth, and Paul Tillich in the daytime while at night canvassing Woodlawn tenements as precinct workers for the Independent Voters of Illinois (contesting in a small way the "Chicago machine"), leading a student waiter strike against the faculty eating club for its discriminatory membership practices, marching on the Illinois State House against the Broyles Bills that sought an anti-Communist pledge for universities, while at the same time challenging Marxist efforts to take control of student programs of social action on the campus. It led us to cycle and hitchhike through Great Britain and the Continent to study "the church and the working classes," in experiments such as the Iona Community,

Christian Worker, and Christian Socialist movements. It entailed an eye-opening visit to the first assembly of the World Council of Churches in Amsterdam (1948), where we met some of the theologians whose books we had read so avidly. Contextual learning at the University of Chicago also meant serving a year of internship in suburban Oak Park and two years as pastors of a working-class congregation in Chicago's stockyard district, while Dot worked concurrently in a settlement house in the steel mill community of South Chicago. These experiences left their mark on us. Thinking and doing are mission oriented, linking theology and ethics, church and world. These dualities cropped up in subject matter chosen for academic endings, a B.D. thesis on theologian and social ethicist Reinhold Niebuhr, and a Ph.D. dissertation on the concept of dehumanization in the thought of Kierkegaard and Marx.[6]

The intimacy of theology and life, text and context, formed and was formed further in a decade of ministry in the "steel valley" of greater Pittsburgh. After Chicago we went to a two-point charge in Homestead and Duquesne, Pennsylvania, with our mixed vision of a mission to the worker and a storefront ministry along the lines of the East Harlem Protestant Parish in New York City. Since the Homestead congregation lost its building as a result of the depression, we were able to try an East Harlem–like experiment—two years of storefront ministry in a former candy store (and numbers racket quarters). However, we soon learned the difference between second and third generation mill-town workers who wanted a building "just like the Catholics," and the welfare and immigrant populations of inner city New York glad to have storeroom space for worship. Hence the move from the storefront to a first unit built in "workingman's paradise," the West Mifflin suburb of Homestead.

Our ten years with steeltown people, through recession, strikes, automation, unemployment, and the attendant demoralization of industrial workers and their families, taught us much about the processes of alienation about which I had so glibly written in the bowels of the University of Chicago library. But through all the economic and social ups and downs, there were countless joys and deep satisfactions. The two parishes lived the rhythms of liturgy and the Christian calendar, the newborn were baptized, the young

6. "Myth and Truth in the Theology of Reinhold Niebuhr," B.D. diss., Univ. of Chicago Divinity School, 1948; "A Comparison and Critique of the Interpretations of Dehumanization in the Thought of Søren Kierkegaard and Karl Marx," Ph.D. diss., Univ. of Chicago Divinity School, 1962.

educated and confirmed, minds stretched and hearts warmed in the gospel, the sick visited, the dead buried, and mission to an industrial community falteringly carried out. One venture in industrial ministry was an adaptation of the approach of the Iona Community on seventy-five acres of land surrounding an old frame church and burying ground in the country twenty miles from the mill towns. Here we formed the "Milliron Community," composed of worker families from the Homestead-Duquesne parish, seeking to recover the discipline of work, worship, study, and play in conjunction with life and ministry in the steel industry.[7]

During this time theological rumination went on, first and foremost with my partner in ministry[8] and more and more with pastoral colleagues. The latter included a number of those in the Pittsburgh area and beyond called "mission pastors" who were involved in one or another kind of outreach ministry.[9] This running conversation with colleagues contributed to some theological clarifications that found their way into a small work, *The Purpose and Work of the Ministry.*[10] Such thoughts could not have been developed or articulated without also the experience and insights of the laity at the very heart of the mission. So, all doctrine finally rises out of the *sensus fidelium,* however subsequently articulated by those charged with the particularities of preaching and teaching.

The situating of theological reflection in the midst of the life and witness of laity and clergy continued in the subsequent years of a teaching ministry. In 1961 we went to Lancaster Theological Seminary where I was called to teach historical theology and Christian ethics. The smaller metropolitan area and a seminary ministry meant a new and different intellectual context for theological inquiry—teacher-student and teacher-teacher—and a new social environment—a conservative middle-class region. The academic environment (including Franklin and Marshall College) was intellectually stimulating, as were especially the demands for careful classroom preparation and exposition. And the churchly and evan-

7. See Gabriel Fackre, *The Purpose and Work of the Ministry* (Philadelphia: Christian Education Press, 1959), 114-41.

8. The joint work *Under the Steeple* (New York: Abingdon Press, 1957) was the result of relating our experiences of the World Council of Churches to questions of mission and unity in a local parish.

9. Among them Frank and Gertrude Pirazzini, George and "Danny" Geisler, Paul and Edith Oberkircher, Martin and Gail Bupp, Hale Schroer, Philip Harner, and mission leaders Purd Deitz and Ralph Weiler.

10. See esp. pp. 114-41.

gelical catholic heritage of the Mercersburg tradition in the seminary confirmed our earlier liturgical and ecumenical direction. The Lancaster city and county ethos took some adjusting to, particularly when the currents of social change in the 1960s swept into this Pennsylvania Dutch community.

During this decade we became deeply involved in the civil rights movement, its demonstrations and drives in town, in Washington, D.C., and in the South. Within that ferment came also the emphasis on *extra*parochial mission in the churches, the struggles of the peace movement, and participatory stirrings among students, women, and elders. For us involvement in these things included the launching of a downtown coffeehouse renewal center, starting a network of freedom schools in the city, organizing a drive to integrate the three junior high schools (successful), a campaign for a black school committee candidate (unsuccessful), and the founding of a citizen's newspaper, the *Lancaster Independent Press* (giving the establishment some "LIP").[11] A less pronounced move in counterculture was our membership in a blue-collar neighborhood church and leadership of an adult church school class that bore with our 1960s-style wrestling with the wrongs and rights of society.

An important community of theological discourse in that time and place was a mix of activist pastors, students, seminary colleagues, and laity. Among the richest occasions for this conversation was a weekly morning "theological tabletalk" group that met for the eucharist and breakfast. Another was a friendship with a center city congregation, Trinity Lutheran Church, and its senior pastor, which institution provided a home for many of the 1960s' social ministries in that city.[12] Encounter was yet another intellectually stimulating environment, the coffeehouse where the interface of theology and life went on in discussions of movies, books, and art,

11. These involvements and experiments appear in various works of the period: *Secular Impact* (Philadelphia: Pilgrim Press, 1978), 74-89 describes the coffeehouse mission, Encounter; *Second Fronts in Metropolitan Mission* (Grand Rapids: Eerdmans, 1968), 17-30 analyzes the Lancaster churches' civil rights mission; *Liberation in Middle America* (Philadelphia: Pilgrim Press, 1971), 92-114 details the same struggle and with it the founding of a citizens' newspaper.

12. Wallace Fisher was the pastor. An author of many books on mission, his best-known, *From Tradition to Mission* (Nashville: Abingdon Press, 1965) is the story of Trinity Church, which under Fisher's leadership with his wife, Margaret, his successor, Larry Lehman, and colleagues Penrose Hoover and Jack Hoffman, has been able to hold in remarkable unity a risk-taking mission commitment with strong preaching and worship, vigorous church growth and giving.

public debate on everything from a Moral Rearmament "invasion" of the city and urban renewal to the compelling issues of civil rights, war and peace, and poverty. A large piece of this was Encounter's "lay corps" of 120 people trained to share the faith in four-hour shifts with the coffee counter drop-in. Later the coffeehouse moved to a larger downtown facility and became headquarters for the city's marginalized communities—a black teenagers' club, a troupe of local actors, and the *Lancaster Independent Press.*[13] What was happening locally had its counterpart for us in the speaking and workshop circuit, in the church renewal movement of the UCC, and on the ecumenical scene in general. We touched these circles regularly as our family journeyed to summer conferences and as Dot and I were part of one or another task force or committee on mission.

Family life was very important in the midst of these comings and goings. Our five children joined us in the mission struggles in the city and beyond, especially in the civil rights and peace movements. And they took their own bruises. Most painful were those that came from their peers whom they left in order to integrate a city grade school and a junior high school, and those whom they met in the sometimes hostile reception of the schools and neighborhoods they entered. These pressures gave special meaning to our times together—at home, in the long drives on summer circuits, and during a period of sabbatical study.

The significance of family life was also related to the compelling needs and visions of the sixties and the mainline churches' involvement in them. Dot and I saw some of the personal and family consequences of this involvement in two intense group experiences in La Foret, Colorado, in 1969, ten-day "marathons" in which we served as theological resources with a psychotherapeutically oriented leadership team. Using a variety of Esalen-like methods, the 160 clergy and spouses were urged to "let it all hang out." When they did, the vocational frustrations and fractured family relationships that came in the wake of heavy social action activity poured forth. Heroic stands urged upon clergy by the regnant mainline theologies meant serious conflict with congregations that had not heard much before about "mission in the world," and reacted accordingly. Contextual ethics that associated with worldly Christianity contributed to pastoral confusion about codes of personal behavior and led to a weakening of marriage covenants in their

13. *Secular Impact,* 74-89.

own lives.[14] Group therapies offered as helps and cures for clergy demoralization shared in the illusions about human nature and antipathy to codes and covenants that marked the culture, further weakening their normativity.

These sobering facts prompted us to speak more often and bring to greater prominence the standards of personal morality, conjugal faithfulness, and the integrity of family life. How important it is for parishioners to get clear signals from us on these things when all around them the culture is sending messages of indifference to and attack upon the biblical codes of personal conduct! The rejection of marital fidelity, the acceptance of sexual promiscuity, and the use of drugs are commonplace assumptions in the world of film, paperback books, afternoon TV soaps, and evening TV series. Only when sexual diseases of all sorts and the abuse of drugs begin to weaken the very structures of government, business, industry, the arts, and sports does the culture have second thoughts about the codes so quickly rejected. Let the church find its voice again on these personal matters as well as in the public issues.

Personal morality is linked to personal faith. We learned to respect piety after a season of secular spirituality that preferred "doing" as a substitute for "being." So the disciplines of daily prayer, Scripture, and devotional reading have come to have an important place in our life together.

In the 1970s and to the present time the formal context of theological thinking has continued to be academic. And the informal setting still goes on in voluntary associations of colleagues in ministry and mission. As theological education and my own teaching methods have become more dialogical, enrichment from student insight has grown accordingly. Classes in systematic theology and seminars in "theology and . . ." have been of great importance[15]—

14. An early effort to challenge the code-less "new morality"—both its "cool" (Hugh Hefner) and "warm" (Joseph Fletcher) varieties—appears as the essay "The New Morality" in *Storm over Ethics* (Philadelphia: United Church Press, 1967), 67-87. Reprinted in *Issues in Sexual Ethics,* ed. Martin Duffy (Souderton, Pa.: United Church People for Biblical Witness, 1979), 14-26.

15. Much of this material was tested in three years of systematics classes at Andover Newton, in 1983–84, 1984–85, 1986–87. I am grateful to the hundreds of students from a broad theological spectrum for very helpful comments and criticism that have had their effect on the end product. Very instructive also was the feedback from members of a seminar, "The Use of the Scripture in Theology," in the spring of 1986, during which we vigorously discussed hermeneutical theory and the exegesis of John 14:6.

especially when second career M.Div. students and working clergy in doctoral programs bring their wealth of experience to the classroom. The presence of women in significant numbers in the seminaries has also added a fresh angle of vision. So too has the special mission-framed and internationally oriented setting of the present Andover Newton with its diverse students and faculty. In the same vein, the school is connected to the imaginative Center for the Laity, which requires faculty to view their work in new categories.[16]

The classroom and seminar table would not be what they are without extracurricular conversation and involvements. A very important exchange for me has been another theological tabletalk group, made up of Boston-area working clergy, Protestant and Roman Catholic, a few faculty and students, and some theologically energetic laity. For twelve years this group has met every Monday morning, methodically taking up formative theological writings, bringing to bear on them the members' day-to-day ministry in the city.

The organization of another citizens' newspaper in the 1970s, this time in the liberal and secular city of Newton,[17] and marches and demonstrations in Boston on issues of peace and justice affected the way I taught and thought about theology. The decade also marked a much closer union of deed and word, conversation and action, than before, symbolized by the United Church of Christ's "Word-in-deed" evangelism movement, in which both of us had an active part. While engaged in "do and tell" mission through an elder center in our congregation, Eliot Church, much of it was through a grassroot movement in the UCC that produced a series of training events, a core of consultants throughout the denomination, a statement of commitment, and an outpouring of literature created by pastors and people, with buttons and banners designed

16. On the Center for the Ministry of the Laity, see its periodical, *Centering* (210 Herrick Road, Newton Centre, MA, 02159).

17. I chaired the organizing committee in its early task of conceptualizing and launching the paper, *The Newton Times*. It survived, then thrived as a citizens' weekly for seven years, doing investigative journalism, supporting peace and justice movements in the Newton and Boston area, attempting to provide interesting local news, all on a volunteer staff basis. The advent of the "throwaway" suburban weekly with its large advertising clientele, staff, and financial resources overtook and displaced the *Times*, especially when in this genre *The Newton Tab* began to do substantial reporting and critical commentary, bringing it national acclaim.

by Dorothy.[18] All this in spirit and content had its effects in a number of places outside the United Church of Christ. The point of the movement was the joining of deeds of mercy and justice with the sharing of the gospel, rather than the polarization of these as in much social action and evangelism.

The Word-in-deed evangelism movement signified something deeper in our own life, and reflected a development in the church at large and the culture beyond that. It came home to all our family in a transitional period between Lancaster and Newton, a six-month stay in Honolulu in 1970 where I taught at the University of Hawaii and served as theologian-in-residence at the Church of the Crossroads. There the religious fevers soon to be felt on the mainland were already running high. Encounters with devotees of Hare Krishna and "Jesus freaks," sundry swamis and gurus, and various cultic and occultic activities, all reflecting a growing spiritual hunger in society, made us very aware of how little prepared many mainline churches were to speak to these matters of basic faith. So in the Church of the Crossroads with its unswerving social witness—the previous year giving sanctuary to GIs protesting the war in Vietnam, and during our time picketing in Kalama Valley to protect the land of native Hawaiian pig farmers against the inroads of lucrative condominium development—efforts were made to "get the Story straight" with lectionary preaching, revived confirmation classes, and courses in basic theology.[19] As one of our

18. See "Banners Tell of a Festive Faith," *The United Church Herald* 13 (Aug. 1970): 24-27, and "Button, Button, Who's Got the Button?" *The Christian Ministry* 1 (July 1970): 44-46; Dorothy Fackre, "Banner of Hope," *AD* (March 1973): 59-62. Dot's banner and button making began in 1968 as part of the raised mission awareness of that time.

19. A summary of evangelism themes appears in my *Do and Tell* (Grand Rapids: Eerdmans, 1973) and *Word in Deed* (Grand Rapids: Eerdmans, 1975). The evangelism resource book developed in the grassroot UCC movement was the *Evangelism Training Manual* (1973), going through many mimeographed editions through the Board for Homeland Ministries of the United Church of Christ. The Board also produced a short film, "Dawn People," which choreographed and portrayed in graphics a three-page summary of the Christian narrative that appears in the preparatory material for the Nairobi Assembly of the World Council of Churches and in the appendix of *CS*, 272-74. See also, "Dawn People: The Gospel Danced on Film," *Youth,* (Nov. 1975): 54-63. Various denominational evangelism programs adopted the "Word in deed" and "Story" categories. See *The New Life Mission Handbook,* Board of Discipleship, United Methodist Church, 1976; *The New World Mission Handbook,* Board of Discipleship, United Methodist Church, 1974; *A Story to Tell,* Training Manual, General Program Council, Re-

children almost joined a Hare Krishna community, and others began to ask intently about the meaning of their own faith, faith issues became very personal. So in a small "catechism for Skye" done for a youth magazine, adorned with poetry, songs, and banner designed by the rest of the members of the family, the germ of this systematics took early form.[20]

The seed was further nourished in the ensuing years in the movement in evangelism previously mentioned, and then by a larger sweep of populist theology in the United Church of Christ. From the mid-seventies to the present time a ground swell in "theological renewal" has taken place in the UCC, calling for the balancing and interrelationship of biblical and theological teaching with the denomination's well-known social witness. While some of this was associated with a dangerous retreat into a privatized spirituality or a reactionary political posture, the major momentum in the UCC was among those firmly committed to the social-ethical role of the church. Striving for theological solidity, social activist clergy and laity spoke more and more of the need for integrity, a church witnessing to *leitourgia* and *kerygma* as well as *diakonia*. Hence, our own involvement in the founding of the Biblical Theological Liturgical Group (affectionately known as the "BTL Club") and the Mercersburg Society, my participation in an agency-sponsored theology project for the denomination, circuit-riding within and beyond the UCC in the cause of theological consciousness-raising, and, most of all, a series of Craigville Colloquies. As an illustration of the kind of context in which the theology found here has been developed, as well as an introduction to the topic of this volume, in another portion of this Introduction I will describe the Craigville theological process.

But Craigville is more than a theological process. As the Cape Cod locale in which this systematics is being written, it represents all the possibilities and ambiguities that attend the venture: *Possibilities,* for the Christian Camp Meeting Association that founded Craigville in 1872 (the "Christian" refers to a small New England denomination, one of the four streams that joined to form the present United Church of Christ) left a goodly heritage of worship and

formed Church in America, 1976; *Being the Christian Story,* A Resource Book in Engagement Evangelism, United Church of Canada, by Gordon Bruce Turner, 1982; *Evangelism Outreach,* American Lutheran Church, 1976.

20. Dorothy Fackre, Gabriel Fackre, Bonnie Fackre, and Gabrielle Fackre, "A Catechism for Today's Storytellers: Prepared for Skye by her Family," *Youth* 23 (July 1972): 23-42.

study, work, and play continued by the UCC Conference Center on the grounds that works with the present CCMA to provide a year-round rhythm of nurture and mission. Thus these pages are written in the midst of a battle with land-hungry developers, efforts to preserve the purity and fast-diminishing levels of the Cape's water supply, and the development of Craigville as a resource for preaching and teaching in the church. *Ambiguities,* for we are talking about a piece of land a mile from the Kennedy compound, located in the playground of the eastern seaboard's middle and upper classes, and for many an escape from the city's inferno and the larger world's crises. The tents and early cabins of the pioneer Craigvillers have become comfortable summer cottages, some of whose residents continue the CCMA and UCC tradition and mission, but many of whom are there just "to have a nice place on the Cape," with the church hosts being an inconvenience to be tolerated. So reality intrudes on our visions, but also puts them in touch with a social context in which the Christian text is to be interpreted.

These first random observations in autobiography pose some deeper questions. One such query put by "the hermeneutics of suspicion" is: Can anything good come from this—theology written and thought by an aging middle-class male? Never mind the proletarian times in this personal history, the will to solidarity with oppressed blacks and women, a partnership of male and female in all that was done and much that was said here. For some influential voices in theology today, the only credentials for sound teaching are a designated biological, economic, or social existence. As ideas are weapons in the war between the oppressor and the oppressed, the belief is held that *true* ideas rise only from the oppressed involved in the struggle against bondage. Thus feminist, black, native American, Asian, Hispanic, and Third World theologies can claim a hearing, for they speak out of the cauldron of oppression and liberation. Not so theology done without these credentials. In the writing of this book these interlocutors have ever been at the author's elbow. The response to the claim and charge can be found only in the pages that follow. However, to read them with an open mind is itself an admission of a flaw in this argument from suspicion, for it assumes that there can be access to truth without the requisite biological, economic, or social qualifications. The contradiction is present in the many books written to argue the case for one or another liberation theology, directed as they almost all are to a readership constituted by the class, race, or sex considered to be oppressor.

The telling point made, however, by this perspectivalist epistemology is that only those who experience suffering can know it in its depths. To fail to hear the cry from the abyss by the poor, oppressed women, people of color, and those of marginalized and disabling condition is an outrage to the gospel. God suffers with them, speaks good news to them, and is engaged with them in their struggle. Thus "suffering and hope" are the right entry point for understanding faith and doing mission.[21] What is so wrong in the theologies that begin on these notes is the exclusionary clause: *Only* those who suffer in the designated ways know God and have hope. Suffering cannot be so neatly defined or confined. Further, Christian hope reaches into ultimate as well as penultimate fulfillments that have to do with the *forgiveness of sin* as well as the *release from bondage,* and liberation at the end of history as well as in it. We cannot draw circles that exclude the God of a larger suffering and a wider and longer hope. To be continued.

Another point of view that is never far from mind in these pages is also very contextually oriented: "Know where you are coming from!" in the slang of the times. This counsel of self-awareness welcomes every perspective, making no claims for a privileged epistemological locus. Come one, come all. Why? Well, in another transient slogan, it's "different strokes for different folks." Truth is what is *true for you.* More accurately, no objective truth claim is possible, so this view contends, in the sense of correspondence between an assertion and the object to which it refers. Theological statements are "meaningful," not true.

The experience of pluralism—"plural shock"—so common in a time of new and disorienting exposure to a variety of worldviews and life-styles, has produced a network of ideas that enables many in this situation to cope with its disorienting effects. In the world of religious thought a spate of new pluralistic theologies has arisen that perform this function. An exegesis and exposition in this book on the "scandals" of particularity and universality will both address the condition and respond to it. For now, we simply record the importance of this interlocutor and anticipate the running dialogue with a relativist perspectivalism.

We note, as well, dissonance between its postulate and premise.

21. Thus Desmond Tutu's *Hope and Suffering* (Grand Rapids: Eerdmans, 1984). Much more will be said about this dual theme in the contextualization sections of this volume.

If the confident declaration of relativity were not assumed to be itself a universal truth by the one making the claim, others accordingly could ignore the assertion as "doing one's own thing," expressing a perspective, but not offering it as a candidate for intellectual discourse and judgment. The position of this book is in head-on collision with this viewpoint. Theological judgments are claims to objective truth as well as testimonies to personal or social meaningfulness. Again, to be continued.

Jesus Christ, the Center

The central truth claim in Christian faith is Jesus Christ. He is the way, the truth, and the life. What that means to me appears throughout this work in one or another of its implications. Whatever the changes in my outlook, life, and work over the years, this has been a constant. Feeding it early was a maternal Baptist piety, the Sunday school classes and Jesus preaching of an evangelical cum pacifist pastor in a Brooklyn church, and six years of summer church camp in Ocean Park, Maine. While the "Americanization" of an immigrant father meant that I was raised in my mother's Hanson Place Baptist Church, I can't help but think that the Pantocrator Christ in the icons of his St. Nicholas Syrian Orthodox Cathedral also had their effect in a liturgical and sacramental disposition, and perhaps too in an iconic literary style.

Nodal points in these early years were a "decision for Christ" at the age of ten followed by immersion, and a "decision for the ministry of Christ" at sixteen along with a determination to follow unswervingly Jesus' counsels of perfection, including the way of nonresistance. At Bucknell University that same year, the piety began to wither, but the pacific Jesus remained firm. This loyalty was strengthened by the campus struggle to release Japansese-American students from West Coast internment camps, and a summer's work with a Quaker Peace Caravan in Pittsburgh, testifying to nonviolence and trying to integrate that city's hospitals. In these last two actions the path of two such "Jesus people" came together, and have been one since.

Another turn on the journey came for both of us when we began to feel the limitations of pacifism as well as of pietism. Were the choices of a follower of the Jesus way as straightforward as they seemed to be, especially when the welfare of another human being is now linked to one's own course of action? What we were experiencing personally by our new bonding we were reading in the books of Reinhold Niebuhr, his theological analysis of the ambiguities in social and political decision making. "No one is righteous, no, not one!" And with it the releasing word, "Your sins are forgiven." While the stock-in-trade of this antiexperiential neoorthodoxy was anything but a "born again" conversion, its radical judgment and word of gracious pardon in Christ spoke to us deeply. Jesus was still to be followed—and in antiestablishment fashion—in a strike against a racist faculty club's membership policy, a march for civil liberties, solidarity with workers in a ministry in the stockyards area. But the gospel is a mercy work done by Christ that covers our own sin, our self-will that persists in the most strenuous endeavors to follow Jesus. And the law as ethic is no longer a counsel of perfection but the guide to achieving realistic advances toward justice and peace, with the attendant use of power, aware always of its corruptibility and need for checks and balances. So our mentors, Reinhold Niebuhr and Jim Adams, helped us to form a growing picture of Christ that sought to be faithful to both the visions and the realities.

That growth took us along a curve of the path in the next decade, the mill town parish experience described earlier. Here the churchly Christ known in the sustained life and worship together of a particular people kept company with the activist figure of earlier days. The sacramental Presence found further support in the Mercersburg atmosphere at Lancaster Seminary, an environment that was similar in some ways to the Christ of Orthodox patrimony. And in the latter period of the Lancaster sixties, and the Newton seventies and eighties, the change agent mandates of the servant Christ got a heavy underscoring. But in the last fifteen years, growth in our understanding of Christ and advance along the way of commitment have had more to do with clarity about the *source* and the *resource* of our knowledge of Christ.

Scripture, the Source

When I was twelve someone gave me a red letter New Testament. At first it confirmed my pietism, then later my pacifism. These particular "isms" may have passed but the biblical framing of my picture of Jesus has not. Scripture is the source for the substance of the gospel and its Center. The more the much-touted worldliness of theology has taken hold in mainstream churches (and I did my own share of such touting),[22] the clearer became the importance to us of the biblical witness to Jesus Christ. Dietrich Bonhoeffer, who sensitized a generation to the worldly Christ, never forgot that, even though many who were drawn to what they thought was his "secular Christianity" did. So too have their successors in our own day, those enamored by current contextualisms and pluralisms. Whatever we say about the Christ hidden in the movements of humanization and liberation and in the cultures and religions of the world is to be judged by the known Christ of Holy Scriptures.

The sounding of strong biblical notes and the contesting of the acculturation of faith brought us into contact and then collegiality with others long known for this emphasis, "the evangelicals." Asked to lecture at the evangelical Gordon-Conwell Seminary, I was introduced as one with "evangelical affinities." Such affinities were strengthened by participation in a coalition of "ecumenicals, evangelicals, and charismatics" put together by Albert Outler in two notable Notre Dame conferences on "the recovery of the sacred." This association led to a friendship with Carl Henry and extended research on his work for an interpretive essay in the *Handbook of Christian Theologians.*[23] Later I was invited as an "evangelical ecumenical" to join with various "ecumenical evangelicals" in presentations to evangelical audiences at the American Academy of Religion and Wheaton College (Illinois) and their resulting publications.[24] I found myself also in (sometimes uneasy) ad hoc alliances with the evangelical caucus in the UCC, represented in a collection of their essays defending classical moral norms, and later in the larger theological renewal efforts in the denomination. An important element in all these new associations, especially for Dot but also for me and for our children, has been a group of British apologists and writers who have influenced modern evangelicalism, primarily C.S. Lewis but also J.R.R. Tolkien, Charles Williams, and Dorothy Sayers. Another is the friendship with William B. Eerdmans, Jr., who, during an occasion in 1966 when I shared a

22. In popular form in *Secular Impact, passim,* and in more scholarly exposition in Gabriel Fackre, *Humiliation and Celebration* (New York: Sheed & Ward, 1969).

23. "Carl Henry," *Handbook of Christian Theologians,* rev. ed., ed. Martin Marty and Dean Peerman (Nashville: Abingdon Press, 1983), 583-607.

24. "The Use of Scripture in My Work in Systematics," in *The Use of the Bible in Theology: Evangelical Options,* ed. Robert K. Johnston (Atlanta: John Knox Press, 1985), 200-226, and "God, The Discloser," in *Christian Faith and Practice in the Modern World,* forthcoming from Eerdmans.

platform with William Stringfellow, invited me to follow Stringfellow into the Eerdmans' "stable." I have been a satisfied occupant of a stall in that ecumenical/evangelical press ever since.

How Scripture is interpreted is, of course, the question, and indeed the burden of this book. We soon enough discovered the variety among evangelicals on this and related matters. The affinity with evangelical witness on the one hand, and a developing awareness of the inhospitable elements within this constituency on the other, have played their part in making evangelicalism yet another crucial partner in conversation in working out this systematic theology. Negatively, this has meant sharp differences with neofundamentalist evangelicals, with a critique worked out in *The Religious Right and Christian Faith.*[25] While we need to appreciate this movement's authority stress on Scripture and its concern for personal morality, we must take strong exception to the political fundamentalism that undercuts its protestations of biblical loyalty by intruding its own political agenda into the message of Scripture, a "secular humanist" wolf in sheep's clothing. So the captivity of the Bible to worldliness can happen not only to self-confessed secularists and relativists but also to evangelicals who contend against them.

Another kind of invitation to cultural captivity by self-declared evangelicalism is of a softer mien, speaking the language of spirituality and "self-esteem." Here smiling preachers in comfortable suburban sanctuaries or soaring cathedrals hawk the wares of pop psychology coated with a biblical veneer. Trading on the spiritual hunger of the day, inquisitiveness about things psychological, and the genuine healing of the mind and heart that faith can bring, they seek to attract people to faith in the packaging of modernity. The appeal of this acculturated Christianity can be seen in the popularity of TV preachers busy merchandising their political and psychological nostrums.[26]

The attention to secular issues is not the problem with these and other evangelical positions. "The world" is the proper setting for understanding and articulating the gospel. Mistaking the *setting* for the *source* and the *substance* is the problem. This role reversal

25. This book is an effort to assess a cultural cum theological phenomenon using the narrative outline of *The Christian Story.* Gabriel Fackre, *The Religious Right and Christian Faith* (Grand Rapids: Eerdmans, 1982).

26. Among the worst offenders is Robert Schuller. See his *Self-Esteem: The New Reformation* (Waco, Tex.: Word Books, 1982) and an evangelical critique by David F. Wells, "Self-Esteem: The New Confusion," *TSF Bulletin* (Nov.-Dec. 1983): 11-12.

ironically is tied up with the bold claim that the gospel, and only the gospel, is being proclaimed by evangelicals, and that "worldliness" (currently called secular humanism), is the enemy. Where no place in the scheme of Christian authority is granted to the world, then no careful weighing of the credentials of partnership is done, and no priorities established. So it enters covertly and begins to take charge of the unacknowledged but real alliance. The dialogue with an evangelical point of view here and throughout the systematics, therefore, will affirm a common commitment to the biblical source and norm, but be wary of such when the text is not brought into self-conscious and self-critical relationship to the cultural context. There are plenty of evangelicals who know and do just that, making for the comradeship between this evangelical ecumenical and those ecumenical evangelicals.

An Inclusive Church, the Resource

Ecumenical means inclusivity, universality of perspective, catholicity. That is the character of the churchly resource emerging in this personal journey. An ecumenical interpretation of Scripture, and finally an ecumenical theology, is not the preserve alone of the official ecumenical movement. That remarkable twentieth-century development has given the term luster. At many points it has provided the habitat and stimulus for the thinking done here about Christian doctrine: attendance at two World Council of Churches' assemblies (Amsterdam and Evanston), an alternate delegate status at another (New Delhi) and a part in preparation for yet two others (Nairobi and Vancouver), involvement in a World Council of Churches' "missionary structure study," lecturing to various city, state, and national councils, serving as a delegate to the Consultation on Church Union (COCU), life in the United Church of Christ that is the confluence of four streams of Protestantism, teaching in the joint doctoral program with Boston College's rich Roman Catholic heritage, being part of a Boston consortium of theological schools of diverse tradition, and engagement over time in numerous ad hoc interchurch ventures. But an ecumenical theology may or may not conform to the specific tendencies or judgments of ecumenical bodies, and it can reach beyond to those belonging to its formal associations.

The commitment to inclusiveness was an important part of our ministry in Duquesne and Homestead. It came out in down-to-earth ways, like paying attention to all the natural subcommunities within a parish. No "clan" is excluded, not the "strawberry social," the "altar," the "pulpit," the "camper," or the "our gang" groups. These were names given to some of the circles of interest we found in our own steel town charge, writing about them in *Under the Steeple.*[27] When any one of them treated its own activity as the be-all and end-all of the church, it fell prey to the reductionism and imperialism that Paul worried over in the Corinthian community. We discovered from Corinth and in the Monongahela Valley that by relativizing their claims, forswearing hegemony over others, being taught by others and living in harmony with them, the clans in a congregation could grow into the fullness intended for the Body. What we had learned about ecumenism from our early World Council experience we saw right there in the parish we were serving. In his Corinthian letter, Paul gives a charter for ecumenical existence and catholic faith: respect for the variety of gifts (1 Cor. 12); sounding the call of Christ to the Body of Christ to be modest in the claims of its parts (1 Cor. 12); claiming the parts for interrelationship (1 Cor. 12–13); facing the difficult fact that such love and mutuality may bring with it priority of witness as the occasion demands (1 Cor. 14).

The riches of this text have been mined throughout our life. In Lancaster days it drew us to the Mercersburg theology and its implications: the integration of patristic, medieval, and Reformation traditions, the companionship of sacrament and Word, a eucharist in its fullness that anticipated the formulations of "COCU" and "BEM."[28] And again in Lancaster, seeing the full picture meant a critique of the institutional church and the concurrent quest for "new forms," as in Encounter and *LIP,* but, at the same time, the refusal to denigrate the parish. We struggled to hold together our worship life at St. Luke's with the coffeehouse–renewal mission. We worked at linking Encounter with the congregations of the city. It meant many actions in the civil rights movement, while resisting the self-righteous polemic and separatism of reformers toward folk in congregations who were not marching and boycotting. In the years that followed, inclusivity was the impetus of Word-in-deed mission. Here we bent our efforts to regain a lost evangelism momentum, and struggled to integrate it with social action concerns. What an uphill battle! The recovery of piety in those days was too

27. See *Under the Steeple,* 13-54.

28. On the Mercersburg theology see the key works: John Nevin, *The Mystical Presence,* The Lancaster Series on the Mercersburg Theology, vol. 2, ed. Bard Thompson and George Bricker

often combined with the rejection of "activism," and the activist, in turn, regularly scorned the pietist. We were convinced that the "prayers" and the "picketers" could and should work in the same harness.[29]

Another effort to hold together what seemed to be contradictory things revolved around the ministry of the laity. Richard Broholm brought to Andover Newton the call to seminary participation in this burgeoning movement. I chaired a faculty committee to institutionalize "the laity project" on campus, and took part in a five-year "model congregations task force" that laid the groundwork for the subsequent Center for the Laity at the school. In these ventures, and in task forces in the center and at Eliot Church on a theology of institutions and science-technology questions, the importance of this new frontier became clear and compelling. Yet again, the ministry of the laity should not demean the pastoral office in a reversal of the old superiority-inferiority ranking fostered by clericalism. We have to recognize the uniqueness of the gifts of the ministry of the laity as well as those of the clergy, and nurture a genuine partnership both in theory and in fact.[30]

Clergy-laity collegiality was just one of the many mandates of inclusiveness that have come in recent years from hearing the voices of the long-voiceless. Thus "inclusive language" is both the meaning and a metaphor of many struggles: silenced and marginalized women, people of color, class, age, and condition. The early stages in the movement for inclusion may require loud and even shrill declamation. How can there be real partnership on the human plane when there is no parity? And parity requires a struggle to be acknowledged as peer. In such a moment the foreground sounds of the marginalized will be, and must be, heard. But finally that priority must be read in the light of the overall inclusive vision. The time should come when membership in the Body means mutual affirmation, colearning, and love. As we are still in the middle of

29. The phrase is that of John Oliver Nelson, founder of Kirkridge, the community in Pennsylvania that has sought to hold together the disciplines of prayer and action.

30. This partnership is espoused by the Center for the Ministry of the Laity, as expressed in the volume written by a faculty-laity task force, *The Laity in Ministry,* ed. George Peck and John Hoffman (Valley Forge, Pa.: Judson Press, 1985). My essay in it grew out of a science-technology group in the Eliot United Church of Christ congregation in Newton that has been meeting for many years in which researchers at Boston hospitals and M.I.T., science teachers, engineers, and others regularly discuss issues in ministry confronted in the workplace.

the battle to right old wrongs, we have yet to understand what this kind of inclusive language and holistic life together might mean. But we know what the imperative is, and we live under the claim to move toward it.

In the foregoing the stress has been on the social, ethical, and institutional underside of the *oikoumene.* All of this has theological import, our main business here. Parochial and extraparochial mission, ministries of clergy and laity, evangelism of word and deed, empowerment of men and women, elder with younger, black with white, mean a healing of fractured *doctrine.* The Christian tradition calls narrowed, reductionist, and fissiparous teaching "heresy." Heresy is a partial perspective passed off as the full truth. So the respective reductionisms in the first major doctrinal debate on Christology: the overhumanizings of Jesus in Ebionism, Adoptionism and their heirs, and the overdivinizings in Docetism, Apollinarianism, and their successors. As Jesus Christ is truly human, truly God, and truly one, so all doctrinal statement reflects this kind of fullness. From creation to consummation we confront the temptation to reductionism and seek to move past it, led by an ecumenical vision. That means listening for the voice of the voiceless, enlarging the networks of communication, openness to the new sounds but not allowing them to drown out legitimate old ones, and always seeking a harmony that echoes the grander chorus of another Land.

The trust in the work of the Spirit through the way of collegiality reminds us again of Paul's counsel to Corinth. A genuinely ecumenical theology rises only out of a fully catholic existence. The social locus of inclusive theology, therefore, is an ecumenical church. The whole people of God with its variety of perspectives must be involved in the making of theology. Some of the strains and stresses entailed by this conviction are described in the story of Craigville that follows. To it and to this personal journey there must always be this postscript: the quest for a full-orbed theology is dogged by a fragmentation that persists to the end. We are *in via,* with all the shortcomings to be expected and all the openness demanded of travel unfinished. *Semper Reformanda!* That is narrative theology in its deepest meaning.

THE CRAIGVILLE PILGRIMAGE

The intellectual and spiritual turmoil in sections of the United Church of Christ of the 1980s tells a lot about the issues that confront Christian faith in the late twentieth century. These things are especially true of a small theological drama that took place in the village of Craigville. While the events and the process they set in motion will be "ancient history" by the time these words are read, they are a sampling of the times and circumstances in which this systematics is written, and a clue to its contents.

On the fiftieth anniversary of the Barmen Declaration[31] several of the rump theological groups in the United Church of Christ sent out an open invitation to a colloquy on the confessional condition of the denomination. The "status confessionis" and how it is reached is a subject of considerable debate. In societies where a highly visible ideology openly threatens the existence of the church and the gospel, the need for a clear affirmation of Christian claims is compelling. So is the unambiguous rejection of alien teachings and their dehumanizing consequences. In such a period the Synod of Barmen took place in 1934 and the Confessing Church was born to confront the blood and soil philosophy and practice in Germany. In late twentieth-century South Africa, where racism poses a like challenge, the World Alliance of Reformed Churches named racism as a "heresy" and indicted its practice in church and society.[32] But what of societies where "both the horns of the devil and all the forked feet" (Reinhold Niebuhr) do not show so prominently? What of churches that are known for their declared *resistance* to dehumanization in its racist, sexist, and classist forms? Can there be need for confession here, too? And if so, what would be its character?

The 170 people from across the denomination who responded to the grassroot effort at self-examination thought there was cause for a declaration of faith, even in such a church. As with the Barmen Confession, the condition that prompted this was an accommodation of the gospel to the culture, one much more subtle than Barmen faced but carrying with it the same chameleonlike accom-

31. The Barmen Declaration was made by members of the Confessing Church in Germany in 1934 at their Synod of Barmen. It forcefully challenged the "blood and soil" philosophy of Nazism on the basis of listening only to "the one Word, Jesus Christ." See "The Theological Declaration of Barmen," *The Book of Confessions,* Presbyterian Church (USA) (New York: Office of the General Assembly, 1983), 8.01–8.28.

32. The World Alliance of Reformed Churches suspended from the privileges of its membership the Nederduitse Gereformeerde Kerk and the Nederduitse Hervormde Kerk van Afrika for corrupting the gospel with racist philosophy. See *Called to Witness to the Gospel Today: Studies from the World Alliance of Reformed Churches* (Geneva: WARC, 1983), 26-30.

modation of faith to fit the tendencies of the times. This acculturation was seen to take two forms. In congregations it meant the temptation to succumb to the narcissism, consumerism, and nationalism of the day, and the attendant loss of Christian substance in preaching, teaching, and practice. A study of the profile of clergy sought by North American denominations judged the norm to be "a pallid but personal faith."[33] In particular, UCC congregations appeared to lack any interest in having pastors knowledgeable in the Bible, theologically aware, or committed to mission. In the corporate structure of the church, its agencies, boards, conferences, and synods cultural captivity took a different form: the rhetoric and some of the reality of social activism were there, but little interest in their biblical and theological grounding and small concern for aspects of the Christian faith other than the social service and social action agendas. A doctoral study by a UCC pastor investigated the published material of the denomination using Avery Dulles's "church model" classification (the church as herald stressing proclamation, as sacrament stressing liturgy and worship, as communion highlighting fellowship, as servant stressing ministry to human need, and as institution specializing in organization); he found the church as servant to be the almost exclusive focus of the United Church of Christ in its corporate expression, with little evidence of interest in the kerygmatic, liturgical, and communal dimensions.[34]

If these readings of the UCC were right, it meant, at best, that the UCC was made up of caring congregations, and was a denomination committed to action for justice and peace. At worst, it bespoke submission to the conventional wisdom of the culture or the counterculture, the church taking its cues from the pop psychology and pop sociology of the day. Here was a social context that pled for a forthright statement of doctrinal identity that brought the ideologies under judgment. It called for not a full-blown "confession," something that would have to grow out of a representative constituency before a clear and present peril, but the fragmentary testimony of a ragged company speaking to those with whom it traveled, "a letter to the churches."

33. The phrase is that of Richard Ostling, *Time* religion editor, in the title of his story on research. See *Time,* Sept. 29, 1980, 85.

34. William Imes, *Concepts of the Church Advocated in the United Church of Christ (USA) and the Evangelical Church of the Union (DDR)* D. Min. Typescript, 1978. For a sharp rebuke of theological acculturation in the Church of the Brethren by Barth/Blumhardt–influenced Vernard Eller, see his *Towering Babble* (Elgin, Ill.: Brethren Press, 1983).

The reader may judge whether the participants achieved this goal in the following epistolary effort.

THE CRAIGVILLE COLLOQUY LETTER TO OUR BROTHERS AND SISTERS IN UNITED CHURCH OF CHRIST

Grace and Peace:

On the 50th anniversary of the Barmen Declaration we have come together at Craigville to listen for God's Word to us, and to speak of the things that make us who we are in Christ.

We praise God for the theological ferment in our Church! When such life comes, and light is sought, we discern the Spirit's work. The struggle to know and do the truth is a gift of God to us. So too are the traditions that have formed us—Congregational, Christian, Evangelical, Reformed, and the diverse communities that have since shaped our life together. We give thanks for the freedom in this family of faith to look for ever-new light and truth from God's eternal Word.

Thankful for the vital signs in our midst, we know too that our weaknesses have been the occasion for God's workings among us. To make confession at Craigville is also to acknowledge our own part in the confusions and captivities of the times. The trumpet has too often given an uncertain sound. As the people of God, clergy and laity, our words have often not been God's Word, and our deeds have often been timid and trivial. Where theological disarray and lackluster witness are our lot, it is "our own fault, our own most grievous fault."

Yet we trust God's promises. Mercy is offered to those who confess their sin. Grace does new things in our midst. Blessing and honor, glory and power be unto God!

In our deliberations we have sought to honor the ties that bind us, and to learn from the diversities that enrich us. We gladly speak here of the affirmations we can make together, and the judgments we share.

Authority

Loyal to our founders' faith, we acknowledge Jesus Christ as our "sole Head, Son of God and Saviour" (Preamble, Para. 2, *The Constitution of the United Church of Christ*). With Barmen we confess fidelity to "the one Word of God which we have to hear and which we have to trust and obey in life and death" (Barmen, 8:11). Christ is the Center to whom we turn in the midst of the clamors, uncertainties and temptations of the hour.

We confess Jesus Christ "as he is attested for us in Holy Scripture" (Barmen, 8:11). As our forebears did, we too look "to the Word of God in the Scriptures" (Preamble, Para. 2). Christ speaks to us unfailingly in the prophetic-apostolic testimony. Under his authority, we hold the Bible as the trustworthy rule of faith and practice. We believe that the ecumenical creeds, the evangelical confessions, and the covenants we have made in our churches at various times and places, aid us in understanding the Word addressed to us. We accept the call to relate that Word to the world of peril and hope in which God has placed us, making the ancient faith our own in this generation "in honesty of thought and expression, and in purity of heart before God" (Preamble, Para. 2).

Affirmation

According to these norms and guides, we call for sound teaching in our Church, and so confess the trinitarian content of our faith. Affirming our Baptism "in the name of the Father and of the Son and of the Holy Spirit" (Matt. 28:19), we believe that the triune God is manifest in the drama of creation, reconciliation and sanctification. Following the recital of these mighty acts in our Statement of Faith, we celebrate the creative and redemptive work of God in our beginnings, the covenant with the people of Israel, the incarnation of the Word in Jesus Christ and the saving deed done in his life, death and resurrection, the coming of the Holy Spirit in church and world, and the promise of God to consummate all things according to the purposes of God. In the United Church of Christ we believe that the divine initiatives cannot be separated from God's call to respond with our own liberating and reconciling deeds in this world, and thus to accept the invitation to the cost and joy of discipleship.

Church

Our faith finds its form in the Christian community. We rejoice and give thanks to God for the gift of the one, holy, catholic and apostolic Church, gathered by the Holy Spirit from the whole human race in all times and places. That Church is called to share the life-giving waters of Baptism and feed us with the life-sustaining bread and wine of Eucharist; to proclaim the Gospel to all the world; to reach out in mission by word and deed, healing and hope, justice and peace. Through Baptism the Church is united to Christ and shares Christ's prophetic, priestly and royal ministry in its servant form. We rejoice that God calls some members for the ministry of Word and Sacrament to build up the Body and equip the saints for ministry in the world. We rejoice that God calls the laity to their threefold ministry, manifesting the Body of Christ in the places of work and play, living and dying.

We confess that although we are part of the Body in this Church, we are not the whole Body. We need always seek Christ's Word and presence in other communities of faith, and be united with all who confess Christ and share in his mission.

Polity

We confess our joy in the rich heritage of the Congregational, Christian, Evangelical, and Reformed traditions and the many diverse peoples who compose the fabric of the United Church of Christ. We are a "coat of many colors" and we give thanks for this diversity. We affirm the value of each voice and tradition that God has brought together and that our unity in Christ informs our faith and practice. In these days together, we have been reminded of the search for unity amidst the marvelous diversity in the United Church of Christ. We acknowledge that our diversity is not only a precious gift of God but that it is sometimes the source of hurt, frustration and anger.

God is gracious. Through God's grace we are able to embrace in forgiveness and to reconcile divisions. In covenant we are continually being called to be present to and for one another. In covenant we are being called to acknowledge that without one another we are incomplete, but together in Christ we are his Body in which each part is honored.

We have not yet reached agreement in our discussions regarding the governance of the Church. We acknowledge a need to develop further our polity; to hold together in mutual accountability all the various parts of our Church. We affirm that the Christian community must conform its life and practice to the Lordship of Jesus Christ and dare not heed the voice of a stranger. We affirm that in the United Church of Christ the Holy Spirit acts in powerful ways as the communities of faith gather for worship and for work, in local churches, in the Associations, in the Conferences, in the General Synod, and in the instrumentalities and Boards. As a servant people, the prayer on the lips of the Church at such times is always: "Come, Holy Spirit!"

Justice

We have not reached agreement on the meaning of peace with justice. We confess however our own involvement with the injustices present in our society. We acknowledge our need to embody God's eternal concern for the least and most vulnerable of our neighbors. This shall require a renewed commitment to the study of the biblical teachings on justice and a fresh determination to do the things that make for peace.

We invite you to join us in reconsidering the meaning of Jesus' call and the summons to the Church to preach good news to the poor, proclaim release to the captives, enable recovery of sight to the blind, set at liberty those who are oppressed, and proclaim the acceptable year of our Lord.

Where justice is compromised and the rights of the weak sacrificed to the demands of the strong, the Church is called to resist. Christ stands alongside those deprived of their just claims. We pray for ears to hear God's voice resounding in the cries of those who are victimized by the cruel misuse of power. God's tears are shed also amidst the indifferent. We share with each of you the ministry of reconciliation. We ask you to consider thoughtfully the meaning and implications of this high calling in the world God loves and to which Jesus Christ comes as the embodiment of hope, the messenger of love, and the guarantor of the divine intention that the bound be set free from the unjust yoke.

In response to the witness of the Holy Scriptures and the example of Jesus Christ, we beseech our government at every level, to be steadfast and persistent in the pursuit of political, economic and social justice with mercy and compassion. We are of a common mind, inviting you to join us in the urgent pursuit of those longings which compel a just peace in the nuclear age. Where justice is withheld among us, God is denied. Where peace is forsaken among us, we forsake Christ, the life of the Church is compromised, and the message of reconciliation is gravely wounded. Let us bear witness to the truth in this.

Ambiguities

We acknowledge with joy that new light is yet to break forth from God's Word. This bright light is a gift for the nurturing of our lives as Christians. At the same time, it is our experience that this vision of the Church is often blurred and incomplete. "For now we see through a glass, dimly" (1 Cor. 13:12). Where our vision is unclear and the voice of the Church uncertain, we are urged not to indifference or compromise, but to our knees; to repentance, to prayer, and an earnest quest, seeking together the way of Christ for us.

We acknowledge with gratitude that in Christ every dividing wall of enmity or hostility is broken down. How do we celebrate this when we are tempted to ignore, avoid or resist some members of the community? Is not such resistance a contradiction of love of neighbor? As brothers and sisters in Christ we are summoned to address one another with humility knowing that our words and actions are subject to the judgment of God. Are we not to trust God to reconcile divisions among us, and when there has been separation or hurt to lead us back to one another as a shepherd searches for the flock? Can we afford to be any longer apart from the promise of the Gospel? Are we not to live this promise in the brilliant light of God's redeeming ways with us? God is faithful and just. Trusting in that faithfulness and the enormity of divine grace, surely we may bear the tension of the paradoxes of salvation not yet fully realized.

Rejections

Ours is an age of a multitude of gods and we are tempted on every side to cling to a false message and a false hope. This is a dangerous path and it is no stranger to any of our congregations. Idolatry can tempt us and lull us to sleep; it offers us false comfort and false security. We ask you to consider with us the idolatries of our time and to reject all that denies the Lordship of Jesus Christ.

We reject "the illusions of self-liberation" (WARC, II, 2, p. 12). With the framers of the Barmen Declaration, we reject the false teaching that there may be "areas of our life in which we would not belong to Jesus Christ, but to other lords; areas in which we would not need justification and sanctification through him" (Barmen, 8:15).

We reject the racism and sexism that demean our lives as those created precious in the sight of God.

We reject materialism and consumerism that put things in place of God and value possessions more than people.

We reject secularism that reduces life to its parts and pieces, and relativism that abandons the search for truth.

We reject militarism that promises "security" by means of a nuclear balance of terror, threatening God's creation with destructive "gods of metal."

We reject identification with any ideology of the right or the left "as though the Church were permitted to abandon the form of its message and order to its own pleasure or to changes in prevailing ideological and political convictions" (Barmen, 8:18).

We reject cultural captivity and accommodations as well as the notion that we can turn aside from the world in indifference, for we remember that "the earth is the Lord's and the fulness thereof . . ." (Psalm 24:1).

We urge the Church in each of its parts to prayerfully consider the meaning for our times of Paul's admonition in Romans 12:2: "... Do not be conformed to this world but be transformed by the renewal of your mind, that you may prove what is the will of God, what is good and acceptable and perfect." Pray that God will help the United Church of Christ discern the things we must reject as well as the things we must affirm, that to which we say "no" and that to which we give our glad assent.

Life Together

For the health of the Church and the integrity of our witness and service, we urge clergy and laity to gather in timely fashion for prayer, study, and mutual care. We encourage the mutual support of clergy for one another in their ministry, and ask the theological faculties to maintain communion with students beyond the years of their formal study. We ask Church and Ministry Committees to nurture Christian love and concern for seminarians during the course of their preparation for ordained tasks in the Church. We hope that retreats and periods of rest, reflection and spiritual renewal will become part of our life together in each Conference, and that the teaching ministry might be affirmed by laity and clergy to the end that our congregational life and our mission be anchored deeply in Scripture and informed generously by the urgent realities of our time.

Doxology

To the truth of the Gospel that has sustained and emboldened the Church in each generation, we too say "yes." With grateful hearts, we affirm the gift of faith present in the United Church of Christ—evangelical, catholic, and reformed—which we are being called to live out in these fragile and bewildering times.

While the way ahead is not always clear to us, we dare to hope and rejoice, believing that we belong to our faithful Saviour, Jesus Christ, our "only comfort in life and death" (Heidelberg Catechism, Ques. 1). We seek to hold together worship, discipleship, proclamation and service, Word and world.

As our forebears have done, we too declare that we shall tread this path with all who are "kindred in Christ" and "share in this confession" (Preamble, Para. 2). We invite you to walk with us in this way.

In Christ,
The Participants in the Craigville Colloquy
Craigville, Massachusetts, May 16, 1984

The letter received attention in the church press because it seemed to be news of something stirring, enlarging the standard picture of the UCC as "the social action church." Appreciative comments came from ecumenical sources that had wondered about the UCC's theological commitments, and from UCC members who saw Craigville as an effort to hold together doctrine and action. But it got its share of brickbats. As the latter are important to the kind of theological method being hammered out here, we mention them and their effect on the subsequent Craigville process.

The Boston Feminist Dialogue group was the first to make its objections known. After studying the document the group issued a statement rejecting the "abstract theology" they perceived in the letter, criticizing the absence of women in the colloquy process, the lack of attention to women's issues, and signs of a less-than-adequate commitment to inclusive language. On the heels of that came objections from both "the left" and "the right" in the church, each side judging the colloquy to be "centrist" and therefore flawed in terms of its particular concerns. Some social action advocates dismissed it as a sell-out to the current wave of neopietism and conservatism, while pietist and political conservatives saw it as the same old theological and social liberalism for which they had always faulted the UCC. A Presbyterian editor perceived it as a move toward denominationalism and away from ecumenism. An exponent of the hermeneutics of suspicion wrote a long article condemning it as a power play of aging white middle-class males trying to reverse the gains in the UCC struggle against racism and sexism in the obscurities of theological jargon.

Pleased by the positive response and expecting the antitheological criticism from predictable sources, Craigvillers were nevertheless disturbed by attacks on their commitment to the action agenda of the UCC and by the allegation that the marginalized did not have a place in the document or a role in the proceedings. Two of the seven-member drafting committee had just been arrested in South Africa embassy protests, and many of the colloquy participants had histories of involvement in the struggles against racism and sexism, poverty and war. Forty women had taken part in the colloquy with significant representation in working groups, planning committee, plenary leadership, and the drafting committee. However, a floor fight that preserved the traditional trinitarian formula for baptism, with its ecumenical implications in mind, provided the evidence some critics needed for the charges of sexism, while others were troubled by the fact that the principal organizers of the colloquy were males. There was no doubt that the "y'all come" invitation to theological dialogue did not produce the hoped-for cross section of people. The planners of "Craigville II" tried to take to heart the word of the critics.

Yes, there would be a second colloquy, for the wide interest evoked by this kind of forum pointed to a sequel and perhaps even an ongoing process. This time it was the Craigville Conference Center that took the initiative, encouraged by the leadership of the BTL and the Mercersburg Society, who recognized the need for more broadly based ventures. To that end the director invited a wide spectrum of people and points of view to plan for a second meeting, one that would continue the original vision. An organizing committee was formed, constituted by both the representatives and the critics of the first colloquy, bringing with them a diversity of perspectives and interests. Included were members of the Boston Feminist Dialogue group, the Biblical Witness Fellowship (the evangelical caucus in the UCC), black and Hispanic clergy, laity leadership, justice and peace activists, representatives of a new "spirituality network" in the UCC, a few BTL and Mercersburg members, and some with no self-chosen identity or advocacy position. They shared a common love for the theological task, but beyond that, what? Here we seek to name some of the characteristics that mark this kind of theological matrix, what can happen in it, and be hoped for out of it. In recounting the events at Craigville II we will describe motifs that were common to both, and express the kind of theological process they entailed.

The planners of Colloquy II were determined to keep the spontaneity and participatoriness of the first gathering. Thus both colloquies opted for a self-select process: "Do you feel called to speak?" Then in response, the community as a whole makes its views known. The influence of the laity movement is at work here, one in which gifts of ministry are discerned by individuals in concert with the community. This mixture of freedom and order seemed to the organizers to be the way the Spirit worked in the life of the church over time, as in the spontaneities rising in the midst of the people in combination with the orderings of Word and Sacrament. This dual premise manifested itself at various points of the Craigville process:

1. In both colloquies the drafting committees were chosen in the main by the New Testament practice of "casting lots."[35] In Collo-

35. Acts 1:26.

quy I, the entire assembly was asked to consider whether its members had a call to be on the drafting committee for the letter. Thirty stepped forward. Straws were drawn from this number and five selected. In Colloquy II each of the ten working groups was asked to select (by any method—from casting lots to agreement to election) a representative among its number who volunteered for the drafting task; from this pool of ten, five were chosen by lots. In both colloquies these five were supplemented by two more persons chosen by the organizing committee for their "poetic or editorial skills" and thus some planning was conjoined to most freedom. In the first colloquy four local church pastors and a conference minister ("bishop") were chosen by the lot-casting method, and the BTL convener chairing the eight hours of committee labor. Theologically, the group included various mainline perspectives, some radical social activists, a leader in the Biblical Witness Fellowship, and a Mercersburg Society founder. In Colloquy II, four local church pastors and a seminary professor were chosen by lot and the comoderator of the colloquy (a local church pastor) and the writer were appointed by the organizing committee, with the comoderator chairing the drafting process. Again the group worked eight hours through the night. On both occasions the committee received reports from colloquy working groups, determined overall themes, parceled out the respective sections to be written by the seven drafters, reviewed and refined those offerings, and then turned the results over to two editors for polishing. The working draft was then submitted to the full colloquy for judgment.

2. In Colloquy II the selection of major speakers/presenters was determined by a churchwide search for one-page papers on the authority of Scripture. Forty-five responded to the invitation placed in the national and regional UCC media. Six were chosen by the organizing committee. The hermeneutical spectrum included feminist, conservative evangelical, critical, activist, ecumenical, and centrist perspectives, reflecting the variety in the denomination and, beyond that, the current debates in biblical interpretation.

3. Both colloquies invited anyone interested in forming a precolloquy study group on the themes to do so, and send the results of the group's deliberation to the organizing committee for publication in a booklet given to colloquy registrants upon arrival. Twenty-one such groups were formed for Colloquy I, with reports of varying lengths received and printed from twelve of the groups. Thirteen groups formed for the second colloquy and three-page papers were received from eleven of them. In Colloquy II the re-

sponse was built around three questions posed by the World Alliance of Reformed Churches: the meaning of Scripture as Word, the relation of Scripture to tradition, and the relation of Scripture and tradition to "lived experience."[36]

4. The heart of both colloquies was the working group. In the refined process of Colloquy II, ten groups were created by random assignment of numbers at registration. These met seven times throughout the colloquy to react to presentations and build toward a working-group statement responding to the three World Alliance questions. Conveners of the working groups representing a variety of views were selected by the organizing committee and oriented to their task by a training period before the colloquy in which they reviewed a spectrum of views on the authority and interpretation of the Bible, examined exegetical resources, and discussed group process.

Registering for the meeting were 140 people from throughout the church—from such distant points as Hawaii and California, with delegations from the South and Midwest, Pennsylvania and Ohio, and of course the New England areas. Strong representation was present from feminist groups and other critics of Craigville I. Mercersburg Society, BTL, and Biblical Witness members were also on hand. Many participants had no affiliation with grassroot movements or advocacy groups but were drawn to the event by the importance of its subject for debates within the UCC, and a need for clarity in their own teaching, preaching, and personal journey. Pastors predominated but laity were present and vocal. Conference ministers, associate conference ministers, and staff were there from twelve of the thirty-nine conferences. A few representatives from major church boards and agencies were on hand, as also were several members of the Executive Council and the assistant to the President of the Church (the president was present at Colloquy I). A handful of seminary students and a few seminary faculty attended. Some members of the EKU-UCC working group that was cultivating links with the Evangelical Church in Germany were present, as their annual meeting had been coordinated with it. While three black participants played a significant role in the life of the colloquy, efforts to secure significant minority representation failed.

Colloquy II began with worship and was suffused throughout

36. *Called to Witness to the Gospel Today,* 14-15.

with regular morning and evening prayers, and included other forms of worship such as an early American gospel chorus; the climax of worship was a closing eucharist. The worship committee took great pains to combine liturgical quality and celebrative and contemplative traditions with vigorous preaching and a variety of perceptions of the colloquy theme, with women and men taking turns at leadership. The variety did produce some tension around inclusive language issues as I shall presently report.

The Colloquy II format provided for six presenters to read twenty-minute papers throughout the first day with ten minutes of plenary response. (Presiding in plenary were the moderator of Colloquy I and a member of the Boston Feminist Dialogue group.) The first working-group meeting was devoted to the exegesis of a common text (John 20:1-18) to give opportunity for methods of interpretation to emerge and encounter one another. Craigville biblical-scholar-in-residence, Willis Elliott, provided exegetical guidelines in an early plenary session in preparation for this work. And a book nook was open during the colloquy with a range of resources on current exegesis and interpretation.

In Colloquy II (as in I), after two days of presentations and working-group conversation, the scribes or conveners of the ten groups made a plenary presentation of agreements and disagreements on the authority of Scripture and turned them over to the drafting committee. Following that the entire colloquy met for a festive meal and an evening off while the drafting committee did its work. The following morning the draft of the statement was presented in plenary, followed by a two-hour discussion about its contents. Amendments and editorial refinements were passed and suggested. At the close of II (as in I), a vote was taken on the substance of this "witness" and the twelve-hundred-word statement was approved with six dissenting votes. (The Colloquy I Letter had been approved by a vote of 140 for, 6 against.) Before we examine the document, we need to mention some of the behind-the-scenes drama. Critics of Colloquy I, determined to have their views represented, registered in significant numbers for Colloquy II and were welcomed by the organizing committee. Members of the Boston Feminist Dialogue group caucused during the meeting and organized a protest over the use of some less-than-inclusive language in one of the worship services, announcing that its group and supporters would stand in silent witness whenever such took place again. The organizing committee had asked the compiler of a UCC inclusive language hymnbook to hold a workshop during the conference to explore these issues, but allowed worship leaders to follow their conscience on this matter, and more traditional usage followed in some cases. Again, members of the feminist group, together with others, approached the organizing committee on the second morning to challenge another feature, the format of the second day, which linked two presentations of a very different sort (the feminist and the evangelical papers), and did not allow sufficient time for working-group response to each. The petitioning group also raised the question of the advisability of a statement from the colloquy, holding that the diversity of views and limited time made such impossible. The organizing committee accepted the first recommendation and changed the format accordingly, but declined to act on the second, maintaining its commitment to a modest "witness to the churches," whatever that might turn out to be.

As it developed, the casting of lots for a drafting committee produced a group composed of five women and two men. That number included vigorous spokespersons for feminist concerns, in particular, and activists in general, as well as other points of view. As a gracious move in response to the preponderance of women on the drafting committee one of the Boston Feminist Dialogue group proposed the addition of another man to the drafting committee to achieve better balance. This proposal was turned down in plenary with an avowal of trust in the Spirit's work through the designated process.

Was this trust justified? I believe it was. But let the reader judge.

A WITNESS TO OUR BROTHERS AND SISTERS IN THE UNITED CHURCH OF CHRIST FROM THE CRAIGVILLE II THEOLOGICAL COLLOQUY SCRIPTURE/WORD IN THE UNITED CHURCH OF CHRIST

Chronicle

The yearning for theological dialogue and clarity among members of the United Church of Christ, the challenge to respond to questions posed by the World Alliance of Reformed Churches, and the momentum generated in Colloquy I, converged in a second Craigville Colloquy on September 4-6, 1985. Preparation and participation began early in the year when an invitation was extended to individuals and groups to consider the following questions: In what way can it be said that Scripture is God's

Word? What is the relationship between the authority of Scripture and the authority of tradition? Between Scripture and the lived experience in diverse social, cultural, and historical situations? . . .

This document can capture only a portion of the passion, the pain, and the power that were shared as 140 people struggled to understand and to be understood. We represented great diversity of experience and theological perspective, but we were not representative of the full diversity of the United Church of Christ, in that most of us were white, middle-class clergy. Many of us arrived expecting to have the rough edges of differences sharpened; others hoped to soften high-contrast distinctions. Through encounters with others, some departed with a surer sense of the boundaries of our own perspectives. Others, through those same encounters, found our perspectives enlarged and enriched. All of us left more sensitive to the mystery of the Word.

Themes of Our Witness

An emerging theme of consensus among us was that the authority of Scripture, the authority of tradition, and the authority of experience are inextricably bound together. Any one or two taken apart from the other(s) would not be faithful to our understanding of how God speaks to us. At the same time, we recognized the centrality of Scripture as the means by which tradition and experience are illumined. Some affirmed that God has also spoken to us through other people and/or life situations which have profoundly illumined our reading of Scripture. For others, Scripture and tradition and experience are so closely related that centrality is not an issue; rather, they see a motion among the three which sometimes brings experience to the fore, sometimes tradition, sometimes Scripture. For yet others, the original text of Scripture is equated with the Word of God.

Another emerging theme was the recognition that, because our contexts differ—age, sex, race, class, condition—we are a diverse people. Accordingly, we recognize that, as a community of faith, we can only realize the fullness and richness of God's Word when we all truly hear and honor these diverse voices of the whole church of God.

The metaphor of a prism may illumine the multiplicity of our experience as a community of faith and covenant. As light is refracted through the prism to produce the full spectrum of color, so the Word of God is refracted through Scripture, bringing forth an array of different expressions. In this way, the prism reminds us of our unity, for only when all the colors are gathered in the testimony of the whole community can we begin to glimpse the fullness of the light of God's Word made known to us. As Paul reminds us, all the parts are necessary for the wholeness of the body of Christ (1 Corinthians 12).

We returned time and again to the conviction that the sovereign triune God is the source and character of the Word. All our judgments are made with a humility that honors the mystery and majesty of that source. For Christian people, the holy God speaks the self-revealing Word in the holy Scriptures, through the testimony of the Holy Spirit. All our words are accountable to that Word spoken in and through the canon. In the trustworthy testimony of prophet, apostle, and countless unnamed biblical people, and in the proclamation arising out of their testimony, human beings witness to the divine light. The Bible therefore, is the matrix out of which our own testimonies of faith are born, by which they are nourished, and in which they grow. In the life of the Christian community, this text is the heart of our teaching and preaching, our prayer, our life, and our mission.

The Christian tradition confesses that, within the canon, the clearest expression of God's Word is the life and ministry, death and resurrection of Jesus Christ. Thus, the church asserts that Jesus Christ is the primary Word of God, in which we know ourselves judged and reconciled by God, and sent out to be reconciled with our neighbors. This message of reconciliation is the lens which allows us to focus our gaze on Scripture itself and on our further reflections on God's Word made manifest in the world. This same message stands as the internal interpretive norm for Scripture, and thus for tradition, experience, and life.

The canon is inextricably bound to the Christian community, known to us both through the stories, creeds and confessions of its history and through our participation in its contemporary life. We encounter the living Word in the sacramental and liturgical life of the body of Christ where the Word, tradition, and experience are bound together. Since we in the community of faith know ourselves to be addressed ever anew by God's Word, new testimonies to God's Word will continue to arise in new historical contexts, and new stories will grow out of our response to the biblical narrative. These testimonies and stories will serve as new earthen vessels to carry the Word of God by which these and all human witnesses are judged.

Commission

Through the illumination of the Holy Spirit, the Scriptures make known to us Jesus Christ, the Incarnate Word of God. That Word calls us to personal repentance and transformation and meets us as we stand with the suffering and oppressed. This same Word commands us to proclaim the Gospel in words and deeds of justice and mercy, to challenge and confront the principalities and powers of evil, and to love our neighbors and our enemies.

Our tradition is more than a mere historical record of the church. We are a people of the resurrection. Our forebears live in Christ, and "we are surrounded by a cloud of witnesses" (Hebrews 12) who encourage us in our struggle with sin and the powers of evil. We are not isolated or alone.

Our experience, personal and corporate, is more than a mere passing of days and years. We are a people created, sustained, and indwelt by the Spirit of God. We must speak our experience to the whole church and to the world, even as we must listen to all who are in Christ and to people of other faiths, so that our smallness of vision will not blind us to the fullness of God's presence.

In all this we confess that although "we see in a mirror dimly" (1 Corinthians 13), we do glimpse God's vision, and together with the universal church, we are called to believe and to act.

We invite churches and members of the United Church of Christ to join our dialogue around these concerns of our common life.

In Christ,
The Participants in the Craigville II Theological Colloquy
Craigville, Mass., September 6, 1985

Sifting and sorting through the document in the light of controversies in the UCC in the wider church, I have found the following to be some of its achievements:

1. A clear declaration of biblical authority, the Scripture as the definitive source of Christian faith and life. The statement speaks in a variety of ways and metaphors of the Bible's normativity: its "centrality," its location as "heart" of our teaching, preaching, and mission, its position as "matrix" of belief and life, its function as standard to which all human testimony is "accountable," its existing as the place where the divine "Word" is heard and the divine "light" shines as God's "self-revelation" happens through the testi-

mony of "prophet and apostle." These various figures and concepts—reflecting traditional, dialectical, and contemporary images and formulations—make the authority of Scripture the ultimate court of appeal in faith and life.

2. Affirmation of a strong assertion of a Christological hermeneutic of Scripture. The basic interpretive principle of scriptural authority is Jesus Christ, the "lens" through which we read the text. What is biblically authoritative is, as Luther put it long ago, what "urges Christ."

3. Affirmation of the role of tradition. The church in its ancient lore and contemporary witness is declared to be a valued guide in understanding and interpreting the Bible. Indeed it is a resource and not the source, "ministerial" not "magisterial," but for all that indispensable.

4. The richness of the church's tradition is to be sought out in the quest for the meaning of the biblical text. Using the image of "prism" the Witness speaks of the illumination of biblical meaning by the variety of perspectives in the church, its meaning coming from the receiving of these diverse gifts, as in 1 Cor. 12.

5. Affirmation of the crucial role of "lived experience" in drawing out the implications and applications of the text. Here the historical and cultural context of understanding Scripture is given its due in an interactionist paragraph, asserting the principle of "hermeneutical circulation," the dynamic interplay of text and ecclesial and social contexts. Yet this inseparability of the three is combined with the assertion that Scripture is primary in its illumination of tradition and experience, and the latter two are "accountable" to Scripture.

6. The ultimate source of authority in "the holy God" challenges too easy association of the human words of the Bible with this sovereignty. That assertion is held together in tension with "the holy Scriptures" as the way through which the divine self-disclosure is mediated.

7. Affirmation of the critical role of justice and peace concerns in the contemporary interpretation of Scripture.

The second colloquy was a continuing learning experience, in the risks of theological conversation among diverse partners, and in the excitement and unpredictability of the grassroot process.

Cosponsors of the first, and in attendance at the second but in reduced numbers, members of the Mercersburg Society voted for the Witness Statement, but experienced trials and tribulations along the way, and mixed feelings afterward. While a strong liturgical and sacramental framework existed throughout the colloquy, and ecumenical and catholic notes in many of the working-group reports, little notice was taken of this in the early draft of the Witness Statement. Representatives of the Mercersburg tradition brought this out in plenary, and proposed an amendment that would take into account the sacramental and liturgical aspects of authority. It was voted down by a majority. But it came up in the subsequent debate, and a distilled version of the proposal was approved by a new majority vote. However, the Mercersburg viewpoint came under fire there, and earlier in several of the working groups, and the traditional language of some of its representatives as well was sharply criticized by feminist participants. Can the churchly and the activist learn from each other and work together? This question has had its effects in formulating the themes for the third colloquy—"the ministry of the whole People of God"—one which will engage these kinds of issues as they surfaced in the important ecumenical study, *Baptism, Eucharist and Ministry,* and the movement to recover the ministry of the laity.[37]

Biblical Witness Fellowship members who were on hand had a mixed reaction. One BWF leader expressed cautious approval of the Witness but doubted its effect on the denomination. On the other hand, the president of BWF, who made one of the presentations, objected in the final debate to the first-draft omission of a moderate inerrantist view in the chronicle of colloquy diversity. This legitimate concern resulted in a floor amendment and in the inclusion of this point in the final edition of the Witness. He and another BWF leader also expressed doubts as to the clarity of the statement on the final authority of Scripture, as its interactionist paragraph was seen to mute the note of biblical centrality.

Many positive testimonies came from others along the spectrum represented at the conference, from feminists to centrists to evan-

37. Craigville Colloquy III was held Sept. 30–Oct. 2, 1986, on "The Ministry of the Whole People of God," with similar processes and dynamics. Critic-in-residence on this occasion was a corps of vocal laity whose strong commitment to the ministry of the laity brought this concern to the fore. The complementarity of the ministries of laity and clergy, both grounded in the ministry of Christ, is affirmed in the colloquy Witness Statement adopted unanimously after the work of an all-night drafting committee chosen by the same lot-drawing process as the earlier colloquies. See *The United Church News* (Dec. 1986): 6. Fourth and fifth colloquies are in the planning stages for 1987 (the Eucharist) and 1988 (Baptism and Mission).

gelicals. However, to honor catholicity, we must hear from the critics. Some both within and without the colloquy saw it as opposed to the things they stood for. These included some self-declared "liberals" who interpreted the biblical and theological ferment in the UCC as a retreat into dogmatism. A contingent arrived at Craigviile and made its point of view known throughout the meeting, arguing in working groups and in plenary for a "common core" view of Christian identity,[38] and appealing for a focus on contemporary issues rather than the "abstract" questions of biblical authority. Failing in an effort to forestall a colloquy statement, they made a skillful parliamentary move at the close to "receive" rather than to adopt the report, and after the defeat of that motion voted against the Witness Statement.

Other critics found fault with the colloquy process. A new denominational newspaper portrayed the event in a front page story as an occasion for partisan disputes. Taking its clue from this report an AP wire service story also featured what were seen to be tense dynamics. In contrast, the *Boston Globe* religion reporter who had been present at both colloquies highlighted the rapproachements and caught the significance of agreement on biblical authority as construed inclusively.

The Bible, the church, and the world, their interrelationships, singularities, and priorities are the issues at the heart of the Craigville process. How the varied gifts brought by the people of God can be offered to one another, and received by them, is the question posed by this kind of experiment. The account of Craigville concludes the autobiographical part of the Introduction and sets the stage for a systematic inquiry into these very issues.

TERMS AND TERRITORY

As the character of God is best rendered in the telling of the Christian Story, so too are the main terms of theology best developed in the unfolding of its plot. We let them take on flesh and blood, therefore, in the exposition to follow. But just as the playbill identifies beforehand its cast of characters, so too preliminary orientation is helpful here. Thus, I include some working definitions in this Introduction. The first has to do with the nature of systematic

38. For an exposition of this view see the typology in Chap. 5.

theology and its relation to some special terms and activities: dogmatics, doctrine, and theology.

Christian pedagogy began in the earliest moments of the church's life with "the apostles' teaching" (Acts 2:42), its precedent being the Teacher himself, Jesus. As Emil Brunner has shown, three concerns of the Christian community molded this teaching in the form of rigorous intellectual discipline: the need to distinguish truth from false belief, the requirement to instruct the faithful and those preparing for the first act of faith, and the necessity for guidance in the understanding of Scripture.[39] We consider now some of the subsequent developments and distinctions.

Dogmatics

A long and still vital tradition describes the disciplined exposition of Christian belief as "dogmatics." Where the ecclesial context is present, and the intention of the author appropriate, the comprehensive ordering of Christian teaching in this way makes sense. However, it requires two features to so qualify. Like its antecedents in the teaching of *dogmata*, or the tenets of a philosophical school, classical dogmatics rose out of a particular confessional or creedal community. Similar to its other root word, which meant public ordinance or decree, *dogma* (and its exposition) is associated with binding rules and clear powers of enforcement. Thus a Reformed dogmatics, Lutheran dogmatics, or Roman Catholic dogmatics expounds the definitive teachings of those churches and establishes boundaries of ecclesial inclusion and exclusion.

Some effort is being made in this century to recover the language of dogma and dogmatics, with Barth's *Church Dogmatics* the best-known attempt.[40] Where there is a base in ecclesial reality and identifiable teaching tradition, one can argue for such a move. Its appeal lies in the forceful declaration of Christian identity. However, where there is no particular churchly framework in either its institutional or pedagogical reality, and where there is neither the way nor the will for ecclesial inclusion/exclusion, dogma and dogmatics do not seem to be appropriate terms for the kind of theo-

39. Emil Brunner, *The Christian Doctrine of God, Dogmatics,* vol. 1, trans. Olive Wyon (Philadelphia: Westminster Press, 1950), 6-13.

40. Karl Barth, *Church Dogmatics,* ed. G. W. Bromiley and T. F. Torrance, trans. G. W. Bromiley et al. (Edinburgh: T. & T. Clark, 1936–1962). Hereafter referred to as *CD*.

logical discourse to follow. The teaching discussed here is not the province alone of a particular church tradition. As oriented to a catholicity of life and thought, it is carried out more in hope than in ecclesial reality. Yet, given the fragmentary but nevertheless real *oikoumene* from which it rises, there is a "can be" as well as an "ought to be" in the theological work done here. Included are not only the associations and hidden bondings of this larger community but also the author's particular denomination, the United Church of Christ, with the anticipations and commitments its name implies. But these informal and formal associations are, at best, portents of a catholicity yet to be. The only real evidence of an undivided church (and that open to question) is to be found in the early centuries. With it just two Christian doctrines can, by our definition, be classified as dogmas: the Person of Christ and the Trinity. As the teaching discussed here is not tied to a specific community, the juridical features of dogma are obviously not applicable. For this reason we look for other language.

Doctrine

Another word that describes the intellectual distillates of basic Christian teaching is *doctrine,* and its discipline of inquiry has been called *sacred doctrine.* Christian doctrine and the articulation of it in methodical ways comes from the same three concerns mentioned earlier—polemical, pedagogical, and expository. We shall make use, therefore, of the terminology of doctrine, but substitute for *sacred doctrine* the term *systematic theology.* First, why *doctrine?*

Doctrine has a similar lineage to that of dogma, but its associations are both richer and more diffuse. Doctrine, like dogma, is ecclesially related. It is Christian teaching done in and for the believing community. However, doctrine in our usage refers to the defining themes of the *church universal* as recovered by ecumenical perception of the past and vision of the future. Doctrines are those reference points in Christian teaching to which the whole church has had recourse, as in the doctrine of God, the doctrine of creation, the doctrine of Christ, the doctrine of the church, etc. As a point of orientation for faith, a doctrine includes a set of assertions about the subject in question: God is triune, creation is essentially good, Christ is the only-begotten of God, the church is the Body of Christ on earth, etc. Where these assertions are maintained and understood aright, there is "sound teaching." Where they are not, there is unsound teaching.

What gives form and force to doctrine is the tradition of the church catholic. In its development, circumstances precipitate an agreement on proposals that then constitute a doctrine, one that on a rare occasion achieves explicit ecumenical consensus, as in the doctrines of the Trinity and the Person of Christ. Those teachings identified in this systematics as doctrine are points of agreement, explicitly or implicitly ecumenical. They are the "grammatical rules" of the larger Christian community.[41] There is much risk in making such a claim: the capacity to find these enduring themes, to do so within the limitations and corruptions introduced by the context in which they were formulated and are appropriated, the particularity of these doctrines rather than others, etc. All this will have to be argued out in what follows.

Doctrinal reference points, while solid, are capable of better and worse perception, and less and more adequate formulation. "Doctrine develops." As time and place position them in fresh perspective, and as a wider community of ecclesial vision develops, we get a longer and fuller view of these points of orientation. That means narrow construals are corrected, and an enriched grasp of Christian teaching is possible. As perduring features of Christian identity, however, doctrine is revisable but not reversible. Earlier identifications of central Christian teaching persist in newer interpretations, and constants are present although to be understood in ever-new ways. How the continuities and discontinuities are identified and related to one another is a very large question. A narrative approach will let these matters come to expression in the story itself.

Theology

We take another step toward defining *systematic theology* by examining a third term, *theology*. The diversity of usage makes the task complex.

In what follows we shall use the word, generally, in two ways, hoping that the context will clarify the specific use. From time to time we shall accord with general usage, defining it in the broadest sense as any conceptuality or discourse about God. However, vis-à-vis doctrine and dogma, a specialized meaning is more appropri-

41. See George Lindbeck's important work *The Nature of Doctrine: Religion and Theology in a Postliberal Age* (Philadelphia: Fortress Press, 1984), 32-45, 73-90.

ate, particularly when preceded by the adjective *systematic.* To this second and more technical usage we now turn.

Classical doctrinal inquiry distinguishes between two kinds of thinking about God: God's own and our own. *Theologia archtypia* is God's self-understanding, sometimes known also as *theologia in se. Theologia ektypia* is our reflection about God. *Theologia in nobis* or *theologia nostra* is our thought about God within the limitations of human existence.[42] Eastern Orthodox theologians make similar distinctions between higher and lower forms, but within the human plane itself: "essential theology" as the normative Christian thought of the Fathers and "secondary theology," as thinking about God that takes the former as its standard. There is a commendable modesty in the references to *theologia ektypia, theologia nostra,* secondary theology. Our theology (in overall meaning) is conditioned thinking about God, bearing the marks of our humanity, and not to be confused with a God's-eye view of things, or a God's-mind understanding of them.

Within that compass we must take into account another set of distinctions. In contemporary discussion, the broad and etymologically grounded meaning of the term has been considerably stretched to include discourse about any ultimate commitment ("god" as one's final loyalty), or assumptions about reality by which one's life is oriented. Thus Marxism, democracy, Freudian psychology, humanism, and atheism have their own kind of "theology." This expanded definition brings political, economic, social, and psychological ideologies into the arena of theological discourse. However, it sometimes muddies the waters, so we shall use it only sparingly and in quotes.

At the other extreme, traditional expositions of Christian doctrine have employed the word *theology* to describe the single doctrine of God, theology as distinguished from Christology, soteriology, eschatology, etc. On rare occasion we shall follow suit, but with the qualifier, "in the narrower sense."

One influential use of the word, emerging by custom as much as by careful definition, is related to cultural developments and institutional patterns. In a society in which religion is experienced in increasingly pluralistic ways, *theology* is associated with the thought patterns of a religious tradition. The interpreters of these traditions are the "Jewish theologian," the "Christian theologian,"

42. T. F. Torrance's comments on these distinctions are helpful. See *Reality and Evangelical Theology* (Philadelphia: Westminster Press, 1982), 21-30.

the Buddhist theologian," etc. (whether or not the tradition in question is theistic or has a doctrine about God). Contributing to this are the intellectual and communal overtones of the word in its use in Judaism and Christianity to describe the centers for preparing its clergy, as in "theological" schools. Theology in this sense is the intentional work of the intellect on and with the beliefs of a religious tradition.

From these various strands we shall craft the meaning of the term and relate it to system and doctrine. Theology, in our secondary and technical sense here, is thinking about God rising from *a given time and place* conditioned by its questions and perspective, and rooted in a *particular religious tradition,* reflecting therein its commitments and community. These volumes constitute then a venture in *Christian* theology, with self-conscious occupancy of a particular commitment and community. Christian theology, as all kinds of theology, is particularist in yet another sense: it emerges from, shows the marks of, and seeks to relate to its own time and place, and is, as such, perspectival. Christian theology, therefore, works with Christian texts in a historical context.

Systematic Theology

Systematic theology in the Christian tradition is ordered thought about Christian teaching set forth in a historical context. Ordering means identifying the defining characteristics of that teaching and showing their interrelationship. Ordering, therefore, is comprehensive in scope, seeking to locate and explicate each key feature, and place it within the whole body of Christian teaching. But this quest for coherence is always carried on perspectively, as it relates to the historical circumstances of the theology and the theologian.

The materials of Christian teaching that are ordered by systematics are the *doctrines* of the Christian community. Doctrines provide the continuity along the path of perspectival discontinuity. Doctrine is the aforementioned body of teaching, latent and patent, which establishes the community's ideational identity. We follow here the distinction of the Eastern Church between essential theology and secondary theology, but do not limit the former to a patristic habitat. Also we attempt to avoid the temptations of static and traditionalist understandings of doctrine in both the East and the West with a commitment to the *development* of doctrine. There the mutual edification of doctrine and theology is important. While doctrine perdures, it develops along the line of specific historical loci as the quest for Christian identity proceeds apace, being formed by polemical, catechetical, and missionary factors in each context. And in yet another sense, we must honor the dynamism of doctrine. Former points of consensus in Christian teaching are refined and enriched by the processes of theological engagement. While not reversed, the doctrinal projectory is altered on the one hand, and extended on the other. These adjustments are the result of the theological struggles of the given time and place, fresh perspective making for new clarity of direction. And in turn, the directionality of doctrine becomes critical for the theological work of a given time and place, keeping it on the path toward its goal. Theology, therefore, takes its signals from doctrine.[43]

Doctrine as the Christian community's defining assumptions and formulations is traceable to a deeper wellspring in the charters of the community. Doctrine is the inner line of an ecclesial resource that is related to the biblical source with its gospel substance and Christological center. In speaking of these themes we have reached the subject of the volume at hand. As prefatory to it we state simply what is to be undertaken. This projected series of volumes is a systematic theology, teaching within the community of faith through the ordered exposition of Christian doctrine as it is related to a given time and place.

43. Cf. David Wells, "The Nature and Function of Theology," in Johnston, *Use of the Bible in Theology*, 174-99, who makes a similar distinction between doctrine and theology, but associates it more closely with what is identified in this work as "gospel," the biblical substance to which church is accountable. See the discussion below in Chaps. 1 and 6.

CHAPTER I

Authority and Revelation

Prolegomena in systematics are regularly devoted to questions of authority. While a case can be made for beginning at any point in the orb of Christian teaching, the method of inquiry is usually positioned before the exposition of its content. How do you arrive at your assertions of what is taught about the being and doing of God? "Theological method" (in this sense of how Christian doctrine is stated and interpreted) is addressed to the question of where we go to find out what is so. It entails decisions about "authority," the places of legitimation for theological assertions. Do we go to Scripture? To tradition? To reason? To personal or social experience? *Why* we go where we go is the warrant for the loci of the authority chosen. The answer to this "why?" is the doctrine of revelation.

While distinguishable, in the final analysis method and content are inseparable; we cannot separate the how and where from the what and why. That fact supports the assertion that we can begin anywhere in doctrinal investigation, and prompts the correlative claim that all theological argument is circular. However, there is something different about the doctrine of revelation. A *theo*logic undergirds the logic of method preceding content. Here a narrative reading of Christian faith is illuminating. The doctrine of revelation is present in every other doctrine, the theme of *disclosure* that develops in the unfolding story of God's *deeds*. Revelation is a tale within a tale. The omnipresence of this story within the Story, the guidance it gives concerning the nature of the Great Narrative, suggests that we put our feet first on this doctrinal path. Where God has disclosed what God has done determines how we go about our theological investigation.

The culture of pluralism and secularity out of which this systematics is written puts forcefully the question of authority. A heterogenous culture with its diversity of worldviews, explicitly religious or otherwise, cannot help but make the ordinary churchgoer wonder: Why do I believe this and not that? The secularization process that joins pluralization (indeed is inseparable from it) prompts both the skeptic and the believer to ask, "Why should I think this rather than that?" Thus the initial systematic question becomes a leading pastoral question. So too within the church, reflecting the cultural pressures, disputes and differences are regularly traceable to matters of authority. Does the Bible take precedence over claimant human experiences? Or the traditions of the church? And even when the Bible is accorded final authority, differing interpretive approaches produce unending disagreements. The heated controversies within evangelical Protestantism have shown that a common loyalty to the Bible, conservatively read, still brings sharp differences on matters of social and personal ethics, revelation, and salvation.[1] To understand these various points of view, and to be able to speak a word within them and to them, is the intent of this volume.

How basic these questions are for the pastor! Every sermon preached, worship service led, class taught, person counseled, program administered, judgment rendered on matters theological and moral, political, economic, social, and personal presupposes a concept of authority. To be muddled about the latter is to be confused about all of the former. What compounds the problem is the unclarity in the churches about Scripture. John Bowden throws down the gauntlet in a dictionary article on "Biblical Criticism": ". . . the churches have largely ignored or shelved the problem of biblical authority, affirming it but not sustaining their claim. . . . There is no disguising the fact that the problems associated with biblical criticism are one of the major factors in the contemporary theological malaise."[2]

Authority in narrative perspective is the question of who *au-*

1. Robert Johnston, *Evangelicals at an Impasse: Biblical Authority in Practice* (Atlanta: John Knox Press, 1978), has persuasively made this case.

2. John Bowden, "Biblical Criticism," in *The Westminster Dictionary of Christian Theology*, ed. Alan Richardson and John Bowden (Philadelphia: Westminster Press, 1983), 68.

thorizes theological assertions. "Fontal authority" is the good and gracious God, the Author of our Story.[3] Yet the "problem of authority" is not God, but our struggle to discern the means God uses to disclose truth. Here is where lines are drawn within the Christian community. Technically, we are speaking of "mediate authority."[4] God's means (revelation) will determine our methods (authority). The divine self-disclosure provides us in our own human arena with accessible touchstones of authority. These points of reference author-ize, in a secondary sense, our theological judgments. They are the "heres" and "theres" through which the Author addresses us. The understanding of the process of derivative authorization is the task before us, the question of theological authority.

Certain theories (and practices) of authority, theological or otherwise, have turned some against the use of the term, and have led to the rejection of the very idea of authority. These critics understand authority as the equivalent of "authoritarian" and "authoritarianism." Therefore, they reject all authority in the interest of parity and partnership.

A case could be made for finding another word if the association of authoritarianism with the word *authority* is so persistent that oppressive usage makes it impossible to hear the questions posed. However, the rejection of authority is itself authorized by *some place* considered trustworthy. Because the choice of one or another final reference point is unavoidable, and the battle to rescue the term from authoritarian overtones is not yet over, we shall continue to employ it here. Further, its linkage with the world of narrative puts it in a new light. Authority is author-ity, the authorship, authorization, of the Christian Story.

In our exploration of theological authority we will focus on the three places or points to which appeal has been made in Christian teaching over two millennia. While others may describe them in different terms and they are found in many and varied forms, we name them *Bible, church,* and *world,* and sometimes *Scripture, tradition,* and *human experience.* Our first sortie into the subject will be to survey the landscape of contemporary debate, showing the range of options in authority as they sort out around these three

3. The phrase is P. T. Forsyth's. See his *The Principle of Authority* (London: Hodder & Stoughton, 1912).

4. See Dennis Campbell, *Authority and the Renewal of American Theology* (Philadelphia: United Church Press, 1976), 2ff.

loyalties. As such, the next chapter will be a classification of views on authority using this triplet as the framework.[5]

Of the making of classifications in contemporary theology there is no end—"models," "typologies," "scenarios," etc. Often (but not always) their appearance can be a sign of significant movement in Christian thought, indicating an awareness of a fuller company of travelers on a common trek, and the desire to engage in conversation along the way. And often implied is a judgment on the validity but partiality of the positions reviewed, an appreciation for the insights of each, but a move to integrate them. Avery Dulles represents this in his important work, *Models of Revelation.*[6] I associate myself with the catholicity of this mood and movement. To describe the range of options in authority is an effort to listen to the sisters and brothers and to learn what can be learned from each point of view. Hearing out the range of opinion within the Christian community as part of the method of exposition is itself a theological judgment. Here it means a churchly and ecumenical perspective. The "we" that occurs regularly with the language of this inquiry is not an editorial "we" but a conversational one.

The conversation in options is, of course, carried on from a specific point of view. In this orienting chapter, I have laid out some of its assumptions in a preliminary way: Scripture is the *source* of authority. By "source" is meant both origin and seat of authority. The Bible is the place from which theology rises, providing it with its language and life, the origin of authority. Scripture is also the point of final adjudication for theological declarations. They stand to be reviewed at this seat, and must pass scrutiny before this judge.

Within this source there is a *center,* a measure by which the Scripture is itself understood. At the seat of biblical authority judgment is rendered by *Jesus Christ.* Here is the norm for the source. We read this Book to see how it bears witness to this One. *Was Christum triebet!* (Luther).

The Bible is the source, of which Christ is the center, and for which the gospel is the *substance.* The Bible is the vehicle for the Good News. That gospel is what we shall call the "Story" of what God has done, is doing, and will do for the world. In macrocosm the narrative ranges from creation to consummation. In microcosm it is the story of the center, the person and the work of Jesus Christ.

5. For a comparable classification see Karl Barth, *CD* IV/3, 97ff.

6. Avery Dulles, *Models of Revelation* (Garden City, N.Y.: Doubleday, 1983).

The gospel substance provides the material out of which doctrine emerges and with which systematic theology works.

A critical factor in authority is the Christian community. For two thousand years it has grappled with the center, substance, and source. The results of that engagement and its continuing process unavoidably influence, and explicitly ought to shape, our theological understanding. As such, the church constitutes the *resource* for our construal of the source and its defining contents. As the Scripture has its focus, so too within the church are to be found points of orientation, customarily called "tradition." Tradition, as tested threads of church conviction, constitutes a *guide* for the resource work of the Christian community. Its authority in that role is proportionate to the fullness of the community that gives it expression. The Vincentian canon is a historic formulation of this ecumenical test—albeit a visionary one—of the ecclesial guide: what is always and everywhere believed by everyone.

Our interaction with source and resource go on in the *setting* in which we live. This environment is the "world" of human experience in all its richness, variety, and poverty. Included are the phenomena of nature and history and the encounter with them in our own time and place through reason and affect, imagination and decision, behavior and interiority. We shall follow Friederich Schleiermacher's distinctions of "thinking," "doing," and "feeling" to describe this rich and varied texture of human experience.[7]

In the general setting of authority are to be found "signs" of special significance. These are the points in human experience in which thinking approaches "the true," doing "the good," and feeling "the beautiful." As such they are of help in the statement of Christian teaching; *aid* is to setting as guide is to resource and substance to source.

Out of a particular setting of authority rises a *perspective,* our historical angle of vision on the source and resource. In this systematics Christian teaching is viewed from a *narrative* perspective, with its motifs of liberation and reconciliation (vis-à-vis bondage and alienation), its formative metaphors of vision and light (vis-à-vis reality and night), and its mode of catholicity.

In our constructive and systematic contribution to the conversation on authority in the Christian community the basic ele-

7. Friederich Schleiermacher, *The Christian Faith,* vol. 1, ed. H. R. Mackintosh and J. D. Steward (New York: Harper & Row, 1963). His categories are "knowing," "doing," and "feeling."

ments—source, resource, setting—are the criteria of authority, necessary parts of any theological statement on the nature of authority and Christian belief. As such they are *principles* integral to the formulation of Christian doctrine: the Scripture principle, the church principle, and the world principle. There is a priority, an order, a distinction of functions, and a way of correlation among them. The Scripture principle takes precedence; the Bible is the source of Christian teaching. The church principle positions the Christian community and its lore as a resource clarifying our understanding of the scriptural source. And the world principle locates the role of human experience as the setting from which and to which the source and resource speak about the substance of faith, and according to its norm. What these elements of authority mean in their particularity and how they interact with one another constitute the inquiry before us.

HERMENEUTICS

While identifying the priorities and functions of the elements of authority is a long and basic step in the work of systematics, it cannot be taken without another leg in motion. Authority cannot be exercised without interpretation, our way of appropriating and rendering intelligible assertions of authority. A position on authority entails a position on interpretation. This holds true for each of the elements, however they are ranked or in whatever way they function. Scripture is interpreted Scripture, the church and its traditions are interpreted church and traditions, and the world is an interpreted world.

A good portion of this book is given over to the interpretation of Scripture. What one considers the source of authority deserves interpretive attention commensurate with its importance. Here we make contact with the wide-ranging discussion of biblical hermeneutics. In doing so we enter a field of dispute that reaches the very spelling of the word (hermeneutics vs. hermeneutic).[8]

Biblical hermeneutics has a long history.[9] In its traditional form

8. "Hermeneutics," in Richard N. Soulen's *Handbook of Biblical Criticism* (Atlanta: John Knox Press, 1976, 1981), 22-86.

9. See Lewis Mudge, "Hermeneutics," in *Westminster Dictionary of Christian Theology,* 250-53, and Milton S. Terry, *Biblical Hermeneutics* (New York: Phillips & Hunt, 1883).

it developed as the study of ways to make sense of the text in which God revealed the truth. What principles must be followed to enable us to see the coherence of Scripture and render it intelligible to reader or hearer? How, in particular, do the unclear and difficult passages get interpreted? Principles such as the fourfold meaning of Scripture and rights of church tradition in biblical interpretation appeared in patristic and medieval hermeneutics. Sixteenth-century Reformers rejected these and called for a return to the sufficiency of Scripture in its plain meaning. Problems of unclarity and disputes among those who professed just these standards brought further hermeneutical refinements in such principles as "the analogy of faith" (the clarification of unclear passages by clear ones based on the unity of Scripture), and "progressive revelation" (what is appropriate at one stage may not be at a subsequent one, or is to be interpreted from the point of view of a subsequent one).

Traditional hermeneutics came under sharp attack with the rise of historical consciousness. The traditional assumption that Scripture contained revealed assertions (often described by critics in the ambiguous phrase "timeless truths")[10] accessible by traditional principles of interpretation was radically questioned on the basis of the historical contingency of all human thought and writing. Biblical texts have their historical contextuality, and so do their readers and hearers. The problems are: How do we get into an ancient context? How do we get what they said in their context out from it and into ours? Early answers given by this historically-attuned perspective were: Get into the ancient text-in-context by historical-critical inquiry. Get out of it with "what it meant," and into our context by an interpretive process that says "what it means." That latter process was and is sometimes identified as "hermeneutics."

But can we ever really get into an ancient text-in-context, or out of our own present context? More radical perspectivalists consider the early historically aware hermeneutics naive. Cultural relativity does not allow for simple access to either end of the hermeneutical loop, ancient text or present context. The interpreter's perceptual apparatus is partial, in both senses—limited and controlled by vested interests. Hermeneutics now becomes one or another pro-

10. So in Albrecht Oepke's article on the subject in Kittel's *Theological Dictionary of the New Testament*, ed. and trans. Geoffrey W. Bromiley, vol. 3 (Grand Rapids: Eerdmans, 1965), 556-92. For exposition of the same see John Baillie, *The Idea of Revelation* (New York: Columbia Univ. Press, 1956), 19-40 and *passim*.

posed strategy to deal with this perceived gap, ranging from declarations of commonality between ancient texts and modern interpreter below the level of intellectual transfer—immersion in a subterranean stream of moral or affective experience—or participation in a shared community of tradition that provides continuity within the discontinuity, to the assertion that the chasm is unbridgeable and that the text is therefore open to limitless interpretation according to the sensibilities and needs of the interpreter.

The various historically conscious hermeneutics have made an important contribution to the interpretation of Scripture. They have brought classic Christian teaching on human finitude and sin to bear on the task of interpretation, reminding the interpreter of the limits of the venture, and encouraging a hermeneutical modesty. If this helps to quell the disease of "theological rabies," it is all to the good. All interpretation is perspectival, limited by our finitude, infected by our sin.

At the same time, modern hermeneutics has contributed to both a malaise and some bad moves in the use of the Bible in theology. It has invited a hermeneutical nihilism that reasons: If we can't get out of our "construals" (a favorite word in relativist times) and get into the text, then "I'll do my own thing," let Scripture serve my purposes. Or it invites an epistemological elitism that declares that the text is available only to those properly credentialed—often meaning those with the right class, sex, race, condition, commitment, or skill. In all cases the text tends to be shut up in the hearer's context, precluding a Word that would be other than the word that accords with the interests or skills of the interpreter, that would enlarge or question them.

The ecclesial consequences of hermeneutical relativism are also worth noting. If either nihilism or elitism is the course taken, there is no need for listening to other points of view in the Christian community. We keep company with those of the same perspective and reject alternative readings as incapable of understanding either the text or our judgment of it because of differing social locations or power agendas. Where the church is confronted by these hermeneutical partisanships it experiences a "balkanization," indeed a "beirutization," in which a variety of subcommunities of interpretation fire away at each other from behind their barricades. Something of an irony attends this exchange, for in spite of the allegations that the text can be understood only from within the specified location of construal, many books are written to convince the multitude outside of it that this is so. The writing of them contradicts the contextual argument, for it assumes that, on the one hand, those outside the perimeters of privilege can hear and be convinced by the argument, and thus are not contextually captive, or, on the other hand, that the rule of total relativity of statement is suspended at this point of argument for the absoluteness of relativity, or of the particular relativist position asserted. If the position argued for is offered truly as only a perspective that can be heard or accepted by those in the proper context, then it should be limited only to that audience as a consciousness-raising device and as a weapon in the war with other perspectives. However, if this is so, other hearers do not have to take it as a serious truth claim, can ignore it, and can prepare their own fortifications for the coming battle.

The hermeneutical approach here attempts to learn from the contemporary insights and debate. Its response to the relativist critique is a hermeneutical catholicity that will be espoused at each turn within the exegetical journey, those turns being identified subsequently as the common, critical, canonical, and contextual senses of the text. Part of that inclusiveness is a willingness to learn some lessons from traditional as well as modern hermeneutical theory. In that respect I offer as a working definition one kindred to traditional formulations. Hermeneutics is the articulation of the set of principles employed by an interpreter in the understanding of Scripture. The full import of this simple definition can become clear only as we investigate the distinctions between internal and external hermeneutics, meaning and significance, the four senses of Scripture, etc., in both the exposition and exegesis to follow.

In passing we note a connection between hermeneutics and systematics that will be argued throughout. Hermeneutics is to Scripture as theological method is to the question of authority. One's theological method is the set of principles set forth, or at work in, the concept of theological authority one espouses. Thus *exegesis,* as the application of hermeneutics to a biblical text, is paralleled by systematics, the application of theological method to the exposition of a Christian doctrine.

REVELATION

Why *these* elements of authority? Wherefore Bible as source, church as resource, and world as setting? The answers to these questions lie in the understanding of the nature of God's disclosive work in the loci of authority. A *doctrine* of revelation undergirds the *principles* of authority. The foundational Scripture principle is grounded in the revelation of God—in the deeds of God and the interpretation of them by inspired "prophet and apostle." The church principle is rooted in the illumination of these deeds and words in the life and witness of the Christian community over time and place. The world principle is warranted by the intimations of divine will and way in universal human experience as it comes to expression in a given time and that place.

Revelation is unveiling *(apokalypsis),* disclosure. Of what? This is the wrong question, according to an era of recent theology that is personalist, historical, and antipropositionalist. The issue is not what but who: Revelation is not the uncovering of some thing, but of Someone. It is the divine *Self-*disclosure. God does not give "information" but "personal communication." That Self-impartation comes in historical events. For some, these are happenings of divine import in the ebb and flow of our larger social history. For others, personal events comprise "history" in which the divine I meets the human Thou. And for yet others, the historical and the personal histories are linked.

While an event-oriented view of revelation made telling criticism of rationalist tendencies and propositional theologies, its limitations have become increasingly apparent. We shall not here polarize the personal and the propositional, nor oppose the deeds to the words of God. God is One who has a Word for us. The Purposer has a Purpose. What that Purpose is cannot be separated from the deeds God does. Revelation, therefore, is understood here as Self-disclosure of what God both does and says.

Learning from the theologies of public event, and joining word to deed, we shall view revelation along the timeline of God's acts. Thus a narrative of revelation keeps company with the epic of redemption. We will then interpret all the familiar terms in the discussion of revelation within the flow of the story. We will view "general revelation" in connection with the chapters on creation and the providential covenant with Noah, and look at "special revelation" in the chapters on the covenant with Israel and the incarnation of the divine Word in Jesus Christ. We will explore the Spirit's work of illumination in the chapters on church, salvation, and consummation, as revelatory signs given in this world and in the world to come, grace pressing toward glory.

Together with a narrative reading of revelation, we shall pursue the same quest for inclusiveness in a doctrine of revelation as sought in the concept of authority. The fullness of linear movement is the theological presupposition of the amplitude reached for in the circles of authority.[11] General revelation, or what shall be called universal revelation, in a world of creation and fall is the warrant for the authority we vest in human experience as the setting for our theological work. *Particular revelation* in the history of prophet and apostle as they encounter and interpret the elect of Israel and the incarnation of the Word in Christ is the assumption behind Scripture as the source of authority. We will identify the specifics of the Spirit's work as *impartation* in creation, *inspiration* in covenant and Christ, and *illumination* in the Christian community from Pentecost to Parousia. Criticized throughout are foreshortened perspectives, those that reduce revelation either to its universality or to its particularity, or obscure one or another of the Spirit's noetic labors.

The realities of sin and finitude persist in the most determined commitment to catholicity. This attempted inclusive doctrine of revelation has its myopias. And it is a process, not product, for revelation happens in the pilgrimage of God. That journey runs from the eternal dynamism within the triune God—the interministry of the three Persons—through the stages of disclosure to the final lucidity when the radiance of God illumines all in all. Within that revelatory trek are the acts of trinitarian coinherence and transparency, creation, election, incarnation, Pentecostal outpouring, saving work in persons and among powers, and the final consummation of the divine purpose. The story of redemption-revelation gives us the guideposts of authority. Random reference will be made throughout this volume to these things, and the developed doctrine of revelation then set forth in Volume 3.

11. See Chap. 6 for an analysis of the relationship.

CHAPTER II

Options in Authority

We enter the question of authority in Christian doctrine by examining a variety of viewpoints on the subject within the church of the closing decades of the twentieth century. While the specific form each takes bears the earmarks of the age, many of the options can be found in different garb at other times and places. Taking the time to listen initially to this wide-ranging conversation itself reflects a conception of authority. As noted earlier, theology in this systematics is done within the Christian community. And the fullness of Christian teaching is related to the catholicity of the corps of teachers.

Our overall system of classification is a "typology," and thus an effort to cover the full range of data. All options in authority are held to fall somewhere within three major types: Bible, church, world. These terms and their rough equivalents, Scripture, tradition, and human experience, refer to touchstones of authority to which one or another exposition of Christian doctrine basically relates. These three macro-options are "ideal types" in that few of the positions we locate within a type do so with exactitude suggested by the distinctions. Yet all fit under a designated rubric to the extent that they give primary allegiance to it rather than to one of the others.

Within each major type are multiple subtypes. The range discussed, the kind of classification employed, and the attention given to a position within that range varies. In the case of biblical authority, the importance of the category within the present systematics and the vigor of the discussion in ecumenical and evangelical circles invite the finer distinctions made and the variety examined. The length of treatment of "moral experience" in the world-type of authority is commensurate with the attention given to it in modern context. The way the subtypes are identified under the heading of "church"—as ecclesial and confessional perspectives rather than schools of thought or theologians—reflects the data of that division.

THE BIBLE

The advocates of Scripture as final arbiter of theological judgments comprise this category. Many who espouse this view, as well as not a few of its critics, perceive "biblical authority" as a monolithic position. Our investigation will show that this is not only a gross oversimplification of the type as such, but also of those within it who define the scriptural standard in the most restricted of terms. Thus Protestant "evangelicals" who are perceived by others (and often themselves) as a bloc vote on the question of authority have rather basic differences on biblical authority, ones that constitute a veritable "battle for the Bible."[1] The disagreements among evangelicals and the larger differences within this type are traceable to how the Bible's authority is understood, or, more exactly, the method employed to interpret it. Thus the rubric *authority* is inseparable from its companion *interpretation.* This is true for advocacies of "the church" and "the world" as well as the Bible. Each type entails differing modes of interpretation that manifest themselves in the variety of subtypes.

In the conjunction of authority and interpretation we confront the much-discussed subject of hermeneutics. The authority issue is the hermeneutical question in that the espousal of a given major type is determined by the method of interpretation—the hermeneutical principles—employed in its outworking. While an "inerrantist" and a "Barthian" find themselves together in significant ways in their common profession of biblical authority (especially vis-à-vis those who look to general human experience for ultimate meaning), significant doctrinal and moral judgments differ be-

1. As in Harold Lindsell, *The Battle for the Bible* (Grand Rapids: Zondervan, 1976). The battlefield imagery is common in the neofundamentalist phenomenon. See Timothy LaHaye, *The Battle for the Mind* (Old Tappan, N.J.: Revell, 1980), and Frances Fitzgerald's perceptive study of it, "A Disciplined Charging Army," *The New Yorker,* May 18, 1981, 53-141. On the concept of neofundamentalism, see Gabriel Fackre, "The Neofundamentalist Phenomenon," *Word and World* 5 (Winter 1985): 12-23.

cause of the hermeneutical (interpretive) assumptions of each. Even inerrantists differ in important ways, as a result of their varying frameworks (transmissive, trajectory, intentional). Therefore hermeneutical issues will face us at every turn of the authority inquiry. We note this in passing at the beginning of our typological investigation, and will examine in much more detail the issue of interpretation in the constructive sections of this volume, venturing theses on "internal" and "external" hermeneutics.

We turn now to the spectrum of options within the type that assigns Scripture the place of normativity in Christian doctrine.

The Oracular View

Oracularity is an identification not customarily applied by either defenders or critics of this most conservative of perspectives on Scripture. Also, other views of authority, such as inerrancy, speak of Scripture as the "oracles of God." Usually the position we are discussing is referred to as "the dictation theory." This description, however, is a category error since it refers to the doctrine of revelation that underlies a postulate on authority, rather than judgment on a way or place of authorization. The connotation of the word *oracular* fits this view as a theory of authority, and does so more closely than those who use it for rhetorical purposes, so we employ it to describe the authority implicate of a dictational view of revelation.

Oracular authority means that the words of the original text are given directly by God to the authors—as dictation to amanuenses—and faithfully preserved over time by the Holy Spirit, coming to subsequent readers and hearers with the absolute stamp of authority. Words of the Bible in their original language (and in popularized versions of this theory, in the translated text also) *are* the oracles of God. We hear them as if they were from the very mind and mouth of deity. As such, one must treat them with the respect due to the holy God who speaks them. "Critical scholarship" or any effort to disallow or disqualify what they say on the subjects about which they deal are illegitimate tamperings with the sacred text.

References to the dictation of Scripture have appeared in dogmatic treatises over the centuries.[2] They often, but not always, pre-

2. Protestant theologians who held this view include P. Van Mastricht, G. Voetius, and J. Cocceius, as cited by Heinrich Heppe, *Reformed Dogmatics*, ed. Ernst Bizer, trans. G. T. Thomson (Grand Rapids: Baker, 1978), 17, 20, 27.

suppose this oracular view, a fact to be determined by the total argument of the expositor and the associated exegetical practice. However, the most rigorous theoreticians and practitioners of the oracular view of sacred text are Islamic fundamentalists and Mormon apologists.[3] The treatment of the Bible as sacred oracle survives and even flourishes in popular Christian fundamentalism, although it is consistently repudiated by the intellectual defenders of fundamentalism and conservative evangelicalism.

Where oracular deliverance was often assumed in traditional pre-Reformation exegesis, space was made for the puzzlements that naturally follow. How does one account for variant reports of historical events, dubious moral practices, and seemingly divergent theological teachings? The answer was that questionable passages had a deeper import. Enter the fourfold method of interpreting Scripture, according to which, beyond the literal sense one can find moral, spiritual, and mystical dimensions, and thus the tropological, allegorical, and anagogical meanings of texts. There may be treasures here in these contentions of multiple meaning, and we shall subsequently search for them. At this point we simply note that pre-Reformation justification of oracularity required a special attunement to truths that transcended the plain meaning of Scripture.

Reformation interpreters called for controls on what they saw as unjustified flights of imagination in this concept of manifold sense and sought a return to the literal meaning alone, a mood that had its effects in the revisionist efforts of the inerrantists and infallibilists we shall now examine.

The Inerrancy View

In order to distinguish their view from a dictation/oracle conception, and yet accord to Scripture the highest of authority, many conservative interpreters have raised "inerrancy" as their battle cry. Indeed, they view interpretatve differences about Scripture as a warfare, with the stakes being the survival of the Christian religion itself.[4] For more than a few inerrantists the term *inerrancy* has

3. Badru D. Kateregga and David W. Shenk, *Islam and Christianity* (Grand Rapids: Eerdmans, 1980), 27, and Robert Hullinger, *Mormon Answer to Skepticism* (St. Louis: Clayton, 1980), 11-16.

4. Lindsell, *Battle*, 200-212. Thus Harold O.J. Brown: "The controversy over inerrancy may appear to be smaller than that over justification in the sixteenth century, especially insofar as both sides are in wide agreement concerning the

become the testing point of evangelical Christianity. And for those who have concluded that "evangelicalism" has become too loose a phenomenon, "fundamentalism" has been resuscitated and linked with loyalty to inerrancy.

Proponents of inerrancy believe that the Bible in its original form is without error in all the matters about which it chooses to speak. Thus, in its "autographs," the writings of the original authors inspired by the Holy Spirit, no mistake of any sort appears. All the information contained in them, from assertions of faith and morals to those of science and history, is protected from error. As God cannot lie, neither can the "epistemic Word." The key to inerrancy, especially vis-à-vis the oracular view, is the description of inerrant Scripture as "protected from error." The words of the autographs are not, as such, transferred from the mind of God to the mind of the author and then to the written text. Rather, the Holy Spirit respects the humanity of the author, allowing the text to emerge along the contours of that mind and within the context of the culture that shapes it. However, *the superintendence* of the writing process is such that no error in that humanly contoured and contexted text is permitted. Thus the words are not dictated—not oracular, but superintended—and in that sense, inerrant.[5]

The rigor of this view, while short of oracularity, is designed to exclude other notions that lay claim to a high view of biblical authority but fall short of these standards. One of them is the "infallibility" position we shall presently examine, which declares that Scripture is infallible or trustworthy in faith and morals, in doctrine and life, but not necessarily inerrant on other matters. This is not good enough for the inerrantist (at least those clearly held to be so in the first two forms we have identified).

As in all views, a revelatory Presence assures the authority of the text, the noetic work of the Holy Spirit. The underpinning of inerrancy is a doctrine of revelation that asserts "plenary verbal inspiration." God's definitive Self-disclosure comes in the unique

trustworthiness and normative authority of the Scripture. Yet, I suggest that, like the Arian controversy, this one has the potential not merely to alter the church somewhat or split it, but to destroy it" ("The Arian Connection: Presuppositions of Errancy," in *Challenges to Inerrancy: A Theological Response,* ed. Gordon Lewis and Bruce Demarest [Chicago: Moody Press, 1984], 384-85).

5. On the repudiation of "dictation" or "mechanical dictation" see Lindsell, *Battle,* 32-35; Roger R. Nicole and J. Ramsey Michaels, eds., *Inerrancy and Common Sense* (Grand Rapids: Baker, 1980), *passim;* Clark Pinnock, *The Scripture Principle* (San Francisco: Harper & Row, 1984), 57-58.

privileged communication of the entirety of Scripture. The inerrancy of the words of its authors is grounded in their protection from error by the power of God. The divine act of superintendence assures their trustworthiness. That reliability is uniform, touching all that Scripture affirms, an autograph in faithfulness guaranteed by a Bible plenarily inspired. We shall return to these themes when treating the doctrine of revelation.

For all its appearances of stringency, this view comes in three different versions: conservative, moderate, and liberal inerrancy. The insistence upon inerrancy in some evangelical quarters as the definitive mark of evangelicalism has no doubt contributed to the broadness of its meaning. It is worth asking if this fluid use has rendered it incapable of performing the function its ardent supporters envisioned. Be that as it may, let us consider the variety of views on inerrancy.

1. Transmissive Inerrancy

We coin a term again to take account of distinctions not always acknowledged by protagonists and antagonists. This transmissive view is the conservative interpretation of the word and idea of inerrancy. With the two others it holds that the autographs are protected from any error in all the subjects with which Scripture deals. While firm distinctions are made between this perspective and "the dictation theory," there is a similar reverence for the working text of the Bible in the hand of the current believer. Its most obvious manifestation is in the zeal to harmonize apparently conflicting accounts of events, reported sayings, doctrinal and moral teachings.[6] Harold Lindsell is a well-known exponent of inerrancy of this sort.

Here again a revelatory assumption is at work underneath the authority thesis. It appears as a latent, and sometimes patent, trust

6. Lindsell, *Battle,* 30ff. Roger Nicole, "The Nature of Inerrancy," in Nicole/Michaels, *Inerrancy and Common Sense,* 71-95. The font of inerrancy teaching in North America is the "Princeton School" of Charles and Alexander Hodge and Benjamin Warfield. See Benjamin Warfield, *The Inspiration and Authority of the Bible,* ed. S. Craig (Phillipsburg, N.J.: Presbyterian and Reformed, 1948). Cf. this Protestant view of superintendence with early Roman Catholic theories of inspiration as "divine assistance against errors" (as in Vincent Conteston, 1681; Johann Jahn, 1802; Jan Herman Janssens, 1818; and Franz Heinrich Reusch, 1870). This was considered a "minimalist" view and condemned by Vatican I. See the discussion of these matters in Robert Gnuse, *The Authority of the Bible* (New York: Paulist Press, 1985), 7-8.

in a "grace of preservation." The Spirit watches over the processes of transmission as well as the writing of Scripture to provide us with an inerrant document. The received text cannot be so subject to the foibles of the transmitters that errors would be allowed to creep into a Bible to which we turn for trustworthy knowledge. Transmissive inerrantists do not want their view to be mistaken for what we have called the oracular view. They acknowledge the human presence in the inspiration of the Bible, noting the vocabulary pool and literary styles of various biblical writers. But the human factor is kept to a minimum. The attention critical scholarship gives to this human aspect, and the "secular humanism" believed to lie behind it make transmissive inerrantists wary of ventures in historical and literary criticism. Further, in reaction to symbolic construals of Scripture, and in the struggle against modern scientific inroads into areas in which the Bible speaks, they stress the plain or literal meaning of the text. Literality when applied to the description of events is usually understood in terms of accurate, unembellished historical reportage.[7] Hence, transmissive inerrancy has figured prominently in efforts to establish the historical veracity of Scripture's accounts of the world's beginnings and endings.[8] In all these things the role of the human in the divine-human confluence that brings Scripture to be is reduced to minimal proportions. The supervision of textual errorlessness in the original and received writings thereby guarantees a flawless text.

2. Trajectory Inerrancy

Also disavowing the oracular/dictation position, a second inerrancy view holds to an errorless text, but develops further the human role in the creation process and casts a more critical eye on the transmission of the text. Here the individuality of the author in both style and substance, the formative features of culture, and the literary devices employed in the writing all bring to greater visibility the finitude of the vehicle the Holy Spirit uses. Supervision of the text and its preservation from error, in this case, allows for some latitude with regard to historical accuracy. Thus one takes

7. Lindsell, *Battle,* 161-83; John W. Haley, *An Examination of the Alleged Discrepancies in the Bible* (Nashville: Goodpasture, 1951), *passim*.

8. R. L. Wysong, *The Creation-Evolution Controversy* (Midland, Mich.: Inquiry Press, 1976), 151ff. For a review of the debate and the literature see Carl Henry, *God, Revelation and Authority,* vol. 6 (Waco, Tex.: Word Books, 1983), 108-228. Hereafter referred to as *GRA*.

into account the use of Oriental hyperbole, the function of narrative in ancient writing, and even the limitations in cosmology that characterize an earlier age. All this can be done, it is believed, in loyalty to the Scripture's accurate testimony to both fact and faith as that is discerned by the best of grammatical-historical study.

Trajectory inerrantists are thereby willing to acknowledge the human factor to a greater extent in the process of transmitting the inspired autographs. Active use of the tools of textual criticism are urged in order to discover the most reliable route of transmission and the documents closest to the inerrant autographs. Indeed there is explicit acknowledgment that errors are discoverable in the text that we now have.[9] But the recognition that the received text is subject to flaws is regularly linked with the following modifications:

1. The reach of error does not include basic Christian doctrine or morals.
2. Where our texts have been tested with regard to historical factualities they have proved 99 percent correct.
3. Because the method of critical scholarship has been used so regularly by secular humanist interpreters, the credibility of its results is in question. Critical scholarship may be used in modest ways, nevertheless, but its results are never decisive.[10]

"Trajectory" is our adjective for this point of view because it does allow for the power of the Spirit's work in the autographs to be given full play along with the extension of divine guidance through the transmissive process. This view affirms solidity of origin and rightness of direction in the inspired autographs and declares for sustained doctrinal accuracy. Inerrancy is a trajectory faithful to the original launch of revelation but "on its own" in flight.

In both trajectory inerrancy and transmissive inerrancy many of the traditional principles of scriptural authority and interpretation are firmly held. *Sola scriptura* is espoused in its conservative meaning: the Bible is the only authority, not the only final authority, with tradition and human experience regularly seen as contenders. The principle of *analogy of faith* is prominent, the clarification of unclear texts by clear ones on the basis of the unity of Scripture. *Perspicuity* is espoused, the lucidity of the text to the eye of the ordinary believer. Also assumed is the Bible as a deposit of true

9. Henry, *GRA*, 4:220-42.
10. Ibid., 385-404.

timeless *propositions* on all matters on which it speaks. Access to Scripture according to these principles is reached by the careful and prayerful use of historical-grammatical means of investigation. Carl Henry, the theologian most influential in the rise of modern evangelicalism in North America, has made a formidable statement of this view.[11]

3. Intentional Inerrancy

We now cross an important line in the debate on the authority of Scripture. While holding to the errorlessness of the Bible, intentional inerrantists assert that the Scripture itself must determine how Scripture is to be interpreted. One must discern the purposed meaning of the text as it is found by a study of the text. The Bible is to be understood according to authorial intent, not the way we choose to understand it.[12] Therefore, we should be wary of treating historical chronicles in the Bible according to the canons of modern historiography. As in earlier inerrancy perspectives, the literary character of the text is given attention; but in this case much more so. Intentional inerrantists are determined to stay within the confines of historic intentionality—poetry read as poetry, history as history, doctrine as doctrine, homily as homily, as these genre are interpreted in the mode of the culture in which they originally appeared.[13] J. Ramsey Michaels is a representative of this position.

The principle of intentionality allows for a form of inerrancy in which one reads ancient texts that include chronicles not meant as "informational" or accurate in the modern sense, but that have theological or moral meaning. For example, the Genesis accounts are not investigated for clues to the age or condition of the earth at its inception but for the theological points the author is making as that affirmation was housed in a primitive cosmology.

11. For his personal cum theological journey see Carl Henry, *Confessions of a Theologian* (Waco, Tex.: Word Books, 1986).

12. In *The Scripture Principle,* Clark Pinnock describes his pilgrimage from a "total inerrancy" or "strict inerrancy" viewpoint to a "moderately phrased category of inerrancy." This means "inerrancy is relative to the intention of the text" (p. 78). For the record of his personal struggle, representative of many in modern evangelicalism, see *The Scripture Principle, passim,* esp. 57-60, 70-79, 126-29, 222-26 and also "How I Use the Bible in Doing Theology," in Robert K. Johnston, ed., *The Use of the Bible in Theology* (Atlanta: John Knox Press, 1985), 18-34.

13. *The Scripture Principle,* 78-79; J. Ramsey Michaels, "Inerrancy or Verbal Inspiration? An Evangelical Dilemma," in Nicole/Michaels, *Inerrancy and Common Sense,* 58ff.; Millard Erickson, *Christian Theology,* vol. 1 (Grand Rapids: Baker, 1983), 233-34.

Intentional inerrantists espouse a plenary verbal inspiration view of Scripture. Sometimes they prefer this focus on the revelatory process rather than on the characterization of its authority in the language of inerrancy.[14] Holding to inspiration in this plenary verbal way is the warrant for arguing that the Scripture should be taken on its own terms rather than using a concept and method it does not itself employ.

This third version of the theory of an errorless Bible stresses even more the human factor in the divine-human process of inspiration. As a consequence, critical scholarship is allowed a more active role. Intentional inerrantists are often in active conversation with the wider academy of biblical scholarship. They do not wage the kind of warfare against it that marks the other two exponents of inerrancy, although they do challenge the antisupernaturalist bias where they believe it enters to distort the results of critical scholarship.[15]

Given these characteristics, the intentional inerrantist is often under attack by the advocates of the transmissive and trajectory viewpoints. Institutions and societies within evangelicalism, especially those that have employed inerrancy as the formula for admission, sometimes bring the intentionalist into sharp collision with the more conservative defenders of inerrancy.

The Infallibilist View

A term akin to *inerrancy,* and even treated by some as synonymous, has achieved some currency as an alternative view on the authority and interpretation of the Bible. "Infallibility" has become for many evangelicals a classification that unambiguously declares for the supremacy of the Bible, but seeks to identify more specifically the sense in which that is so. Infallibilists declare Scripture to be normative in matters of "faith and life," or "theology and morals," or "soteric knowledge." To believe that the Bible is the "Word of God" is to be obedient to its affirmations as to who God is, what God does and will do, and what God wants us to do.[16] In matters of

14. Ramsey Michaels, in Nicole/Michaels, *Inerrancy and Common Sense,* 49-70.

15. Ibid., 67-70.

16. An intense debate goes on among evangelicals on the difference between inerrancy and infallibility. A book by Jack B. Rogers and Donald K. McKim, *The Authority and Interpretation of the Bible: An Historical Approach* (San Francisco: Harper & Row, 1979), was for awhile the center of the controversy. Rogers and McKim argue that "the central Christian tradition" beginning in the early church

physics and chemistry, astronomy and paleontology, historiography as exact chronicle, one must turn to the physicist and chemist, the astronomer, paleontologist, and historian, with the respect due the rules of these disciplines. When the Scripture touches on these subjects, its words are within the limits of the science and history of its own times—including prescientific worldviews and preempirical narrative-making. Since the Bible was not written to provide general encyclopedic information but to make available the knowledge of salvation, we look to it for that "Word of God." We acknowledge its authority on ultimate matters and recognize its timeboundedness on penultimate ones. Infallibilists, therefore, are not exercised by apparent historical inaccuracies or premodern scientific judgments in the biblical text, nor do they seek avidly to reconcile conflicting accounts. The Word of God brings to us saving knowledge through a human medium, and is not to be confused with, or considered destroyed by, the manifest limitations of the human aspects of the texts.

While historical-critical scholarship is not the foundation for this theological program, nor in high profile in theological judgments, infallibilists generally assign it a role in the investigation of Scripture. Indeed its findings are often taken with great seriousness, although those accepted are on the conservative end of the scale. Its exponents frequently play an active part in modern societies of biblical scholarship. Like the intentional inerrantists, they recognize the influence of philosophical and theological assumptions in the world of critical scholarship and strive therefore to relativize

and continuing through Augustine and Anselm to Luther and Calvin understood Scripture to be "wholly authoritative as a means of bringing people to salvation and guiding them in the life of faith" (p. 457). While there is no intention to deceive in the Bible, making it in that sense "errorless," it shares the science and historiography of the period in which it was written and thus is capable of "mistakes" in these fields and was accepted as so timebound in the central tradition. Inerrantists of the transmission and trajectory sort have sprung to the defense of "an errorless Bible." For rejoinders see *Biblical Authority: A Critique of the Rogers/McKim Proposal* (Grand Rapids: Zondervan, 1982) and Lewis/Demarest, *Challenges to Inerrancy*, esp. 285-316. Exponents of the infallibilist view include G. C. Berkouwer, who moved from an earlier inerrantist view to an infallibilist position (*Holy Scripture* [Grand Rapids: Eerdmans, 1975]); Bernard Ramm, *Protestant Biblical Interpretation* (Grand Rapids: Baker, 1970); Dewey Beegle, *Scripture, Tradition and Infallibility* (Grand Rapids: Eerdmans, 1973); Stephen Davis, *The Debate about the Bible* (Philadelphia: Westminster Press, 1977); and Donald Bloesch, *The Essentials of Evangelical Theology*, vol. 1 (San Francisco: Harper & Row, 1978), 51-87.

their influence on critical results. But they acknowledge also, and more so, the achievements of the Enlightenment in this area of biblical study and make use of its tools of learning, with the qualifications noted.[17]

As in the case of inerrancy, the infallibility view has conservative, moderate, and liberal versions. We shall identify them as unitive, essentialist, and Christocentric. Like the inerrantists, the interpreters of a soteric Scripture do not always develop these differences explicitly, but their premises are apparent in the different approaches undertaken.

1. Unitive Infallibility

In this first version are often found former inerrantists who have concluded that position to be untenable but strive to maintain strong biblical authority in matters of faith, theology, and moral judgment. They have decided that (a) the scientific and chronological opinions of Scripture are separable from its ultimate affirmations and mandates and (b) that there is an overall coherence to the Scripture in its views on a given matter of faith and life. Those who expound this position will speak of "the biblical view of God" or "Scripture's doctrine of human nature," or "the Bible's teaching" on the atonement, personal salvation, the church, etc. Continuities throughout Scripture are established by the principles of propositionality, perspicuity, and the analogy of faith, as these are further aided by historical-critical as well as grammatical-historical modes of study.

2. Essentialist Infallibility

When critical scholarship plays a larger role, as it does in infallibilist hermeneutics, one must confront the implications of the diversity found in Scripture. Some infallibilists therefore look for determinative assertions of Scripture amid the apparent differences in theological and moral judgment. A case in point is the status and role of women in church and society. Are all of Paul's judgments on these matters infallible? If the answer is "No," then the assumption of across-the-board authority of the Bible's teaching on matters of faith and life must be modified. The tack often taken is a focus on one rather than another theological and moral affirmation, the one chosen representing a larger vision of the matter

17. For a strong defense of some aspects of the Enlightenment see Bernard Ramm, *After Fundamentalism: The Future of Evangelical Theology* (San Francisco: Harper & Row, 1983), 2-71.

at hand. For example, proponents identify Paul's assertion of the status of women in Galatians 3:28 as the comprehensive guide, rejecting or reinterpreting views short of that. Not all that appears in the Old or New Testament on doctrinal and moral matters, therefore, is considered inspired. This is more than the "progressive revelation" of inerrantists and conservative infallibilists in which the true but partial nature of earlier assertions is filled out and reconstrued in the light of later disclosure. In essentialism, New Testament teaching as well as Old Testament teaching can be questioned (sometimes described as "law") if it does not meet the standard of truth.

How are these standards determined? By Scripture itself. The Bible establishes the heart of the matter in doctrine and morals, those affirmations that are central within its own diverse patterns of thought. What those defining characteristics are is very often influenced by the tradition in which the essentialist stands, sometimes explicitly, otherwise implicitly. These refrains are "the essentials," the *"sedes doctrina,"* "the fundamentals." An essentialist view of Scripture is sometimes held functionally even by those who are critical of the infallibilists' selectivity. Donald Bloesch's *Essentials of Evangelical Theology,* while influenced by the Christological accents of Karl Barth, is a work in this tradition with wide impact.[18]

3. Christocentric Infallibility

By what criterion are the essentials themselves established? According to the Christocentric view, Jesus Christ is the standard of (a) what is essential in Scripture, (b) how these core teachings are to be construed, and (c) what new understanding of Christian doctrine is accepted and what old rejected.

Here again the status of women in biblical teaching is instructive, for it has been a significant factor in inerrantist-infallibilist debate and movements. Infallibilists who believe that the Bible is doctrinally normative but are influenced by the struggle for the rights of women anguish over the biblical texts that appear to le-

18. While Donald Bloesch draws heavily on a "christological hermeneutic" and might be classified in the following type, the way this works is more as a Calvinist coextensiveness with the continuing doctrinal specifics of Scripture than in terms of a Lutheran selectivity and reappropriation of it. See his *Essentials of Evangelical Theology, passim,* and his "The Primacy of Scripture," in *The Authoritative Word,* ed. Donald McKim (Grand Rapids: Eerdmans, 1983), 117-54 and "A Christological Hermeneutic: Crisis and Conflict in Hermeneutics," in Johnston, *Use of the Bible,* 78-102.

gitimate the second-class status of women. Historical and contextual reassessment has contributed to the emergence of the essentialist view itself. In the Christocentric modulation of infallibilism, a move is made beyond others by fixing "Christ" as the principle of selection for identifying and interpreting the essentials. Who he was and what he did to affirm the dignity of women, and the implications of his saving work for establishing equality (e.g., Gal. 3:28) become the point of reference for making doctrinal and moral judgments. Received notions that diminish women in church or culture are rejected as incommensurate with a Christocentric standard. Further, this lens as the instrument of scrutiny of the whole Scripture enables the infallibilist to see things heretofore unnoticed: the parity of male and female in creation, the appearance of women as the first witnesses of Jesus' resurrection, the legitimation of women in various forms of ministry in the New Testament, and the discerning of female gender characterizations of deity in the Bible. Paul Jewett is a well-known exponent of Christocentric infallibilism.[19]

Inerrantists, particularly in the transmissive and trajectory camps, are sharp critics of infallibilism in all its forms: unitive, essentialist, and Christocentric. Charges made include:

1. The insistence that biblical statements on science and history are inextricable from its views on faith and morals so no such distinctions as those made by the infallibilists are permissable.
2. Finding the core doctrinal and practical teachings within the Bible entails a "pick and choose" method that puts sinful humans in charge of God's epistemic Word.
3. God is the author of light and not darkness so the whole Bible must be a reflection of that light with "no shadow of turning" (James 1:17 KJV).
4. While the authenticity of evangelical faith in those who do not espouse inerrancy might be acknowledged, selective use of Scripture puts their feet on a "slippery slope" that leads persons and institutions on the way to infidelity.

19. Paul K. Jewett, *Man as Male and Female* (Grand Rapids: Eerdmans, 1975) and *The Ordination of Women* (Grand Rapids: Eerdmans, 1980). See also Letha Scanzoni and Nancy Hardesty, *All We Are Meant To Be* (Waco, Tex.: Word Books, 1975) and Virginia Ramey Mollenkott, *Women, Men and the Bible* (Nashville: Abingdon Press, 1971), 10-21.

The Conceptual View

All the foregoing perspectives associate the authority of Scripture intimately with the words of the text; the way the Bible expresses itself as well as its contents count as authoritative. While the inerrantists and infallibilists may disagree with what features of the text are authoritative, the text is never dissociated from the contents as if the matter could be had without the form in which it was cast. However, for the next point of view the form is adiaphorous. We must look behind, not in, the medium for the message. The ideas that shine through the text are the important thing; the text is the catalyst for discovering them.

As David Kelsey points out in his description of this position ("concepts as content"),[20] the search for concepts is associated in part with the mid-century "biblical theology" movement, although we shall relate that development more closely to another type. An important feature of that movement was its effort to distinguish Christian faith from other worldviews, with special insistence on the differences between Hebrew and Greek mentalities.[21] Biblical concepts were explored in word studies and such extensive publishing projects as Kittel's *Theological Dictionary* of the Old and New Testaments. The biblical concepts of God, Christ, salvation, human nature, and the world's destiny were familiar subjects of inquiry, and continue to be so.[22] Traditional theology made the same kinds of assumptions, of course, that there are singular teachings of Scripture on each of these subjects and many others, but their truthfulness was set within a more encompassing theory of authority in which concepts were/are legitimated as propositions within the field of an inerrant or infallible text. In the conceptual view the ideas are distilled from a text in which no claims to either

20. David H. Kelsey, *The Uses of Scripture in Recent Theology* (Philadelphia: Fortress Press, 1975), 24-28.

21. As in Thorlief Bowman, *Hebrew Thought Compared with Greek,* trans. Jules L. Moreau (London: SCM Press, 1960). This distinction has been heavily criticized as an oversimplification.

22. Representative works include J. K. S. Reid, *The Biblical Doctrine of Ministry* (Edinburgh: Oliver & Boyd, 1955); Alan Richardson, *The Biblical Doctrine of Work* (London: SCM Press, 1954); Thomas F. Torrance, *The Biblical Doctrine of Baptism* (Edinburgh: St. Andrews Press, 1958). Reinhold Niebuhr's Gifford lectures in Edinburgh may have contributed to this wave of conceptual hermeneutics in Great Britain. See his formative interpretation of "the biblical doctrine of man" in *The Nature and Destiny of Man,* 2 vols. (New York: Scribners, 1941, 1943).

inerrancy or infallibility are made. Further, concepts tend to be at a higher level of abstraction than the propositions of traditional theology.

One version of the conceptual view aims to go beyond standard doctrinal fare for its subject matter, seeking instead refrains that permeate Scripture. Thus recurrent "motifs" or themes are traced throughout Scripture. The "motif analysis" of the Lundensian theology exemplifies this view. Anders Nygren focused on the theme of *agape* and Gustaf Aulén located the classic view of the atonement in the New Testament and the Christian tradition.[23]

The conceptual view has its special revelatory underpinnings. God's Self-disclosure comes in the inspiration of ideas. The gift of revelatory insight is given to human minds, either those of the authors of the texts or in biblical figures and their traditions. Revelation by indirection rather than direction characterizes most of the conceptual protagonists, since virtually all deny inherited views of the inspiration of Scripture. The written text is the human witness to revelation. In this process, individual and corporate, the privileged ideas rise to visibility, stamped with biblical authority.

The time in which the conceptual view enjoyed prominence is one in which Christian identity was either in poor repair or under heavy attack. In other times and from other considerations the conceptual view comes under criticism. Some deny that there is sufficient unity within biblical teaching to warrant a statement of "*the* biblical concept" of anything. Others question the detachability of concepts from the language that conveys them, or doubt the wisdom of associating biblical faith with discursive categories. Still others object to the claim that the Bible is in any sense the reservoir of identifiable cognitive truth claims. Views to the right consider the conceptual view a long step in the slippery slope toward infidelity.

The Historical View

In the early decades of the twentieth century a variety of theologians and schools of Christian thought turned to an orientation to "history." Revelation is what God did and does, not what God said, thereby questioning all the foregoing views.[24] Oracularity, iner-

23. Anders Nygren, *Agape and Eros,* trans. Philip S. Watson (Philadelphia: Westminster Press, 1953); Gustaf Aulén, *Christus Victor,* trans. Eric H. Wahlstrom (Philadelphia: Fortress Press, 1960).

24. See, e.g., William Temple, *Nature, Man and God* (London: Macmillan, 1934), 312-13, and John Baillie, *The Idea of Revelation in Recent Thought* (New York: Columbia Univ. Press, 1956), 62-82.

rancy, infallibility, and conceptuality hold that the Bible is the source of abiding theological assertions, however differently these truths are distributed within, or extracted from, the biblical texts. Not so the historical view, which holds that Scripture is a recital of the *acts of God* accompanied by their interpretation.

What are these divine actions? The historical view stresses deeds of deliverance. Scripture is the record of the saving acts of God, happenings in which divine benevolence changes untoward circumstances. The central events of this "salvation history" or holy history *(heilsgeschichte)* are Israel (and within Israel—exodus, conquest, exile, restoration) and Jesus Christ. Given early formulation in the nineteenth-century Erlangen School, especially by Hans von Hoffman, the holy history view came to high visibility later in the writing of such biblical scholars and theologians as Gerhard von Rad, Oscar Cullmann, G. Ernest Wright, and James Muilenburg.[25] The work of C. H. Dodd on the New Testament *kerygma* was a variation on this theme. The prominence of biblical scholars in the articulation of these ideas produced the label "biblical theology movement" in North America and Great Britain. The extent to which it did or did not constitute a genuine movement, did or did not thrive for a while and then recede, has been the subject of various tracts by defenders, critics, and reinterpreters.[26] Whatever one makes of this debate, themes about holy history have had a lasting effect in the theology of Karl Barth, and a continuing influence on some versions of "narrative theology," in "the canonical approach" to Scripture (in spite of the strong criticism of it coming from this quarter), in efforts by various evangelical theologians

25. Oscar Cullmann, *Christ and Time,* rev. ed. (Philadelphia: Westminster Press, 1964); Oscar Cullmann, *Salvation in History,* trans. Sidney G. Sowers (New York: Harper & Row, 1967); G. Ernest Wright, *The God Who Acts: Biblical Theology as Recital,* Studies in Biblical Theology no. 8 (London: SCM Press, 1952; G. Ernest Wright and Reginald H. Fuller, *The Book of the Acts of God* (Garden City, N.Y.: Doubleday, Anchor Books, 1960); Gerhardt von Rad, *Old Testament Theology,* vols. 1 and 2, trans. D. M. G. Stalker (New York: Harper & Brothers, 1962–65); Walter Eichrodt, *Theology of the Old Testament,* vols. 1 and 2, trans. J. D. Baker (Philadelphia: Westminster Press, 1961–67); C. H. Dodd, *The Authority of the Bible* (London: Nesbitt & Co., 1928, 1938); Bernhard W. Anderson, *The Unfolding Drama of the Bible* (New York: Association Press, 1971, 1957).

26. E.g., Brevard S. Childs, *Biblical Theology in Crisis* (Philadelphia: Westminster Press, 1970); James Barr, "Biblical Theology," in the *Interpreter's Dictionary of the Bible,* Supplementary Vol. (Nashville: Abingdon Press, 1976), 104-11; James D. Smart, *The Past, Present and Future of Biblical Theology* (Philadelphia: Westminster Press, 1979); Langdon Gilkey, "Cosmology, Ontology, and the Travail of Biblical Language," *Journal of Religion* 41 (1961): 194-205.

attempting to move out of inerrantist and infallibilist frameworks, in some strands of Roman Catholic theology, and in the liturgical renewal movement.

While the accent is on the events of salvation history, the historical view does not necessarily reduce authority to bare events. Scriptural interpretation of these happenings also have authority. Truth comes in words that say what the events meant to the one experiencing or confronting them. In some cases these subjective interpretations of objective events are given lasting status, while for others they are "confessional," human witnesses that need to be appropriated differently in succeeding contexts. For yet others, the prophetic and apostolic testimony to the deeds of God is considered an early effort at interpretation that, as such, does not have the normative weight granted to it by the first two variants, but is only one of many ventures in contextualization.

Salvation history perspectives do not exhaust the historical view. In some cases the "acts of God" include the subset of events from Exodus to Easter that constitute deliverance—but go beyond them to "universal history." A version of this is found in second-century baptismal rules of faith and in early economic trinitarianism. Here the divine deeds include the trajectory from creation to consummation. Extending further, other forms of the historical view include general providential activity and a more detailed periodization of universal history in orthodox theologies of one sort or another, the federal theology of Coccieus, and sundry millenarian and dispensationalist theories. In all cases the thread of salvation history is still found at the center, but elaborated beyond that. In more traditional forms, revelatory authority is given to the interpreting words as well as to the recorded deeds.

The theology of Wolfhart Pannenberg represents a unique contemporary version of the universal history perspective, although so redesigned as to make one wary of too simple categorization. The scope of revelation is universal history, but its center is Jesus, understood against the background of Israel's tradition and expectation. Yet he construes the biblical interpretations of particular events as promissory. They serve as signs of a yet-to-be definitive Word to come at the end of history. And their own weight as authoritative is not self-authenticating, but to be validated by accepted standards of rational discourse and evidence.[27]

27. Wolfhart Pannenberg, *Basic Questions in Theology* (Philadelphia: Fortress Press, 1970), 15-80. Pannenberg's programmatic essay, "Redemptive Event and History," appears in *Essays in Old Testament Hermeneutics*, trans. Shirley C. Guth-

Overall in the historical view, Scripture is accorded the status of primary authority in matters of faith, in the sense that it is a reliable record of the central happenings and a trustworthy interpretation of what God did, does, and will do.[28] The extent to which the theological commentary on these acts is accorded authority, and how that authority functions, varies with the exponent.

Views to the right of this perspective challenge it for not taking into account adequately the centrality and adequacy of biblical propositions about God's plans and purposes, soteric or otherwise. Views to the left of it question the meaningfulness of the very concept "acts of God," the extent to which it does justice to the non-historical elements of Scripture and whether it has fixed upon the true center of the Scripture, Jesus Christ, and has understood how we gain access to the focal point.

The Christological View

The Christological view of Scripture is a capacious category encompassing a variety of interpretive options and a range of theological views. What they have in common is the understanding of Scripture as a medium for knowing Jesus Christ. However, this view is not to be confused with others that also hold Christ to be normative but join to that standard a content that extends beyond the norm, either the Scripture in its entirety or a definitive thread of teaching within it. For the present position Christ is the Word that alone constitutes the content of Scripture. The Christocentric version of the infallibility view understands Jesus Christ as the lens for understanding the larger data of the Bible, whereas this Christological view construes Jesus Christ as the datum itself.

Some of the Christological subsets we will examine are them-

rie, Jr., ed. J. L. Mays (Richmond: John Knox Press, 1963), 314-35. The position is developed by members of "the Pannenberg working circle" in *Revelation as History*, ed. Wolfhart Pannenberg, Rolf Rendtorff, Trutz Rendtorff, and Ulrich Wilkens, trans. David Granskou (New York: Macmillan, 1968). A helpful interpretive volume is *Theology as History*, ed. James M. Robinson and John B. Cobb, Jr. (New York: Harper & Row, 1967), esp. Robinson's chapter, "Revelation as Word and History" (pp. 1-100). On the Christological "center" see Wolfhart Pannenberg, *Jesus—God and Man*, trans. Lewis Wilkins and Duane A. Priebe (Philadelphia: Westminster Press, 1968).

28. In *Salvation in History*, 39, Cullmann accents the similarities of his view with those of Pannenberg. On this matter they do converge, however different the range of history focused upon.

selves locked in controversy, even though each warrants its position by an appeal to Christ. A few espouse a Christological interpretation as a way of throwing off old dogmatic formulations. Others see it as an opening for the use of critical scholarship. Still others find it as a way of stressing the moral significance of Scripture. In each of these cases, human experience is given a much fuller play in the understanding of Scripture than the earlier mentioned positions. At the same time other Christological views wage a battle against the role of human experience in interpreting Scripture, because they see its presence as a captivity of Christ by the experiencer. Indeed the original impetus for the twentieth-century "crisis theology" was the over-againstness of Christ and culture. Both ends of the spectrum within this type, therefore, appeal to Christ as the true meaning of Scripture.[29]

1. Christ as the Addressing Word

The richness of Karl Barth's thought makes it difficult to fit into the overall schema we have developed here. We could make an argument for his inclusion in the historical view, in spite of his disagreements with most of its exponents. Barth employs the promise-fulfillment framework associated with it, and speaks of holy history. Some interpret his thought as a narrative theology in which "an agent is rendered," Jesus Christ.[30] Others who take an infallibilist position have drawn heavily on Barth, including the defense of propositionalist assumptions in his theology.[31] Still others are convinced that Barth's thought never escapes the influence of the Enlightenment, placing him, with Bultmann, as prey to an existentialist subjectivity, a child of modernity who would let contemporary experience take away biblical authority.[32] All of this is a warning to avoid too easy categorizations. We place him on our range of options, therefore, with hesitation and qualification, judging that "Christ as the addressing Word" comes closest to his view of biblical authority.

29. For those various appeals to Christ vis-à-vis culture see H. Richard Niebuhr, *Christ and Culture* (New York: Harper & Row, 1951).

30. See David H. Kelsey, "Rendering an Agent," in *Uses of Scripture,* 39-55, and the work of Hans W. Frei, *The Identity of Jesus Christ* (Philadelphia: Fortress Press, 1975).

31. Ramm, *After Fundamentalism, passim*.

32. Cornelius Van Til, *The New Modernism: An Appraisal of the Theology of Barth and Brunner* (Phillipsburg, N.J.: Presbyterian and Reformed, 1973).

Jesus Christ as attested in Scripture is the one Word we have to hear. Barth's declaration in the Barmen text he drafted expresses his Christological center. What does this mean? Various things:

1. Scripture is authoritative in the church because it is the canon asserting itself in the community by the Self-communication of God through it. The Word was uttered so unambiguously here that the church could do nothing else but acknowledge that fact, legitimating the present text. If a manuscript with apostolic credentials were to be discovered, and the Word were to be spoken through it by the power of the Spirit, such a document, authorized by the church-in-council, would have to be added to the present corpus. The canon is self-validating. Or better, the Word speaking through the canonical words is Self-authenticating. The authority of the Scriptures is established by Jesus Christ, the Word of God, the Second Person of the Trinity, the Son of God addressing us through it.[33]

2. The Bible is authoritative because its *content* is Jesus Christ. As Jesus Christ is the Word of God, all that is true in the Bible is the manifestation of who he is. As the divine Self-disclosure, Jesus Christ is whatever is revealed to be true in the assertions made about God-in-revelatory-action.[34]

3. The Bible is authoritative because it is *witness* to Jesus Christ. The center of the divine Self-disclosure is open to us in the life, death, and resurrection of Jesus Christ. As God incarnate, Jesus Christ unveils to humankind what God chooses to reveal of the divine being. Jesus Christ, therefore, is the divine revelation. To know it is to know him. The Bible enjoys primal authority because it is the port of entry to who Christ is and what he did.[35]

4. As the definitive disclosure of God's will and way, the biblical narrative of Christ—his deeds and words and the apostolic testimony to it—constitutes the norm of all that Scripture has to say.

33. Karl Barth, *CD* I/1, trans. G. T. Thomson (Edinburgh: T. & T. Clark, 1936), 27, 121ff., 135; *CD* IV/2, trans. G. W. Bromiley (Edinburgh: T. & T. Clark, 1956), 123; *CD* IV/3, trans. G. W. Bromiley (Edinburgh: T. & T. Clark, 1961–62).

34. *CD* I/1, 427, 439; *CD* II/2, trans. G. W. Bromiley, J. C. Campbell, Ian Wilson, J. Strathearn McNabe, H. Knight, and R. A. Stewart (Edinburgh: T. & T. Clark, 1957), 4ff.

35. *CD* II/1, trans. T. H. L. Parker, W. B. Johnson, H. Knight, and J. L. M. Haire (Edinburgh: T. & T. Clark, 1957), 172ff.; *CD* III/3, trans. G. W. Bromiley and R. Ehrlich (Edinburgh: T. & T. Clark, 1960), 200-204; *CD* IV/3a, 96, 11, 44, 99-103, 113.

Anything in the Bible that does not cohere with this centerpoint is not the Word of God.[36]

5. Just as in Jesus Christ, God incarnate is both fully human and fully divine, so the written Word has a dual character. The Bible as a form of the Word is the Word in human words, reflecting thereby the Christological paradox. This human witness cannot be confused with the Word any more than the human mode of Jesus' existence can be mistaken for deity. We must avoid Monophysitism or Docetism in understanding the Bible by recognizing the full finitude of the biblical texts, including their capacity to err in things scientific, historical, and even theological. This humanity of the written Word legitimates the use of critical scholarship. The Bible takes its shape from the Christological paradox: the God-Man addresses us through its pages in the human-divine modes that Christ is.[37]

6. Because Christ is the active Word of God, the Bible is the living Word of God. The Word comes to us as a happening, not in a static way. Because God is free and sovereign, the Word is an event that takes place when and where God chooses to let it be. The Word is not under human control but under God's Self-control. The Word is spoken at God's behest and not ours. The Bible cannot be said to be a deposit of God's information, which would leave it at the mercy of human devices and designs. The Bible *becomes* the Word of God in an event of divine free Self-determination. Incapable of being harnessed to our purposes, the Word happens when so appointed in the divine freedom.[38]

7. There is no human precondition to the happening of the Word. However, the promise of the Scripture and the history of the speaking of the Word are associated with its life in the proclamation of the community. The preached Word, with the exegetical disciplines associated therewith, has been and can become again the occasion for the event of the Word. The authority of Scripture is inseparable from the exegeted and articulated Bible, as it is regularly expounded in the life of the congregation. In this sense Christ comes to us through the church's proclamation.[39]

36. *CD* I/1, 121-23; *CD* I/2, trans. G. T. Thomson and H. Knight (Edinburgh: T. & T. Clark, 1956), 817; *CD* II/1, 18ff.; *CD* II/2, 52-53; *CD* IV/3, 32, 39, 44, 48, 49-53, 86-103.

37. *CD* I/1, 129-33; *CD* III/3, 200-204.

38. *CD* I/1, 105; *CD* IV/2, trans. G. W. Bromiley (Edinburgh: T. & T. Clark, 1956), 303ff.; *CD* IV/3a, 22, 31-38, 44-47, 74-80, 83-86.

39. *CD* I/1, 98ff.; *CD* IV/2, 538-49; *CD* 3a, 96.

In outlining these aspects of Christ as the addressing Word, we have expressed the threefold form of the Word that Barth explicitly describes.[40] The Word, he says, happens in the revealed Word of the incarnation, the written Word of Scripture, and the proclaimed Word in the engagement of the community with its Center. The written Word is the reference point in our midst that occasions that living engagement, the gift to us of access to the revelation in Jesus Christ. And that revelation is known only through the Word incarnate twenty centuries ago in Jesus of Nazareth living, dying, rising.

The authority of the Bible therefore is at the initiative of the Word of God speaking through the words of Scripture in the rich and varied senses indicated. The dynamism of this view makes it impossible to distinguish authority from revelation. Authority is the act of revelation, not separable from it or identifiable in words, doctrine, ideas, motifs, events, principles, behavior, feelings. "God is known by God alone." So too, the description of this entire project as "the theology of revelation."

Because inseparability has been mistaken for indistinguishability, this view regularly invites misunderstanding from its enemies and missteps by its friends. Its foes wrongly accuse it of either biblicism, on the one hand, or subjectivism, on the other. Barthians of a less-than-dialectical mind have dissolved the connection between revelation and authority, either removing the latter by a stress upon an elusive revelatory dynamism, opening themselves to the criticism of subjectivity, or identifying too simplistically that dynamism with one or another loci of authority—propositions, moral visions, principles and behavior, or personal experience, evangelical or existential. Both the richness and profundity of Barth's thought and its unclarity and instability make it a major force, perhaps *the* major force, in the church's twentieth-century struggle with the issues of authority and revelation.

2. *Christ as the Call to Decision*

Rudolph Bultmann has shaped and expressed most clearly the decisional version of the Christological view of Scripture. Because he is similar to Barth in subtlety of thought and the variety of friendly and unfriendly interpreters, we walk cautiously into our characterization. Søren Kierkegaard will provide some help as his ideas have influenced Bultmann.

Kierkegaard waged an intellectual and spiritual warfare against

40. *CD* I/1, 98ff.

two phenomena of his time: Hegelian philosophy and "the crowd"—the "Christian crowd" of the Danish established church, and the larger crowd of "society," "the masses," "the press," "the state."[41] He believed that the truth had eluded both the Christian believer and the ordinary human being of his day with respect to their moral life, and beyond that in their religious and, finally, Christian "existence." The passion and subjectivity required to be a genuine human being first, and then to be a Christian, were missing. He declared that the "philosopher" (Hegel and the Hegelians, in particular) encourages people to escape living with risk and involvement by inviting them on a speculative journey devoid of personal concern.[42] The "crowd" is the temptation to dissolve the self into the herd of groupthink. Kierkegaard set himself the task of calling his contemporaries to grasp what they did and thought as a call to personal decision, worked out in fear and trembling.

Self-hood before God is what it is because God can be met only in a way commensurate with who God is and how God works: the One who comes to us in the suffering and passion of the cross.[43] Thus the way of being human, and finally the mode of faith itself, is along the path of "subjectivity," a personal, engaged, passionate, choosing, suffering, deciding self.[44] The posture appropriate to knowing God is as a solitary figure on a barren Danish moor, alone and exposed before God, with no support offered by other people or security to fall back upon, and no escape to the position of a noninvolved spectator. God's way in lonely passion and crucifixion with us defines the way we are to encounter God. No serene walk in the garden with Deity, but rather a treading of water over the fathomless depths. Socrates knew how to be human holding "an objective uncertainty in passionate inwardness."[45] So the Christian before the paradox of the incarnation is engaged in suffering subjectivity. Truth, human or divine, "is subjectivity." Without it we

41. As I have argued in "A Comparison and Critique of the Interpretation of Dehumanization in the Thought of Søren Kierkegaard and Karl Marx," Ph.D. diss., Univ. of Chicago Divinity School, 1962.

42. The refrain is throughout Kierkegaard's works but is dealt with at length in Søren Kierkegaard's *Concluding Unscientific Postscript,* trans. D. Swenson and W. Lowrie (Princeton: Princeton Univ. Press, 1944).

43. As in his expounding of the proposition *"quidquid cognoscitur per modem cognoscitus, cognoscitur,"* ibid., 51.

44. Ibid., 33.

45. Ibid., 182.

cheat God of the strenuous activity that is the *conditio sine qua non* of knowing the Truth.

Many of these themes recur in Bultmann's thought, with refinements traceable to the philosophy of Heidegger, whose own thought was shaped by Kierkegaard. Bultmann finds the heart of the Bible to be our meeting with Jesus, the preacher of the kingdom.[46] In him we confront an either/or, and are brought to a crisis of decision. Called in our present situation to radical obedience, we meet the personal claim God makes upon us and face its concomitant warning not to fall back on any tempting security measures. We know in our situation what is right and wrong. Yet we avoid making the hard decision to act in accord with what we know. The Word of the kingdom becomes one of judgment on our fears, and our failure to choose. And a Word of forgiveness is joined to the judgment.[47] All our life is viewed in its relationship to God with the acceptance and the claim that comes into this situation. Christian faith is this Jesus-encounter with its deep seriousness, the call to be an actor not an observer on the scene of life. Our struggles with theodicy are representative of all existential questions. The problem of suffering is not an occasion for speculation but for committing oneself to the God who demands we view every event in our life as gift and claim, acceptance and choice.[48]

This Christological reading of the authority of Scripture is joined to Bultmann's demythologizing program. In the world of science and technology we live with modernity's closed system of causality and therefore cannot accept the Bible's worldview of miracles and divine acts. We must construe Scripture in a different framework consonant with today's empiricism.[49] For Bultmann the framework is supplied by existential premises of Kierkegaard cum Heidegger. The authority of the Bible, therefore, is its capacity through mythological story to bring us before the decisive moment when in self-examination, fear, and trembling we see our life before God. In

46. Not "the personality of Jesus," for "I do think indeed that we can now know almost nothing concerning the life and personality of Jesus." Rudolph Bultmann, *Jesus and the Word,* trans. Louise Pettibone Smith and Erminie Huntress Lantero (New York: Scribner's, 1958), 8. The encounter is with "his teaching, his message" (p. 12).

47. Ibid., 133-219.

48. Ibid., 27-56.

49. Rudolph Bultmann, *Jesus Christ and Mythology* (New York: Scribner's, 1958) and "New Testament and Mythology," in *Kerygma and Myth,* ed. Hans Werner-Bartsch (New York: Harper & Brothers, Harper Torchbook, 1961).

this gracious and fearful moment comes a gift and claim, each calling for personal decision. We stand before an either/or.

One clear difference between Bultmann and Kierkegaard is the status of the objective assertions of the Bible. For Kierkegaard, the incarnation is not an unbelievable myth but a real action of God altering the relation of the world to God. However, it is of such a paradoxical nature that it resists the curiosity of speculative reason and the captivity into which such reason takes its objects. For Bultmann the authority of the Christ who calls us to decision does not depend on either a discreet act in the history of God or a supernatural intrusion into the causal chain. While Bultmann treats these biblical assertions mythologically, statements about the reality of God do not seem to undergo the same transmutation. The gift and command have their source in ontological reality, One who so calls us to choose.[50] Some of Bultmann's followers, however, take his existential Christology to what appears to be its logical end point: what we have in the Bible are entirely mythical statements with their only referent being human experience, an "I may" and an "I must" that makes and keeps human life human.[51]

However modified, Bultmann's interpretation of the authority of Scripture has to do with its power to confront us in Christ with the call to decide. As with the first Christological subset (represented by Barth) so here, too, authority and revelation are inseparable. Revelation is the authority of this experience of gift and claim. But there is a world of difference between "addressing Word" and "call to decision." Barth refuses to identify the moment of encounter with our *experience* of it. Bultmann, influenced by Kierkegaard's preoccupation with passion, inner suffering, and subjectivity takes an existential and therefore experiential turn, stopping short of a total psychologizing of the event that would eliminate any objective transcendent source. However, Bultmann's critics declare that the moment in which this One comes to us is so laden with philosophical and experiential factors that both the transcendent Referent and the Christological point of meeting are obscured or rendered unnecessary. Barth in particular saw Bultmann's Christological prin-

50. For a careful study of this, see Helmut Gollwitzer, *The Existence of God as Confessed by Faith,* trans. James W. Leitch (Philadelphia: Westminster Press, 1965), 15-34.

51. Herbert Braun, "The Problem of a New Testament Theology," trans. Jack Sanders, in James M. Robinson, et al., *The Bultmann School of Biblical Interpretation: New Directions?* (New York: Harper & Row, 1965), 169-83.

ciple as the chief subverter of biblical authority. And Bultmann in turn read Barth's venture as an exercise in biblicism.

3. The Jesus of History

In the personal journey of the Introduction we met the "red letter New Testament." It enjoyed widespread popularity in the early decades of the twentieth century, and continues to have a following. What is the Bible all about? The answer leaps from the page in the bold and colorful print of Jesus' own words. The Bible is the setting for these jewels, the teachings of the Master. And while not so marked in red, the behavior of Jesus provides the background for interpreting the words. Beyond that, all of Scripture is to be measured by the Galilean profile. What does not fit the picture is not authoritative. Matters that go beyond the specifics of Jesus' model behavior and teaching (e.g., the "Old Testament God of wrath," Paul's bloody metaphors of the atonement, etc.) are either rejected or reread in the Jesus framework (with the Paul of 1 Cor. 13 and Psalm 23 representing the truer picture of each testament) and thus found to have deeper meaning, one coherent with the picture of Jesus. The Bible is a trustworthy guide to the extent that it measures up to the example of Jesus. But, finally, these various acceptable threads of teaching throughout the Scripture are not more than what is found already in the bold red letters.

This Christological key, perhaps more accurately a "Jesusological" one, took recent shape in the nineteenth and twentieth centuries in association with theologies that reacted against orthodoxy. Thus the "Jesus of history" was set against the "Christ of faith." "Biographies" of Jesus were popular, ones that stressed the moral and practical implications of the Bible and bewailed the "abstractions," "dogmatism," and "irrelevance" of traditional Christianity. What needed to be done was to distill the biblical essence, the Teacher's principles of love to God and neighbor. In its mildest forms, Jesus' religion was equated with good citizenship standards. More intensely, it demanded a discipleship without regard to consequences. Its most rigorous expression was the determined effort to pursue a Sermon on the Mount ethic of cheek-turning, second-mile, coat-sharing nonresistance (or "nonviolent resistance"). Thus emerged a spectrum of views that ran from Bruce Barton's salesman figure to Harry Emerson Fosdick's pacifist Jesus.[52]

52. Bruce Barton, *The Man Nobody Knows* (Indianapolis: Bobbs-Merrill, 1925) and Harry Emerson Fosdick, *The Man from Nazareth: As His Contemporaries Saw Him* (New York: Harper & Brothers, 1949).

In one form or another this view of the authority of Jesus as example and teacher became a leading theme in the preaching and teaching of liberal Protestantism. It found a response as well in wider communities of ethical concern, among secular commentators and people of other religions who credited Christianity with at least a founder of moral grandeur. In later decades this "exemplarist" view of Jesus and biblical authority became influential among Roman Catholic interpreters.[53] Its critics hold that both the bad news of divine judgment and the Good News of salvation are eroded by this position in which a "God without wrath brought men without sin into a kingdom without judgment through the ministrations of a Christ without a cross."[54]

4. *The Historical Jesus*

The Jesus of the red letter New Testament, discovered readily on the pages of the Bible or formed by early efforts in historical inquiry, came under sharp attack from a later scholarship. As investigative tools improved, the "old quest" was judged to be more the projection of the values of the quester than the discovery of "the real Jesus," autobiography rather than a biography.

If we have any idea who Jesus is, some said, he would not be much of a model. The biblical Jesus is a stranger to us all, an interim apocalyptic visionary.[55] Other scholars concluded that the nature of the writing we have about Jesus, constructed as it is by the early Christian communities, precludes any discovery of the elusive figure behind this veil of primitive interpretation.[56] Must we then not settle for "the Christ of faith" handed on to us in the early church's proclamation? Or perhaps an intuitive bonding with the spirit of the strange Galilean?[57]

No, declared others who launched a modest but determined "new quest." Following a programmatic essay by Ernst

53. Hans Küng, *On Being a Christian,* trans. Edward Quinn (Garden City, N.Y.: Doubleday, 1976).

54. H. Richard Niebuhr, *The Kingdom of God in America* (New York: Harper & Brothers, Harper Torchbook, 1957), 193.

55. Albert Schweitzer, *The Quest of the Historical Jesus* (London: A. & C. Black, 1931), 1-12.

56. Martin Kähler, *The So-Called Historical Jesus and the Historical Biblical Christ,* trans. Carl E. Braaten (Philadelphia: Fortress Press, 1964), 42-91.

57. Albert Schweitzer, *Out of My Life and Thought,* trans. C. T. Campion (New York: The New American Library, Mentor Book, 1953), 48-51.

Käsemann,[58] a significant stream of New Testament studies argued that while no career of Jesus could be charted, nor his inner attitudes confidently described, elements of his teaching might be identified. So, too, a few aspects of his self-understanding and his behavior and relationship with others could be indicated.

The growing body of new quest literature has becomes the resource for yet another Jesus-centerea interpretation of Scripture. Using currently available methods of historical-critical inquiry and insights from a new literary criticism, a major interpretive proposal began to take shape. In the Christological volumes of Edward Schillebeeckx we see the method and the results in a developed way and in a systematic framework.[59] Jesus emerges as the "eschatological prophet," the final announcer of a coming kingdom, the reign of God already present in Jesus' relationship with the sick, hopeless, and marginalized, and in his own "Abba" encounter with God. The "resurrection experiences" of this figure, communicated to us in culturally formed symbols and traditions, had an impact on his followers sufficient to assure them, and in turn all later Christian believers, that Christ is now alive with God.

In Schillebeeckx's reconstruction of the picture of Christ we have a statement of the authority of the Bible for its readers today. The Scripture is authoritative to the extent that it accords with the Jesus of history as he is recovered for us in the careful compilation of the results of the new quest. In these we are given the "historical Jesus." However, the recovery is not the end of the matter. Living and writing in a critical era that has posed the questions of "the hermeneutical gap," Schillebeeckx cannot simply offer these results as the meaning of the Bible for people today. That meaning must be communicated in contemporary terms, a task accomplished by finding theological equivalents that capture the current significance of the ancient portrayal of the eschatological prophet. Schillebeeckx finds the carrier of this contemporary import in a modified version of liberation themes, one that includes deliverance from death, illness, and sin as well as sociopolitical liberation, a salvation characterized overall as good news of hope in the face of human

58. Ernst Käsemann, "The Problem of the Historical Jesus," in *Essays on New Testament Themes*, trans. W. J. Montague (London: SCM Press, 1964), 15-47.

59. Esp. Edward Schillebeeckx, *Jesus: An Experiment in Christology*, trans. Hubert Hoskins (New York: Seabury Press, 1979). For an analysis and evaluation of some of the themes in Schillebeeckx's Christology see Gabriel Fackre, "Bones Strong and Weak in the Skeletal Structure of Schillebeeckx's Christology," *Journal of Ecumenical Studies* 21 (Spring 1984): 248-77.

hopelessness. While the Bible speaks of many things, the figure of Jesus is the criterion for identifying the valid from the invalid. As in its old quest predecessor, the pre-Easter Jesus furnishes the content for making this distinction.

Schillebeeckx has been attacked from within the Roman Catholic Church by those who contend that he has gone against the church's magisterium and its specific dogmas, questioning his loyalty to the office itself. Other critics to the right declare that he has allowed human experience to legislate the meaning of Scripture, either in obeisance to academic scholarship or in contemporary liberation categories.[60] Critics on the left find that his picture of Jesus reflects the values of a middle-class male perspective and thus is subject to the same autobiographical critique mounted against the old quest.[61]

5. *Jesus the Liberator*

The old and new quest Christologies do not exhaust the Jesus of history/historical Jesus mode we are examining. In fact the most aggressive statement in the late twentieth century of the Christological view is found in "liberation theology"—Third World, black, and feminist. Other versions of liberation theology belong elsewhere in our typology, depending on the extent to which the experiential factor is more prominent than the biblical source, or whether liberation themes are found in combination with other motifs. Here we treat those views in which Jesus, his flesh and blood reality as witnessed to in Scripture, is the decisive theological authority.

The liberator view begins one step behind the assumptions of Jesus research. It holds that the most careful reading of the New Testament materials on Jesus cannot itself avoid being historically conditioned by the setting and power interests of the expositor. Thus both popular and scholarly treatments of the New Testament figure show class, race, and sex biases. This can be seen in blatant ways such as Bruce Barton's interpretation of Jesus as a hard-working capitalist, or in more covert fashion in the "abstract" Christol-

60. Leonard Swidler and Piet Fransen, *Authority in the Church and the Schillebeeckx Case* (New York: Crossroad, 1982). For a general background to the Vatican concern that prompted the inquiry into Schillebeeckx's works see Joseph Cardinal Ratzinger with Vittorio Messori, *The Ratzinger Report,* trans. Salvator Attanasio and Graham Harrison (San Francisco: Ignatius Press, 1985).

61. Rosemary Radford Ruether, "Is a New Christian Consensus Possible?" in Hans Küng, Edward Schillebeeckx, et al., *Consensus in Theology?* ed. Leonard Swidler (Philadelphia: Westminster Press, 1980), 63-68.

ogies or orthodox belief, "commonsense" readings of Scripture, the red letter Jesus, or in sophisticated reconstructions. All views promote the vested interest of the interpreter by what they say or fail to say. Thus a "hermeneutics of suspicion" is applied to claims that the interpreter has discovered "objective" data in the Bible. In this case, Christological proposals are seen as value-laden instruments of self-interpretation. Thus, the first move of any interpretation of the Bible is to expose the interpreter's social location and agenda.[62]

The second move is to take up a stance that will reveal who the real Jesus is, one that will get at the root figure on the one hand, and be able to render that figure meaningful in contemporary context, on the other. The truth about Jesus discloses itself to those who suffer with the hidden Christ in the places of oppression and in the struggle for deliverance. As liberator of the oppressed, Christ is found in solidarity with the poor and disenfranchised. His true identity is known only to those present there with him and committed to his struggle. The understanding of Scripture and all the doing of authentic theology, therefore, must be "critical reflection on praxis."[63]

The One who emerges in this encounter becomes the interpreter of the rest of the biblical text. What does not fit this Christological norm cannot be gospel. What is other than it, but kindred to it, is read in its light. Sometimes the Jesus standard itself is construed in the light of the prior liberation event, the exodus. Read as a paradigm of liberation, the release of a people from slave status, exodus cum Jesus becomes the criterion for scriptural truth.

A cluster of present theologies that stress liberation employ this Christological principle of interpretation. Third World liberation teaching often focuses on the historical Jesus as a key to Scripture. Gustavo Gutiérrez has given powerful expression to this position.[64] Black theology has also made extensive use of the theme of Jesus

62. Juan Luis Segundo, *The Liberation of Theology,* trans. John Drury (Maryknoll, N.Y.: Orbis Books, 1975), 7-96.

63. Gustavo Gutiérrez, *A Theology of Liberation,* trans. and ed. Sister Caridad Inda and John Eagleson (Maryknoll, N.Y.: Orbis Books, 1971), 6-21.

64. In addition to *A Theology of Liberation* see also *The Power of the Poor in History* (Maryknoll, N.Y.: Orbis Books, 1983) and *We Drink from Our Own Wells* (Maryknoll, N.Y.: Orbis Books, 1975). For an Asian version of Christ the Liberator themes see Ahn Byung-Mu, "Jesus and the Minjung in the Gospel of Mark," in *Minjung Theology,* ed. the Commission on Theological Concerns of the Christian Conference of Asia, with preface by James H. Cone (Maryknoll, N.Y.: Orbis Books, 1981), 138-52.

as liberator, joining it to the exodus theme. The history of slavery for the North American black community gives special power to this conjunction. James Cone is a well-known interpreter of this view.[65] Feminist theologians have made selective use of the Jesus model, but issues about Jesus' masculinity, the employment of the new literary criticism in interpreting Scripture, and the accent on affect submerged by discursive-masculine models of traditional theology often mute the Christological note. Letty Mandeville Russell gives a Christological accent to her feminist position.[66] We shall return to these developments in the experiential section on authority. In all forms in question the Bible is authoritative to the extent that it directly or indirectly bears witness to this figure who liberates those in bondage. Jesus can be so found in Scripture by those who know the boot of the oppressor on their own neck, or are in solidarity with the oppressed. In this position "from below," we can see Jesus to be the bringer of the rule of righteousness. Such a perspective from the underside of history constitutes the "epistemological privilege" of the disenfranchised, why there must be "preferential option for the poor," not only in the struggle for liberation but also in understanding the meaning of Scripture.

Combinationist Views

Our final category under biblical primacy is a comprehensive one, and that in several senses. While holding to the primacy of Scripture, this set of perspectives self-consciously includes other elements of authority as criteria for valid theological assertions. Using our threefold division, that means that either "the church" or "the world," or both, are joined to the Bible as factors in theological decision-making, albeit ministerial to the scriptural source and standard.

All of the foregoing views are "combinationist" in some sense. As interpretations of Scripture, they draw upon experiential and/or ecclesial factors to state and argue their cases. The difference is that (a) the focus upon an internal biblical framework or refrain obscures or plays down the worldly or churchly elements acknowl-

65. James H. Cone, *A Black Theology of Liberation* (Philadelphia: Lippincott, 1970); *For My People: Black Theology in the Black Church* (Maryknoll, N.Y.: Orbis Books, 1984), 53-77; *Speaking the Truth: Ecumenism, Liberation, and Black Theology* (Grand Rapids: Eerdmans, 1986), 1-49.

66. Letty M. Russell, *Human Liberation in a Feminist Perspective* (Philadelphia: Westminster Press, 1974), 131-54.

edged to be present, or (b) the church and world elements are there, but not acknowledged, (c) the experiential and ecclesial are self-consciously rejected as authoritative, but nevertheless function covertly, (d) the churchly or worldly context for biblical text is strongly asserted but the focus or functional standard is Scripture as such or a norm within it. The options in the present category are those that avow and actively employ the role of the church and its traditions, and/or the world of human experience, as an integral part of theological method.

This rubric is also comprehensive in the sense that a great variety of subsets work in combinationist fashion, many more than are found in the previous views that include such subsets. Further, these varied perspectives themselves represent a range of interpretive streams. We shall attempt to cover this range, seeking to include both very standard positions and those that are relatively new but increasingly influential, under these headings: traditional, ecumenical, canonical, symbolical, and contextual.

Before moving to the description of each, I interject a brief discussion of a familiar theme in the Protestant heritage, having reserved it for this point in the analysis because the question is posed most sharply by the combinationist views, at least those that are Protestant.

Sola Scriptura

On the face of it, and in much formal Protestant argument, "sola Scriptura" carries a radically exclusivist meaning. It seems to assert that the Bible alone can be recognized in the making of doctrine. Along with its frequent companions, *sola fide, sola gratia,* and *solus Christus,* it suggests the solitary grandeur of Scripture in matters of authority, comparable to the no-nonsense assertion of salvation by faith alone, grace alone, and Christ alone, with all partnerships, including junior ones, disallowed.

If "sola" means that kind of exclusivity, how then do we account for the citation of ancient Christian tradition and allusion to the "Fathers" in the theological and exegetical expositions of Luther and Calvin? How can Reformation confessions and orthodox interpreters assign the role of instruction and even relative normativity to classical creeds and to the confessions and catechisms of the Reformation themselves? How in these same strongly Protestant circles can the act of preaching and the stewardship of the same by the pastoral office not be at least a tacit acknowledgment of the role of the church in the interpretation of Scripture? How can both modern evangelicals and firm defenders of the Lutheran tradition today include the role of tradition in their concept of authority while still espousing *sola Scriptura?*[67] And how can both early and later Protestant interpreters have recourse to experience as a factor in authority in any of its varied forms—whether it be in a reason-oriented apologetics, moral substantiation of faith, or the corroboration of scriptural truth by a "heart strangely warmed"? Either there is a fundamental confusion in these matters, or the principle of *sola Scriptura* is not what it is made out to be by either friends who deny to the church or world any role in issues of authority, or by critics who accuse Protestants of ignoring just these things.[68]

The kind of distinction cited in the chapter on definitions, which will be developed in the constructive section of this volume, is an effort to throw some light on these questions and to find a way to honor the interests of the Reformation, sometimes obscured by the polemics and the unclarity of later defenders of the Protestant heritage. At issue in the Reformation was the *source,* construed in both its revelatory and authority dimensions. Does God disclose the truth in deeds and disclosures among prophet and apostle with its fruit in the biblical deposit and, in a second revelatory deposit in the church, manifest in ecclesial dogma and the teaching office? This two-source view of revelation and authority (which may or may not have been the official position of the church at the time of the Reformation, and may or may not have been the teaching of the Tridentine response to the Reformers—both issues are in dispute) was anathema to the Reformers. In theory, even in its most sophisticated formulation by Trent (which sought to maintain the Bible as the norm that is not itself governed by the church albeit properly interpreted only by it) it seemed to them to deny the premise of definitive biblical authority. And in practice it appeared to provide a church hierarchy with a warrant to control the scriptural text. Also in declarations that suggested a parity of Scripture and tradition within that same church, the choice between a clear and present authority with long-standing revelatory credentials, and an ancient complex and inaccessible book with its acknowledged re-

67. In the former case, Pinnock, *The Scripture Principle,* 79-82, and in the latter case, Carl Braaten, "Prologomena to Christian Dogmatics," in Carl Braaten and Robert Jenson, eds., *Christian Dogmatics,* vol. 1 (Philadelphia: Fortress Press, 1984), 1-78.

68. See Gnuse, *Authority of the Bible,* 114ff.

velatory status, there is clearly "no contest." In this setting, the assertion of the Bible as the sole source of authority with its unique revelatory status as the disclosive work of the Holy Spirit had to be made. Scripture alone meant just that, the Bible as the sole occupant of the seat of *adjudicating* authority and the only origin of Christian teaching. However, to declare for this singularity does not require the exclusion of other elements in the formation of theological judgment. While Scripture is the sole teaching authority, contra the functional occupancy of this role by the then church's magisterium, this point of decision does not preclude a *process* for discerning the Bible's meaning that includes the community of faith and its wisdom. Nor does it exclude from that process any means to be found in a fallen but still graced creation that can also aid in the discernment and clarification of Scripture's intent. Thus the church's most widely esteemed lore—its historic creeds, its confessional and catechetical tradition with its pedagogical and proclamatory offices, and the life of the whole people of God in worship and work *(sensus fidelium)*—are *ministerial* to the understanding of a Scripture that remains always *magisterial.*[69]

Further, a subsidiary role, both clarifying and confirming, is played in Reformation theology by the larger web of human experience—rational, moral, and affective. But this latter is no more the *source* of authority than is tradition, always standing under the judgment of Scripture with its special revelatory warrants. Nevertheless, it functions in a way that is different from either Scripture or tradition by relating the biblical text to the human context, contemporary and common. We argue, therefore, like the position being developed here, that the Reformation held tradition to be the resource for understanding the biblical source, with human experience functioning as the setting into which the source speaks. When *sola Scriptura* is understood in this way, as referring to the sole source of authority, and the ancillary functions of tradition and experience acknowledged as well but defined carefully in terms of their respective functions, the apparent dissonance between the Reformation formula and the practice of the Reformers disappears. Again, a step is made toward a catholicity of interpretation sought in the present ecumenical movement and represented by this venture in systematics.

Let us return now to a discussion of the subsets of the combinationist view.

69. A distinction made by Clark Pinnock.

1. Traditional

"Traditional" here refers to those positions in church theology—Roman Catholic, Eastern Orthodox, Lutheran, Reformed, and others—that give precedence to Scripture, in some sense, but also turn to second and third touchstones of authority. But we include as well under this general heading less official/ecclesial versions of theology that, like the venerable traditions, employ multiple reference points while maintaining biblical primacy. As we yet have to examine the views of church and world priority, it would be premature to go into the details of standard combinationist types, traditional or ecumenical. We make an exception in the case of canonical and symbolical options because their relative newness requires some description.

The ecclesial-traditional type is more widespread than often recognized. For example, one could make a case that the classical Roman Catholic position espouses this view. Thus the Tridentine formulation that Scripture is the "norm which governs and is not governed" *(norma normans et non normata),* in spite of the prominent role of the magisterium, clearly makes the Bible the formal standard for theology, however that may be qualified in practice or nuanced by a two-source theory of communicated revelation. How different is this methodologically, as Robert Gnuse points out, than the stance of the Lutheran Book of Concord, which says that the Bible is the *norma normans* and the ancient creeds and Reformation confessions are the *norma normata?*[70] The difference comes, of course, in how this is played out, both in method and content of interpretation.

The same kind of scriptural precedence with a contributory role for tradition can be found in Eastern Orthodox formulations, official and unofficial, with an outworking, nevertheless, that consistently gives precedence to tradition over Scripture, as in Roman Catholic tendencies. In a later section of the typology we shall call these the "traditionalist" Roman Catholic and Eastern Orthodox views (also Protestant). But the point here is that official Roman Catholic teaching from Trent to Vatican II, and strongly so in the "progressive" wing of post–Vatican II Catholic interpretation and an influential construal of the Orthodox tradition represent a combinationist view of biblical authority.

In all cases—Roman Catholic, Eastern Orthodox, and Protes-

70. Gnuse, *Authority of the Bible,* 8.

tant—combinationism often includes human experience. Identified frequently as "reason" and sometimes as "experience" with warrants in a doctrine of natural grace, common grace, general revelation, etc., some form of universal human capacitation is welcomed as an aid in theological decision-making.

The place of reason also appears in the insistence on the role of philosophy in the theological enterprise (as junior partner), or more recently the facilitating of theology by sociological, psychological, aesthetic, and political insights, and the appeal to standards of logic and evidence. This recourse to natural reason or general experience should be distinguished from the legitimation of reason and experience by its baptism in the waters of faith, as in the reason entailed in "faith seeking understanding," or "experience" as the avenue of confirmation used by the Spirit or in the special grace of conversion in "born again" Christianity.

In "the Methodist quadrilateral"—Scripture, tradition, reason, experience—"experience" is understood in accord with Wesley and Methodism's "heart strangely warmed." It is an inner witness to the truth of scriptural affirmations, either convincing one formerly unconvinced or convicting one personally of a truth otherwise held, as the *Christian* experience of the "inner testimony of the Holy Spirit" to biblical revelation. It is not a reference to a general human capacitation as an element of authority alongside Scripture and tradition, thereby providing additional data for doctrine. In the case of "reason," however, the role of wider data and reflection, including philosophy, is acknowledged and brought into conversation with Scripture and tradition, albeit always accountable to the scriptural source. Popular discussion of the quadrilateral, prompted by the too facile conjunction of the four elements, sometimes does not make these important distinctions of kind between the elements of *authority*—Scripture, tradition and "reason" (here called "world" or "human experience"), and its underpinning with the process of *revelation*—Christian "experience" (in this volume identified as personal "illumination").

A part of traditional combinationism are the many nonecclesial theological enterprises that make little reference to, or use of, church lore, do their work with an eye on the biblical horizon but draw heavily on other resources. Found here are numerous philosophical theologies, and more recently political theologies, which root their view in Christian cum biblical soil but till it with a variety of other kinds of tools. Hence the more "traditional" forms of Platonic, Aristotelian, Kantian, Hegelian, process, existentialist, Marxist-influenced, and Jungian-shaped Christian theology. Affective and moral rather than rational forms of experience take on greater prominence in some viewpoints, ancient and modern, as in mystical, pietist, "experientialist," and ethically oriented theologies. In many of these, considering their nonecclesial bent, human experience moves into a highly active "resource" role for interpreting the biblical source, and the church and its traditions become the "setting" that provides the idiom and community out of which theology is formed. Critics of this view frequently question whether the aggressive move made by human experience in these views displaces, or tends to displace, the Bible as source of authority.

2. Ecumenical

The difference between "ecumenical" and churchly "tradition" is the former's self-conscious and often institutional effort to define authority in an ecclesial context, but to do it in a developing ecumenical fashion rather than in a confessionally particularist way. With the ecumenical, as with the traditional, two or more criteria of authority are at work, often identified as "Scripture and tradition," sometimes as "Scripture, tradition, and reason," and more recently as "Scripture, tradition, and lived experience."[71] This book falls into this subtype of biblical authority, as the divisions Scripture, tradition, and human experience or Bible, church, and world suggest. The major portion of the volume is devoted to the exposition of this view and its warrants, so we reserve comment on it for the later exposition.

Two important ecumenical statements that indicate the direction of the ecumenical trajectory are the formal declaration of a "COCU consensus" on authority and the position on authority developed by the Faith and Order Commission of the World Council of Churches as represented in its various statements on the subject, the working premises of its document *Baptism, Eucharist and Ministry,* and materials emerging in preparation for its project "Toward a Common Expression of the Apostolic Faith Today."[72]

71. The World Alliance of Reformed Churches, *Called to Witness to the Gospel Today* (Geneva: World Alliance of Reformed Churches, 1983).

72. *Baptism, Eucharist and Ministry,* Faith and Order Paper no. 111 (Geneva: World Council of Churches, 1982), *passim.* See also *Churches Respond to BEM,* 2 vols., ed. Max Thurian (Geneva: World Council of Churches, 1986); *The COCU Consensus,* ed. Gerald F. Moede (Princeton: Consultation on Church Union, 1985), 29-33. The WCC's *The Bible: Its Authority in The Ecumenical Movement* shows the direction of ecumenical thinking.

3. Canonical

An increasingly influential view of scriptural authority that has taken shape in the last decades of the twentieth century is described variously as "a canonical approach to Scripture" or "canon criticism."[73] We place it here among the combinationist perspectives because of its strong emphasis on the place of the Christian community in the formation and interpretation of the Bible. In describing the canonical approach we draw primarily on the work of Brevard Childs.[74]

Canon criticism as a pursuit within biblical studies emerged as a corrective to deficiencies perceived in the theory and practice of historical criticism, and out of concern for the availability of Scripture to its faith community. Canon critics believe that preoccupation with the historically contexted prehistory of the biblical text ignores certain facts about the formation of the Bible as canon, and the needs of the church in its present dealing with Scripture as its teaching authority. The historical-critical method claims to understand Scripture by reconstructing its origins in a given historical context, and by tracing the subsequent path of that response through other points in time and place. Canon advocates assert that insufficient attention is given in this approach to the often concealed "footprints" of canonical editors who, with a different agenda, have significantly influenced both the process and the product. With respect to the New Testament canon, for example, a process of organizing and refining the original data has gone on from the earliest oral stages through literary crystallization, redaction, and collection into a body of writing, a process calculated to establish over time the theological identity of the Christian community. This project incorporates the contextualization of text according to the questions and conditions of a given ecclesial cum social context into its overall momentum toward establishing a theological norm

73. Brevard Childs, *Introduction to the Old Testament as Scripture* (Philadelphia: Fortress Press, 1979) and *The New Testament as Canon: An Introduction* (Philadelphia: Fortress Press, 1984); James A. Sanders, *Canon and Community* (Philadelphia: Fortress Press, 1984) and *From Sacred Story to Sacred Text* (Philadelphia: Fortress Press, 1987).

74. Childs's canonical approach has been influential in the present work. James A. Sanders's excellent work *From Sacred Story to Sacred Text* (Philadelphia: Fortress Press, 1987) came to my attention after this book was completed. See his discussion of "canonical hermeneutics," 87-105. Cf. also the concentric circles here to his hermeneutical comments in *Canon and Community* (Philadelphia: Fortress Press, 1984), 77-78.

for a community of varied circumstances and future existence. The areas specifically addressed to historical context that engage the attention of historical critics are "loosened" in this process with its wider and longer constituencies, and with its need for continuities of belief beyond the discontinuities of setting.[75] These constituencies and continuities, however, are not rigidly defined. Doctrinal identity has more the character of the boundaries within which the faith of the community can live and work rather than a definition of the particulars within those borders.[76]

The word "canon" serves to identify the interest in latitudinal and longitudinal normativity, on the one hand, and the establishment of limits for it in a designated body of writings. The concepts of "rule" and of a "list of writings" are the two standard meanings of the word that cohere with these two purposes. A canonical approach will, therefore, attend carefully to the "final form" of the individual books of the Bible, and do the same with regard to the canons of the two Testaments, separate and together. What books are selected, how they are arranged, the internal relations and juxtapositions (e.g., the diverse perceptions of Jesus in the four Gospels, the relation of the pastoral to the Pauline corpus, the rationale for including James together with Pauline literature, the superscriptions, introductions, conclusions, etc.), shed light on how they are to be understood by the community that accepted them as normative, and what their significance is for us today. So too, the final form of the individual writings show evidence of shaping toward a meaning beyond the circumstances that occasioned them, either in their various strands or the audience to which the writing was addressed as a whole. That evidence has to do with teaching which has continuing meaning for the Christian community and relevance to a wider circle of contemporaries, thus making it as normative for the Christian community as such. This canonical mode of thought presupposes, of course, a unity within manifest diversity, one often lost by those who assume that biblical writing has only a highly particular ecclesial and social context.[77]

That there is such a process contributing to defining characteristics from the earliest oral period and proceeding to the postapostolic editing and establishing of a list of books means that we cannot understand the Bible apart from the church. In fact, it becomes

75. Childs's *The New Testament as Canon,* 23.

76. Ibid., 28-29.

77. Ibid., 29-30.

very difficult, if not impossible, to separate them. It can be said, of course, that the Spirit-empowered apostolic message propelled itself forward, prompting the canonical legitimation. But if these forces were already at work in the establishment of what we know as apostolic teaching, then this distinction between receiver and received cannot be so neatly made. In any case, our point here is that the intimacy of Scripture and tradition, the Bible and the church, makes the canonical option a form of the combinationist view.

We should note another feature of this same conjunction as found in some of the special accents of B. Childs. For him, a commitment by the present interpreter to the Bible as a rule of belief, to the church as the principal community of interpretation, and to Christ and the gospel as its orientation point further accents the churchly features of this view of biblical authority.[78]

Critics of the canonical approach question the coherence and consistency of its use, the importance of canonical influences in either understanding the Bible or communicating its significance to people today.[79] Associated with this is an often embattled defense of the historical-critical viewpoint. Foes of the canonical approach hold it to be in danger of retreating into or being undermined by a precritical mindset. Others, on the right, see canon criticism as allowing too much room for historical-critical methods, thereby undercutting biblical authority. From the same group comes the charge that the church has replaced the Bible as the source of authority.[80]

4. *Symbolist*

Where the emphasis on subjective appropriation has been prominent in the types examined, it is customarily joined to objective truth claims of one sort or another. But now we come to a theory of biblical interpretation that, in many cases, looks to Scripture as "performative" rather than assertional. It functions as "meaningful" rather than satisfying an interest in the objectively "truthful." Indeed in this view truthfulness has often come to signify meaningfulness. The Scripture is "true to me" or "true for us" (our com-

78. Ibid., 26-44.

79. James Barr, *Holy Scripture: Canon, Authority, Criticism* (Philadelphia: Westminster Press, 1983), 75-104.

80. Carl F. H. Henry, "Canonical Theology: An Evangelical Appraisal," unpublished paper delivered at Yale Divinity School evangelical colloquy, 1984.

munity) rather than "true to life" in the sense of conformity to an objective referent. One could argue that the elimination of an objective truth claim for Scripture puts this view in our third major type—the world as authority—rather than under scriptural primacy, for our human experience appears to be the arbiter of theological judgments. However, I have placed it here as a combinationist view of biblical authority because the experience to which reference is made is brought into relationship to a focal text, the Bible, and some of its exponents vehemently protest allegations of subjectivism.

Theological developments of this sort have been influenced by second thoughts about the impact of science and technology in the West. Rationality, cold logic, and dispassionate empirical inquiry, the dominance of the "left brain," masculine hegemony—all these have come under attack for their cultural failures. Most intense criticism has come from the voices of those long silenced—women, minority groups, the poor. Brought to the fore have been affect, feeling, right-brain functions, the contributions of women, the insights of the marginalized. Methodologically, this has meant much more attention to the role of symbol in religion. With it have come whole theologies of narrative, metaphor, and symbol.[81] A symbolist interpretation of the Bible focuses on the literary forms of the text, drawing attention to the places in Scripture where imagination takes hold, *poesis* moves to the fore, the total self is engaged, metaphor abounds, tales are told. Dominic Crossan is a well-known exponent of this view in its narrative expression. What counts is not an intellectual content abstracted from the text but how the Scripture evokes response in the reader or hearer. Discursive thought is not disdained, but reckoned as "second order" discourse. The symbol is the first order expression intimate with reality. After that the "symbol gives rise to thought" (Paul Ricoeur). An encounter with a Picasso painting, one that discloses dimensions of being otherwise not discoverable, that changes the discoverer, is comparable to the way the Bible yields its treasures.

Symbolical and existential views of biblical authority have similarities in their stress on personal appropriation. But there are significant differences. The symbolist view employs artistic categories that as "the aesthetic stage" Kierkegaard found to be sus-

81. See Avery Dulles, *Models of Revelation* (Garden City, N.Y.: Doubleday, 1983), 131-54; also my "Narrative Theology: An Overview," *Interpretation* 37 (Oct. 1983), *passim*.

pect.[82] The moral and the paradoxical are to the fore in "Christ as the addressing Word" and "Christ as the call to decision." And most important, all addressing and many decisional modes of interpretation do not normally question the objectivity of the referent. In the present case the meaning of the text is identified with its performative power, conceived in either personal or communal ways. Thus the authority of Scripture is related to how it works in a life-changing way, rather than whether it gives the reader content about transcendent reality.

In a symbolist approach to Scripture the literal meaning of a text does not determine its availability. For example, some exponents of feminist theology have taken up this view. A feminist reading encourages an imaginative grasp of the women present but often silent in biblical stories, encouraging the discovery of their "hidden histories." Other feminist interpretation goes beyond that, exposing the "texts of terror" that oppress women. And yet further, a symbolist approach for some allows for the liberating powers of feminist imagination to perceive humanizing possibilities in texts otherwise hidden to the eyes of the oppressor. Phyllis Trible and Elisabeth Schüssler Fiorenza have been influential figures in these developments.[83]

In the symbolist view, the meaning of the text is "polyvalent," susceptible to many construals according to the creativity of the engagement between the text and the imaginative reader. Critics to the right hold that the interests and experience of the interpreter so control the biblical text that scriptural authority and its cognitive claims are dissolved. Critics to the left hold that the Scripture is not needed as an authority in any sense, since our human experience as such is trustworthy.

5. Contextual

A primary expression of the combinationist view is found in many of the self-identified contextual theologies of the late decades of the twentieth century. While social context is very important in other combinationist views (post–Vatican II Roman Catholic theologies

82. Søren Kierkegaard, *Stages on Life's Way,* trans. Walter Lowry (Princeton: Princeton Univ. Press, 1946).

83. Elisabeth Schüssler Fiorenza, *In Memory of Her* (New York: Crossroad, 1983); Phyllis Trible, *God and the Rhetoric of Sexuality* (Philadelphia: Fortress Press, 1978) and *Texts of Terror* (Philadelphia: Fortress Press, 1984); Sharon Ringe, "Standing toward the Text," *Theology Today* 42 (Jan. 1987): 552-57.

and various ecumenical theologies), liberation theologies that hold Scripture to be normative are the best-known representatives of the position. Here one must interpret the text of Scripture in the context of culture. The conjoining of "Bible" and "world" in this authority structure happens (1) in the original text: What are the social circumstances that shape them? (2) in evaluating other readings of the text: How does the social location of a given assertion about the meaning of Scripture affect the interpretation? and (3) in the right interpretation of Scripture: Is it done in the center for the struggle against systemic oppression?

This last subtype in our review of options in authority gives us a chance to see a feature of the conversation on authority that tends to be concealed by the typological methods we are employing. Viewpoints are never as precisely aligned within a category as our classification suggests. That may be because we have not thought them out consistently, or because the views are in flux, or because they combine perspectives in a way more subtle than these categories allow. Typologies seek to identify tendencies, making distinctions that help us to sort complex data. They are heuristic, helping us to make our way into the conversation and establish our own point of view within in.

To illustrate the mobility within a type and between types to be found in the discussion on authority we will listen in on the exchange within feminist liberation hermeneutics that begins within a combinationist view of biblical authority and moves out of it to other perspectives.

The hermeneutical debate within feminism is charted in two important collections of essays, *The Feminist Interpretation of the Bible,* edited by Letty M. Russell (Philadephia: Westminster Press, 1985) and *Feminist Perspectives in Biblical Scholarship,* edited by Adela Yarbro Collins (Chico, Calif.: Scholars Press, 1985). Formative works in feminist hermeneutics include Phyllis Trible, *Texts of Terror* (Philadephia: Fortress Press, 1985) and Elizabeth Schüssler Fiorenza, *In Memory of Her* (New York: Crossroad, 1983). Works that may indicate future directions of feminist conceptions of authority are Rosemary Radford Ruether's two recent books, *Womenguides: Readings toward a Feminist Theology* (Boston: Beacon Press, 1985), and *Women-Church* (San Francisco: Harper & Row, 1985); Elisabeth Schüssler Fiorenza, *Bread Not Stone* (Boston: Beacon Press, 1984); and Sharon D. Welch, *Communities of Resistance and Solidarity: A Feminist Theology of Liberation* (Maryknoll, N.Y.: Orbis Books, 1985). A perspective that has not been given much attention in the wider debate is that of evangelical women, one with its own range from the more conservative Susan T. Foh, *Women and the Word of God: A Response to Biblical Feminism* (Grand Rapids: Baker, 1979) through evangelical feminists Nancy Hardesty and Letha Scanzoni, and Virginia Ramey Mollenkott, *The Divine Feminine* (New York: Crossroad, 1983) to radical Third World women critical of North American feminism.[84] We note in passing that there are sharp criticisms of feminist hermeneutics, such as those of Donald Bloesch who alludes to "parallels between ideological feminism and German Christianity."[85]

The feminist debate on biblical authority has produced various typologies to distinguish approaches within feminism or between feminism and alternative conceptions. For example, Katherine Doob Sakenfeld distinguishes among (1) "looking for texts about women to counteract famous texts used against women," (2) "looking to the Bible generally . . . for a theological perspective offering a critique of patriarchy," and (3) "looking to texts about women to learn from the intersection of histories and stories of ancient and modern women living in patriarchal cultures."[86] Carolyn Osiek's models include (1) rejectionist, (2) loyalist, (3) revisionist, (4) sublimationist, and (5) liberationist.[87] Fiorenza distinguishes between the following options in hermeneutics with which feminists have to deal: doctrinal, positivist-historical, dialogical-hermeneutical, liberation. We shall take into account these classifications in working out developments in feminist hermeneutics and comment on their meaning from the point of view of this systematics. Thus this section is not only descriptive in nature but begins to indicate the normative judgments on authority and interpretation that are to come.

If the last third of the twentieth century is taken as the major period of the rise of feminist critical consciousness, then its early

84. In a national gathering on liberation theologies sponsored by the Boston Theological Institute in the fall of 1986 some of the sharpest exchanges were between Latin American liberation theologians, women and men, and North American feminists, around both theological and class issues.

85. Donald Bloesch, *The Battle for the Trinity* (Ann Arbor: Servant Publications, 1985), 77. See also 69-87.

86. Katherine Doob Sakenfeld, "Feminist Use of Biblical Materials," in *The Feminist Interpretation of the Bible,* ed. Letty M. Russell (Philadelphia: Westminster Press, 1985), 56ff.

87. Carolyn Osiek, "The Feminist and the Bible," in *Feminist Perspectives in Biblical Scholarship,* ed. Adela Yarbro Collins (Chico, Calif.: Scholars Press, 1985), 97-105.

years were characterized to a large extent by the combinationist type of biblical authority. Protestant feminism and Roman Catholic feminism influenced by Vatican II developments regularly assumed the normativity of Scripture but read Scripture within the setting of self-conscious women's experience and the growing attention to a "women-church" ecclesial resource. Many Christian feminists who live and work in mainstream Christian communities, as well as all evangelical feminists and many Third World liberation-oriented women still hold this view. A thread of liberating texts within an overall rationale of "Christ the Liberator" or a focus on "the Reign of God" provide the reference point for Scripture. This makes possible four points: (1) The acceptance of texts that cohere with this criteria and therefore are subject to elaboration in terms of it. (2) The search for possible meanings in manifestly androcentric texts, often with the help of historical-critical or literary-critical scholarship. The latter discovers cicumstances within the ancient situation that either do not appear to have an agenda of male power interests, or whose patriachy is historically conditioned and therefore not of abiding normativity, or are indeed through and through patriarchal and therefore lesson-filled as "texts of terror." (3) A way of rendering visible the invisible but real presence of nonandrocentric meanings and even feminist accents in texts overladen with inherited masculine interpretations, recovered through a reading done in the matrix of feminist experience. (4) A feminist symbolical reading of Scripture that acknowledges it to be the formative language world of the Christian community and thus the place where women of the church come, not for conceptual orientation but for evocative and transformative encounter.

More recent developments in feminist thought, both Christian and Jewish, have raised questions about the primacy of biblical authority. As an evangelical feminist reviewing *The Feminist Interpretation of Scripture* asks, "Is the Bible a collection of patriarchal writings . . . ? If so, how can the Bible be authoritative for Christians?"[88]

The movement from biblical normativity in its earlier form to another understanding of Scripture can be seen in Letty Russell's

88. *Daughters of Sarah* (July/Aug. 1984): 29. For indications of a developing Christian feminism that seeks to integrate classical teachings on the Trinity, the Person and Work of Christ, and other orthodox beliefs with a commitment to inclusivity see Karen and Leif Torjesen, "Inclusive Orthodoxy: Recovering a Suppressed Tradition," *The Other Side* (Dec. 1986): 14-18.

application of the theme of partnership to hermeneutics. Continuing a long-standing commitment to Scripture, one that expressed itself in careful exegesis "in the context of involvement" in her ministry in the East Harlem Protestant Parish, she asserts

> in spite of the patriarchal nature of biblical texts, I myself have no intention of giving up on the biblical basis of my theology. With Rosemary Ruether, I would argue that the Bible has a critical or liberating tradition embodied in its "prophetic-messianic" message of continuing self-critique. . . . It is found in God's intention for the mending of all creation. The Bible has authority in my life because it makes sense of my experience and speaks to me about the meaning and purpose of my humanity in Jesus Christ.[89]

However, this commitment to Scripture is now situated in a "new paradigm" of biblical interpretation: "partnership" rather than hierarchy. In clarifying this, Russell refers to David Kelsey's "performative" view of Scripture in which authority means "an imaginative construal" of the Bible in which "the claim must include intelligible discourse capable of consistent formulation and reasoned elaboration and justification . . . [reflecting] the structure of tradition as scripture is used to nurture and reform the identity of a particular faith community; and be seriously imaginable in the cultural context in which the interpretation takes place."[90] She sees this as similar to Sally McFague's view of interpretive framework as a "constellation of beliefs, values and methods," and compares it as well to Bruce Birch's "de-absolutized canon which allows for the honoring of the ancient witness to the degree that it reveals the basic truths of our faith, while at the same time honoring the power and authority of our own experience of God."[91] What this means is that no one element in the configuration of authority can take precedence. Partnership means parity and dynamic interaction.

> Experience, tradition, biblical witness and intellectual research enrich each other in their rainbow of order (but not subordinated) diversity, in a synergistic perspective of authority in community. . . . In the perspective of authority in community, the interpretive key is no longer one external or internal biblical

89. Russell, "Authority and the Challenge of Feminist Interpretation" in *Feminist Interpretation of the Bible,* 138.

90. Ibid., 141

91. Ibid., 146.

key, but rather a configuration of sources of faith that seek to enrich the way God may be present to us.[92]

In this conception of authority, "the biblical witness" remains a necessary partner in the process of arriving at theological judgments. Further, it provides the vision, the historical events, the stories, its key figure, and much of the language for describing the message and evoking commitment—God's intent for creation, shalom, Jesus Christ. The right reading of the message entails the partnership of other elements: "experience, tradition, . . . and intellectual research." As such we are still potentially in a combinationist view of biblical authority. However, because partnership is equal, no one of these is subordinate to the other. In principle, tradition, historical research, and experience have authority equal to Scripture. In fact, tradition is not given this parity, for patriarchy has so dominated it that one can use only selective and radical reinterpretations of the historical tradition. Functionally, *tradition* means the developing tradition of "communities of oppression," where women and men are struggling for equality and mutuality, becoming "prisms through which God's action in the mending of creation is to be understood."[93] *Experience* is not human experience in general, or Christian experience in its various permutations, but the experience of oppressed women struggling for liberation with others of marginal race and class (age and condition also by implication). Historical reconstruction enters the picture, but for vocational reasons "Ruether and I (in contrast to Fiorenza) are far more likely to appeal to theological principles than historical reconstructions because we are theologians."[94]

While Russell is often identified as a feminist theologian closer to the tradition and to scriptural authority than other well-known exponents of feminism, her current views do not seem to fit the combinationist category, either formally or functionally. And it poses two questions: (1) Does the formal declaration of equal partnership of four elements (biblical witness, experience, tradition, historical research—a foursome that sounds similar to the Methodist quadrilateral) hold up in the functional outworking of this hermeneutic? It would seem that feminist-interpreted experience of oppression/liberation provides the framework for evaluating the other three elements, including Scripture. In this respect it appears

92. Ibid.
93. Ibid., 142-43.
94. Ibid., 145.

decisively to shape the intellectual content of the meaning of God's intention and thus the import of Jesus Christ. (2) Does the assertion of partnership as a paradigm of authority meet the standard Russell espouses of a legitimate imaginative construal: intelligibility, capability of consistent formulation, reasoned elaboration, and justification? Theological authority by its nature and by its history is recourse to a place for adjudicating assertions of ultimacy. The point that Russell has made so well is that the way to that place is by partnership. She rightly challenges patriarchy as a way and identifies it as another form of triumphalism.

The quest for inclusivity in this systematics is the same kind of challenge as that mounted by Russell to all forms of hegemony. Her call, and that of other feminists, must be heard if we are to listen rightly for the biblical Word. However, partnership is a *process*, a life together on a journey. It does not furnish the pole star by which that journey is made. All theories of authority, including partnership ones, finally appeal to some orientation points. Descriptively, what seems to be developing in Russell's present view is the primacy of "women-church," as the community of oppression, struggle, and liberation, one that supplies the principle of selection and interpretation of the other partners. Normatively, the Scripture has become the resource to the biblical source in providing the text that is used by an experiential context. This rearranges the priorities espoused in the current work. The differences are:

1. The faith community that constitutes the resource for interpreting Scripture is a catholic community, not limited to a self-identified "community of struggle." This more inclusive community offers access to dimensions of biblical meaning that go beyond those aspects stressed by communities of struggle, beyond the political, economic, and social forms of suffering (to issues of natural evil), and are not limited to the problem of suffering (including also the issues of sin, death, and error). This wider constituency enables us to hear biblical notes that are not in the auditory range of ecclesial communities that exclude these questions and their questioners. But this wider community will itself miss fundamental aspects of the Word if it does not at the same time attend to the witness of the communities of struggle. This is especially so because they address directly the culture's defining issue of human suffering in its stark modern form.

2. All human beings have an accessibility to the text made possible by the image of God sustained through a common (Christic)

grace that makes Scripture intelligible to common inquiry. Ordinary people can hear something of what a text says through the disciplines of common sense, can learn about the results of critical research, and can be convinced of the truth in texts that come through perspectives different from their own. Perspicuity stands, therefore, against privileged readings of texts or privileged communities of interpreters. At the same time it recognizes that only a full ecclesial community of inquiry can bring out the richness of textual meaning, therefore requiring the catalytic action of diverse interpretive subcommunities, including feminist communities of struggle.

3. The Scripture has its own freedom and integrity beyond both our partial and inclusive communal readings. As the fruit of special revelatory action it is the source of insight about the being and doing of God as read through the lens of Jesus Christ. It provides the content of our claims, and produces fresh understanding of it. The text interpreted in accord with the substance and in the light of the center addresses ever-fresh personal and social contexts. The new light shed on its meaning, however, is inseparable from contextual concerns. A critical struggle of our own time is the liberation of women from patriarchy and the consequent broadening of our understanding of Scripture.

While Letty Russell associates herself with Rosemary Ruether in a "prophetic-messianic" understanding of scriptural authority, Ruether in her more recent *Womenguides* and *Women-Church* takes some new steps. She asserts that "feminist theology must create a new canon. . . . Feminist theology demands a new collection of texts to make women's experience visible. Feminist theology cannot be done from the existing base of the Christian Bible."[95] In *Womenguides* she has set out to produce "a working handbook from which a new canon might emerge."[96] Drawing on goddess traditions, Gnostic writings, streams of Christian interpretation considered heretical or treated as marginal, and current feminist writings and other sources that call into question patriarchal captivity, she urges the development of a body of women-church lore (within the "borders of Western Christian culture") that will constitute a new canon. Its emergence will allow women to

95. *Womenguides: Readings toward a Feminist Theology* (Boston: Beacon Press, 1985), ix-x.

96. Ibid., ix.

> read canonical patriarchal texts in a new light. They lose their normative status and we read them critically in the light of that larger reality that they hide and deny. In the process a new norm emerges on which to construct a new community, a new theology, eventually a new canon. This new norm makes women as subjects the center rather than the margin. Women are empowered to define themselves rather than be defined by others. Women's speech and presence are normative rather than aberrant.[97]

Ruether's frank appeal for a new canon rooted in feminist experience and interpretation is related to perspectivalist assumptions associated with a "critical consciousness." In this view all readings of Scripture are inseparable from interest-laden social locations. Something objective called "the Word of God" cannot be juxtaposed to human experience. Scripture is not independent of "experience." Rather, "human experience is both the starting point and the ending point of the circle of interpretation."[98] It is a matter of fact that symbols and interpretation merge and disappear to the extent that they are found meaningful by human beings. But more, according to this view the contention that Scripture stands independent of our experience and in judgment upon it is a standard ploy of patriarchy. As canons shaped and interpreted by a dominant male ethos, their claim to primacy is patriarchal experience codified in tradition legitimating itself, silencing and finally destroying women. As Scripture is always experientially interpreted as rising from the interest of our social location, the patriarchal hegemony can be broken only by a radically new perspective.

> Thus the criticism of the tradition in the context of women's experience does not merely add another point of view to the prevailing one. Women's experience explodes as a critical force, exposing classical theology, including its foundation in tradition and Scripture, as shaped by male experience rather than human experience. Women's experience makes the androcentric bias of the original formulations and the ongoing interpretation of the tradition visible, rather than hidden behind the mystification of divine authority. It throws the universality of the claims of the tradition in question.[99]

97. Ibid., xi.

98. Rosemary Radford Ruether, "Feminist Interpretation: A Method of Correlation," in Russell, *Feminist Interpretation of the Bible*, 111.

99. Ibid., 113.

Women's experience so understood is not the experience of women in general, but "the experience which arises when women become critically aware of these falsifying and alienating experiences imposed upon them by a male-dominated culture."[100]

Read with a feminist critical consciousness, and within communities of women-church, Scripture yields a view of a "prophetic-messianic tradition." This is not a canon within the canon, but a "perspective and process through which biblical tradition constantly re-evaluates, in new contexts, what is truly the liberating Word of God over against both the deformations of contemporary society and also the limitations of past biblical tradition."[101] And it is not only for women and their communities of struggle, but also for any faithful articulation of the Christian (or Jewish) message. "The task of feminist hermeneutics is also to establish this theory of interpretation as normative and indispensable to the understanding of the faith in seminaries where interpretation is taught and in churches and synagogues where the good news is preached."[102]

In these formulations that either work within the biblical tradition or seek to alter it by the creation of a new canon, we have moved out of the present combinationist view that holds Scripture to be normative for faith and its theological work. The "prophetic-messianic message" does not require the particulars of a revelatory history with its focal point in Christ or the biblical testimony to it. Rather, the latter provides the form in which a feminist critical consciousness emerges. The same consciousness and commitment could express itself in the Jewish tradition with its symbols and history, reinterpreted in the normative framework provided by women's experience. The context of critical consciousness/feminist experience determines the meaning of these (and other) religious texts. In the feminist conversation we have moved from "the Bible" as source of authority to "the world" as source of authority, with the hermeneutical locale being women's experience critically developed.

To anticipate our argument, the difference between Ruether's view and the one set forth here lies in diverse doctrines of revelation. These in turn issue in different conceptions of authority. Human experience as such—including men's as well as women's—

100. Ibid., 115.
101. Ibid., 117.
102. Ibid., 124.

as understood in *The Christian Story* is in thrall to our self-serving agendas and cannot as such disclose ultimate truth. Hence we have a narrative that tells of an engagement of the Creator with human experience, its critical turning points being in actions with the people of Israel and in Christ, a story passed on to us through a book and a community. The events that comprise this narrative, and the reports and experiences of them in Scripture and tradition, are indeed influenced and distorted by the experiential medium through which they pass from their Author to us. But the message reaches us even through the distortions and limitations, so the act of faith in a revelatory Source. Actually it is similar to Ruether's own confidence that women's experience, critically perceived, carries the same disclosive power. The difference is the locale of disclosure. In the classical Christian tradition, understood in the inclusive perspective here espoused, the corrective to distortive reading of a text is (a) the text's own accessibility to a committed common sense, and (b) the inclusivity of the community of interpretation. The inclusivity requires a corrective by women's critical experience of the bondage of Scripture to the history of male control, and the will to see new vistas of meaning that women's experience can disclose only through the epistemological ministry given to them in the Body of Christ.

Elisabeth Schüssler Fiorenza's *In Memory of Her* entered the feminist discussion on the authority of Scripture in 1983 with a clarity of analysis and impressiveness of research that refocused the discussion of the issues and forced the academic and theological establishments to give greater attention to the charges of androcentrism of the biblical text. On the larger questions of authority, Fiorenza described four approaches: (1) A doctrinal model that holds Scripture to be revelation itself in terms of "timeless truth" established by proof text. (2) The positivist historical exegesis model that seeks by "factual, objective and value free" methods to arrive at what the text says without ideological construal and against dogmatic positions such as those espoused by the first view. (3) The dialogical-hermeneutical model, which is more wary of the impact of the community on both the ancient text and the contemporary interpreter. It seeks to ascertain the confessional and social factors that entered into the dialogue between the textual trajectory and its communities of form or redaction on the one hand, and the same factors at work as preunderstanding in our approach to the ancient texts as we try to carry over its importance for our circumstances. However, this approach assumes that the search for the meaning of the text in its original context is worth attempting and therefore in some sense achievable in spite of our social contingency, and that a hermeneutical translation of its significance for all people in our time and place is also reachable. (4) The liberation model, which rejects all value-free appropriation of biblical texts and assumes the partisanship for or against the oppressed that is at work in both the text and its interpretation in any subsequent context, and therefore the necessity to read Scripture from an advocacy position.

Fiorenza works out her own version of the liberation perspective in critical encounter with such other formative feminist thinkers as Russell, Ruether, Mary Daly, and Phyllis Trible. Acknowledging differences between Russell and Ruether, she nevertheless views them as exponents of a "neo-orthodox model of feminist interpretation" because they attempt to recover from the Scripture a kernel of theological truth, "the prophetic-messianic message" variously characterized and often idealized. She believes this to be inadequate because (a) oppressive elements within the prophetic tradition are not examined critically, (b) an abstract dehistoricized "archimedian point" as such within Scripture is assumed, (c) its formulation excludes learnings from postbiblical feminism, such as the recovery of the goddess traditions, and (d) it serves as an apology for biblical authority instead of looking for another fundamental orientation point for a feminist liberation hermeneutics, "women's struggle for liberation from all patriarchal oppression."[103]

Phyllis Trible, a biblical scholar who like Fiorenza attends to the text critically and avows the inseparability of form and content, employing the tools of rhetorical criticism, "nevertheless shares with Russell and Ruether an understanding of the hermeneutical process that is rooted in neo-orthodox theology."[104] Thus while Trible acknowledges the patriarchal domination of Scripture, she concentrates on recovering the countervoices to misogyny, accessible through methods of the new literary criticism. Thus Fiorenza links her with Russell and Ruether in declaring for an overall ahistorical refrain in Scripture that is liberating and tends to furnish warrants for the authority of Scripture. Further, her concentration on literary exposition of the text ignores the necessary historical-critical task of showing the patriarchal forces at work in the social contexts in which the text took rise.

103. *In Memory of Her* (New York: Crossroad, 1983), 32.
104. Ibid., 19.

Fiorenza's own conception of authority is illumined initially by her engagement with the thought of Mary Daly. She observes that withdrawal of feminists from the structure of patriarchy to define their own space on the margins means leaving these formative institutions in the hands of the foe, and thus consigning to bondage countless women who presently have neither the will nor the way to obtain the purity of feminist ethos demanded by Daly. Included in this deserted terrain is the religious structure so formative of values in the West, Christianity. Within it is the Bible, which has contributed to the oppression of women. This is especially the case recently with the use of the Bible by the influential wave of political fundamentalism bent upon further oppressing women. What is also missing in Daly's schismatic move is the refusal to acknowledge the historical roots from which women as well as men come, the necessity of claiming that heritage as belonging also to women and the possibility that women have made contributions to it, and perspectives that can be claimed as antecedents to the present feminist community of struggle within the church. Strategy-wise, contra Daly, Fiorenza opts to work within the Christian ethos, exposing patriarchy as a demonic political-economic-social system (including racist, classist, militarist, and other forms of oppression to which women are subjected within patriarchy, thus linking the struggle of women with other victims of systemic injustice), working from within "women-church" in its effort to develop its own networks of support with and beyond the circle of Christianity. Women-church is

> the movement of self-identified women and women-identified men in biblical religion. The ecclesia of women is part of the wider women's movement in society and in religions that conceives itself not just as a civil rights movement but as a women's liberation movement. Its goal is not simply the "full humanity" of women, since humanity as we know it is male defined, but women's self-affirmation, power, and liberation from all patriarchal alienation, marginalization and oppression.[105]

The Bible is a major factor in women-church's encounter with the oppressive Christian past that still functions in the church's life and witness. As a biblical scholar, Fiorenza has chosen to focus on this inheritance. Clarity about epistemological, and thus derivative,

105. Elisabeth Schüssler Fiorenza, "The Will to Choose or Reject: Continuing Our Critical Work," in Russell, *Feminist Interpretation of the Bible,* 126.

authority assumptions is necessary for this task. Important as well is a use of historical-critical tools that is informed by the feminist epistemological and hermeneutical assumptions.

A feminist liberation model of biblical interpretation must reject the primary authority of the Bible asserted by the traditionalist doctrinal model, uncritically encouraged or allowed for by the model of positivist historical exegesis and dialogical-hermeneutical interpretation models, and inadequately challenged by the neoorthodox feminist models of Russell, Ruether, and Trible. "The locus or place of revelation and grace is therefore not the Bible or the tradition of a patriarchal church, but the ecclesia of women and the lives of women who live the 'option of our women selves.' It is not simply 'the experience' of women, but the experience of women (and all those oppressed) struggling for liberation from patriarchal oppression."[106] The warrant for anything found in Scripture that can aid this struggle is not its existence in the Bible as "some special canon of text that can claim divine authority. Rather it is the experience of women themselves in their struggles for liberation."[107] Or again, "insofar as the model here locates revelation not in biblical texts but in the experience of women struggling for liberation from patriarchy, it requires that feminist critical hermeneutics of liberation read the Bible in the context of believing communities of women in the context of women-church."[108]

Fiorenza summarizes this conception of the authority and interpretation of Scripture in her distinction between Scripture as prototype and as archetype. She rejects Scripture as archetype, which she holds to be an ideal form that establishes "an unchanging timeless pattern . . . [an] abiding timeless pattern or principle."[109] A prototype is an open-ended paradigm that sets experience in motion and invites transformation. "Rather than reduce its pluriformity and richness to abstract principle or an ontological immutable archetype, I suggest the notion of historical prototype open to its own transformation."[110]

Historical-critical inquiry is a valuable instrument for the interpretation of Scripture, according to Fiorenza's revelatory premises, as long as it is employed with a feminist critical consciousness.

106. Ibid., 128.
107. Ibid., 135.
108. Ibid., 136.
109. *In Memory of Her*, 33.
110. *Feminist Interpretation of the Bible*, 135.

Much of the past and present exercise of critical instruments has been under the control of patriarchal assumptions hidden under claims of academic disinterestedness. While critical methods have performed a function in challenging ecclesiastical and dogmatic control of texts, a male bias has been working to obscure the presence of women and the more emancipated aspects of the text and tradition, silencing the voice of women in critical inquiry itself. Historical-critical inquiries are themselves value-laden, reflecting the patriarchal system that houses it. Let it be used to investigate Christian origins, but not consider itself above the struggle for liberation, identifying honestly its social location and power interests in taking sides in the current struggle, thereby allowing that struggle to illumine what is found in the texts themselves.

Fiorenza has made a significant contribution to the understanding of aspects of Scripture heretofore not adequately grasped. By careful scholarship and imaginative interpretation of parts of the New Testament, she has uncovered the presence and leadership of women in the early Christian communities. Further, she has convincingly exposed male bias in a traditional exegesis and theology that has obscured this presence of leadership. She has made a good case for the role that patriarchal premises have played in the formation of Scripture itself, one that has hidden the formative place of women in Christian origins. For those that accept the function of critical scholarship, believe that the understanding of texts as well as the interpretation of doctrine is corrigible and enrichable, and hold that perspectival experience is an instrument of the Spirit shedding new light on old texts, there is every reason to welcome these insights. Further, while denying an "archimedian point" in Scripture itself or within Scripture, Fiorenza does stress the importance of Jesus' attitude in dealings with women and the "discipleship of equals" he encouraged. In so doing she does make a modest use of a Christological reference point in developing her own theses. Again, she does find a place for the church in her authority structure, and calls rightful attention to those who have been oppressed as an epistemologically significant constituency within that church. These are concerns and accents that must be vital parts of any concept of the authority and interpretation of Scripture.

To this important partner in the conversation on authority we pose some questions from the perspective of the present work: (1) The uncovering of the hidden history of women in Christian origins suggests that women were formative in early interpretations of

Christian faith in the missionary community, as in the Markan and Johannine Gospels. So too in Paul's own divided mind, especially in the use of the baptismal confession that seems to be at the center of the egalitarian affirmation in Galatians 3:28. The same thing is true in the motifs of *agape,* and in many of the metaphors in early Christian writing.[111] While the institutional structures and theological decisions of the church show the distorted influence of cultural patriarchies, was the original trajectory of Christian teaching (shaped in part by women) reversed, and the continuing influence of women on Christian teaching removed in the subsequent core doctrines? To say or imply that the purity of the gospel is to be found only in Christian origins with subsequent Christian history discovered to be a perversion, is a view not unknown in reform movements in the church. However, this notion is finally ahistorical. It also has Manichaean features that divide the world into the advocates of light and night, obscuring the ambiguities in all human movements. As Fiorenza was able to discover the impact of women in Christian origins by an imaginative reconstruction of them, it is possible that other research can discover a similar formative presence in the life and witness of the church in the patriarchal forms that housed Christian identity since its presumed egalitarian and communal origins. Fiorenza's success in discerning the presence and power of women in the church's charter itself encourages the effort to discern their subsequent presence and influence. This judgment is made in part from a conception of authority that holds that the church catholic is a legitimate resource for interpreting faith. Such a resource means that the Spirit's gift of illumination continues in the Christian community from the beginning, distributed among the whole people of God. Women and men throughout time are not denied access to the substance of faith, the gospel, however distorted their time-bound theological constructs may be. Fiorenza has shown that the gospel within Scripture took form in a more inclusive horizon than earlier perceived. This *consensus fidelium* of the "missionary church" as it is empowered by the Spirit is not so easily destroyed by human machinations.

On this point the canonical approach to Scripture is germane. The text that Fiorenza has examined is the Christian canon, the corpus of writing deemed authoritative for the community. While

111. *In Memory of Her, passim*.

she has shown how redactors and later editors have hidden the role of women, it is also clear that they have given high visibility to the interpretive center within Scripture, Jesus Christ, and have not eliminated the range of data that give encouragement and access to the discoveries she has made. If the canon-forming community, for all its patriarchal limitations, can be open to these vistas, there is no reason in principle to require that the same community subsequently extinguish these features. To believe that the Holy Spirit lives in the church is to believe that it cannot destroy them.

(2) The metaphors and commitments of oppression and liberation are the right ones for the systemic suffering to which women have been and are subjected. Women-church communities can be apt modes for addressing the issues. Are they also adequate to the range of other concerns that constitute the life of women? It is not the business of a white male to define what "being human" means, as Fiorenza says. However, the community of which both Christian women and men are a part, shaped (if we are right in our first point) by the agenda of both women and men, has included "other concerns." In fact, the New Testament reports that it was women who were the first to perceive the risen Christ and thus to witness the victory over death for which the Christian faith stands. While the resurrection of Christ means more—for example, it gives hope in the struggle of liberation—it means no less than hope in the face of physical death. Every woman shall die and those she loves shall die. No resolution of systemic injustice will deal with these quandaries. It is no accident that a woman, Elisabeth Kubler-Ross, who initially concerned herself with the human aspects of "death and dying" (though not the systemic factors) moved beyond ministry to grief to transcendent questions of life after death.[112] The categories of oppression and injustice are not adequate to deal with the personal meeting with death. Sadly, when finitude has become the only issue in religion, it has obscured the historical suffering of women and has turned religion into an ideological smokescreen. But one reductionism does not justify another. Christian women who live out of the Christian heritage will want to draw on its full resources, those that confront death as well as social suffering. This

112. That she has had to turn to other religions and conceptions of transcendence for this search is the price we have paid in the Christian community for not providing our own vigorous options. The result of the current Western secularity, which has a built-in resistance to its own religious heritage, is also a contributing factor.

is especially true for women pastors in whose daily ministry must meet death and dying as well as injustice and oppression.

Related closely to death, indeed on the way to it, is suffering that has traditionally been identified as "natural evil" or the "tragic dimension of life." Human effort can moderate the natural suffering that comes in the form of disease, aging, or destruction wrought by natural disasters. And the instruments of healing and help before these hurts are impacted by social, economic, and political factors that entail a liberation struggle (the equal access of women to medical technology, protection against environmental factors that make for the ill health of women, etc.). However, communities of struggle and liberation cannot extirpate natural suffering beyond human control. We need conceptualities that enable us to come to terms with these inevitabilities. The Christian tradition has resources for facing these enigmas, beyond accommodation to their factualities, as in the traditions of prayer and healing. Women should not be excluded a priori from a consideration of critical issues of natural suffering as well as death, and therefore cut off from a tradition with resources to address them. Again, the woman pastor faces these questions day in and day out.

The universalities of death and natural evil are joined by that of sin. Male frameworks in exegesis and theology have employed the traditional teaching about sin to diminish women. Attributing the origins of sin to Eve as the temptress is a particularly vicious tradition. And the use of the teaching about pride as the original sin with respect to women and other human beings seeking social, political, and economic power in order to keep them in subservience—by recommending humility, servanthood, and self-effacement as virtues of the powerless—is another male ideology rightly exposed by a feminist critical consciousness.[113] However, the narcissistic self-will in every human being, pride understood as egocentricity or self-idolatry, puts the self at the center in the place of God and therefore puts down other human beings—that is the assumption on which the Christian Story is grounded. God's action in the narrative of faith overcomes sin and its wages, reconciling the estrangement between humanity and God, the alienation between humans and each other and with nature. So another question: (3) Can a conceptuality that holds the problem of women to

113. Judith Plaskow, *Sex, Sin and Grace: Womens' Experience and the Theologies of Reinhold Niebuhr and Paul Tillich* (Washington: Univ. Press of America, 1980).

be essentially the struggle of the oppressed against the oppressor—the victim against the wielder of arrogant power—do justice to the universal problem of sin and alienation from God to which the narrative addresses itself? And what of the reconceptualization of sin in feminist thought that conceives of it as the weakness of will rather than pride, the failure to assert one's interest before the oppressor? Is the sin of pride only the sin of the powerful, and thus only laid at the door of patriarchy with its manifest arrogance of power?

Scripture interpreted in the classical tradition does not exempt anyone from the tendency to self-elevation, the root meaning of sin, one found below the level of its particularization in the arrogance of the powerful and the apathy of the powerless. Historically, movements of social change that have divided the world into the righteous and unrighteous, the saints and the sinners, obscure the powerful currents of negative self-assertion within the champions of justice as well as in its foes. In so doing they deny themselves a crucial resource in the battle, namely, the principle of self-criticism. The doctrine of sin is a Christian assertion validated by both honest self-examination and careful empirical scrutiny. Movements for liberation will weaken their own impact if they deny to themselves a recognition of the presence of an imperial self-will in their own ranks as well as in those of the enemy, or conceive of the sin of the movement for change as only apathy rather than itself being subject to the temptations of self-elevation. Thus quite apart from how we all stand before God by virtue of our universal sin and how this impacts on our understanding of the gospel, there are pragmatic questions of the empowerment of social movements in the wisdom of the tradition, in this case, an awareness of the fact of sin as well as of social suffering.

(4) How can women-church change the wider church and avoid the errors learned in the history of sectarian Christianity? (The exclusion of the critic from the larger church and thus the loss of its prophetic witness, on the one hand, or the withdrawal of the critic to form its own marginal enclave of the pure.) Or, is women-church a subcommunity of another fundamental worldview with its own constituency rather than a basic part of the Christian community? If this is the case it does not need to attend to the issues of sectarian exclusion or departure.

The wider Christian community that women-church judges oppressive needs the relationship to and criticism of women-church. Given the finitude and sin that marks any human institution, including the church, the witness to the oppression of women requires those who experience that reality and have the perspective associated with it. The humanity of the church means limited angles of vision and the presence of self-interest with its dangerous consequences when associated with power and its pyramiding. Justice for women, including responsibility in the interpretation of biblical texts, has waited upon the development of a self-conscious constituency of women within the church, as in the culture, to make that witness. The church will have a reduced view of its own gospel if it does not make a place for women-church and its witness, a new "critic-in-residence."

(5) If a women's community of struggle and liberation within the church brings to the fore its particular interpretations of the gospel, who will keep alive the memories in the Body of Christ of the other dimensions of the gospel: its Easter message of triumph over the universal plight of death, its address to the universal quandaries of natural evil, its word of judgment on the universal sin of self-idolatry and word of forgiveness to that sin and guilt by the act of suffering love on the cross? The stewardship of the fullness of the gospel requires the catholicity of the Body of Christ. The church needs in its midst sisters and brothers whose tradition and location will assure attention to those aspects that might otherwise be neglected. Women-church needs the inclusivity of the Christian community to keep before it dimensions of the human question and the gospel that speaks to it, that are not to the fore in its own interpretation of faith. The same wholeness of community is necessary for probing the depth of the community's charter, the Scripture. Without women-church, that larger community will not grapple with the levels of the biblical witness to the problems and power of women that Fiorenza and others have pressed us to confront. But without those who have struggled and know liberation from personal sin and guilt before God (Luther and Wesley) the common understanding of these aspects of faith would be the poorer. Hermeneutical richness is in proportion to the wholeness of the people of God, the quest for which continues to the End.

There are glimpses in Christian history of this life together, as there are lessons of the way toward its fracture. The orders within the Roman Catholic Church (also in Eastern Orthodoxy and to a small extent in Protestantism) are creative experiments in how visions within the community are recognized and commissioned as vital parts of the larger Body. The Wesleyan movement within Anglicanism, and Methodism's own class meetings, are examples of how the critic-in-residence sought to remain in dialectical relationship to the wider Christian community. So too are the renewal movements in our own time that have sought to maintain connections with the local church or the larger ecclesiastical establishment—those of the sixties, the base communities in Latin America, the charismatic communities, and intentional communities of all sorts, vis-à-vis their larger fellowship. Can these movements survive in this relationship to "the establishment"? In every case there were and are signs of separation. The judgments of the critic seemed too harsh for the larger community, or the larger community too intractable for the critic. Thus the Methodist center of vitality becomes the chapel founded down the street from the Anglican church, the revival movement creates a new denomination by choice or necessity, the renewal center or base community becomes its own separated church or "the real church." The same questions are facing and will face women-church. This systematics is a commitment to the catholicity of the church. The Craigville Colloquies mentioned earlier are test points for its thesis.

(6) Does the concept of authority and its revelatory presupposition set Fiorenza's proposal for women-church on a sectarian course that moves it not only out of the mainstream of the Christian community but outside the church itself? If the norm of women-church is its own experience of struggle and liberation, one that views Scripture and tradition as a patriarchal foe, will it be able to continue, or will it choose to continue within the larger community? How will its institutional destiny be different from that of Mary Daly's marginal communities?

As the implications of a feminist experiential center of authority are worked out in Ruether's thought, there is a self-conscious effort to include texts outside the biblical canon as "womenguides." If there are no special revelatory grounds for the normative claims of Scripture (or tradition), then this move seems to be a logical one. Since Fiorenza shares Ruether's judgment about the relativity of biblical authority and the normativity of feminist critical experience, texts that express this matrix, in or out of the Christian community, become theologically legitimate orientation points. This view stands in opposition to the narrative integral to historic Christian faith. Its chapter on the fall puts in question the final authority of any human experience, given the universal distortions by sin. Its chapters on Israel and Christ assert the opening of vistas into ultimacy by acts of disclosure accessible to us through the prophetic-apostolic witness. If this narrative is shared by the historic Christian communities, women-church's alternative framework of authority puts it on a collision course with these communities.

(7) Is there an opening toward the kind of catholicity here espoused in one of the fundamental assumptions of Fiorenza's critical approach to Scripture: the accountability of perspectival readings of the text to the evidence? In a revealing account of a student who questioned the value of critical scholarship because of its male control, Fiorenza judges inadequate the Rankean program of disinterested scholarship, employs a hermeneutics of suspicion on the presumed unbiased results of New Testament research by a male establishment, and appeals for the exposure of the scholar's own "values, interests, commitments, presuppositions and socio-political location."[114] However, she also notes "historical narrative and judgments are not totally relativist and can be distinguished from fictive accounts. They are open to and necessarily subject to scholarly scrutiny. . . . Historical judgments are inter-subjectively understandable and inter-subjectively verifiable."[115] She lists critera for such scrutiny, including knowledge of the sources, comprehensiveness of research, integration of data, and consistency and coherence of reasoning.

Fiorenza's judgment that interpretations of textual meaning are accountable to standards beyond those of a perspectival (including presumably a feminist perspectival) reading raises a question whether the definitive community of authority is really women-church. Biblical interpretations of a community of struggle and liberation must pass muster before the standards of evidence and reason, and accommodate themselves to the research data. Assertions cannot hang in the air but are reviewable by the evidence and logic of a community of scholarly inquiry. Unless it includes only feminist critical scholars or women-identified critical scholars, that means either the accountability of women-church to male dominated research establishments or the belief that there is an evidence and logic that asserts itself in a value-free way, as a Rankean might declare.

Fiorenza's working assumption that (a) there are data to which a perspectival reading is accountable, and (b) that it requires a larger community of inquiry to grasp that data, indeed an inter-

114. Elisabeth Schüssler Fiorenza, "Remembering the Past in Creating the Future: Historical-Critical Scholarship and Feminist Biblical Interpretation," in Collins, *Feminist Perspectives on Biblical Scholarship,* 53.

115. Ibid., 53.

perspectival one (all historians should state their perspectives), is similar to the view espoused here. The difference is the community in question. Ours is not the scholarly community but the church catholic, a community of Christians, ecumenical in time and place. Critical scholarship is a component within that, as we shall argue, serving the well-being of the text's meaning, but not constituting the magisterium that determines textual meaning or significance. The grounds for its contribution, as well as that of commonsense reading, lie in the concept of a damaged but not destroyed image that is intersubjective, warranting civil conversation about interests examinable by evidence and reason. However, these texts are those of the book of the Christian community. A grasp of their full meaning is a process in which the variety of perspectives that constitute the faith community, empowered by the Spirit common to their community, enters a conversation that renders judgments that are by virtue of this catholicity called "intersubjectively understandable and verifiable." This work is devoted to the exposition of that view. These pages on the dynamic within a contextual-combinationist type seemed an apt place to begin the conversation with alternatives. However, we have other perspectives within the two remaining major types to examine before we develop in detail this book's point of view.

THE CHURCH

Our next major type gives the church pride of place in theological decision making. The Christian community, finally, adjudicates Christian doctrine. Indeed the Bible and the world may play a role in this authority structure, even a very prominent one, but the arbiter of what is declared to be valid for Christian identity is the church. The Scripture may be held to be inspired and even inerrant, but its proper understanding is to be found only in the counsels of the community. Or a large role may be given to experience, but experience is to be had, or its truth grasped, only within the framework of the church.

Church authority, as we define it here, may be formal, highly structured, and have a long history and many credentials. Or it may be very loose, informal, and of brief duration. While outwardly very different, defenders of a traditionalist Roman Catholic view and devotees of intense group experience in a Protestant house church both locate final authority in the common life of the Christian community. Furthermore, ecclesial authority may be explicit, as in the first instance, or implicit, as is often the case of Protestant subcommunities whose official standard is the Scriptures. Authority in the church-type may be formal or functional, and can be vested in documents and historical decisions—official or unofficial—of the community, in a teaching office of a corporate or personal nature, or in a very wide and even vague entity such as "the mind of the church." We shall begin with the more structured and go to the less formal expressions of ecclesial authority, discovering, nevertheless, an elusive quality in the most formal, and some element of structure in the most informal and transient.

Presupposed in both formal and functional church authority is a doctrine of revelation. Although not often stated as such, there is an epistemological "continuing incarnation" in which trustworthy access to ultimate truth comes through some locale of the Body of Christ on earth. Where "inspiration" is associated with Scripture in the first type, the same kind of definitive revelatory authority is associated with the church in the second. *Ecclesial* apostle and prophet, in effect, are the conduits of revelation.

Traditionalist Views

1. *Roman Catholic*

The traditionalist view is but one within Roman Catholicism, contrary to the popular Protestant assumption that it is *the* Roman Catholic view. There are grounds for considering it the dominant pre–Vatican II understanding. But many Roman Catholic theologians consider even this a caricature insofar as it neglects the primacy of Scripture to be found in the long tradition of the church and its official statements (as we noted in our discussion of combinationist views).

We return to a discussion of the decisions of the Council of Trent. A traditionalist interpretation of the key paragraph on revelation and authority holds that the deposit of a revelation is preserved *partly* in the Scriptures and *partly* in church tradition. The council's final phrasing of the revealed status of written Scripture and unwritten oral tradition join these two with an *et* (having replaced the first draft's *partim partim* with this word), thus leaving open the relation of each to the other, and to the anterior deposit of apostolic truth. However, a post–Tridentine interpretation of this action gave much Roman Catholic teaching up to the mid-twentieth century a traditionalist cast by reintroducing the "partly-partly" concept in its interpretation of the relation of Scripture to tradition, each conceived as carrying a portion of the God-given apostolic tradition, with the subsequent living traditions of the church required to supplement and clarify the apostolic tradition conveyed through the Bible.[116]

While the living traditions of the church may include the life of worship, the piety of the people, and actions of discipleship and mission, traditionalists fix upon the official distillation of this more amorphous flow. Two closely related aspects are constitutive of tradition: the dogmas of the church and its teaching office. Dogma as the defined teaching of the church, promulgated by the pope in concert with the bishops, makes up the "extraordinary magisterium." The latter establishing and interpreting organ, the "ordinary magisterium," is the authoritative process inseparable from the authoritative doctrinal product. Behind this conception of authority lies a view of revelation as the communication of propositions. The triune God discloses the deposit of faith to prophets and apostles who in turn pass them on in written Scripture and unwritten traditions. The revelatory momentum continues (somewhat like the trajectory conception of inerrancy through the Bible) through the apostolic ministry, rendering infallible those teachings by ex cathedra statements from the papal chair.

Other readings of Trent reject the partly-partly interpretation, holding that all the essential apostolic teaching is found in each of the two authoritative sources: all the gospel is found in the Scripture and in tradition. An implication of this view that affects day-to-day issues is that assertions of faith declared to be authoritative must be related somehow to Scripture. This implies that present dogma must be read in the light of the biblical norm, and future dogma must show its scriptural credentials. Vatican II–influenced streams of interpretation of this sort prompt our inclusion of a Roman Catholic perspective within the overall category of biblical primacy.

However, this same more scripturally decisive view is subject to a certain ambiguity as it is expounded by "centrists" and "progressives," and as it is given a traditionalist turn by conservative defenders. These views of Scripture do insist that all that is neces-

116. See Joseph Rupert Geiselmann, "Scripture, Tradition and the Church: An Ecumenical Problem," in *Christianity Divided,* ed. D.J. Callahan, Heiko A. Oberman, and Daniel J. O'Hanlon (New York: Sheed & Ward, 1961), 39-72.

sary for salvation is found in the Bible, defined as inspired. But the saving content of Scripture is properly discerned only by the church through its teaching office. What a text truly says can only, in the last analysis, be established by that office. Specific texts have been given a magisterial interpretation only in a few cases. However, the definition of the dogmas of the church established directly or traceable to Scripture is in the hands of the magisterium. As such, the magisterium holds the teaching key to the Bible. Moderates and progressives point out that the use of this power functions only out of an anterior *consensus fidelium* formed from the life, belief, and worship of the whole people of God. Further, they argue for the importance of the contribution of theological and biblical scholars to the processes of establishing authoritative teaching. But the arbiter of what is taught as Catholic truth is the officially designated magisterium.[117]

In both "hard" and "soft" traditionalism so identified, the church is the defining source of theology. What we have already construed as the self-interpreting power of the Scriptures is now subject to another final court of appeal that can declare conclusions drawn in the former way to be in error. Major type one, the supreme authority of Scripture, therefore, is often seen by traditionalist Roman Catholics as an "individualism" in which the pride of human beings asserts itself over the proper God-given authority of the church, which is to say its teaching office. (I shall argue subsequently that there is another way to deal with the concerns of both Protestants and Roman Catholics.)

An additional reason is sometimes given for the precedence of the church. Exponents point out that the Bible was declared authoritative by an ecclesial canonization process. As such, its authority is derived from the church, and therefore subject to interpretation by the same body that gave it canonical status.

2. Eastern Orthodox

Concern about departure from the Orthodox heritage has prompted some of its theologians to call for a return to patristic modes of authority conceived in a traditionalist fashion. As in Roman Catholic traditionalism, here too a great respect is accorded to Scripture. The Bible is acknowledged to be inspired and even inerrant, although these categories are seen to be more the legalistic language

117. For a careful exposition of this view see Raymond E. Brown, *Biblical Exegesis and Church Doctrine* (New York: Paulist Press, 1985), 26-53.

of the Western church than the customary way of speaking in the mystical ethos of Orthodoxy.[118] Scripture is considered the fundamental criterion of faith.[119] However, as in the traditionalist Latin view, here also the *valid* interpretation of Scripture can be done only by the church. But this interpretive primacy is understood in a different way. Traditionalist Orthodox theologians are at pains to distinguish their views from the Roman Catholic view of tradition, classical or contemporary. The difference lies in the Orthodox understanding of the *unity* of Scripture and tradition, where the processes of tradition are found and the voice of tradition is heard.

The bond that joins Scripture and church tradition is sometimes identified simply as Tradition. Behind the manifestation of the scriptural writings and the particular lore of the Orthodox Church, constituted as it is by the writings of the Fathers, the apostolic succession of bishops, the liturgies of the church, etc., there is a *mystical process* at work that is the source of all authoritative teaching. Tradition, understood in this way, is the standard that determines the validity or invalidity of doctrinal assertions.[120]

But how do we finally discover this higher Tradition? The answer is "the mind of the Church." This mind of the church is first and foremost the *sensus patrium,* the exposition of faith by the Fathers as found in their writings and formulated in the decisions of the first six ecumenical councils, as these are appropriated by the Orthodox theology that rises out of it, and from the spirituality and liturgical life of that church. At the heart of these various characterizations is: (1) The normativity of the patristic witness. Nothing can be said, including nothing about the meaning of biblical texts, that could violate the Fathers' positions, both those expressed in conciliar decisions and in their more wide-ranging writings. (2) The central place given to spirituality in the church as it is embodied in the liturgical rhythms of priests and people, and in the life of the monk. (3) The role of apostolic succession and the bishops' function within that as the articulator of doctrine, yet the limited nature of this role. The bishop has a spiritual, not a legal, significance in the maintenance of true doctrine, both as individual bishop and in the corporate episcopate. There is no legal

118. Archimandrite Chrysostomos and Heiromonk Auxentios, *Scripture and Tradition* (Etna, Calif.: Center for Traditionalist Orthodox Studies, 1984), 55-56.

119. Georges Florovosky, *Bible, Church, Tradition: An Eastern Orthodox View* (Belmont, Mass.: Nordland, 1972), 17-36.

120. Chrysostomos and Auxentios, *Scripture and Tradition,* 45-75.

teaching office to be found here. Indeed there is a very strong rejection of a "personal magisterium" in which a chief bishop would speak *ex cathedra* and claim infallibility for such declaration. (4) The desire to keep the authority of the church fluid, not tied down to specifics in a body of writing, a person or a group of people or a charter. Thus even the most conservative Orthodox writer will speak of the *living* Tradition, or the authority of the church as processive rather than sedimented.

Since these assembled themes are linked to the stress on the unity of Scripture and Tradition, we are led to ask how the authority of the church or tradition in the church relates to the authority of Scripture. The answer is threefold: (1) the church's tradition never adds anything to Scripture. There is no new revelation to be affixed to that recorded in the Bible. The Fathers and the councils do not add to biblical revelation new truth not already there. (2) As inspired, the Bible (the canon for many Orthodox includes the Apocrypha, but for others this material is edifying for piety but not authoritative in doctrine) is the "criterion" for doctrine. As the Fathers appeal to it in their theological work, so today Orthodox theologians are always bound by this written text. The meaning of that text is not discerned necessarily by the ordinary reader using commonsense standards, nor by the tools of critical scholarship, nor any combination thereof, but only as it witnesses to Tradition as it is determined by patristic and early conciliar formulations appropriated and distilled in the mystical process of living and dying in Orthodoxy. Thus a joint authority of Scripture and Tradition means that the church, construed in the Orthodox sense of that term, constitutes the final court of appeal for theological judgments. This court, of course, must work within the limits of the law, and that law is laid down in the Scripture. Given the rich and varied character of the biblical materials, a broadly conceived church process charged with identifying the Tradition within it has a powerful mandate indeed. While each is given a function in the "unity of Scripture and Tradition"—Scripture a criteriological one and Tradition an interpretive one—the interpretive one functions as the decisive authority.

An aggressive Orthodox traditionalism bewails a more irenic view to be found in some places in that communion. That irenicism may occur within the overall framework of the traditionalist viewpoint, holding the church to be definitive in the authority structure. However, "church" here may move further beyond the range of the Orthodox Church than the traditionalist would allow, including

Roman Catholic and possibly Protestant elements as well. One step beyond that are Orthodox thinkers who have entered vigorously into the ecumenical movement. Their perspective can be seen in some of the formulations developing in the World Council of Churches, where the influence of the concept of tradition is at work, but defined in such a way as to include both Protestant and Orthodox concerns.[121] In the latter case, a larger "Tradition" lies behind and is found within both scriptural writings and the living traditions of the Christian community, thereby making contact with a point in the traditionalist view (the distinction between Tradition and traditions). In World Council thinking this Orthodox stream of thought connects with a Protestant concept of the Word witnessed to by the words of Scripture, or the gospel set forth by Scripture and interpreted by tradition. We shall return to some of these points in the constructive section of this volume. Here we note them as a divergence within Eastern Orthodoxy from the presently identified traditionalist point of view.

Functionalist Views (Protestant)

A Protestant category may seem to be out of place under the rubric of churchly primacy. Reformation teaching gives precedence to Scripture. In fact, some of those we place in this ecclesial subtype would vociferously declare for nothing less than biblical primacy, including *sola Scriptura* in its most conservative sense. However, we are entering a section that includes views that *implicitly* rather than explicitly espouse an ecclesial standard.

The priority of the church happens in various ways. Sometimes it expresses itself by the decisiveness of a doctrinal deposit or a confessional tradition. Sometimes authority is rendered with less denominationally defined tests, but ones that still function ecclesially. Others have a much more amorphous criteria. In whatever form, Scripture takes a secondary place to an ecclesial standard.

1. Interconfessional Perspectives

At some points in church history and theological controversy movements form to protect what they believe to be "the fundamentals." Confessional boundaries are thereby crossed, or nonconfessional

121. World Council of Churches, *The Bible: Its Authority in the Ecumenical Movement,* ed. Ellen Flesseman-van Leer, Faith and Order Paper no. 9 (Geneva: World Council of Churches, 1980).

bodies with no tightly defined body of doctrine (i.e., Baptist and Free Church traditions) join with others in order to call for subscription to a set of beliefs held to be essential to the survival of faith itself. The fundamentalist movement in North America is a case in point with its list of doctrines considered definitive of the gospel.[122] Scripture is understood in the light of these fundamentals. Loyalty to the Bible is determined by adherence to them, and as such they constitute a confessional authority exercising covert hegemony.

Sometimes an interconfessional arbiter of faith has more to do with theological method than the traditional loci of content. Processes of authority take ecclesial form, with their rules of exclusion and inclusion. Theological credibility and ecclesial fellowship are determined by adherence to an orthodoxy of theological method—usually one found on the extreme right or the extreme left of the spectrum we are now examining. Thus a subcommunity of people not organized along confessional lines but bound by methodological loyalties establishes the credentials for orthodox belief. Strict inerrancy has become this kind of norm in some evangelical circles. Elsewhere a form of ecclesial experience—explicit feminist experience or implicit masculine value systems, ethnic origins, race, class, and condition—becomes the criterion for acceptance and rejection, both ideationally and socially. In both cases the standard is sometimes embodied in movements with carefully honed arguments, litanies of response, oaths of allegiance, and networks of belief, practiced and enforced. Sometimes these implicit interconfessional communities represent the ecclesial principle of authority more forcefully than do institutionally defined or confessionally articulated ecclesiasticisms.

2. *Informal Perspectives*

Very close to the implicit nonconfessional networks of ecclesial authority is what we call here the informal implicit perspective. Its representatives may be other than Protestant (as in Roman Catholic renewalist movements), although they are predominantly in the Protestant stream if we include in that category post-Reformation and "third force" denominations and movements. The phenomenon may occur within a denomination or outside of it.

122. John Gerstner, "Theological Boundaries: The Reformed Perspective," in David F. Wells and John D. Woodbridge, eds., *The Evangelicals,* rev. ed. (Grand Rapids: Baker, 1975), 29-37.

Community control is exercised in various ways. It can appear in a "house church," in a short-term "intense group experience," in a barrio "base community," or in a suburban "charismatic fellowship." Whether for a protracted time or limited period, the group in question establishes the boundaries of theological acceptability. Whatever other formal criteria of belief may be held—the Bible, the creeds and teaching office of the larger church, etc.—the community so organized and its experience of reality constitute the authoritative "plausibility structure" (Peter Berger). Within this environment one person may become the magisterium. When the community is not a subgroup within a congregation or alongside of it, it may be the congregation itself or its pastor that serve as doctrinal authority.

A very influential form of pastoral papacy outside the small-group context can be found in the modern electronic church. Here the boundaries of informal ecclesial life are established by the reach of the television signal or radio beam. Networking is a literal as well as a figurative description of the formation of the ecclesial constituency. The line taken in matters cultural and political as well as theological becomes the criterion of authority, including the proper interpretation of Scripture, but ranging far beyond that in its supplementary wisdom about the ways of God in the ways of the world.[123]

In all of the aforementioned, a community of faith takes form either within or outside of official structures, one that makes the rules for theological inquiry and sets the limits of acceptable doctrine. When the church speaks, God speaks.

The length and depth of our review of church-type authority, relative to the treatment of both Bible and world types, is not a measure of the importance of the former. It reflects the limits of the author's range of involvement in, and knowledge of, the varieties of ecclesial authority. For all of one's ecumenical commitment, our grasp of the issues of authority is shaped by a social location short of catholicity. The "text-context" question and Word-world dynamic are here very formative for me, and therefore I have given more space to "Bible" and "world." Nevertheless, the church category will emerge very prominently in the constructive section of this

123. See Jeffrey K. Hadden and Charles E. Swann, *Prime Time Preachers* (Reading, Mass.: Addison-Wesley, 1981) and Fackre, *The Religious Right and Christian Faith* (Grand Rapids: Eerdmans, 1982), 31-35, 104-6, and *passim*.

work, indicating the ecumenical impulse that moves it, even from within the limitations of social location.

THE WORLD

"Experience" as a criterion for theological assertions is notoriously difficult to describe, as a study of its use by "the Chicago School" has shown.[124] We must carefully establish how we are using the synonymous terms *world* and *experience* or *human experience.*

Earlier we alluded to experience as it functions in the Methodist quadrilateral. There it does not appear as a distinct touchstone of authority comparable to Scripture, tradition, and reason. "Experience" is specifically Christian experience, conceived as essentially interior (although also with strong moral import). Our usage here is different. Like "empiricism," it encompasses all human capacities of discerning truth: rational and moral as well as religious, aesthetic, and other forms of affectivity. However, in the context of the question of authority in Christian belief, "empirical" or "experiential" refers to human discernment that does not depend upon the specific standards of Bible or church, Scripture or tradition. By and large, this means *universal* human experience beyond these reference points. However, it can include *particular* experiences—those of other religions or sectors of human experience (race, class, sex, age, condition, disposition)—considered to be privileged in their disclosures. And extra-Christian experience encompasses in this reckoning "reason," as the frequent juxtaposition or partnership of "reason and revelation" suggests, for in it we find not only the rational capacity but the human quest for truth as such. We include in human experience the *entirety* of our capacity and predisposition to determine what is ultimately so—the rational, moral, and affective dimensions of our humanity. This is "the world" that offers itself as authority in Christian debate about sources and standards of authority.

By including reason within experience we not only differ from the distinction between or alliance of the two, as in the quadrilateral, but from the distinction and sometimes opposition of them in some more general usage. Thus "experience" for some refers to "precognitive" or "unthematized" sensibilities of a religious, moral,

124. Owen C. Thomas, "Theology and Experience," *Harvard Theological Review* 78 (1985): 179-210.

or aesthetic sort.[125] Similarly, others differentiate experience from ratiocination as two modes of encounter with reality, the former more trustworthy and the latter less so. In both cases, experience is associated with "feeling" and reason with discourse and intellectual functions.

There is no question that we must recognize distinguishable human dimensions here, identified variously as the "heart" and the "head," emotion and ratiocination, affect and intellect, feeling and reason. Yet these functions are not absolutely separable as modern sociopsychology and biblical understandings of human nature both conclude. Feeling is formed by structures of meaning culturally and linguistically shaped, and these in turn are influenced by sensory stimuli we receive as feeling.[126] So, too, is the unity of self in biblical understandings. Here we use the general term *experience* to describe the total human encounter with our environment in its web of interrelationships. With that meeting, we shall also try to do justice to the assertiveness of one or another aspect of experience—rational, moral, and affective.

With respect to the type now under discussion, experience constitutes the source of authority. From it we are urged to receive the fundamental data for the work of theology, and to it we are asked to return to corroborate our proposals. While Scripture and tradition enter the process of theological decision making, providing the *arena* of experience and the *symbols* of its communal or personal expression, the content is supplied by the wider experiential matrix. The world is the source and the Bible and/or the church are the setting.

Presupposed in this concept of authority is a doctrine of revelation. In some cases, this means that God the fontal Source of our mediate worldly source discloses what is to be known through human experience as it appears in the forms of Scripture and Christian tradition. What is available in these particular symbols and this history is also accessible outside of it, and is to be interpreted

125. David Tracy, *Blessed Rage for Order: The New Pluralism in Theology* (New York: Seabury Press, 1975); Langdon Gilkey, *Naming the Whirlwind: The Renewal of God Language* (Indianapolis: Bobbs-Merrill, 1969); Karl Rahner, *Foundations of Christian Faith: An Introduction to the Idea of Christianity*, trans. William V. Dych (New York: Seabury Press, 1978).

126. For assessments of experience divorced from its cultural and linguistic habitat see George Lindbeck, *The Nature of Doctrine* (Philadelphia: Fortress Press, 1984) and Francis Schüssler Fiorenza, *Foundational Theology: Jesus and the Church* (New York: Crossroad, 1984).

with categories drawn from the universal world of human experience. Or, God discloses truth in some particular experience outside the boundaries of Christian faith and life, and the understanding gained from that source is used as the framework for interpreting Christian faith and life.

As this authority type is a major interlocutor for our systematics, a detour here is appropriate to clarify the assumptions on the basis of which we encounter and assert the experiential options. Narratively stated, what we are calling "experience" or "world" is humanity-in-creation, essentially good because the good God brought it to be. Yet the fall into self-will has so damaged the human relation to the rest of the creation and to its Creator that humanity has lost the capacity to discern clearly, as well as to pursue faithfully, the divine intention. This means that human experience, "the world," is not a trustworthy arbiter of the divine purpose. The self-inflicted tribulation that haunts creation is a sign of its loss of vision and a will too weakened ("bent") to follow it. But the human venture goes forward nevertheless, with sufficient light to live and to hope toward a better future. God lets the story unfold, restraining chaos and making and keeping human life sufficiently human for that new future by the common graces of light and life that buoy up our faltering experiences. Along this way come breakthroughs of particular grace that constitute the turning points of the narrative, in Israel and finally in Jesus Christ. With them is given the special light of prophetic and apostolic disclosure that transcends the broken lights in creation, clarifies their ambiguities, and challenges the misperceptions associated with them through the fall. As the work of the one God—the power of the Purpose, the Spirit of the Son—"special revelation" therefore keeps company with universal revelation. Human experience is the *setting* of the theological venture whose *source* is the apostolic testimony.

Invariably the exponents of human experience as source ask those who affirm a biblical source of authority the question: Are not the biblical events and testimonies themselves entwined in human experience? And if that is the case, how can any distinctions of the sort just made be held to exist? If particular divine disclosure is itself embedded in history, is not special appeal to the Bible itself finally just an appeal to human experience?

The answer to these questions is in the narrative. The whole story is of God's relation to *us,* happenings taking place through our human experience. However, the divine initiative is not so captive to human experience that it cannot employ it as a medium for its message. God works in, with, and under human experience in order to disclose what is otherwise obscured by it. Human experience continues to envelop the redemptive and revelatory points of entry but cannot screen from us God's disclosive intentions.

The issue here in the doctrine of revelation is the same as that faced in other doctrines. One of the first struggles in early Christian thought had to do with the relation of human experience to divine action in the debate about the Person of Christ. Is the deed of God that is Jesus Christ a foreign body within the realm of experience, as Docetists, Apollinarians, and others insisted, by diminishing the human reality of Jesus? Or is Jesus essentially bound to and a creature of human experience, as Ebionites, Adoptionists, and others maintained? The Christian community rejected both positions, setting a significant precedent not only for Christology but also for theological epistemology. As in the incarnation, Christ's humanity is inseparable from his divinity, so our reception of revelation is bound up with divine deeds disclosed through human experience. In that unity the presence of God carries with it the power of God, and makes possible the knowledge of God in and through the experiential medium. This is the assumption of special revelation, one that does not deny the universality of human experience, and thus its role at some point in the authority structure of faith (no epistemological Docetism). But at the same time it will not grant that experience the right to exclude the divine Presence and its power to reveal (no epistemological Ebionism). Our third authority type, the world, rejects this assertion and interpretation, holding that Scripture and tradition are separable from or subsidiary to human experience and must be interpreted in terms of categories drawn from the world.

The exponents of experiential authority are manifold. In sifting and sorting the subtypes we adapt distinctions made by Friedrich Schleiermacher. Appeals to experience in theology tend to organize themselves around three kinds of human capacity and action: "thinking," "doing," and "feeling."[127] We will also employ these categories without Schleiermacher's theological framework for them. We use them in the broadest sense: those who have recourse to "thinking" give reason final authority; those who espouse "doing" turn to moral attitude and behavior as definitive; those who appeal

127. Friedrich Ernst Daniel Schleiermacher, *The Christian Faith,* ed. H. R. Mackintosh and J. S. Stewart (Philadelphia: Fortress Press and Edinburgh: T. & T. Clark, 1928, 1976), 7-12. His "Knowing" is our "thinking."

to "feeling" hold that authority resides in human affect. There is a rough correspondence here to long-standing philosophical distinctions between the true, the good, and the beautiful, although the "beautiful" does not adequately encompass an affectivity that ranges widely across a spectrum from aesthetic through "religious" to the "emotional" and "visceral."

Thinking

The appeal to human experience as "thinking" describes what is often known as "reason." Reason has a variety of connotations: the exercise of the laws of logic, cerebral processes applied to ultimate matters, thematization of intuitive encounters with reality, rigorous empirical investigation, the subjection of all private claims of truth to standards of public inquiry. We include all of these in our category of thinking but with special focus on the use of rational processes to construct *interpretive frameworks* that seek to give an account of the reality to which the Christian religion points. Assumed here is the human capacity to read the meaning of "life, death, and destiny" out of the data available to human beings, on the condition that rational faculties take charge of that inquiry. Here, briefly, are some of the currently active versions of this subtype.

1. Philosophical Views

Philosophy in its classical sense is the attempt to discern by rational means the first principles of being and knowing. What are the most universal premises about reality and our access to it? In the theological community some continue the Platonic and Aristotelian answers to these questions. Others carry forward more recent Kantian and Hegelian traditions. Existentialism and process thought are among the more influential current points of view pressing for a philosophical interpretation of Christian belief. In this subtype the Bible is read through the lens of a philosophical system, and Christian tradition is rethought in terms of its major themes. We illustrate this option in authority by "process theology."

John Cobb's Christological restatement in *Christ in a Pluralistic Age*[128] illustrates the way in which one can use Alfred North Whitehead's philosophy to reinterpret Scripture and a major teaching from the Christian tradition. Cobb employs a formulation from the

128. John Cobb, *Christ in a Pluralistic Age* (Philadelphia: Westminster Press, 1975).

patristic Logos Christology as a starting point. The *logos* as the ancient idea of universal order is reconceived as "the principle of concretion" and organ of novelty. The Logos is the "primordial nature of God," the envisaging and ordering of the infinite range of potentiality or "eternal objects." The Logos is no static display of possibility but the lure toward optimal creative transformation drawing "actual entities" (the Whiteheadian description of rudimentary being) out of the past and into the future. When the Logos, supplying the actual entity with its "initial aim," brings to be an occasion that is more than the repetition of habitual existence, thus increasing the richness of its experience and the width of its scope of possibility, an event takes place that can be identified as "creative transformation," one whose enabler can be called the "incarnate Logos." While the immanent or incarnate Logos is active in all becoming, the initial subjective aim supplied by it to actual entities at the level of physical objects is only the reenactment of the immediate past. It is on the "level of life," and eminently human life, that the opportunity for novelty happens, although the leap from organic to inorganic is itself a sign of creative transformation. Whenever there is a new actualization of possibility in which the past is appropriated in fresh configuration with novel potentiality, there is Christ. Since this event reaches toward both past occasions and future possibilities and the God who orders the past and envisages the future, Christians read this dynamic as the love known to them in Jesus of Nazareth.

As Jesus is a fundamental reference point for the philosophical reformulation of the Logos themes, attention must be turned to the past data about him found in the New Testament accounts and the church's Christological traditions. For evidence about the Nazarene carpenter Cobb turns to four perspectives on the New Testament material, those of biblical scholars Rudolf Bultmann, Norman Perrin, and Ernest Colwell, and, for an outsider's view, to the Marxist philosopher Milan Machovec. He finds his sources to be in agreement on these things: Jesus of Nazareth proclaimed the coming kingdom of God and its urgent call for individual decision; the kingdom's defining characteristic is care for and mercy toward others. While these ideas are in continuity with Judaism, Jesus creatively transforms them, articulating them in the language of the everyday world with a special sense of commanding authority from and unity with God, and joins them to conduct that reflects the teaching. The New Testament data and the transforming influence this figure have had on global history, and still have in personal encounter with us, are such as to suggest a special relation of the incarnate Logos to Jesus of Nazareth. The incarnate Logos so acts as to win a total response to its lure of creative novelty. The self so involved can be said to be constituted by the Logos. Cobb finds that in all the evidence that can be amassed about Jesus, especially his "certainty of God's will" and "the authority of direct insight," there is the indication that the Logos is not just one aspect of the self's existence but that it constitutes the self as such. "There might be someone of whom history has left no record who was constituted much as Jesus was, but that is idle speculation. So far as we know, Jesus is unique."[129]

Where there is this kind of coalescence of the self and the Logos with its "unique cumulative richness and aliveness of experience" there is produced "a field of force of truly unusual magnitude sustained and extended through repeated acts of remembrance."[130] This effect in history is the "work of Christ," the creative transformation of the prophetic tradition's vision of reality that has passed through the Greco-Roman world into the West and finally into its present global sphere of influence. Its source is in part the remembered teaching of Jesus and in part Jesus' "causal efficacy," an experiential "force field" Cobb interprets in terms of a Pauline Christ-mysticism of forgiveness as release from preoccupation with the past and anxiety about the future. It is the double impact of both Jesus' words and transmitted experience that has prompted the church to formulate its two-nature doctrine of the Person of Christ and has given rise to understandings of the Work of Christ that stress either the pedagogical or the sacramental. While Cobb perceives these conceptualities now to be defunct, they do testify to the importance of the human figure of Jesus on the one hand, and the gracious power that flows from him to us on the other.

Cobb affirms, "Apart from Christ there is no hope for a better future."[131] Since the Logos confronts every settled entity with possibilities for creative becoming, the power named Christ is the only factor that saves the world from "slow inertial decay." Four "images of hope" that work to that end today are: (1) The City of God as it is embodied in Paolo Soleri's model of "archology," the vertical city rising from the Arizona desert, a vision of environmentally integrated urban living, the "plumbing of the City of God." (2) The

129. Ibid., 142.
130. Ibid., 145.
131. Ibid., 186.

creative transformation of Christian faith by the assimilation of the achievement of Buddhism, "enlightenment . . . associated with . . . detachment, openness, release, quiescence, serenity, and silence . . . [the] subjective expression of the Buddha nature."[132] Christian engagement with Buddhist insight could eventuate in a postpersonal existence that transcends the restrictive sense of selfhood in Christian tradition. (3) The kingdom of heaven understood in Whiteheadian terms as "the consequent nature of God," the preservation and growth of all that is of value and importance in the pulsing immediacy of God's memory. (4) The "resurrection of the dead" as brought to theological awareness by Pannenberg and reinterpreted by Cobb in terms of parapsychological phenomena. Thus we are to understand Jesus' own resurrection in terms of visionary appearances of ontological validity, one which gives us hope for a personal existence beyond this life, albeit not in terms of the tradition's temporal end of history or resurrected body but as participating after death in a transphysical realm in transpersonal unity.

In Cobb's philosophical theology, various aspects of classical doctrines of Christ and accents with the biblical testimony are appropriated and reworked in Whiteheadian language and conceptuality. A philosophical framework developed in the ethos of modern science-technology and evolutionary theory provides the intellectual content for the assertion of faith, with the adaptation of the results to a culture "profane and pluralistic."

2. *Social-Political Views*

For some the quest for universal frameworks of a philosophical sort is misguided. Encompassing intellectual schemes of this sort are held to be decisively shaped by sociological and political dynamics. Abstract "philosophy" is seen to have provided a legitimation for existing power relationships. In the place of these "ideological" ventures the meaning of Christian faith must be set forth in a sociopolitical framework that supports the oppressed in their struggle for justice. At the present time in the Third World and in ecumenical discussion, a powerful candidate for a social-political reinterpretation in which human experience is final authority is found in various versions of liberation theology. The type cited here is to be distinguished from both biblical "Jesus as liberator" views and ecclesial varieties of liberation theology that also

132. Ibid., 207.

use sociopolitical interpretation tools, but do so as aid to rather than source of authority.

As an example we cite an expression of liberation theology that employs Marxist analytical tools for the understanding of Christian faith.[133] These advocates of liberation reject traditional Marxist dismissal of religion as opiate and other atheist assumptions in the belief that modes of social analysis can be separated from the total worldview and used with Christian premises.

Thus, they adopt Marx's interpretation of history in its theory of oppressed-oppressor class conflict, presently taking form as the struggle of the proletariat against the bourgeoisie, moving climactically toward the expropriation of the expropriators, the collective ownership of the means of production, the withering away of the state, and finally the appearance of a classless society. Christian eschatology alters the expectations of the paradisical state anticipated in Marxist projections, providing a critical principle within the new society that holds its achievements to be always short of the reign of God. Christians with this interpretive framework participate in liberation movements of the disenfranchised. The close association of a social theory with the mission of the church and its gospel is justified on the grounds that (1) all theology by its silence or selectivity is already aligned to one or another theory (since experience is inseparable from the gospel), and an explicit critical affirmation is better than the uncriticized but nonetheless real functioning of one legitimating the status quo, (2) the convergence of Marxist analysis with the cause of the poor makes possible the Christian use of the same, and (3) the benefits of Marxist analysis have been established, having proven its feasibility in praxis in the church's struggle for and with the poor.

Where this sociopolitical understanding of experience is rigorously applied to Christian teaching, major doctrines are rethought in terms of the oppressor-oppression problematic. God is thought of as the One active in history to bring sociopolitical liberation to the oppressed, being in solidarity with them in their suffering and slavery. Sin is essentially the act of oppression and in the oppressor. Salvation is liberation from historical oppression, or shows its reality fundamentally through this process. The knowledge that God

133. José Porfirio Miranda, *Marx and the Bible: A Critique of the Philosophy of Oppression,* trans. John Eagleson (Maryknoll, N.Y.: Orbis Books, 1974) and *Marx against the Marxists,* trans. John Drury (Maryknoll, N.Y.: Orbis Books, 1980).

is at work bringing liberation is known, for Christians, in the person of Jesus Christ. (For others in many versions of this position, the truth can be known also by others in their own paradigms.) In his attitude, behavior, and teaching, and in the resurrection experiences of his followers he is seen to be the liberator. Of particular importance is Jesus' preaching of Good News for the poor in the coming of the kingdom of God, the message of a promised world of justice. Commitment to Christ means solidarity with the oppressed, working toward their release from bondage, and viewing that goal and steps toward it as the inbreaking of the kingdom. The transcendent dimensions of the coming rule of God constitute a principle of criticism for any partial achievements along the way, rather than fulfillment in the next world. The latter shows up regularly as ideology promoted by oppressive forms of Christianity that deflect the proletariat from their determination to throw off the shackles of a system of private ownership of the means of production that is the source of injustice. Thus the mission of the church and the message of Christian faith are authoritative to the degree that they support the proletariat in their struggle against capitalism and its minions.

3. Cultural Views

Rational frameworks do not have to be encompassing interpretations of reality, philosophical, social-political, or other. They can be basic premises about the way things are, devoid of explicit schemas and their elaboration. A worldview of this sort consists of a controlling assumption, on the basis of which all experience is understood and by which behavior is guided. One such lens through which the Christian religion has been interpreted is the postulate of secularity. As the secular premise has had wide and varied influence in twentieth-century theology we use it as our prime example of a formative cultural scenario.

"Secularity" is the presupposition that the time-space continuum constitutes the sum and substance of reality.[134] "Transcendence" as a reality that reaches beyond finitude is a fiction. References to the infinite, the transcendent, the eternal, or the supernatural when they occur in religion and in Christian thought are either abandoned entirely, as in outrightly humanist or "death of God" forms

134. For discussion of theories of secularization and a definition of the term see Gabriel Fackre, *Humiliation and Celebration: Post-Radical Themes in Doctrine, Morals and Mission* (New York: Sheed & Ward, 1969), 15-27.

of theology,[135] refined, as in naturalist or neonaturalist theologies,[136] or are retained but removed from the realm of truth claims, serving as evocative of desired relationships to this-worldly realities or expressive of dimensions of human reality.[137]

While the aforementioned restate Christian assertions in immanentist fashion, more conservative renderings of a secular framework do not reject the transcendent presuppositions of classical Christian faith but hold that a secular society requires the translation of its assertions into terms meaningful to a secular society. This is accommodation to the idiom of secularity, not the excision of the transcendent claims of Christian faith by the premise of secularity.

While the secularization theologies in the first category often trace their lineage to Dietrich Bonhoeffer, the idiomatic secular theologies that retain a transcendent ontology are closer to Bonhoeffer's own view. However, his was a much more dialectical conception than that of most who claim him as mentor.[138] Because of the effort to maintain both the ontological referent and the biblical framework as the principle orientation points in authority, this kind of secular theology belongs more appropriately to our first major type, a combinationist view that seeks to relate Scripture to human experience. In the present case experience is itself normative, with the Bible reread in a secular framework.

4. *Logic and Evidence Views*

Some empirical views in the thinking mode do not espouse a comprehensive theory or a wide-ranging premise, but focus instead on an intellectual method. Theological assertions must pass muster before the rigors of either public evidence or the laws of logic. In its most radical expression theological propositions must rise from empirical and logical procedures. In its more familiar form the material for theological work is found elsewhere, in Scripture or

135. Notably Thomas H. H. Altizer and William Hamilton, *Radical Theology and the Death of God* (Indianapolis: Bobbs-Merrill, 1966) and Thomas Altizer, *The Gospel of Christian Atheism* (Philadelphia: Westminster Press, 1966).

136. Henry Nelson Wieman, *The Source of Human Good* (Chicago: Univ. of Chicago Press, 1946).

137. Paul Van Buren, *The Secular Meaning of the Gospel* (New York: Macmillan, 1963) and *Theological Explorations* (London: SCM Press, 1968).

138. For a critique of the use of Bonhoeffer by secular theologies see Fackre, *Humiliation and Celebration,* 91-122.

church tradition, but its validity is submitted to testing by empirical and rational processes.

A very diverse "rationalist" subcommunity can be found in this type. It encompasses those who reduce the specifics of theological assertion to a minimum that can pass this kind of scrutiny and also those who believe that much traditional belief, including an inerrant Bible, can and must be legitimated by evidence and logic.

Included in the first case are rationalist versions of theology with Enlightenment roots such as Deism and early Unitarianism, which screened out any propositions of traditional Christianity that did not seem justified by the investigative methods of eighteenth- and nineteenth-century "reason." This procedure left a residue consisting of belief in God, virtue, and immortality, or "the moral and spiritual teachings of Jesus." Later versions of antitraditional theology sought to establish more restrictive standards of evidence, declaring that only assertions validated by "the scientific method" of hypotheses tested by publicly verifiable examination of empirical data should be theologically valid. This adherence to the scientific method was often allied to the premises of secularity as in the neonaturalisms of the mid-twentieth century.[139]

Other theological positions that claim to be accountable to strict standards of evidence and logic argue that key features of the Christian tradition can pass such scrutiny. We choose as our example the "evangelical rationalists."

Evangelical rationalists are those who hold strongly to revelation as a source of theological propositions, indeed revelation deposited in the propositions of an inerrant Scripture. However, as strongly as the revelational source is asserted, the standard for determining the truth or falsity of even these central faith statements is "reason." If a theological assertion, even one with the highest credentials, such as the inerrancy of Scripture, cannot be shown to be reasonable—that is, not backed up by evidence or proven to be in violation of any of the laws of logic—that assertion cannot stand. What is considered the most persuasive evidence might not meet what others define as that—validation by miracle and the fulfillment of prophecy—but appeal is made in any case to public evidence and the canons of logic. Thus the revelatory declarations of traditional Christianity are treated as hypotheses subject to rational tests. Christian apologists in this tradition declare that no one has yet

139. See the early work of Henry Nelson Wieman, *The Wrestle of Religion with Truth* (New York: Macmillan, 1927).

shown Christianity to be irrational, and the careful pursuit of evidence and the laws of logic demonstrate alternative views to be less than reasonable.[140]

There are, of course, many versions of Christian faith that include the role of reason in theological method, but do not locate it as final arbiter of what is true and false. In the case under discussion, "thinking" plays this role of source (origin and/or standard of authority). Similarly, all of the scenarios in the present category hold that the rational expression of human experience is the determinative point of adjudication for theological assertions.

Doing

"Doing" is the experiential authority when conduct warranted by universal experience or particular experience outside of Scripture and tradition is the origin and test of Christian teaching. This moral behavior is seen to arise out of moral attitudes, but the consequences are given the highest priority. And they have to do with moral acts in relation to other humans, to the environment, and to the self. An act is moral if it contributes to the well-being of these relationships.

The function of moral authority in Christian theology is often associated with appeals to Scripture and tradition. "By their fruits you shall know them" is often cited as warrant for the moral test of doctrine. Exponents of this view regularly cite imperatives found in the Ten Commandments, prophetic teaching, Jesus' behavior and preaching of the kingdom, Paul's hymn to love, and early Christian conduct. However, these biblical warrants do not establish in their own right either the need for, or content of, moral norms. Authority is lodged in a more universal experience or extrabiblical sector of experience that validates and provides the interpretive framework for scriptural and ecclesial norms.

The role of doing in theological criteriology has taken on increasing prominence since the eighteenth century. While "thinking" perspectives tend to attribute this to the impact of Kantian philosophy, cultural factors have played their part in its heightening in-

140. For an examination of some approaches to evangelical apologetics, see Gordon R. Lewis, *Testing Christianity's Truth Claims* (Chicago: Moody Press, 1976). Among the evangelicals surveyed in this work, J. Oliver Buswell, Jr., Stewart C. Hackett, and Gordon H. Clark represent what we have called here the "evangelical rationalists."

fluence, either providing hospitable soil for Kantian themes or more directly shaping the emphasis on moral imperative. Thus the rise of science and technology from its Enlightenment setting and socioeconomic context raised the stakes of moral choice. The technological products of modernity not only extended the toolmaker's hand but also the decision-maker's arm, dramatically increasing the capacity for both good and ill. Medical and surgical instruments to extend human life evolved along with the weapons that could more effectively end it. The consequences of attitude and action in control of these new powers gave higher priority to the moral measure of religion and of theological assertions.

With the growing capabilities in communication and transportation made possible by the new technology came an increasing interaction and independence of human communities. Predictably, observers of the developing social and economic networks began to inquire about the moral effects of these systems of interdependence. Following the early utopian socialists, on the one hand, and the more pedestrian data-gathering of British students of industrialization, theoreticians such as Marx and Engels concluded that socioeconomic factors profoundly affect the human condition. In the emerging discipline of sociology the impact of social configurations was further charted by many who entered this field with moral concern, and whose studies, in turn, were used to challenge the destructive effects of industrialization.[141]

With a tradition of moral passion, it was not long before elements of church and theological leadership in a culture of advancing technology began to align themselves with other communities of moral sensibility, including movements among victims. Part of this moral reaction included the use of tools of social analysis, sometimes informed by a theory of class conflict and aspiration for a classless society.

When moral passion and social theory were joined to advances in the secularization process with its attraction of secularity as an

141. Paul Underwood Kellogg, ed., *The Pittsburgh Survey: Findings in Six Volumes* (New York: Charities Publications, 1910), sponsored by the Russell Sage Foundation, is a case in point. The Homestead steel strike of 1892 brought attention to the conditions in mill towns in the United States. See esp. the following volumes in this series: John Fitch, *The Steelworkers,* and Margaret Byington, *Homestead: The Households of a Mill Town.* See also Karl Marx's use of studies of industrial conditions in England in *Capital: A Critique of Political Economy,* vol. 1, trans. Samuel Moore and Edward Aveling, ed. Frederick Engels, rev. ed. by Ernst Untermann (Chicago: Charles H. Kerr & Co., 1909).

interpretation of reality, culture-sensitive theologians followed suit. Theological assertions in these quarters came to be assessed in terms of their contribution to the struggles of victims. In the early decades of the twentieth century that meant primarily the worker, but also women and oppressed minority groups. In questions of war and peace, modern technology made possible the extermination of vast numbers of people. World War I was the first mass application of new technology to the instruments of war-making. It was no accident that out of this emerged a pacifist community of Christian conscience with its principle of selection and interpretation of Christian teaching.

As the effects of technology on other parts of the globe widened, so too did the moral priority. Societies so affected were confronted with the exploitation of their lands and peoples by the Western entrepreneur on the one hand, and the missionary zeal of an ideology from the East that offered itself as an alternative. In many places the Third World began to define itself over against both the Eagle and the Bear. The employment of analytical tools in the quest for economic justice from the latter, and the attraction of the democratic processes and aspirations of the former dwelt in uneasy alliance in the developing countries. In some parts of the Third World the religious community, with its people suffering from hunger and poverty, began to use the social theories of activist elements in its own society, formulating liberation theologies that utilize Marxist social analysis. In some cases, theological ideas became weapons in the class war, the test of their validity or invalidity being their function in the struggle.

Parallel to the economic interpretation of moral issues, movements developed in the West and also in Western theology to confront other kinds of oppression. Moral outrage grew among socially marginalized people. Racial communities, long voiceless and maltreated, preeminently black people in Western countries but also other dehumanized people—native American, Hispanic, Asian-American, women, students, the disabled, elders, prisoners, and even "middle Americans"—began to find their voice, assert their dignity, and demand power in the decision-making processes that affect their lives.[142] Church groups and their theologians as well

142. On the latter—middle Americans—often ignored in a catalog of the disinherited, see Gabriel Fackre, *Liberation in Middle America* (Philadelphia: Pilgrim Press, 1971), *passim,* and a citation of the studies and literature in this field, pp. 121-22.

as theological thought in general responded in kind by making one or more of these constituencies the focus of theological reflection. Truth claims were tested by the extent to which they expressed the cause of those involved in the struggle for freedom and justice, and conformed to the intellectual framework that supported this struggle. In this view a designated sector of experience and its interpretive framework therefore becomes the test for theological assertions.

Paralleling developments in the West and class movements in the Third World, were and are racial, sexual, ethnic, and national movements of self-affirmation. Sometimes class analysis was combined with other considerations. Often African and Asian movements in theology seek to distinguish themselves from Western as well as other Third World economically-oriented movements and interpretations. Here "religion" appears as a critical factor one seen to be ignored by Marxist-influenced liberation theologies. World religions in Asian and African societies become focal points for the indigenization of faith. Sometimes a more general category such as "people's theology" takes on prominence, combining economic, political, social, and religious factors as in the Minjung theology found in parts of Asia.[143] In all these developments, however, the overall concern for human dignity points toward a moral criteriology.

Modern technology has dramatically accelerated one particular moral concern—warfare. The leap forward in nuclear capability in the period since the end of World War II has produced such awesome potential for mass destruction that a major new movement for peace in both secular and religious communities has emerged. In the theological domain "peace theologies" have taken form around this momentum. Those that fit our present experiential category make theology a megaphone for this concern. Doctrine is reinterpreted in the light of the peace mandates and often in the pacifist imperative. Where this kind of moral passion is joined to a secularity premise the whole of the theological enterprise may be made to rest upon the issues of nuclear extinction.

As we review theologies that make justice and/or peace *the* interpretative category, similar efforts should be kept in mind that also are moved by moral passion but do not make moral experience the sole criterion for theology. These views come in two forms: (1) the justice and peace issues (or others) may be one of a variety of foci; and (2) the justice and peace issues (or others) may be understood as the *setting* in which all theology is to be done but not the

143. *Minjung Theology, passim*.

source of it. So, in this volume "suffering and hope" are integral to the "perspective." However, the definition of *perspective* rests finally on criteria from a source and substance other than the moral experiences of contemporaneity. Examples of this kind of perspectival treatment with ultimate warrants in Scripture and tradition related to a setting in which justice and peace imperatives are claimant are the Roman Catholic bishops' pastoral letters of 1983 and 1987 on peace and economic justice.[144]

Moral Experientialism and the Religious Right

As the plight of marginalized peoples came to high visibility in the latter part of the twentieth century and moral theologies took advocacy positions for them, a reaction appeared in the churches and in the arena of theology. Two developments, distinguishable but also invariably joined, gained headway in North America. One was a return to the traditional values of country, home, job, and conservative political and economic perspective; the other was a reassertion of personal virtues, especially with regard to sexuality. These trends congealed in a phenomenon in North America known as the Christian Right or the Religious Right.[145]

The Religious Right emerged as a protest movement against what it judged to be an attack on biblical faith on the one hand, and the erosion of moral and spiritual values, on the other. Against what it perceived to be the destruction of biblical authority, it asserted a hard-line inerrancy view. And it juxtaposed to the secularity and relativity it saw in society the assertion of moral absolutes. In contrast to the critique of established authority—political, economic, social—by moral experientialists in theology and church life, it supported traditional authorities, advocating authoritative leadership in affairs of state, military supremacy of the United States, the forward advance of capitalism and its industrial hierarchy, the return to patriarchy in the family. All this is summed up in the "mighty man" philosophy of the Reverend Jerry Falwell.[146]

The political programs and religious crusades of the Religious

144. *The Challenge of Peace: God's Promise and Our Response: A Pastoral Letter on War and Peace, 1983. Economic Justice For All: Catholic Social Teaching and the U.S. Economy, 1987.*

145. Robert C. Liebman and Robert Wuthnow, *The New Christian Right: Mobilization and Legitimation* (New York: Aldine, 1983), and Fackre, *Religious Right and Christian Faith*.

146. Jerry Falwell, *Listen, America* (Waco, Tex.: Word Books, 1980), 14.

Right often focus on the restoration of traditional views of family and sex. Campaigns against homosexuality, antiabortion crusades, antismut campaigns, the monitoring of media, the highlighting of sexually connected diseases such as AIDS and herpes were and are planks in their sociopolitical platform.

While the Religious Right's major assumption is the decay of religion and society as caused by "secular humanism," its politicizing of fundamentalist doctrine introduced more and more elements of the moral experientialism we are describing in this section. That is, the authority of the biblical text came to be read increasingly in terms of commitment to the positions, movements, experiences, and indeed the victim experiences of the contemporary context (viz., the fetus). What was asserted to be functionally authoritative about Scripture were those concerns of moral passion that often found themselves on the agenda of single issue politics, the "Moral Majority," the "Liberty Federation" and even a presidential campaign for a political fundamentalist with a large television constituency.[147] The sign of loyalty to the Bible increasingly became the endorsement of the political and social programs of the New Right in the United States. This translation of loyalties to Scripture into the coin of specific political allegiances provided evidence for critics who charged the Religious Right with the very secular humanism they themselves attacked. In our present categories this meant substituting the authority of the experience of doing for the authority of Scripture, hence the strange bedfellows of Left and Right found in this house of experiential authority.

We have spent greater time on this dimension of experiential authority because of its prominence in contemporary Christian thought. Further, the heightened peril and promise of life on this planet by dint of advances in science and technology have pushed these moral questions dramatically to the foreground. In the "perspective" in authority in this volume the moral setting will play a crucial role.

Feeling

The human capacity to which we now turn is difficult to characterize. Some employ the term we are using for the entire category

147. For perceptions and portraits of the candidacy of Pat Robertson from the political right and the Religious Right, see "CBN's Pat Robertson: Headed for the White House?" *Conservative Digest* (Aug.-Sept. 1985), and "Pat Robertson: What He Would Do If He Were President," *Charisma* (May 1986): 30-35.

of human verification: "experience" as the interiorizing of truth. In the Christian religion truth becomes personally real when it is felt. For others experience means mystical feeling, not as the verification of an authority external to it but as a direct route to religious reality. Still others understand experience to include all affectivity, calling it "emotion," juxtaposing it to moral and rational considerations. But in so doing they cast suspicion upon it, given the pejorative associations of the word *emotion.* We are, therefore, on uneven terrain here when we seek to describe this view of authority in terms of inherited language, for its overtones carry such evaluative freight that they obscure what we are seeking to describe. Even Schleiermacher, whose rubrics we are using, left an uncertain legacy, sometimes distinguishing feeling from thinking and doing but at other times rendering the word in such a way as to include features of the other two to avoid charges of anti-intellectualism or anti-moralism.

In our scheme we understand feeling as a variety of the overall experiential norm in theology (one that includes the moral and rational), having to do with *affect* as the basic warrant for theological judgments. Truth rises out of and is tested by its feeling resonance. Does it move, touch, overwhelm one, or reach, disturb, entice, sensitize, open up the self? Do we know, below and beyond the level of moral and rational discourse, that this is intuitively so? We enter, therefore, a subjective realm, passing from softer sensibilities to more wrenching and upsetting ones. Some may understand feeling in aesthetic categories, drawing on the metaphor of disclosure or reminiscent of the contemplation of a painting, a piece of sculpture, a sunset, or a flower, or feeling may refer to a "flood" of emotion caused by personal or social tragedy or triumph. Feeling can allude to any point along the spectrum of religious experience, the sense of the numinous, the fascinating and mysterious, the awesome, the compelling, ultimate concern or absolute dependence, the passion or outrage of the committed, or the radical change of heart of the converted. Or it can simply be "this speaks to me" or "makes sense of my experience."

An important line runs straight through the various appeals to feeling, distinguishing views that belong in the present category from those that do not. This is the distinction between "testing" and "attesting." In attestation, affective experience is the medium through which the Holy Spirit works to "convict" a person of a truth held to be true on such other grounds as Scripture or tradition. Or, the attesting of truth by the Spirit through affective experience may mean the tip point in the process of decision-making in which other warrants have been active (again Scripture and tradition) but not decisive, so that the acceptance of a truth claim takes place. In such a case the "convincement" of a particular claim may be at issue, or the "conversion" to a whole new worldview may be at stake. In both cases truth warranted otherwise also by Bible and/or church becomes truth "for me." In neither case is affect either the source of truth apart from Scripture and tradition or the test of truth from Scripture and tradition by a source outside of them. Affect is the medium for conviction and conversion that comes from Another and is tested by warrants from a source and resource that is other, not a message that constitutes its own authority.

Without the attestation that brings truth home, that makes truth for all also truth for me, the revelatory pilgrimage is unreached. Personal appropriation of Christian truth claims makes them valid, vital. This linkage of mediatory feeling to the assertions of Christian teaching is why their status as objective truth claims is better described as *affirmation* rather than proposition.

In the Christian tradition this form of experiential attestation by feeling is associated with the turning points in the careers of major figures in the church, the conversion "experience" of an Augustine, Luther, or Wesley. So too is it connected with a tradition of intense personal experience in which conversion is the sign and seal of authentic faith. In a less pronounced emphasis on primordial experience but with a strong accent on the interiorization of theological truths comes the accent on trust *(fiducia)* as a necessary companion to the assent of the will and belief *(assensus* and *notitia)* of the mind. This may be understood to be either moments of luminous corroboration at the beginning of our faith journey, or attestation *in via.* To the latter belong Kierkegaard's focus on "subjectivity," the inward appropriation without which there would be no truth since "subjectivity is truth."

Parallel and sometimes inseparable from these converting and convicting experiences is the feeling characteristic of mystical traditions in Christianity. Here in disciplines of the spirit and journeys of the heart the believer is introduced to the inner meaning of theological teaching. We are speaking of the mystical spirituality of Eastern Orthodoxy and the saints of the medieval church, in which the authority of Scripture and tradition is presupposed, often within the framework of a community's life of worship. In popular discussion of experiential attestation the mystical and fiducial are often identified with the terms "spirituality" and "piety." In the former case the metaphors of descent and ascent prevail, in the latter the figures of journey and pilgrimage. However, movements in depth or length do not themselves constitute primary theological authority, for that is vested in scriptural or ecclesial charters. They do constitute individual validation that renders revealed truth active in the life of the self, true for me as well as true for all. In this attestatory sense feeling does not belong in the present category.

On the other side of the dividing line within affectivity are those positions that view feeling as the source and test of theological claims. In its most radical form religious feeling, or more widely construed personal or social feeling, is the touchstone of authority. These are the points of view represented under the present heading.

Advocates of an affective experientialism are very diverse, often carrying on sustained debate with one another about the nature of Christian faith. Following Avery Dulles's organization of the "models of revelation" that deal with the doctrinal underside of concepts of authority, many of the exponents of his "new awareness" and "inner experience" categories and some of those in the "dialectical presence" category so qualify. Recent experientialist theologians (Gabriel Moran, William Thompson, Gregory Baum, and Ray Hart) strike notes similar to those heard in the earlier Schleiermacher tradition, although the latter's accent on the religious consciousness and the singularities of the Christian tradition is expanded to include wider awareness of ultimacy. While exponents of "the new hermeneutic" belong essentially to the Christological cum biblical type earlier discussed, the more stress is laid upon the "language event" as a species of the genus of human imagination, the closer its interpreters come to affirming an affective source of authority. To these schools of thought we can also add many representatives of the "life story" and "canonical story" types of narrative theology, some versions of Jungian-influenced theology, and some forms of feminist theology.[148]

One can also find elements of affective experientialism in Paul Tillich and Karl Rahner. Finally, however, church authority and biblical referentiality weigh more heavily in Rahner's theology. The subtlety and complexity of Tillich's thought makes his placement in this schema difficult. I prefer to locate him in the broadly experientialist stream, but "combinationist" within that in every

148. Fackre, "Narrative Theology: An Overview," 343-51.

sense—both Scripture and tradition functioning as resource not source, with philosophical, political, and psychological aspects of "thinking," a social ethical aspect of "doing," as well as the anxiety/ecstasy accents in "feeling."

Characteristics that are shared by the variety of affect-oriented theologies include the following:

1. The language and lore of the Christian community are performative, not propositional. They are for "recognition," not "cognition." They do not exist to give us information about divine reality but to put us in touch with divine reality. A true encounter with them is one that "shakes," "stimulates," "awakens," "disturbs," "overwhelms," "awes," "satisfies," "gives enjoyment," "fascinates," "anguishes," "exhilarates," "enlivens." First and foremost, they engage our imagination, not our intellect. As such our meeting with the Ultimate is "unthematized" and its significance is in the new consciousness they bring to be.

2. The new awareness is not a religious aestheticism, an experience for its own sake. Rather, its authenticity is commensurate with its life-changing quality. When one is so shaken and awakened, the self is purified and transformed. We are different in our attitudes and behavior. Imagination, therefore, is not divorced from action but energizes and redirects it. And it does so in a life that is for others. Recognition is of reality, human as well as divine.

3. The primary medium through which divine reality raises awareness and changes life direction is the "symbol." A symbol is "an externally perceived sign that works mysteriously on the human consciousness so as to suggest more than it can clearly describe or define . . . pregnant with a plenitude of meaning which is evoked rather than explicitly stated . . . [tapping] a vast potential of semantic energy."[149] Symbols exist in a variety of ways as visible objects of nature or human design, persons and actions, figurative speech and writing, etc. Much of the affective experientialism in the theology of the late twentieth century focuses on the function of language and literary symbolism such as metaphor and myth. It also contributes to the renewed interest in religious ritual, and has influenced discussion of worship and sacramental theology. In the literary and ritual exploration of symbol, the "originative" language of the Christian tradition and its subsequent employment by believers is sometimes described as of "first-order" discourse close

149. Dulles, *Models of Revelation,* 131-132.

to its affective sources and contrasted with the cerebral distancing that goes on in the second order reflection of formal theology.

4. The performative function of religious symbol is twofold. On the one hand, it is *expressive* of a dimension of reality otherwise inaccessible to us. It brings us into relation with that reality as no other route can, and in this sense is revelatory or disclosive. At the same time it is *evocative,* drawing a response from us, awakening new sensibilities, altering old perceptions, and forming new behavior.

5. Affective experientialists deal in the main with Christian symbols. For most of them their own Christian tradition has been and will continue to be the experiential catalyst. However, they do not deny the same accessibility to reality to those of other religious traditions or nonreligious worldviews. Because human experience is the source of authority, equivalent myths and metaphors can be equally performative. The test is affectivity as earlier construed. A frequent correlate of this universalist judgment is that disclosive and evocative symbols are community phenomena. They emerge within historic traditions and are primarily associated with historic religious communities.

6. A chief foe, perhaps the chief foe, of affective experientialists is a discursive approach to ultimate reality. A "left-brain" intellectualized ideology has taken religious symbols captive, treating them as propositions that purport to give information about the being and doing of God. Thus first-order symbols are mistaken for second-order conceptuality. Symbols are performative, not propositional. Such a view of religious language, however, is not an anti-intellectualism. Symbols do not provide conceptual content, but they evoke it. While Ricoeur's famous phrase carries in his own theology more weight than given by those in the present category, it does express the point: "Symbol gives rise to thought." In affective experientialism "the thought" is not integral to or intellectually testable by the symbol, but is provided by categories appropriate to disciplined inquiry—philosophical, political, psychological, sociological. One cannot accept the distinction between "symbolic truth" and "the truth of the symbol" made by Wilbur Urban and others, which assumes that there is a conceptual motif integral to a religious metaphor, rather than the latter furnished by extrinsic sources of human thought.

In passing we note that affect plays an important part in this systematics. A narrative perspective draws on the wisdom of the symbolic tradition, acknowledging and using metaphor as an expressive and evocative medium. However, feeling is not the source of authority, but its setting. The biblical source is symbolic discourse that not only evokes but also entails intellectual content. Scripture has propositional weight as well as performative power. Narrative symbol brings us into relationship with the narrative God as no abstract discourse can. But that symbol carries with it an objective as well as a subjective truth claim.

Can a concept of authority honor the insights of our worldly setting—its philosophical, political, and psychological frameworks, its moral passions and movements, its affective sensibilities—while at the same time taking as its measure the biblical source and Christological norm and the church and its tradition as its guide? What follows is an effort to learn from the conversation on authority going on within the Christian community and an attempt to set forth such a view. The spectrum of views considered in this chapter will appear in the agreements, disagreements, and reconceptualization to follow.

CHAPTER III

The Text of Authority

A pastoral systematics will stay close to the life-world of the steward of Christian identity. We begin the constructive section on authority, therefore, at the place where the pastor weekly confronts the authority question in a pointed way: preaching from the biblical text. To the extent that the sermon engages the meaning and significance of the scriptural passage, a *teaching* component enters the preaching act. In it fundamental theological issues are posed to the speaker and hearer. With them comes the question of the authority of the text vis-à-vis (a) the experience the preacher and the congregation bring to it, (b) the impact of the church and its tradition upon it, and (c) the principles of interpreting it. Weekly the pastor is faced with the kind of alternatives just explored.

Our review of options prepares us for the interpretation of the text in another way as well. If we are determined to hear out our brothers and sisters, we will reflect this in the way we interpret a text and thus in the concept of authority we espouse. What follows is that kind of understanding of scriptural interpretation and theological authority which includes the contribution of various perspectives. Inclusivity here means four "senses" of Scripture: *common, critical, canonical,* and *contextual.* (We shall consider this subject in the present chapter and the one following.) The same quest for catholicity is at work in the encompassing concept of authority, one which seeks to learn from the exponents of the three major types in their various subsets. We sort their functions and priorities according to this schema: Scripture as *source,* gospel as *substance,* Christ as *center,* the church as *resource,* tradition as *guide,* the world as *setting,* gracious signs therein as *aid,* liberation/reconciliation, narrative, and ecumenicity as elements of *perspective.*

In Chapter 5 we shall take a text that poses sharply the questions of authority and revelation and put the method to work, looking for its meaning and significance.

FOURFOLD INTERPRETATION

The multiple meaning of Scripture sought in patristic and medieval exegesis has few defenders today. However, it did represent an effort at inclusivity from which we can learn.[1] While no simple connection should be made between literal, allegorical, anagogical, and tropological levels of meaning and the senses discussed here, there is a common impulse to widen the range of discourse, and a continuity in some of the themes.[2] However, the practice of the ancient fourfold method did make for the erosion of textual meaning. A rebuke of fanciful exegesis was in order. The Reformation made it, and called for a return to "plain meaning." While attempting to recover some of the value of a more expansive method of interpretation, we shall do it with an eye on the *sensus literalis* as it is discernable by "the whole people of God." But a more full-orbed understanding of perspicuity is needed than the view of it found in too much of the Protestant tradition, shaped as it has been by Western culture's individualism.

The commitment by the Reformers to *sola Scriptura* in its plain meaning did not, in fact, prevent them from drawing on historic creeds, classically formulated doctrines such as the Trinity and the Person of Christ, their own confessions and catechisms, an emphasis on the importance of preaching for understanding the Bible, a

1. Note the appeal for its reconsideration by David Steinmetz, "The Superiority of Pre-critical Exegesis," *Theology Today* 37 (April 1980): 27-38.

2. The discontinuities in setting and the developments in understanding between now and then caution against any simplistic comparisons. However, some continuities in history seem to be reflected in common hermeneutical features. A quest for both common sense and critical sense is parallel to the concern for "plain meaning" and "author's intention" in an earlier hermeneutics. Also, the tropological meaning with its moral accent is in continuity with the social contextuality we shall speak about. Again, the allegorical meaning of a text sought to bring it into relationship to the teaching lore of the church, paralleling the canonical sense described in this work that explores the text within a theological framework. The eschatological cum mystical direction of anagogical exegesis shares the personal contextualization of a text discussed in this book, i.e., how Scripture finally "comes home" in its fateful individual significance. While these parallels are intriguing, we shall not attempt to forcefit the senses identified here into the mold of its classical antecedents.

recourse to learning, an appeal to the lens of Christ, and a reliance on the internal testimony of the Holy Spirit as aids to understanding the text. We use these same assists here also as steps in the hermeneutical process, finding a place for them under the rubrics "critical, canonical," and "contextual"—ones that keep company with the common sense of the text.

Our first step into the interpretive arena is to make a basic distinction between the "meaning" and the "significance" of a biblical text.[3] In the wider debate in literary criticism a case is made for the differentiation between the intended meaning of a text and the drawing of inferences from it, or making of applications of it, in a way faithful to but not explicitly purposed by "authorial intention." We agree with it. Since the "author" of a specific biblical text is often not so easily established in the present state of biblical studies, we speak here instead of "textual intention."[4] The meaning of a text is its own purposed exposition as that lives and grows through

3. The use of *meaning* and *significance* is influenced by the argument of E. D. Hirsch, Jr., for the difference between the author's meaning of a text and its implication for others. Hirsch says,

> *Meaning* is that which is represented by a text; it is what the author meant by his use of a particular sign sequence; it is what the signs represent. *Significance,* on the other hand, names a relationship between that meaning and a person, or a conception, or a situation, or indeed anything imaginable. Authors, who like everyone else change their attitudes, feelings, opinions, and value criteria in the course of time, will obviously in the course of time tend to view their own work in different contexts. Clearly what changes for them is not the meaning of the work, but rather their relationship to that meaning. Significance always implies a relationship, and one constant, unchanging pole of that relationship is what the text means. Failure to consider this simple and essential distinction has been the source of enormous confusion in hermeneutic theory. (*Validity in Interpretation* [New Haven: Yale Univ. Press, 1967], 8; see also 5-67, 140-44, 211-12)

Hirsch says he is indebted for this distinction to Gottlob Frege and his article, "Über Sin und Bedeutung," *Zeitschrift für Philosophie und Philosophisch Kritik* 100 (1892), ET in H. Feigl and W. Sellars, *Readings in Philosophical Analysis* (New York, 1949).

4. The parallel to Hirsch's determinate and persisting authorial meaning thus is not the intention of a human author of a biblical text as such, but the intention of the divine Author as that is expressed in the history of the text's coming to be, culminating in the redactional and canonical editors' final form. This Authorial intention by which all claims to contextual significance are judged is discerned by the common, critical, and canonical inquiries presently to be explored. For a challenge to Hirsch's distinction, see David Couzins Hoy, *The Critical Circle: Literature and Philosophical Hermeneutics* (Berkeley and Los Angeles: Univ. of California Press, 1982), 11-40.

the varied significances possible to it in changing historical contexts. To this integrity of the text the interpreter turns when seeking to discern its significance in a new setting. For biblical texts, rooted finally in the purposes of God, authorial intention is really *Authorial* intention.

Biblical hermeneutics is the activity that seeks to discern the Author's intention in both the text and its contextualization. As such it interprets the text's *meaning* and *significance.* We shall call the investigation of a text's meaning *internal hermeneutics,* and the inquiry into its significance *external hermeneutics.* In both cases the inquiry is guided by a set of principles of interpretation that constitute a hermeneutical framework or a *hermeneutics,* a term we will discuss in more detail later. When these principles are applied to a particular text in the search for its meaning and significance, the general practice of internal hermeneutics becomes the specific practice of *exegesis.* Exegesis is the textual individuation of internal and external hermeneutics.[5]

We first meet the multiple sense of textual meaning in internal hermeneutics. This field of biblical interpretation seeks the meaning of the text by the pursuit of its *common* sense, its *critical* sense, and its *canonical* sense. Taken together they constitute the *meaning* of a text.

Common Sense

In hermeneutical discussion the phrase *common sense* is associated with the philosophical school of Scottish "commonsense realism" of Thomas Reid (1710–1796) and Dugald Stewart (1753–1828), who sought to offer an alternative to Hume's skeptical epistemology and Berkeley's idealism. They insist that our working assumption in human interaction—that there are objects that correspond to our sense perceptions—is trustworthy. So too is the belief in the reality of other minds and the identity of the self that persists through changing experiences. That these things are so cannot be established by airtight proof but depends on an intuitive judgment

5. "Broadly speaking, exegesis is the process by which a text, as a concrete expression of a 'sender' to a 'receiver,' is systematically explained." "Exegesis," *Handbook of Biblical Criticism,* ed. Richard Soulen (Atlanta: John Knox Press, 1981), 66. See pp. 66-69 of this same article for a comprehensive view of the methods and tools of exegesis. Cf. John H. Hayes and Carl R. Holladay, *Biblical Exegesis: A Beginner's Handbook* (Atlanta: John Knox Press, 1982), *passim.* For an evangelical view, see Bernard Ramm, *Protestant Biblical Interpretation,* 3d rev. ed. (Grand Rapids: Baker, 1970), 10-11.

validated practically by living with it. Commonsense realism meant, therefore, that we proceed by a "chaste induction" in confronting every issue, trusting that sincere minds furnished with similar inductive capacities will come to the same conclusions. Scottish realism held that ordinary people in any time and place could discover universal truths. Its populist impulse was very influential in eighteenth- and nineteenth-century political life in America. Its impact in the religious sphere was through the "Princeton School" of Charles and Alexander Hodge and Benjamin Warfield, who believed that one could construct a "science of theology" from a rigorous inductive study of Scripture, just as the natural sciences gathered and tested their facts.

While there is a similarity to the democratic premise and universal presupposition of Scottish realism in our usage here, we are tracing the commonsense lineage back to the plain meaning tradition of the Reformation, on the one hand, and, on the other, reinterpreting it in the light of subsequent historicist, existential, and communitarian developments. Common sense in this hermeneutics is associated with the common life of a believing community in its catholicity rather than the prerogative of isolated individuals pursuing a disinterested investigation. The common sense of a biblical text demands a larger view of commonality.

However, while we must reject the too facile assumptions of a Scottish realism that was itself the creature of one historical period with its conditioned needs and sensibilities, we can learn something from those aspects of it that speak to the particular challenges of our own time. One of these is the rationale for cross-cultural communication and even intracultural civility. Without the assumption that some common understanding is possible between times, places, and perspectives we are locked into our respective "communities of interpretation"[6] with no hope of conceptual inter-

6. An incisive discussion of this dilemma appears in Anthony Thiselton's essay, "Reader-Response Hermeneutics, Action Models, and the Parables of Jesus," in *The Responsibility of Hermeneutics* by Roger Lundin, Anthony C. Thiselton, and Clarence Walhout (Grand Rapids: Eerdmans, 1985), 79-113. As an interpreter of Hans Georg Gadamer *(The Two Horizons* [Grand Rapids: Eerdmans, 1980], 344-51 and *passim),* Thiselton's comments on him in this later work touching the question of determinate meaning are interesting:

> A third model, put forward by Gadamer, is that in which the distinction between meaning and application disappears. But in spite of the enormous value of Gadamer's work, he can leave no room for hermeneutical norms of a kind which would help us to decide what might constitute *responsible* interpretation in any given case. By his own admission, his hermeneutics yields no more than a description of the interpretive process. (P. 110)

course, and finally into a hermeneutical solipsism. A radical perspectivalist view denies us access to ancient wisdom. Further, it justifies the existence of warring ideological camps who have no hope of getting out of their frameworks and into others through a

On radical reader response theory he adds, "Finally the reader-interpreted models of Rorty and Fish, while rightly rejecting a falsely optimistic textual objectivism, leave us in an entirely relativistic world where we can no more than live out our interpretive acts without even asking questions about validity, norms, or truth in any ultimately serious sense" (p. 110).

For Thiselton's comments on Hirsch see pp. 98, 110. His alternative to both highly subjective or simplistically objective views is that of an "action model." Thus

> the action model helps us to see in what sense recontextualization changes the meaning and in what sense it does not. For example, a statement that asserts a state of affairs retains the case at the time of the utterance. "Caesar crossed the Rubicon" and "Jesus was crucified under Pontius Pilate" do not change in meaning as acts of asserting a state of affairs whether or not they are subsequently recontextualized. Even the three parables of Luke 15, the lost sheep (vv. 1-7), the lost coin (vv. 8-10), and the lost son and the elder brother (vv. 11-32), serve in their Lukan context in effect to assert that God rejoices to welcome the sinner, and at the level of assertion this truth transcends subsequent recontextualization. Nevertheless within the pages of the New Testament the action of the parable of the lost sheep, already a defense against pharisaic criticism of grace (Luke 15:1-7), becomes recontextualized in Matthew as the verbal action of a pastoral charge to care for the weak and erring and "not to despise one of these little ones" (Matthew 18:10-14). The performative act of pastoral charge is derivative from, and congruent with, the actions of the Lukan context, but the recontextualization in Matthew provides a new and different action at a different level of function. Questions about hermeneutical "control" or criteria of congruency are more specific and tangible when applied to the functions of different sorts of acts than the vague and often circular questions about whether some "interpretation" is congruent with the text. (If we could know the answer to this, we should less readily need to raise the question in the first place.) The action model asks not whether *text* and *interpretation* are congruent, but whether the primary action and the truth-claims in which it is embedded have been reduced or changed in different contexts. (Pp. 110-11)

The action test in recontextualization is a helpful one. It does not appear to question the distinction between meaning and significance as we have here understood it. It presupposes a determinate meaning ("God rejoices to welcome the sinner, and at the level of assertion this truth transcends subsequent recontextualization"). Any purported statement of its significance in a new setting must reflect the action imperative implied in the original setting as that is appropriate to the new one. Robert Alter's brilliant analysis of the deconstructionist efforts to appropriate Midrash and the rabbinic tradition (as influenced by Jacques Derrida) parallels Thiselton's critique of reader-response theory. See Alter, "Old Rabbis, New Critics," *The New Republic,* Jan. 5 and 12, 1987, 27-33.

forum of common inquiry. The effect of this view on the social intercourse and civil exchange necessary for a pluralistic society could be profound. And a consistent radical perspectivalism disdainful of any commonsense discourse finally ends in the narcissism and individualism so rife in modern society. If all is incommunicable "interpretation," mine or yours, then "I'll do my thing and you do yours."[7]

Common sense, Scottish or otherwise, holds that intracommunity and interpersonal communication is possible because there is some common ground shareable in space and over time. Our perceptual apparatus is not so alienated from either the data or from one another that it precludes understanding. Thus my hope that this page communicates some of its intended sense is not a futile intellectual exercise. For Christian faith the warrants of this commonsense hope, and the reason for efforts in cross-cultural and cross-temporal understanding, lie in a doctrine of general or universal revelation. The image of God in us is not so delimited by historical finitude or damaged by sin that a common grace cannot facilitate common understandings. Put narratively, God gives us enough light on the path to the future that selves and societies can make their way forward. To be continued.

The common sense of Scripture is the aspect of a text's meaning that is accessible to committed and collegial readers or hearers capable of the rudiments of communication. These rudiments include the understanding of texts, read or heard, according to the elementary structures of grammar, the simplest rules of logic, the linguistic conventions of the receiving culture as it seeks to capture equivalences in the sending culture, and the place of the text in the circles of literary unity. Thus the requirements for understanding the textual meanings of Scripture are the same as those for understanding the words on this page, or for that matter any page from the daily newspaper to other literary documents. Assertions found in these settings become intelligible to the reader or hearer by knowing the meaning of the words used according to the language in which it is articulated, the conventions employed for ascribing meaning to the configuration of sounds that constitute that language, the rules of grammar applicable to the same, and the laws of logic that govern intelligible communication. Understanding also

7. For a study and critique of these tendencies in American society see Robert Bellah et al., *Habits of the Heart: Individualism and Commitment in American Life* (Berkeley and Los Angeles: Univ. of California Press, 1985).

requires the principle of literary contextuality: a word's meaning is related to its usage in a sentence, a sentence in a paragraph, a paragraph in the next larger unit of meaning, and so on to the outer boundaries of the literature involved.

To the extent that the genre requires and the literary unit gives knowledge of the historical circumstance of the text, then the who, what, where, and why of the text enters significantly into the determining of plain meaning. For the *critical* sense about which we shall presently speak, accessible only to those with special expertise, information about the historical context is sought from sources outside the text or its literary context. But we are not yet talking about critical meaning here and therefore historical information is germane to common sense to the extent that it is available in the writing in question.

The availability of Scripture to "ordinary people," and therefore its plain meaning, is a fundamental Reformation belief. It is the priesthood of all believers applied to matters of epistemology as well as soteriology. This equality of access to the knowledge of God among the people has been understood and expressed variously as the perspicuity of Scripture, the *sensus literalis,* plain meaning, natural meaning, or the commonsense reading of the text. In most Reformation usage, and here also, plain meaning is for "the priesthood," the whole of the believing community. The illumination that makes the Bible readable is a gift of the Holy Spirit given within the Body of Christ. While the common sense of Scripture depends on methods of investigation common to the grasp of any written material, we cannot divorce it from the common life of the community whose Book it is. This ecclesial concept of common sense is based on the doctrine of revelation to be developed, one in which the "noetic" and "fiducial" work of the Holy Spirit makes possible both the understanding of Scripture and the conviction of its truth.[8]

The natural sense of the text has been buffeted by modern hermeneutical winds, being either radically reinterpreted or disdainfully dismissed. Some consider plain meaning the special province of the critical scholar. Finding out "what it meant" in an ancient historical context is the task of discovering the "literal sense" of a

8. It also presupposes a doctrine of revelation in which accessibility to the original inspiration is assured by the Spirit in the transmission of the text. We will address these connections in Volume 3 of this series.

text.[9] Others believe the contextuality of both the text and the interpreter render the hermeneutical gap unbridgeable, making foolhardy any claim to the discernment of a transferable plain meaning. Others change the textual expectation from meaning to "meaningfulness," treating the text as affectively disclosive or evocative rather than objectively true or false, and thus patient of infinite interpretations. Meanwhile traditionalist defenders of the literal sense hold it to be recoverable as the designated author's own intention, the sum and substance of the text's meaning as well as its significance.

The view set forth here differs from all of the above. It respects the historical consciousness of modernity that necessitates the historical study of texts and requires a self-critical understanding of the receptor's contextualized appropriation process. But it also seeks to honor the transcultural concerns of traditional hermeneutics. The latter comes to the fore in the recognition of a common sense in a biblical text, a sense common to both the creator and the receiver and, as such, available to the ordinary people of God in any and every time and place.

As we have noted, a commonsense understanding of a biblical text today cannot be a repristination of an earlier formulation of it. God's narrative moves on. Important learnings in the sociology of knowledge, cultural anthropology, biblical studies, and in the larger life of the church require the rethinking of plain meaning when that journey forward is honored. Among them are the critical disciplines that have developed since the Enlightenment and the ecumenical momentum that opens us to insights beyond both our ecclesial parochialisms and our individualisms. How can a commonsense approach to the text be reconceived with this partnership of traditional and contemporary elements?

From the tradition we continue the following assumptions: (1) No elite group takes the text out of the hands of the faithful. The Bible is the "church's book" in this wide-ranging sense, belonging to the *laos,* the whole people of God. This belief in the ministry of the laity—the epistemological ministry, in this case—is not only as important today as it was in the effort to recover it in the sixteenth century but more so, given the renewal of attention to the dignity

9. E.g., Raymond Brown, *The Critical Meaning of the Bible* (New York: Paulist Press, 1981), 29-30, and also his *Biblical Exegesis and Church Doctrine* (New York: Paulist Press, 1985), 10-25.

and gifts of the whole people of God.[10] (2) The transcultural aspect of biblical truth is basic to the Scripture's meaning. The Bible as the Word of God can speak to any time and place. The truth, while not reducible to its conformity to objective referents, does not exclude it, and therefore has a "propositional" aspect, or, more exactly, "affirmational." (3) Textual meaning is accessible to ordinary people through the methods of communication common to their day-to-day life: understanding of words according to cultural conventions, observance of logic, as in the principle of noncontradiction, and employment of literary contextuality. (4) The rudimentary rules of communication through texts and across personal and social boundaries are based on that measure of commonality in human perceivers and that measure of trustworthiness in the results of perception that warrant the effort in intelligible cross-cultural and personal intracultural communication. A doctrine of general revelation undergirds this assumption.

The absence of historical consciousness and the presence of an individualistic worldview, and the negligence of "involvement" as it is understood in Reformation and subsequent participatory movements require revisions of inherited notions of commonsense meaning. We have already mentioned some of these, but will sort them out more carefully here.

1. The common sense of Scripture is discernible through the eyes of the people, the people of God. The sight belongs to the Body of Christ. The careful scrutiny of a text in its literary context by observing the standards of intelligible discourse and the rules of logic constitutes the ground rules for any kind of responsible inquiry, common or critical. Yet the spaces open in Scripture for alternative readings and the character of Scripture as a document of ultimate concern mean that one's interpretive horizon will significantly influence what is discerned. As the Scripture of the church, the Bible is rightly interpreted from within the stream of this community's life. This assertion of hermeneutical method is grounded in a doctrine of revelation, specifically the teaching concerning the gift of illumination given to the church by the Spirit.

10. Representing the explosion of literature in the 1980s seeking to recover the ministry of the laity are George Peck and John Hoffman, eds., *The Laity in Ministry* (Philadelphia: Judson Press, 1984). See also *The COCU Consensus*, ed. Gerald F. Moede (Princeton: Consultation on Church Union, 1985), 40-45 and *Baptism, Eucharist and Ministry*, Faith and Order Paper no. 111 (Geneva: World Council of Churches, 1982), 20-24.

2. The common sense of Scripture is discernible through the eyes of committed persons in the people of God. The personal engagement "in fear and trembling" with the Scripture is a spiritual posture commensurate with a text of ultimate concern. As the Word comes to us in passion and personal claim, so we orient ourselves in like manner to its medium (1 Cor. 2:10). But piety is no substitute for the hard work of careful study. That investigation is the necessary *but not sufficient* entry to the common sense of the text. This assertion is also grounded in the doctrine of revelation, the illumination of persons through the internal work of the Spirit.

3. The common sense of Scripture is discernible through the eyes of the *whole* people of God. We are to conceive "perspicuity" corporately rather than individualistically. Common sense is commonality of sense. It requires a variety of perspectives. An individual reading of a text is a partial reading, limited by the angle of vision and affected by factors of self-interest. This given of historicity, however, is not the final fate of the perceiver, a captivity from which there is no hope of escape. Partial perspectives are teachable. That pedagogy is done in and by the Christian community. It entails the catholicity of which we have spoken, the exposure to the variety of perspectival gifts within the Body of Christ. The common sense is a collegial sense. Here again is a revelatory assumption, related on the one hand to the doctrines of creation and fall and on the other to the noetic work of the Spirit in the church.

4. The common sense of Scripture is discernible to the extent that the whole people of God offer their gifts with the commitment appropriate to them. The passion of our second point here joins the participatory motif of the third. What is there in the text to be seen by the community is accessible to the degree that there is solidarity with the moil and toil, and the joys and satisfactions, of the social locus in which a gift of discernment is given. Those who are excluded must help those who are not to see the Word of inclusion; those who suffer the ravages of war must help those who cannot see the gospel of peace; those who have struggled with sin must help those resting comfortably in their righteousness who cannot hear the Good News of forgiveness; those who are powerless and oppressed by the tyrant must help to open the eyes of the indifferent, the accomplice, and the powerful to the fact and ravages of oppression.

5. The advocates of the common sense of Scripture must have enough common sense to recognize the limits of common sense. While the *esse* of textual meaning is open to the people of God in

the ways described, there is a *bene esse* possible through the textual specialist's instruments of inquiry. Thus the sharpening of the tools of investigation is done by the critical scholar. This capacity for discernment is also a gift given to the Body of Christ.

As we have indicated, a doctrine of revelation underlies these various assertions. More attention will be given to it in Volume 3 of *The Christian Story*. Here we quickly sketch overall features to which passing allusion has been made. A process of universal revelation makes possible sufficient commonality across time and place to render transcultural communication possible. Our common image of God that constitutes us as human is not so shattered by sin or delimited by finitude that we are closed in upon ourselves and incapable of cross-temporal and cross-spatial understanding. Intellectual inquiry that rises out of one historical setting to discover the setting of another time and place achieves enough measure of objectivity to enable the study of a text. Thus a grace common (but Christic) in creation makes the being and well-being of the literal sense possible through the commonalities assumed by both ordinary communication and the extraordinary ventures of the scholar.

The conjunction of the fact of creation with the fact of the fall is another revelatory premise that gives further endorsement to both the ordinary and extraordinary reaches for plain meaning. That is, both finitude and sin make for the tendency of particular construals of textual meaning to claim too much for themselves. The partiality of perspective and its will-to-power over others require both the check of other viewpoints on the latter and a balance of the former. Just as the earlier-mentioned grace in creation and this latter realism about human nature makes political democracy both possible and necessary,[11] so the task of discerning a biblical text's plain meaning requires the gifts of all of the people. The discovery of the natural meaning of the text requires the maximum participation of the community of faith to draw out the commonality of its sense. As finitude and sin persist to the end, total lucidity awaits the eschaton. Until then the common sense of a text is a common journey with it.

The grace common to creation, and the fall that militates against it, reappears in the life of the Christian community as sanctifying grace. In the work of sanctifying a people—setting them apart as

11. Reinhold Niebuhr, *The Children of Light and the Children of Darkness* (New York: Scribner's, 1944).

those who witness to the special revelation in Jesus Christ—the Spirit's gift of discernment is given. Thus as the charter of the community is the result of prophetic-apostolic *inspiration,* so its interpretation is made possible through the grace of *illumination.*[12] This light is given to those personally engaged with the text, publicly involved in the life of the people of God, and in solidarity with the experiential matrix in which they find themselves or to which they are called. Coming in this pneumatic flow within the committed community, the Bible is the church's book, and the community is its proper interpreter. But the community in its *wholeness* is that interpreter. Sanctifying grace comes through the distribution of the gifts throughout the community. Further, the sin of *hauteur* continues to do its work even within a people set apart. Paul's discourse on the manifoldness of the gifts, and the tendency of each to claim too much for itself, provides an enduring insight into the

12. To anticipate the theses to be developed in Volume 3 around the three revelatory themes of impartation, inspiration, and illumination: (1) a common-sense view of Scripture, in its largest sense, asserts the communicability of textual meaning over time and place. While contested by various epistemological relativisms, the exponents of the same when communicating to "the public," that is, those beyond their own social location or community of epistemological privilege, regularly violate their contentions, assuming that outside readers can understand their statements. The belief that Scripture as a text from another culture can be understood in our own time and place shares in this assumption. As such, a doctrine of general revelation is presupposed. We shall identify the gift given therein as the grace of "impartation." (2) While such impartation establishes the possibility of cross-cultural communication through Scripture, yet other work of the Holy Spirit assures its reality. Thus the grace of "inspiration" gives the prophetic-apostolic witness within Scripture its perduring status. The affirmations and images of the canonical text, while culture-grounded, are not culture-captive, and therefore free to carry their intended meaning over time and place. We are speaking of the "need to know" assertions in the biblical story line, the gospel. (3) The receivability by the reader and interpreter of the prophetic-apostolic witness in any and every place is aided by the Holy Spirit's work of "illumination." Illumination is the gift of preservation of the Authorial intention of the substance of faith, the gospel, in both transmission and reception. Illumination, we here argue, happens in a catholic mode. In transmission that means "authoritative" editions of the Scripture, ones that reflect the catholicity of the church. In reception that means interpretations that reflect the widest possible conversation in the Christian community. (4) Given the finitude and sin that persist to the conclusion of the Christian Story, the grace of illumination gives "insight" into Authorial intention, not the final eschatological "sight." As such, transmission and interpretation are always subject to correction. But as narrative moving toward resolution under the grace of preservation, insight is trustworthy, as a trajectory on course, although not at end.

relation of the parts to the whole within the body of Christ (1 Cor. 12–13). The correction of imperial construals of a text and the enlargement of delimited individual interpretations come through the inclusivity of the gift of discernment.

The common sense of the text is the beginning point in a journey of meaning. It tells us *what it says.* It gets the whole people of God "aboard." It provides the raw materials for textual meaning discerning the text's *esse.* But the continuation of a hermeneutical pilgrimage entails other steps to be taken. The next one is the quest for the *critical sense.*

Critical Sense

The critical sense of the text includes a move *behind* the world of the text, a reach into regions that are not accessible to those untrained in the skills needed for such travel. Here the biblical scholar goes with a knowledge of its complex trails and with the equipment necessary to negotiate them.

Long before the appearance of modern critical methods for the penetration of this difficult terrain, a scholarly tradition among plain meaning advocates saw the importance of proficiency in the original languages, the value of word studies, knowledge of the customs and history of scriptural locale, and the accuracy of textual transmission and translation. Conservative interpreters still stress these things.[13] Heavy emphasis is placed upon the knowledge of the original language by pastors in their exegetical preaching and in the leadership of Bible study groups. Familiarity with the history, customs, and geography of "Bible lands" is urged upon the laity. So that they might better understand the background of Scripture this information is made available to them through Bible encyclopedias, handbooks, dictionaries, concordances, and other helps. To the extent that scrutiny by learned methods occurs even in traditionalist readings, criticism has joined common sense as a mode of expounding Scripture. Often it is even given the prerogative of passing judgment on the deliverances of common sense as they are available to uneducated laity. These tools are advocated, for example, by conservative scholars who practice or rely upon "lower criticism" or textual criticism, the search for a manuscript reading that approaches the purity of the inerrant autographs. Some conservative scholars so stress these resources for preachers that one

13. Ramm, *Protestant Biblical Interpretation,* 14-22.

can easily conclude that they alone can unlock the secrets of Scripture.

While the distinction between "lower" and "higher" criticism is not used much any longer, it does suggest a transition from the exacting scholarly work of the foregoing (and not only that of textual criticism) to the kind of critical inquiry felt by many conservative interpreters to undercut biblical authority. The variety of critical disciplines involved and the fluidity of the meaning in terms employed for it makes it very difficult to find a modern equivalent for the "higher" category. Friend and foe alike sometimes describe it as the "historical-critical method." But this does not do sufficient justice to the literary-critical features of the *hard* or the "higher" criticism we now speak of, as distinct from the *soft* criticism of the "lower." Further, it is so closely associated historically with an antitheological bias, including in some cases rejection in principle of divine agency, that it would seem to militate as a discipline against the enterprise and the premises of many of those who employ it. "Historical criticism" is a more modest term, but this refers to a subset of the overall discipline we are describing, ranged alongside of or including literary criticism but adding as well tradition, redaction, textual, grammatical, and canon criticism.[14]

What characterizes various expressions of the hard or higher criticism (primarily historical, literary, tradition, form, redaction, and canon in the former listing) is the inquiry made into the "world in back of the text," using methods common to investigation of other texts and data derived from other disciplines. In this pursuit the Bible is treated as any other writing in the reach behind the "front" of it—the "common (sense) front"[15]—to understand it better. That reach can go two ways, "before" and "below," depending on whether one views the text horizontally or vertically. In the former case, a diachronic study searches out the prehistory of the text. Who was its author or were the authors and/or editor or editors, what was the circumstance of its writing, who was its original audience or were its audiences along the path of its oral and written trajectory, what were their circumstances, and how did these factors shape the form in which it appeared? The information gained thereby sheds historical light on the text in the search for

14. A description of each of these is found in Hayes and Holladay, *Biblical Exegesis,* 30-103.

15. Cf. "in front of the text" in David Tracy, *The Analogical Imagination: Christian Theology and the Culture of Pluralism* (New York: Crossroad, 1981), 122-24.

what it meant. In the latter case, a synchronic investigation studies the world underneath the text, that is, the text as a literary entity in its own right or with its own foundation, searching for its patterns and dynamics, indeed probing for its "deep structures." The knowledge gained from these inquiries helps the reader to a better literary understanding of the text or *how it works.* Thus with the new set of metaphors, used in one way or another in the scholarship so identified—back-front, length-depth—a more fully developed complex of inquiries carries forward what used to be called higher criticism. We shall here call the overall phenomenon with its distinguishable but conjoined diachronic and synchronic features "historical-literary criticism."

The search for the world in back of the text, especially its prehistory, began in earnest in the West during the Enlightenment, traced variously to the work of Semler or in anticipatory form in Spinoza.[16] Associated with the stress upon "reason," especially as it sought to contest "dogma," the study of the Bible became increasingly the quest for the natural explanation of the text, how it functions as a human document. Thus scholars rejected efforts to harmonize, explain away, or allegorize the apparent contradictions or inaccuracies in the interests of the perfection considered necessary to an inspired work. To err is human. Again, just as other documents are illumined by knowledge of their backgrounds in authorship, circumstance, and audience, so too Scripture is best seen in its natural setting, and as the forces that played upon its origins are explored. In the most drastic move to render the Bible one with its natural circumstances and human peers, the "principle of analogy" was called into play. On its basis, no explanation of an event is acceptable that does not conform to our contemporary experience. Maximally, it disallows the introduction of any divine agency in the description of events, even though that agency may work within the causal nexus.

We find a place in this theory of biblical interpretation for a historical-literary approach in the "critical sense" of the text. Its use, freed from ideological accompaniments, contributes to the *well*-being of the understanding of the text. Freedom means a refusal to abandon reference to God's action in, with, and under the phe-

16. See John Bowden, "Biblical Criticism," *Westminster Dictionary of Christian Theology,* ed. Alan Richardson and John Bowden (Philadelphia: Westminster Press, 1983), 65-69. For a traditional reading of it see Milton S. Terry, *Biblical Hermeneutics* (New York: Phillip & Hall, 1883), 707-12, 714.

nomena discerned by critical instruments. Providence works through processes of nature and history, the Holy Spirit through the literary patterns and dimensions of texts and their reception, and the eternal Word incarnate in the human being and doing of Jesus of Nazareth. Denial of these things comes from a secular worldview not integral to critical inquiry but affixing itself to it.

Freedom from ideology also means that a *closed* system of causality is not a necessary assumption of critical inquiry. From within its own premise of empirical investigation, no claim of divine action within the causal sequence, as in the miraculous, can, in principle, be excluded. What another generation declared to be "natural laws" that deny the possibility of biblical miracles, a chastened scientific method now more modestly calls the probabilities of nature, "statistical regularities" rather than ironclad rules, regularities subject to an altered reading if the evidence warrants it. To this more restrained empiricism from within the field of scientific inquiry comes a wider historical judgment that contemporaneity tends regularly to declare itself definitive of reality, a judgment that subsequent experience consistently rebuts. Historical wisdom learns to appreciate over time the sometimes superior insight of the past and is trained as well to be skeptical of the "tyranny of the present." Thus the principle of analogy that requires the reports of another era to be obedient to contemporary experience, especially when it carries with it a discredited positivism, is not necessary to the wise use of critical method.

In the space granted for the freedom of the past by the modesties of empirical method, Christian faith discerns the deeds of God that Scripture records and interprets. Yet it is just here that the issue of faith and reason is joined, and the boundaries for the latter are so often set by the former. When the principle of analogy is construed as an absolute and as the standard of scientific inquiry, universal human experience moves to the position of final authority. Yet it is precisely this experience, distorted by sin, that has put the Christian narrative on its course. The deeds of God are done to disclose things no longer accessible to experience as such, and to deliver it from the consequences of its alienated state. Related as these disclosures and deliverances are to the testimony of Scripture, critical scholarship, even in its modest employment relatively free of ideology, standing alone, is an expression of trust in reason as the way to reality and therefore cannot be given the final word. It makes its contribution to a process but does not exercise hegemony over it.

A factor that makes for the relativizing of historical-literary criticism is the insight of yet another critical perspective, a sociological and political "critical consciousness." In this form of criticism a hermeneutics of suspicion ferrets out the vested interests that are at work in the compiling and reception of sacred Scriptures, especially as they are concealed by pietisms and moralisms. This kind of critical awareness challenges a too-simple commonsense reading of texts. But the force of its argument is brought to bear on the "assured results of historical criticism" as well. Here it discovers the limited perspective and power agendas that operate in the search for what are presumed to be objective data.

With lines from Feuerbach, Marx, Nietzsche, and Freud, developed and modified by Third World, black, feminist, and other liberation theologies, and also pluralist theologies, texts and their receptors are confronted with questions of self-interest. Does Israel's declaration of its divine election and its consequent claims to the Promised Land hide a raw political imperialism that justifies acts of violence against inhabitants who stand in their way? Does the sense of inferiority of an emerging Christian community in a hostile majority society put in its mouth inordinate and even preposterous claims to the singularity and superiority of its message and its Savior? Do the limitations and prejudices of male biblical writers assure the diminishment of women and therefore the invisibility of this gender in its teaching and corporate life? Do the class interests of both the writers of Scripture and the leaders of its community obscure the justice issues and weaken or eliminate concern for the underclass? Is the Caucasian imprint so deeply on Scripture that other races cannot recognize themselves in it? Is Scripture so wed to its Hebrew context that equivalent values in other cultures and religions are obscured and denied? All these questions put to the text are also asked of its investigators and interpreters, whoever they may be, traditionalist defenders of the common sense of Scripture looking for "what it says," or scholars who offer a critical path to "what it meant" or "how it works." In contrast to all these, a critical consciousness looks for *whose it is.*

As a community of scholarly criticism represents sharpening of the tools of reason, so the *communities of critical consciousness* are associated with the honing of conscience and the raised awareness of those who personally experience the oppressive use of Scripture. The poor, the victimized, the colonized who know oppression firsthand are positioned to ask these kinds of painful questions. Thus the "doing" and "feeling" aspects of human experience as well as its thinking feature take a radically critical form at this point in the internal hermeneutical process.

The warrants for the critical modes and mentality lie in the Christian narrative of creation and fall, and thus in a doctrine of revelation. In passing we note some of its features as it touches the issues of "reason and revelation," a subject to be addressed at length in the volume to follow. The image of God given to humanity in creation is broken but not destroyed by the fall. A common grace sustains it so that the story may proceed apace with humanity furnished enough light to see the path ahead and make its way upon it. The humanity of Scripture is a proper object of scrutiny by the dimmed but sustained light of reason. As Christ the eternal Logos of God is the source of both the light revealed in Scripture and the light in creation, their interrelationship is not out of order. As Christ is our Judge as well as our Advocate, the critical function is also fitting. This is especially true because our capacity for self-deception is infinite. We need all the help we can get for *self*-criticism.

The central chapter of the Story, as well as that of creation and fall, gives us perspective on the relation of reason to the charter of faith. The Easter victory of the incarnate Logos assures us that this good Word from God is not so frail that it must be protected by us from the sound criticisms of reason. To find frailties—scientific, historical, moral, and theological—in the human organ of the Word cannot injure either the organ or the Word. These flaws include the mixed motives and imbalanced modalities of sex, race, ethnicity, age, class, and condition. "God *chose* the weak things of the world . . ." (1 Cor. 1:27, NIV). The way of this narrative is the work of God through the vulnerabilities of human history. To face these vulnerabilities is not to refute the Story but to honor its historical reality. Reason is the gift given for this scrutiny. Herein is the friendship of the Word in creation with the Word incarnate.

Because the critical tools and consciousness are shaped by a reason that is in the last analysis itself in the domain of the fall, the final Critic and Judge must be the Word made flesh, risen in his glorified humanity and speaking not from but into a rebel world. This Word utters the gospel by the power of the Holy Spirit in the events of election and incarnation and in the inspired prophetic and apostolic testimony to and around them, a Word received in the illumination given to us through the whole Christian community, by the power of the Holy Spirit.

Thus there is a "strangership" as well as a friendship. The Word in the world speaks, but through a distorting medium. When reason seeks to speak in its own right of ultimate matters, its reach exceeds its grasp, crippled as it is by the fall. The Word of Scripture tells us things that the wisdom of the world cannot know. In this realm "reason [is] within the bounds of religion."[17] "Criticism" that purports to be the source of ultimate truth is yet one more example of the imperial will at work in a fallen world.

Criticism of Scripture that rises out of the Christian community, working within its narrative, taking up responsibility within its life, is of special value in strengthening the Body of Christ's vitality. As a member of the household of faith the critic is a "critic-in-residence."[18] When the church at large graciously receives the critic's irritating judgments it learns lessons that enrich its own life. When it is intolerant of such criticism, and the critic in turn reacts in a self-righteous and finally sectarian fashion, the ways part—to the injury of all parties. Biblical critics-in-residence should be a valued part of the catholicity of the church's encounter with the Bible, contributing their special gifts of *bene esse,* the critical sense of the scriptural text.

Canonical Sense

The canonical reading of the text places it in the environment of the Bible as a whole, the Christian canon, relating it to other texts throughout Scripture that bear upon it and to its Christological center and gospel substance. The position taken here is shaped by various strands: The traditional hermeneutical principle of "Scripture is its own best interpreter," including its accent on "the analogy of faith"—the clarification of obscure passages by clear ones; the "canonical approach"—earlier described; the "theological exegesis" that has stressed the Christological center of Scripture and/or the trinitarian and covenantal narrative that runs through it.

The three moves made in canonical investigation—the relation of a text to material germane to it in the whole canon, to the gospel

17. See the important work of Nicholas Wolterstorff, *Reason within the Bounds of Religion* (Grand Rapids: Eerdmans, 1984). Wolterstorff argues that the Christian scholar must be conscious of and employ "control beliefs" in the conversation with the academy.

18. The phrase is that of Donald Michael, "Twentieth Century Institutions: Prerequisites for a Creative and Responsible Society," in *Human Values and Advancing Technology,* comp. Cameron P. Hall (New York: Friendship Press, 1969), 103-4.

as the Christian narrative substance, and to Christ as its Center—are relative to the raw materials of textual meaning and its refinement, and therefore assume the common and critical senses. The canonical sense is the capstone of the hermeneutics of meaning. However, canonical factors are already at work implicitly in the common and critical ventures themselves, as theological cum ecclesial preunderstandings run deep in any approach to Scripture. But they are brought self-consciously to the fore in the canonical sense, and applied with rigor. Insofar as the effort is successful, the *plene esse* of textual meaning is the result.

"Full being," like its companions "being" and "well-being," are of course relative, since disclosure short of the reign of God is always "through a mirror dimly." Therefore the *esse* is composed of raw materials of greater or lesser extent, the *bene esse* is not well but "weller," and the full in fact at best is only "fuller." The canonical full/fuller orders the refined materials so that they are serviceable for the church's sound teaching. Its goal is to interpret the text in conformity with the Author's intended meaning.

The canonical cum common and critical sense is the *truth* of the text as well as its culminating meaning. As such it is the *vere esse* as well as the *plene esse.* The meaning is what the Author intends us to believe. The meaning and truth of the text so perceived persists over time. It is, therefore, as *truth for all,* the point of adjudication of the "significances" of the text that vary according to personal and social context—the *truth for me* and the *truth for us.* Such a persistence through the varying contexts does not preclude, however, the development of meaning along the established trajectory, extending it according to the contextual enrichments that are possible along the way. We shall return to these themes at the close of our canonical discussion and again in our contextual inquiry.

The process of canonical interpretation as the search for the full meaning takes *what it says* (common sense), *what it meant* (critical sense—historical), *whose it is* (critical sense—critical consciousness), *how it works* (critical sense—literary sense) and joins it to *what it meant to mean* (canonical sense) in a pilgrimage toward *what it means.*

Once again the Christian community plays a crucial role in the search for textual meaning. In the quest for the canonical sense, "theological exegesis" through the light cast by the great theologians of the church (Origen, Augustine, Calvin, Luther, Barth), often dismissed as "precritical," has a place alongside the technical commentaries that illuminate the text critically. So, too, familiarity with the doctrinal distinctives of the church is important exegetically. And the contemporary debates about the substance of faith and its center are germane as well. Hence the longitudinal and latitudinal aspects of the community enter the picture. Here the pastor plays an important role in bringing training and familiarity with this lore to the congregation. The creedal and confessional tradition of a congregation also makes its contribution. The inherited formulations of substance and center brought to bear by pastoral custodianship and general catechesis, significant as they are to the canonical task, are always held in creative tension with the phenomenon of Scripture itself.

As mentioned earlier, our references to Scripture, Bible, and now "canon" are to be construed ecumenically. There is a catholic agreement on a Christian corpus, thirty-nine books in the Old Testament and twenty-seven in the New. The apocrypha is still in dispute, accepted by one sector of the church but not another, although increasingly recognized as "edifying" where not authoritative. Canon also means the *Christian canon.* The Hebrew Scriptures and the New Testament are not entities apart. We follow here Childs's important observation that the Old Testament has an integrity of its own and should not be swallowed up by a Christian hermeneutics that dissolves that integrity, but rather is to be affirmed in its own right. The warrant for this is the separate identity given to it by the Christian canon itself.[19] However, it cannot help being read by the Christian interpreter in any other way than in accordance with Christian vision formed in that community and by that commitment. That total canonical framework must be honestly identified as such. The use of the term "Old Testament" for the Hebrew Scriptures is a historic sign of this recognition and merits retention. The New Testament also has its own identity. Yet it cannot and should not be understood in any other way than as shaped by, and requiring for its interpretation, the Old Testament horizon, and has been so placed by canonical decision. A canonical interpretation, therefore, is a text read for its full meaning in light of the Christian community's chosen setting for it in the Old and New Testaments, and with the help of canonical themes therein.

Since the canonical framework is determinative of a final judgment on textual meaning and truth, we shall devote a longer section to its exposition, giving particular attention to the substance

19. Brevard Childs, *Old Testament Theology and Canonical Context* (Philadelphia: Fortress Press, 1985), 7-19.

and center of the canonical circle, formative as they are for canonical meaning and for the larger theological task. This will take us into the subject of interrelationships of the three major elements of authority—Bible, church, and world. The church plays an important part in the interpretation of all the elements of the canonical sense. And the world, in turn, shapes the church's perception.

Gospel: The Substance

The Good News of God is the message of the Bible. It threads its way through the canon from beginning to end. From the Genesis accounts of creation to the closing chapter of Revelation, this book tells of the good will and way of God, creating, redeeming, sanctifying. The gospel is the Evangel of God's purposes enacted and fulfilled. It takes us from its origins in the Godhead through creation, fall, and covenant to the consummation of the divine hope. Christians know that the news of what transpires is good because the story turns on a liberating and reconciling event. In it the foes of the divine purpose meet their match in the life, death, and resurrection of Jesus Christ. The Scripture exists to bear witness to the unfolding drama, being inspired of God in order to teach us this gospel (2 Tim. 3:16). As such, it functions in the way its Author intended when it opens this vista before us, visible by the light of resurrection morning. The canonical sense of a text, therefore, is the way in which it works to proclaim the gospel according to the standard established by Christ. A text is theologically disclosive when it articulates the gospel of Jesus Christ.

By interpreting the gospel as the Great Narrative we take our canonical framework seriously and also express the inclusive theme that marks this systematics. Canonical and holistic intention takes the various "gospel" interpretations in the New Testament and places them in an encompassing framework. Thus the announcement of the Good News of the coming kingdom in Jesus' preaching (Mark 1:14; Luke 17–21), the declaration of the risen Christ, and the message of his saving work as the gospel (Rom. 3:21-26; Gal. 3:10-14) by the apostles, the Good News of the earliest kerygma in its various forms (Acts 2:32-36)—all are included in the canonical story. The history of Christian theology might well be written by the accent given to one or another of these usages, and the content poured into them: the gospel as proclamation of the kingdom, as the incarnation of the Word, as the reconciliation wrought by Jesus on the cross, as the Good News of Christ's Easter victory over evil and death, as justification of the sinner, as liberation of the poor and oppressed. Here we strive to honor each to the extent that it can be justified from the canonical text or by inference from it, refusing to reduce the gospel to one of its textualizations or contextualizations, and attempting to interrelate them by way of their narrative flow. The full Evangel is the whole story.

The understanding of the evangelical heart of Scripture as the Great Narrative, therefore, stands in dialectical relation to a familiar delimitation of it to Christ's redemptive work. Within that central act there is no news that is not decisively good, hence its association in both Scripture and tradition. Yes, the work of Christ, indeed, "Christ," is the gospel. As the hymn writer puts it, the story is "of Jesus and his love."[20] Yet the Bible is the full canon, not only the four Gospels, including therein the fore and aft of the center that makes for the full narrative. As another hymn writer suggests, "the story we have to tell to the nations" is of epic and even cosmic proportions. In it "the darkness shall turn to the dawning, and the dawning to noonday bright, when Christ's great Kingdom shall come on earth, the Kingdom of love and light."[21]

Consonant with the fullness of the story we do not confine the gospel deeds of God only to the particularities of deliverance, as in conventional "holy history" viewpoints. Its critics rightly complain that important sections of the Old Testament, such as Proverbs, Job, and the Psalms,[22] are not covered by the narrowed trail of *heilsgeschichte.* These omissions are made only if the history of God's acts excludes creation, and with it the universal ("general") revelation of the kind implicit in the patterns of truth manifest in the wisdom literature, in the piety of Psalms, and in the problem of Job. The Good News of God's gracious working includes scattering the seeds of light that shine even in the universal night of the fall. These seeds are the gifts to all of intimations of the same Word that became incarnate. So the story has it in the Johannine prologue (John 1:1-14), one of the places where this larger Evangel is identified.

As an evangelical principle of interpretation, the gospel story has New Testament origins. The whole is viewed from the point of turning in the narrative. The sweep of the story is seen in the earliest proclamation of the Christian community, the *kerygma.*

20. Katherine Hankey, "I Love to Tell the Story."

21. Colin Sterne, "We've a Story to Tell to the Nations."

22. Oscar Cullmann, *The Christology of the New Testament,* trans. Shirley C. Guthrie and Charles A. M. Hall (Philadelphia: Westminster Press, 1959), 195-237.

"Jesus is Lord!" is its confessional core.[23] But its understanding comes only when answers to these questions are given: Over what? From what? To what? They are to be found in the earliest kerygma: *over* the foes of God—sin, evil and death; *from* out of the divine purpose that engages our resistance, in a special journey with Israel; *through* suffering to victory at the center of the story; then *to* a birthing by the Spirit of a new community and a call *into* it; on *toward* the consummation of the purpose of creation in the reconciling of all things. So it is in the Petrine account in and after Pentecost (Acts 2:14-40; 3:12-26). This is also true in the variety of places in the New Testament in which the highlights of the story are mentioned according to a particular organizing motif, as in Paul's reference to the first and second Adam (1 Cor. 15:45).

The sequencing of the books of the New Testament by a canonical hand makes its contribution to the total gospel narrative, continuing the story developing in the Old Testament canon. The creation, fall, and covenant in that stretch of the drama are continued in the New Testament with the Good News of Jesus, its sequel in the church's beginnings in the historical Book of Acts, the witness to the justifying and sanctifying grace at work in the lives and communities of believers and beyond recounted in the Epistles, and finally the Revelation of the end in which the purposes of creation are fulfilled. The story is in the *ordering* as well as in the *telling.*

Before long the narrative of Christian identity moved out of the texts developing into the canon and into the "rules" of faith. Why such *regulae* for the churches of Rome, Corinth, Antioch, and elsewhere? For one, new members of the Body of Christ had to be trained in Christian identity. Hence the baptismal confessions, terse statements of the heart of the matter. For another, it was necessary to clarify distinctions between Christian profession of faith and alternative worldviews, especially when the concurrent religions and philosophies began to make inroads into the understanding of Christian identity. Thus the intellectual work of the patristic defenders of the faith, which relied heavily on the rule of faith for defining the Christian community vis-à-vis alternative worldviews. As these formulations in each regional Christian community had to show their connection with Christian origins, like the approved

23. J. N. D. Kelly, *Early Christian Doctrines* (New York: Harper & Brothers, 1958), 37-40, 88-90; Jaroslav Pelikan, *The Christian Tradition,* vol. 1 (Chicago: Univ. of Chicago Press, 1971), 117-20, 150-51.

books of the Christian canon, a rule had to be "apostolic." While claims of apostolic authorship are unfounded, the intent to establish them as such was to show how they did contain definitive apostolic teaching. As they outline the narrative of the apostolic community, they do have these credentials. Thus the Roman rule that became the core of a more universal confession of faith can claim title to being the germ of "the Apostles' Creed."[24]

In the creed are the lineaments of the Story: creation, Christ, church, salvation, consummation. Its threefold division embodies the very nature of God, an economic Trinity whose outworking of God the Creator, Redeemer, and Sanctifier reflects the inner-trinitarian being of Father, Son, and Holy Spirit. Indeed, the doctrine of the Trinity developed concurrently with the formulation of the apostolic rule, both giving further force to the narrative identity of Christian belief.

The deficiencies of the creed remind us that we have moved from the source to the resource level of authority, as these bear on questions of canonical intention. By citing the early rules and patristic writers in the refinement of our understanding of the gospel, we see again in this key hermeneutical principle the role played by the church. As "tradition" it is a guide, the resource in grasping the truth of the scriptural source, a help to finding our way into the heart of the matter. But the creed is the fruit of "illumination" and not "inspiration." As such it is incomplete and subject to correction. Its lack of attention to the life and ministry of Christ has often been noted.[25] Also missing entirely is the place given to Israel in the biblical account, to which two-thirds of the Christian canon is devoted. No doubt the separation trauma of the new people from the old contributed to this absence. Thus contextuality leaves its mark in the finitude of church teaching. Its influence, which continues in the Nicene Creed and much subsequent ordering of Christian teaching, has affected relationships with Judaism and contributed to the anti-Semitic aberrations within Christianity. Because we must always return to Scripture itself and its own statement of the substance, the church's renderings of that substance,

24. Adolf Harnack, *History of Dogma,* vol. 1, trans. Neil Buchanan (New York: Dover Publications, 1961), 157ff. See also Bjarne Skard, *The Incarnation: Christology of the Ecumenical Creeds,* trans. Herman Jorgensen (Minneapolis: Augsburg, 1960), 31-69.

25. For comments on some of its shortcomings see Hendrikus Berkhof, *Christian Faith,* trans. Sierd Wordstra (Grand Rapids: Eerdmans, 1979), 136-221, 293-94, 306-7.

even the most helpful ones, as in the creedal clarifications of the gospel, are accountable to a higher authority, in this case the canonical articulation of the narrative of faith, with its recognition of "the covenant chapter," and a fuller accounting of the Christological chapter in the economy of the triune God.

Church tradition after the creeds continues to play a resource role in the understanding of the gospel. As expressions of less catholicity than the "undivided church," they do not have the "exemplar" status in the Christian paradigm that the early creeds enjoy.[26] But as more developed in the narrative flow of the God-story, they add dimensions of understanding of the gospel. We look to these subsequent forms of gospel faith both to document the importance of the central Christian kerygma as an interpretive principle of Scripture and to discern meanings of it otherwise not readily accessible.

Subsequent creeds, confessions, and covenants in various sections of the church continue the kerygmatic core of Christian teaching and rule of faith. The Athanasian Creed is itself an exposition of its trinitarian form. Reformation confessions include its basic affirmations.[27] Covenants within the Free Church tradition presuppose its structure.[28] Contemporary statements of faith sometimes self-consciously employ a narrative framework.[29] Along with this kind of ecclesial statement, works in dogmatic and systematic theology organize their *loci* as places in the narrative of God that become occasions for doctrinal expositions.[30]

26. Peter Toon, *The Development of Doctrine in the Church* (Grand Rapids: Eerdmans, 1979), 116-20.

27. See Philip Schaff, *The Creeds of Christendom,* vol. 3 of *The Evangelical Protestant Creeds* (Grand Rapids: Baker, 1966).

28. Williston Walker, *The Creeds and Platforms of Congregationalism* (Boston: Pilgrim Press, 1960).

29. As in "The Statement of Faith" of the United Church of Christ in Louis Gunnemann, *The Shaping of the United Church of Christ* (New York: United Church Press, 1977), 69-70. Note also "A Declaration of Faith" (Presbyterian Church in the United States) in the proposed *Book of Confessions with Related Documents* (Atlanta: Materials Distribution Service, PCUS, 1976), 149-72.

30. For a discerning analysis of how systematic theologies are customarily organized according to the "logical order" of doctrine, and how doctrine develops, see James Orr, *The Progress of Dogma* (New York: A. C. Armstrong & Son, 1901), 21-32. Thus the sequence of doctrines in a representative older work, Heinnrich Heppe, *Reformed Dogmatics,* rev. ed. by Ernest Bitzer, trans. G. T. Thompson (Grand Rapids: Baker, 1978), and a representative current one, *Christian Dogmatics,* ed. Carl E. Braaten and Robert W. Jenson, 2 vols. (Philadelphia: Fortress Press, 1985).

As earlier noted, from time to time theological movements explicitly lift up the narrative features of faith. This number includes the federal theology, various covenantal theologies, the *heilsgeschichte* schools of nineteenth- and twentieth-century theology, and in an idiosyncratic fashion the various dispensational theologies. So too modern evangelical theologies in the infallibilist tradition tend to center on the epic of God's soteric deeds as the material principle of authority within the formal principle of scriptural authority. And those that protest this move from an inerrantist perspective often function with the same substance of the source.[31]

In these many and varied ways the church official and unofficial seeks to distill the essence of Scripture in formularies and schemas of a narrative sort. Formally or functionally, the Bible is viewed as the bearer of a message. Its authority is inextricable from the disclosure of what God has done, is doing, and will do to achieve the divine goal of the coming together of creation and Creator. Scripture tells that Story. This long tradition of the summary of faith in narrative mode helps us to see that recital in the biblical materials themselves, although how that is seen always corrects the limitations and distortions of the accounts of it in Christian tradition. The gospel understood as the full narrative of God's movement among us is the *scopus* of Scripture, its raison d'être, its purpose.

We have used interchangeably the biblical word *gospel* and the term *narrative*. Employing the latter is itself an interpretive move coming from a *perspective* in contemporary theology, a subject to be further explored in external hermeneutics. As such it illustrates yet another influence of the resource on the source of theology, for here a current in contemporary Christian theology leaves its mark on the inner sanctum of biblical understanding, canonical intention. Indeed, insofar as narrative is an interpretive theme related to cultural sensibilities, it shows the impact of human experience on the construal of biblical authority. Thus all the elements of authority make their presence felt in the inner ring of authority itself. But as priorities keep company with diversities, here at the core the way church and world relate to the Bible in larger compass—as resource, setting, and source—obtains as well. *Narrative* is a legitimate translation of *gospel* to the extent that it clarifies for us the biblical intention of the term and/or enriches our understanding of it. To that end we give some attention to the use of the narrative metaphor in twentieth-century theology.

31. So Carl Henry's narrative of faith in *God, Revelation and Authority*, vol. 4 (Waco, Tex.: Word Books, 1979), 468-69.

The Gospel as Narrative

Understanding the gospel as narrative is part of a complex of hermeneutical themes broadly described as "narrative theology." In the overview volume of this series I used a typology to distinguish "canonical story," "life story," and "community story."[32] *Canonical story* makes use of biblical micro-narratives, with special interest in Jesus' parables but also including stories throughout the two Testaments about persons and events, historical or otherwise. *Life story* narratology focuses on the personal or social recitals in religious practice in general or in the Christian tradition in particular, discovering theological value and meaning in the tale of the individual's spiritual journey or a group's struggles and hopes. *Community story* is the genre represented in this work: the Great Narrative of the deeds of God evolving from within the early kerygma through the Christian community's various expressions of it noted earlier. As such it functions as the "perspective" in hermeneutics and systematics, seeking to be both faithful to Scripture and fruitful in interpreting the faith to the contemporary world in its own drama of suffering and hope. In volume one we visualized the plot line in the following way:

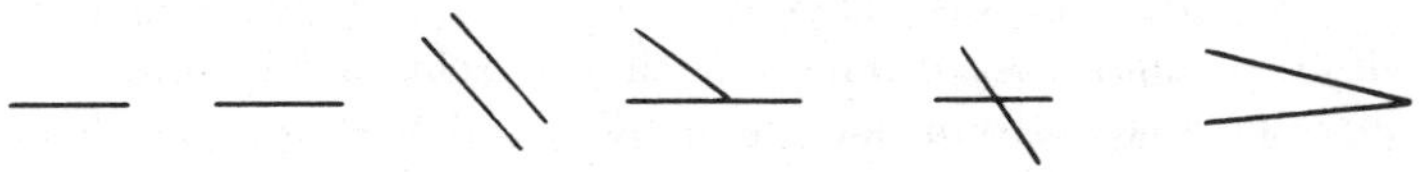

Common to all three varieties of narrative theology is the story structure: a plot with characters moving over time and place through conflict toward resolution. Narrative also engages human affect in ways that other forms of theology cannot, taking the hearer and reader into the earthy and human moil and toil, employing its language of metaphor and symbol. The various forms of narrative theology all teach that through this medium they engage ultimate reality at a profounder level than do discursive modes of communication.

Beyond these commonalities are significant and even fundamental divergences. Some advocates of life story and canonical story juxtapose the small tales of human life and biblical lore to the overarching biblical epic, considering the latter as distant myth or

32. Fackre, *CS,* 4-10. See also Gabriel Fackre, "Narrative Theology: An Overview," *Interpretation* 37 (Oct. 1983): 340-52.

allegory divorced from the experiential matrix in which theology is properly done. Others in the same vein do not count "the big story" of community narrative as narrative theology at all, limiting the term to personal narratives of religious commitment. On the other hand, exponents of the biblical macro-story often do not give much attention to the function of language and the relation of the story form in both its wider expression (life story) or narrower manifestations (biblical stories), with their own exclusive concentration on the Christian cult epic. We can learn from a deeper interchange that must go on among these exponents and their emphases. We strive to profit from this three-way encounter in the exposition of a community story model throughout this systematics, using metaphors from personal and social experience and drawing from the wells of biblical tales and those who interpret them. However, the antisystematic and contradiscursive tendencies in life story and canonical story modes seriously weaken them as theological options. Where they reject the truth claims of the biblical God-story, replacing them with experiential alternatives, narrative theology falls into the reductionism of the world-type options earlier considered.

Among the advantages of a community story model grounded in Scripture, two are worth noting here.

1. Narrative theology takes account of the revelatory dynamisms within Scripture. An example is the interrelationship of the two Testaments. To account for the validity of the Old yet the definitiveness of the New, many commentators, including very conservative ones, employ organic metaphors and categories borrowed from nineteenth- and twentieth-century scientific and philosophical conceptualities: the "growth" of religious understanding in liberal versions, and "progressive revelation" in orthodox appropriations. While these notions do succeed in honoring the validity of the Hebrew Scriptures together with the definitiveness of the New Testament, they are too influenced by the simplistic developmentalism in the organic hypothesis, one that does disservice to its theological users. We can see this in "the escalator theory of progress" found in some theologies of history, or its counterpart in personal soteriology, an evolutionary concept of sanctification moving ineluctably toward the state of perfection. Narrative, with its movement toward resolution, preserves the theme of advance but allows for a complex relationship between past, present, and future, including the active influence of the past on the future (as in the prophetic, priestly, and royal shapings of Jesus' ministry)

and the movement of the future to the past as well (as in the transformation of these categories by the work of Christ). It also allows the tensions, fits, and starts, reversals as well as advances that make for drama, a dynamism too often obscured by the one-way movement of development and growth. Narrative, therefore, takes better account of the *redemptive* movement of God in history than do static views that deny movement, or dynamic ones influenced by organicism that miss the fitful and catastrophic aspects of the struggle forward, the turning points and the ambiguities of advance.

In the Christian narrative the foes that resist divine purpose are very much part of the movement forward. As a result, the fundamental change of direction effected by the person and work of Christ is recognized by narrative better than the straight line or growth conceptualities that make no place for decisive events. And the ambiguity in advance toward resolution is there in narrative, doing justice to the assertion within the canonical epic that Satan will resist the divine purpose to the end, and even contest the divine regency in a closing conflict of Armageddon proportions. These things have a profound implication for the conception of God in the gospel itself. Straightline views that see the history of God with us as either a linear outworking of a supralapsarian project or as a seed-flower exfoliation of immanent powers are not faithful to the central disclosure point of Scripture, the decisive battle fought and won there by Jesus Christ. Thus the history of God is the story of God, replete with drama that moves through radical conflict toward a denouement.

2. The timeliness of narrative is also part of its usefulness as an interpretive framework. We shall explore the lineaments of our own historical context in a subsequent section. For now we simply note that ours is an epoch in which both the fact of and sensibility to "suffering and hope" make narrative and its idiom a particularly appropriate mode of communication.

As Scripture does not explicitly use "story" in its statement of the gospel, we are employing a framework from human experience to explicate that message. So "the world" enters in a subsidiary way into the articulation of the gospel. The warrants for it are in the doctrine of revelation in which the light of God is given in creation—general revelation—enabling us to employ in modest setting elements of human experience. The emergence of narrative as "narrative theology" indicates the testing at work within the Christian community of this as a mode of interpreting the faith. The jury is still out as to whether such a perspective is viable for communicating the gospel and does not subvert it by allowing the setting to control the source, or the resource to pretend that it is more than it is. Thus we conclude these comments with a commitment always to return to the canonical content and language of the gospel to inform and hold accountable our experiential helps, in this case a narrative perspective.

Christ: The Center

Jesus Christ is central to this hermeneutics. He is "the one Word we have to hear and to trust and to obey in life and in death."[33] The signatories of Barmen experienced *in extremis* distortions of biblical faith and cultural idolatries that can never be forgotten when Christians confront the issue of authority. They remembered the most primitive Christian confession when the gospel was imperilled. In less directly threatened but no less tempting times, our teaching and preaching must also keep that confession firm: "Jesus Christ is Lord."

The Christological center is the point of orientation within the substance of biblical faith. How a given text is understood as gospel within the canon is determined within the light of the triune God seen through "the lens" of Jesus Christ. The Christological *center*, therefore, is the *norm* of the *substance* and the *source*.

But why Christ? We are at the heart of the doctrine of revelation as well as at the center of the concept of authority. Jesus Christ is the act in the drama of God that delivers us from sin, evil, and death, and discloses that truth to us. We are brought to believe the gospel by the Holy Spirit whose power opens a shaft of this light of Christ through the night of our ignorance and error. This work of illumination turns us *(epistrophe)* toward its radiance—conversion—and warms us personally in it—conviction. Our being convinced of the truth of the gospel of Christ rests finally, therefore, on the "internal testimony of the Holy Spirit." Yet the pneumatic work that precipitates the commitment of personal faith is related to the *external* testimony of the Holy Spirit, a witness that engages us through the community of sister and brother believers. We come to faith in a common life of worship and witness formed by a particular historical setting with the graces of the Spirit at work therein. This community and our own encounter with Christ within

33. "The Theological Declaration of Barmen" in Arthur Cochrane, *The Church's Confession under Hilter* (Philadelphia: Westminster Press, 1962), 237-42.

it is, in turn, oriented to the book of the gospel of Jesus Christ gifted with the inspiration of the Spirit that makes possible our illumination by the same Spirit.

In answering the question "Why?", the diverse revelatory elements appear with their special functions and ordering: illumination in person-in-Christian-community, inspiration in Scripture, and impartation in our worldly context, with their orienting actions in the election of Israel and incarnation in Christ. We return from the revelatory grounding of faith to the structures of authority to show how these same elements express themselves in a correlative fashion. Thus, the personal commitment to the central authority of Christ coming to be from encounter with the gospel of the Scripture in the church as it lives in the world looks to how the Christ of the Bible himself interprets Scripture, and how the church in the world enters into the conversation on the Christological norm. In this investigation we shall give attention to the warrants within Bible, church, and world for the centrality of Christ, and the content of the Christ so warranted. The length of the section reflects the importance of the center under discussion, and as such provides a showcase for the inclusivity of the hermeneutical method employed.

The Authority of Christ in Scripture

How does the Christ who claims us by the testimony of the Spirit speak to us about the interpretation of Scripture? As it is through Scripture that we have come to know the Christ of the gospel, we turn to the canonical evidence of Jesus' own way of interpreting the sacred writings. The citations that time, of course, were texts from Hebrew writings.

A review of the passages in which the canonical Jesus alludes to tradition that was to become part of the Christian source of authority gives a clear and compelling answer to our question:

Matthew 4:4, 6-7, 10; 5:21, 27, 31, 33, 38, 43; 7:12; 8:17; 9:13; 11:10, 13, 17, 22-24; 12:3-7, 18-21, 39-42; 13:14-15, 35; 15:4-9; 16:4; 19:5, 7, 18-19; 21:13, 16, 42; 22:29-32, 35-40, 44; 24:15, 24, 31; 27:46.

Mark 2:25-26; 4:12; 7:6-7, 9-10; 9:12; 10:3-6; 11:17; 12:10-11, 24-27, 29-31, 35-37; 14:21, 27, 49; 15:34.

Luke 4:4, 8, 10-12, 17-19, 25-28; 6:3-4; 7:22-23, 27, 32; 10:13-15, 26-28; 11:29-32, 49; 13:4, 28-29, 34; 16:16, 29-31; 17:26-30; 18:20; 19:46; 20:17-18, 28, 37-38, 41-44; 22:37; 23:46; 24:25-27, 44-47.

John 5:39-40; 9:2-3; 13:18; 14:6; 15:25.

The pattern that emerges is one in which a text is interpreted as a witness to Jesus Christ. The immediate occasion for the reference often has to do with the fulfillment of prophecy. However, the working assumption behind each citation is that the sacred writings are to be resituated in a new stream of interpretation. That stream is the Good News of God's deliverance in Jesus Christ, the center of the narrative in which Israel and its charter have a crucial place. Since it is a developing story whose pivotal point is Christ, we are to view from this angle of vision what precedes it as well as what follows it. Thus we are to honor as authoritative writing the available texts of the chosen people in whose history God has worked in an anticipatory fashion. We must fully respect their integrity. But for Christians, they are always read as the Old Testament in the light of its sequel and through its Christological lens. By the same reckoning, we are also to understand writing that comes after the center, both within and beyond the particular revelatory track, from this central point.

In our reference to these texts we are working in a commonsense fashion seeking "what they say" to establish the *esse* of a textual reading. A fuller grasp of that sense would require the investigation of each within its contexting literary units. Yet our task here is not to expound their individual meaning, but to illustrate the act of referencing that goes on in them: Christ interprets Hebrew Scripture from the angle of his own person and work.

The same Christological pattern of interpretation found in the Gospels is present in the rest of the New Testament. Where interpretation of the central message goes on—in contrast to supporting textual arguments for day-to-day practice questions and matters of "general revelation"—quotations and references to Hebrew writings are read through the lens of Christ.

Acts 2:17-21, 25-28, 30-31, 34-36, 39; 3:13, 22-23, 25; 4:11, 24-27; 5:30; 7:2-53; 8:32-33; 13:16-27, 33-41, 47; 14:15; 15:14-19; 17:31; 26:16-18; 28:26-28.

Romans 1:17; 2:16; 3:10; 4:3, 7, 11, 13, 17-18; 5:5; 7:7, 10, 22; 8:20, 22, 36; 9–11; 13:8-10; 14:11; 15:9-12, 21.

1 Corinthians 1:19, 31; 2:9; 3:9, 15, 18; 8:6; 9:9; 10:1-13; 13:1; 14:21; 15:25-28, 42-45, 54-55.

2 Corinthians 3:3, 6-7, 17; 4:6, 13; 6:2, 17-18; 9:7-10; 11:2-3.

Galatians 2:6, 16; 3:10-17; 4:21-30; 5:14; 6:16.

Ephesians 1:22; 2:17; 4:8; 5:2, 31-32; 6:14-15.

Colossians 1:17; 2:3; 3:1, 10.

2 Thessalonians 2:4, 8; 3:16.

2 Timothy 2:19; 3:8.

Titus 2:14.

Hebrews 1:5-14; 2:6-9, 12-18; 3:3-11, 15-19; 4:3-10; 5:5-10; 6:8, 13-14, 19-20; 7:1-28; 8:1-13; 9:1-27; 10:1-39; 11:1-40; 12:1-28; 13:15, 20.

James 1:10-11; 2:8, 11, 21, 23, 25; 4:6; 5:11, 17-18.

1 Peter 1:16, 24-25; 2:3-10; 2:22-25; 3:6, 10-12, 14-15, 20; 4:14, 18; 5:5, 7.

2 Peter 2:5-7, 15-16, 22; 3:5-8, 12-13.

Jude 9, 11, 14-15, 23.

Revelation 1:4-8, 13, 15-17; 2:7-8, 10-14, 17-18, 20, 23, 26; 3:5, 7, 9, 12, 14, 17, 19; 4:1-2, 5-9; 5:1, 5-6, 8-10; 6:2, 6, 8, 10, 12-13, 15-17; 7:1, 3, 14, 16-17; 8:3, 5, 7-8, 10; 9:2-4, 6-9, 13, 20; 10:5, 9, 11; 11:1-2, 4-8, 11-12, 15, 18-19; 12:2-5, 7, 9-10, 12, 14; 13:1, 5, 7, 9-10, 14-15; 14:1, 8, 10-11, 14-15, 20; 15:1, 3-5, 8; 16:1-4, 6-7, 10, 12-13, 15-18; 17:1-2, 4, 8, 12, 14; 18:2-7, 9, 11-12, 15, 17, 19-24; 19:2-3, 5, 7, 11-12, 15-17; 20:4, 8-9, 11-12, 15; 21:1-8, 10, 12, 15, 19, 23, 25, 27; 22:2-4, 11-14, 16-17.

In the whole of the New Testament the touchstone of authoritative interpretation for the received texts of Scripture is the person and work of Jesus Christ.

Critical scholarship enters the quest for biblical evidence about the Christological norm. Of special value is the study of the prehistory of Jesus texts, given attention elsewhere in this volume. In the "Jesus research" of the twentieth century a figure emerges who preaches the coming of the kingdom of God, points to signs of its appearing in his person and ministry, claims an authority convergent with its inbreaking, in loyalties expected and sins forgiven, and has an unparalleled intimacy with the heavenly Father. These findings, "meager" though they be and subject to correction and revision by the nature and history of critical inquiry, do show the possible origins of New Testament developments in Christology. Here is a story within a story, the trek of early perceptions of Jesus to their later point of understanding. The service performed by critical scholarship locates germinal elements in the final New Testament picture of Christ. The particulars of kingdom preaching, the imminence and inbreaking of the end and Jesus' inseparability from it are coherent with the claims to the decisiveness of God's deed in this moment of history, and Jesus' key position in it.

The Authority of Christ for Church and World

The centrality of the Christological standard can be seen in the rallying cry of the postapostolic communities to which we referred earlier. "Jesus is Lord" for these early Christians was an epistemological as well as a soteriological affirmation. In the face of other allegiances with which they had to contend, including those that made inroads into the life and belief of these communities, confessing Christians witnessed to their first loyalty. This was the aperture through which they viewed ultimate reality: not the emperor, not a cultus, not a philosophy, not the savior of the hour, but Jesus Christ is Lord and therefore Revealer.[34]

Where the understanding of Scripture was the particular issue, as in facing Gnostic reinterpretations, the defenders of a developing orthodoxy appealed to the rule of faith, but consistently stressed within it the Christological norm. Deviance came down, almost always, to the failure to affirm the biblical Christ. Four centuries of debate about the Person of Christ, the "Christological controversies," prove that this is the interpretive center of Christian teaching. While the rule of faith provided the summary of the essentials, the central paragraph was the focal point. *Nicenum* refined and enlarged it, asserting Christ to be *homoousios* with the Father. And the Chalcedonian definition sought to clarify further the divine and human natures, their unity and interrelationship. The conclusions reached in the debate, however modest—the placing of "no trespassing" signs on either side of the humanity and divinity—have had a lasting influence on the fact and character of Christological normativity.

Numerous subsequent expositions illustrate the fuller understanding of the Christological principle in Scripture made possible by Christian tradition. We mention only a few in passing. Of special interest are the Reformers, whose faithfulness to Scripture and resistance to the volatilization of its plain meaning led them in this direction. On the one hand, they wanted a principle for understanding obscure and even troublesome passages earlier allegorizing had sought to deal with. On the other hand, they sought to free Scripture to speak its evangelical message. In a Christological reading they found a way to combine these, as in Luther's figure of Christ the "babe" lying in the "manger" of the Bible. In another metaphor, Luther calls Christ the "nutcracker": To get a tasty kernel within the hardened shell of text, let Christ hammer away!

While Calvin is not as well known as Luther for accenting the Christological viewpoint of Scripture, one can find it in his exegetical comments and labors. He believes that the Bible as a whole is the "armament of Christ." Or, in our own metaphor, paralleling

34. Cullmann, *Christology of the New Testament*, 221-34, 249-69.

Luther's, all of Scripture is pregnant with Christological meaning, not only the child to be delivered from it. The womb itself is coextensive with Christ. Thus the full body of the text is accordingly given high honor.

The Calvinist interpreter approaches the search for truth in the Bible's pages differently than the nut-cracking procedures of a Luther. For Calvin, what Scripture says, Christ says, while for Luther, what Christ says, Scripture says. Calvin and his heirs tend to take the text as it is. At its best, that entails waiting for the truth that must come from it, even though it may not be there yet in our present understanding. It also means giving full attention to the Old Testament, seeking to understand it on its own terms. At its worst, it means that whatever is perceived as Scripture's plain meaning has to be Christ's own Word, as is. The oracular and inerrancy traditions stem largely from this Calvinist heritage. So too do the multitude of idiosyncratically formed sects that make one or another text the basis for their practice, without having applied the Christological hammer.

For Luther and his heirs Scripture must show its Christological credentials. At its best, this method reinterprets texts by the standard of "Christ," and must do so before it treats them as authoritative. It rejects interpretations that fall short, and even rejects the text itself if it does not pass the scrutiny of Jesus Christ. At its worst, an exclusivist use of the norm diminishes the significance of anything in Scripture that does not pass Christological muster as we understand it, thus tending to call in question implicitly some or all of the Hebrew Scriptures, and to treat as "law" sections that do not fit the picture of Christ. Or it understands "Christ" in such a narrow fashion, as for example reduced to "justification by faith," that it misses the fullness of Christ, especially aspects from other parts of the New Testament (James, the Synoptics) and the prophetic teachings of the Old Testament.

Must these perceptions be polarized? By no means. Karl Barth and Hans Asmussen—Reformed and Lutheran—modeled a better way in their joint work on the Christological witness of the Barmen declaration. We follow this way of partnership in our effort to say how the Christological standard works.

In modern theology the Christological norm is found in many and diverse places. P. T. Forsyth, on one hand, and the Jesus biographers on the other, anticipated many of the twentieth-century developments in orthodox retrieval and in liberal and liberation streams, the one accenting the Christ of faith and the other the Jesus of history. Barth, most of all, called attention to the addressing

Word, Jesus Christ. Here not only those who call themselves "Barthians" but also a contingent of modern evangelicals find in the Christological norm a way of freedom from the preoccupations of inerrancy. In another modern stream of interpretation the liberation theologies often make use of the Christological standard, although, as noted, in active conjunction with an experiential framework. What these modern movements succeed in doing, however we might finally judge their theological adequacy, is to show the implications of this norm in both ecclesial and experiential settings, thereby enriching our grasp of the canonical intention for textual meaning.

Wherever the church lifts up the authority of Christ, the world also makes its impact felt. The different faces of the world show themselves in this interrelationship. The world's worst face is manifest in its *opposition* to the purposes of God, the working of its fallen state in such wise that it imperils the witness of the church. So culture forces the church to point to its center and write on its banner—Jesus is Lord! We listen to this one Word! Just so is the juxtaposition of Christ to the idolatrous claims of ancient and modern cultures. Yet the world can be less the foe and more the enigma. So the church speaks of Christ in terms set by the questions the world poses at a given time and place. The authority of the Easter Christ addresses the ancient fears of demons and death, the crucified Christ confronts sin and death that come to consciousness in the middle ages and the Reformation, and the Galilean Christ enters into the plight of the needy neighbor discerned in times of modern tribulation. Or the world may provide tools of reason better to develop the picture of the New Testament Christ—the contribution of Jesus research. And finally the world can offer interpretive categories for bringing out the significance and enriching the meaning of Christ in a given time and place. Hence, the philosophical concept of *homoousios* in the fourth century, and the political-social themes of liberation and reconciliation in the twentieth. These relationships of the world to the assertion of the authority of Christ are similar to the types of Christ-culture encounter identified by H. Richard Niebuhr, especially the Christ against culture and the Christ transforming culture.[35] We shall meet them all again in our examination of the content of Christ.

35. H. Richard Niebuhr, *Christ and Culture* (New York: Harper & Brothers, 1951).

The Content of Christ

We have examined the evidence within the canon for the employment of a Christological norm in the interpretation of Scripture, as the church's reflection upon it has clarified and deepened the procedure, and as a wider human experience has made its impact on it. Now we shall investigate the *content* of "Christ" as it functions to establish authoritative textual meaning. Already in our inquiry into the "whether" of Christ's authority we have entered into the "what" and "who" of the matter, for these questions are inseparable. But our analysis must be more thorough.

Our first step into discerning the content of Christ will be an examination of the canonical understanding of it in a commonsense reading of appropriate material. This includes the New Testament portrayal of Jesus' own self-understanding, his deeds, preaching, and praying, and the explicitly apostolic interpretation of who he is and what he did—including the strands of Old Testament tradition on which they drew. To this we shall add important clarifications of Christological content from critical sources, a summary of some data from contemporary Jesus research in the New Testament, and an influential background theme to Christology garnered from Old Testament canon critical study. From there we shall move to the contributions of church thinking in the formation of Christological content as these are shaped by one or another historical context.

Who, then, is the canonical Jesus? Is it Mark's preacher and actor of the kingdom? Matthew's teacher of righteousness? Luke's healer and helper? John's revealer? Is it Peter's risen Lord? Paul's crucified savior? The Apocalypse's judge of the living and the dead? He is all these and more, speaks the inclusive Word of the canon. The presence of four Gospel stories rather than a single account of Jesus' career should alert us to that. So also should the shower of metaphors and motifs that descend onto the pages of the New Testament: Messiah, Lord, Son of God, Son of man, Master, Shepherd, Servant, Word, Prophet, Priest, King; the one who receives judgment and punishment, offers a sacrifice, makes a purchase, pays a debt, ransoms, liberates, reconciles, brings victory and peace, life and light. Does one preclude all others? Sundry theories of Jesus' person and work have said so, each finding meaningful a root metaphor or regnant motif, rightly, in many cases, bringing forward an accent too long neglected. But in the polemics of that moment the advocates of these accents often have been scornful of other perceptions that were not, and are not, finally inimical. If the canon can make room for them, why not also our feeble theological formulations?

To attempt that is the work of a doctrine of Christ. Anticipations of it are in the Christology section of Volume 1, and further development is projected for a later volume in this series. In this brief commentary we simply indicate a way to go about identifying the canonical picture of Christ that is foundational to a doctrine of Person and Work.

Jesus' Self-Testimony in Word and Deed

Following the precedent of the previous inquiry into the Christological norm, we begin the quest for evidence on the content of that norm by reference to Jesus' own testimony. That means learning the things that constitute who he is from what he does and what he says—about his message and about himself.

The canonical Jesus begins his self-definition in an early temple encounter in which the singularity of his capacities and mission start to emerge (Luke 2:4-52). Our view of his direction and special status are significantly shaped by the pictures of the beginnings of his ministry: baptism (Matt. 3:13-17; Mark 1:9-11; Luke 3:21-22; John 1:31-34), temptations (Matt. 4:1-11; Mark 1:12-13; Luke 4:1-13), first announcement of message and mission (Matt. 4:13-17). Soon come the healings (Matt. 4:23; 9:35; Luke 6:19; 9:6, 11; John 7:23) and revealing qualities of relationship to those in sin and misery (Matt. 5:1-12; John 8:1-11), interpreted by Jesus as indicators of his message (Matt. 5:13-16; John 9:1-41; 10:25) and a clue to his own role in the outworking of its scenarios (Matt. 5:17). Who he is is manifest by how he relates to his companions (John 14–17) and his critics (Matt. 21:23-27; 22:15-22; Mark 11:2-3; 12:13-27; Luke 20:1-8, 20-26), and finally how he meets his destiny at the hands of his enemies (Matt. 26:36-46; Mark 14:32-42, 53-65; 15:2-15, 31-32; Luke 22:40-46). A high point of his relationship to his disciples, in which he gives culminating comments about his status and role in a ritual act, is at the celebration of "the Lord's supper" (Matt. 26:13-30; Mark 14:12-26; John 13:21-30). His words on the cross give the last earthly perspective on the meaning of Jesus (Matt. 27:46; Mark 15:34; Luke 23:34, 43, 46; John 19:30). But the risen Christ places all that has gone before in post-Easter perspective in key encounters with his followers (Matt. 28:1-10, 16-20; Mark 16:1-8; Luke 24:1-53). Through this the canonical Jesus tells us who he is.

Joining the canonical Jesus' self-indicators in words and deed are the apostolic testimonies to his import. That is the point of it all, according to the one who has communicated the most to us: "For I determined not to know anything among you, save Jesus Christ, and him crucified" (1 Cor. 2:2). And Jesus himself turns to another, the one who became the leader of that community, for early work at this witness: "Who do men say that the Son of man is?" (Matt. 16:13). And the work begins, "You are the Christ, the Son of the living God" (Matt. 16:16). Thus we feed into the content of the Christological norm the canon's report of what the designated apostolic writers had to say about the meaning of Christ, and also the accounts within the literature of the New Testament of what apostolic and other members of the early Christian community had to say about Jesus Christ.

Following a pattern already discernible in Jesus' self-interpretation, the apostolic construals develop a double focus: who is Jesus vis-à-vis what came before, and what did he do of special consequence within that forward movement? They speak of the status (who) and the role (what) of this figure in a developing narrative.

The status of Jesus, as viewed in the overall apostolic testimony of the New Testament canon, revolves around his relationship to the history of Israel, as that history is bound up with the God of Israel. It entails, in turn, the history of God with the world out of which the engagement with Israel is itself born. Who is Jesus vis-à-vis these two converging histories? Paul answers: "The gospel of God which he promised beforehand through his prophets in the holy scriptures, the gospel concerning his Son who was descended from David according to the flesh and designated Son of God in power according to the Spirit of holiness by his resurrection from the dead, Jesus Christ our Lord" (Rom. 1:1-4). The Good News is about the point of interesection of two journeys, human and divine, that become one Great Narrative.

As the apostolic seers of this vision begin to interpret it we hear the insistence on the human and historical reality of Jesus. He is one of us (1 Tim. 2:5; 3:16; Gal. 4:4-5; Phil. 2:8; Rom. 8:3; Heb. 2:14; 4:15; 1 John 4:2). His humanity takes up residence amid our toils and tribulations. On the other hand, the daring claim is made that a Galilean stands in special relationship to God's dealings with Israel and thus with all of us (Heb. 1:3; 7:3; Rev. 22:13). Jesus is Emmanuel, God with us (John 5:11; 12:45; Matt. 16:16; Heb. 7:3).

Closely tied to apostolic perceptions of Jesus' status are their understandings of the role he plays in the conjoined histories of humanity and deity. Jesus is Deliverer from our foes, sin, evil, and death. What he did, moreover, is related to how God worked among the covenant people. As such the latter provided "types" of Jesus' redemptive work. The cult life of Israel, especially in its sacrificial, priestly, and temple features (Heb. 9:28; Titus 2:14; 1 John 1:7; 3:5; Rev. 7:14), anticipated the cross. But Calvary could also be thought of in the framework of Israel's judges, and thus the figures of law, judgment, and penalty (Acts 10:42; 17:31; Rom. 3:20; 1 Cor. 5:10). And still others employed figures of speech and frameworks of interpretation about the role of Christ taken from the general existence of the people of God, running from pedagogy and commerce to war and peace (Matt. 5-7; Titus 2:14; Col. 2:15; Eph. 2:14).

The figure who emerges from this canonically rendered apostolic witness in its plain meaning as related to Jesus' career and his own interpretations of it heard by us through the same canonical framework in its natural meaning constitutes the *esse,* the content, of Christological norm. But that *esse* is itself on a journey reaching out toward its deepenings and enlargements, the *bene esse* of our understanding of Christ the Center, as made possible by the efforts of critical scholarship. We cite two resources in this respect, learnings from of the "new quest" for the historical Jesus and perspectives from the Old Testament as given by a canon critical approach to it.

The New Quest

Earlier we alluded to Jesus research as it bears on the fact of Christological centrality; here we will add a few things that contribute to the content of the Christological norm. The relatively recent phenomenon of the "new quest" is often dated from a key essay by Ernst Käsemann in 1953. Since then great amounts of labor have been expended in tracking back across the prehistory of the Jesus texts to discern at least the lineaments of Jesus' teaching and relationship to others. For the assimilation of its findings, including what appears to be a majority consensus about certain features of Jesus' life and ministry, we turn to Edward Schillebeeckx's massive studies, *Jesus* and *Christ.* Here a systematician argues for the crucial role of historical-critical studies and shows his respect for the discipline by a laborious accumulation of the results available to that date. In doing this he brings out both the advantages and problems associated with this method, so his groundwork is of great help in dealing with questions of theological authority.[36]

36. Edward Schillebeeckx, *Jesus: An Experiment in Christology,* trans. Hubert Hoskins (New York: Seabury Press, 1979), *passim,* and Fackre, "Bones Strong and Weak in the Skeletal Structure of Schillebeeckx's Christology," *Journal of Ecumenical Studies* 21 (Spring 1984), *passim*.

Recurring themes in Jesus research include the identification of Jesus' mission as preaching the kingdom of God; the special relationships of, care for, and affirmation of the outcast, the sinner, and the sufferer in his ministry; his unique "Abba experience," which reflects and embodies a sense of special authority, one manifest also in his teaching and action. Let us look more closely at these three points.

1. Jesus preached the coming of the realm of God in which peace is made, justice is done, wrongs are righted, sins are forgiven, the world is made whole. The coming of this rule is imminent, and its firstfruits already apparent; the kingdom is here as well as near. A case can be made (although it is not integral to this majority view among Jesus researchers) that the disciples saw Jesus or Jesus saw himself as the "eschatological prophet" who brings the last warning and invitation to Israel to participate in this coming reign of God. The Good News is that the kingdom is coming. But this announcement carries with it the imperative: "Repent and believe." Whatever the details of Jesus' self-perception or the disciples' perception of him as an eschatological prophet or otherwise, there is a singular authority associated with the bearing of this news.

A demonstration of the presence of the kingdom and a guide to participation in it is Jesus' ministry of healing. Here is the irresistible arrival of the new age, the defeat of Satan and all the foes that resist the powers to heal and exorcise. The mending of bodies is a portent of a world rendered whole, the firstfruits of what shall be, the assurance of things to come.

2. In a similar way, Jesus reached out to the defeated, rejected, hurt, and helpless. This caring for and bonding with the disinherited are also the way of the kingdom and the God who brings it. And they are the manner of life for those who would enter the new realm. The wounded and those who minister to them, the poor and the poor in spirit, those who suffer from the oppressions of this world, and those who suffer for righteousness' sake will inherit the kingdom. As God loves the neighbor in need and even the enemy of the divine purpose, so we must reflect that in our attitude and conduct toward others.

3. Finally, we can trace all of Jesus' perceptions and proclamations to the character of the God in whom he trusted. One stream of scholarship holds that the personal relationship Christ enjoyed with his heavenly Father was basic to his self-understanding. Hence, much stress is placed upon Jesus' unique Abba experience. By his intimate address of God in prayer ("Daddy"), unique in the traditions of Israel, Jesus saw himself in terms of a singular relationship

to God. While he was to teach his disciples to pray the same way, he was the one who pioneered this special bonding. A new chapter in humankind's life with God was begun with the openness and unity with deity.

Reflecting this same unusual unity of Jesus with God is his forgiveness of sin. Here intimacy becomes a veritable union. What is the prerogative of God alone in the ruling tradition of Judaism is now associated with Jesus by his own assurance of pardon to others. Predictably, this fusion of Jesus' declaration with the divine prerogative invoked charges of blasphemy.

The association of Jesus' ministry with the coming of the kingdom links his intimate Abba experience and his commission to forgive sins, and asserts both the singularity of his ministry and its inseparability from God-in-action.

Meager though these results of critical scholarship are, they can be taken up into the developing understanding of the content of the Christological center. This modest reconstruction contributes to the rational clarification of the canonical venture. Thus two histories come together: a prophetic witness to God and a divine action itself in the witnessing. Also to be found are the prophetic future-orientation and behavior commensurate with it, the priestly care for the sinner and sufferer, and the royal confidence that the worst the world can hurl at God's cause shall not overcome it, continuing Old Testament offices and providing materials for later apostolic interpretations and subsequent ecclesial teaching touchstones.

Other scholarly reconstructions enrich the picture. Now the research on the varied traditions within early Christian communities is germane: the miracle worker of the Lukan tradition, the crucified and risen Lord of the Matthean stream, the divine logos of the Johannine community. Are these and others like them then different Christologies within the New Testament? Yes and no. Yes, they are varied perceptions of Christ according to the needs of a given historical context and a particular Christian community. No, they are not, as such, irreconcilable faiths with separate Christ figures. We may view various New Testament characterizations of Jesus as elements within a more fully developed final picture of the person and work of Christ. Critical scholarship can make significant clarifications of the content of Jesus Christ.

Canonical Theology in the Old Testament

As Brevard Childs observes, the Hebrew Scriptures in becoming the Old Testament of the Christian canon are read very differently from Judaism's interpretation of the same material.[37] And the same thing is true—and more radically so—about Islam's reading of it. One notable difference is the effort by Christian interpreters to find an overall theological coherence in this body of writing, an Old Testament theology. Childs takes up this task anew from the point of view of his canonical approach, discovering not a closed system of thought as much as a multifaceted treatment of common themes. We make use of some of his postulates here, placing them in the narrative framework used throughout this systematics. The latter is particularly apt for the present effort to see the Old Testament contribution to understanding the content of Christ.

Who is this God of the Old Testament and how is "Yahweh" known? In many and varied ways the divine being is disclosed through creation, in the wisdom granted to human beings, in acts in history, in a Name known most decisively through the redemptive deeds done among a special people of God, Israel. The pattern emerging is of One who takes initiatives in deliverance and disclosure, is full of surprises, conceals as well as reveals, speaks words of promise and keeps them, is dynamic in transcendence and immanence, and mysterious in distance and presence. "It was not by chance that the Christian church felt constrained to respond to this biblical witness in trinitarian terminology."[38]

Childs's exposition of the Old Testament theology that is the context for the New and shapes the Christological norm, continues with the identification of the purposes of God disclosed in the knowledge of God. God's intention is for the world to know and be one with God and with itself, a vision described as *shalom.* As the description of this purpose is always against the background of humanity's violation of it, it is portrayed as salvation from the destruction of this relationship, redemption from the blindness, self-will, and faithlessness of human beings, a healing that includes the forgiveness of sin and the reconciliation of all things.[39]

The will of God in a world at war with the primal purpose comes to expression in the context of God's covenant with Israel. Here initiative is taken to disclose God's graciousness and embody it in deliverance from captivity, patience in the face of rebuff. Grace invites the response of thankfulness, a communal life of grateful worship in the cultus and grateful obedience in conduct. The shape

37. Childs, *Old Testament Theology in Canonical Context,* 9-10.

38. Ibid., 41.

39. Ibid., 43-50.

of the expected response is given in the Law, the requirements of love to God and neighbor, and also in the ritual and purity laws.[40] The particular bonding with Israel does not preclude the covenant of the Creator with all humankind before and concurrent with the Abrahamic-Mosaic stream. This covenant act whose graces are manifest in human wisdom and human experience in general, the care of, disclosures to, and accountability of the whole human race are sometimes described as the covenants with Adam and Noah. Yet the gift to and claim upon Israel are related to Israel's role as that of "a light to the Gentiles," a particularity within the universality of the divine working.[41]

The New Testament story of the "new covenant" in Christ, with its own grace and gratitude, covenant community, imperatives and issues of particularity and universality cannot be understood apart from the momentum toward these things in the Old Testament.

Life in a covenant means "life under threat." Israel in its special relationship and the world in the universal embrace of a righteous God means accountability, and sin means judgment. The Lord is of purer eyes than to behold iniquity and will not tolerate an ungrateful disobedience. The curse of covenant unfaithfulness, warnings of which come most powerfully in prophetic denunciation and apocalyptic forecast, means desolation for the wrongdoing and does not preclude the very destruction of humankind. So the background here for the Christ whose love burns "like coals of fire," who "will come to judge the quick and the dead."[42]

The last word in Old Testament theology, one that never comes easily and is never disjoined from accountability and judgment, is hope. Being in covenant is "life under promise." Beyond the losing is the promise of saving. This future-oriented salvation is portrayed in many ways but is common to the prophetic writings, the Psalms, the Pentateuch, and historical books. A refrain is life together with one another and God and in and with the land. While this fulfillment has historical referents, clear notes of transcendence can also be heard, a shalom that goes beyond any worldly actualization of it and overcomes death itself. Associated with these features of eschatological promise is, from time to time, a promised figure, a righteous ruler in David's line who will reign in this kingdom "with justice and with righteousness" (Isa. 9:7) and whose qualities re-

40. Ibid., 51-203.
41. Ibid., 204-21.
42. Ibid., 223-35.

flect the righteous but long-suffering God, one "humble and riding on an ass" (Zech. 9:9ff.), a suffering servant "wounded for our transgressions . . . a lamb . . . led to the slaughter" (Isa. 53:5ff.). Although the "messiah" concept employed in the New Testament comes from a period after the Old Testament writings, its origins lie in this thread of expectation. The messianic theme together with the larger eschatological hope constitute the heritage within which the New Testament Christological horizon grew.[43]

The canon critic who traces the outlines of the Old Testament theology contributes significantly to our understanding of the content of Christ. We see the forces at work in shaping the New Testament portraiture, and are aided in our own understanding of Christ, which we must work out in the setting of the entire canon.

Christ and Church/World

What we have identified to this point as the picture of the normative Christ has not been without the influence of the Christian community's perceptions, as that community has viewed the content of Christ from different points in its own pilgrimage. We now bring to clearer awareness perspectives on the meaning of Christ offered by the church at key times and places that enrich our grasp of who Jesus Christ is and what he does. We give special attention to three stretches of Christian history: the first four centuries of Christological controversy, the Reformation wrestle with the saving work of Christ, and twentieth-century social accents on the being and doing of Jesus. In the last case, we will examine the impact of culture (at work in all ecclesial appropriation), especially the effect of moral experience on the church's Christological judgments.

The pattern of understanding Jesus in the light of the overall narrative of God's relation to the world, present in the self-testimony of the canonical Christ and the apostolic witness of the New Testament, and suggested by the scholarly reconstruction of the historical Jesus and interpretation of Old Testament backgrounds, comes to more formal definition in the later community's doctrinal statements of the Person and Work of Christ. The Person of Christ has to do with the status of Jesus vis-à-vis the divine and human "biographies." The "Work of Christ" deals with what is done by the One who is among us, the *role* developing out of the divine-human *status*.

The first four centuries of theological debate within the church

43. Ibid., 236-47.

gave pride of place to the status of Christ as divine-human Person. As in the maturation of the self in its early stages, so in the childhood of the Christian community, self-identity with respect to one's surroundings, and in particular with other identities, is to the fore.[44] While discussed in the philosophical idiom of the day, with its special language and meanings of "nature," "substance," "essence," and "person," the issue was the same as that appearing in the earlier biblical metaphors and motifs: How can this human Jesus whom we have seen and heard among us be at one and the same time the veritable presence of the one God?

So the debate unfolded, with the enigma producing its predictable partisans. Ebionites, Adoptionists, and Arians, according to the stages of the debate, spoke about Jesus in such a way as to suggest the collapse of the divine story into the human one. Docetists, modalists, and Apollinarians were so taken with the divine action in Christ that the human factor disappeared from view. In the last major round of dispute, those with a tilt toward the human narrative sought mightily to affirm both, but in such a fashion that their unity was put in doubt: thus the "Nestorian" way. On the other hand, efforts to assert the human story while insisting upon the consuming presence of the divine seemed to merge the former into the latter: so the "Monophysite" option. Against these and their predecessor reductionisms the Chalcedonian formula left us the classical statement of the Christological paradox, affirming the unique duality in unity of the twin narratives in the figure of Jesus. Jesus Christ is "one Person," in "two natures," and these "without confusion, separation, change or division."[45] This struggle and its result have given us a fuller understanding of the content of the biblical portrayal of the status of Jesus Christ, one that has shaped the perception of what is to be found in the biblical text. Ecclesial probes do not determine what is there, but guide us toward discovering the depths of the biblical data. In that subsidiary role they are always subject themselves to correction and enlargement from testing against the *esse* of the Jesus content. As one of the few universal formulations of Christian content, however, the boundary-drawing function of Chalcedon, and before it Nicea, is of the

44. Formulated by George Herbert Mead, *Mind, Self and Society*, ed. Charles M. Morris (Chicago: Univ. of Chicago Press, 1934), 150-64.

45. "The Definition of Chalcedon," in *Creeds of the Churches*, ed. John H. Leith, 3d ed. (Atlanta: John Knox Press, 1982), 34-36. See also Pelikan, *Christian Tradition*, 263-66, 340-41.

highest interpretive standing within the resource role of tradition, an "exemplar" within the hermeneutical process.

The Reformation insights on the Work of Christ do not carry the authority of an ecumenical consensus to which the Nicene-Chalcedonian judgments can lay claim. However, they are formative of the view of Christ in this work. And a good case can be made that they capture the spirit of a much wider pattern of belief in the church, one that could yet reach catholicity. Each stream of interpretation in a divided Christendom offers its gift to the larger community. The issues that the Reformers brought to the attention of the whole church are related to the atoning work of Christ.

With the above qualifications acknowledged, the ecclesial guide to the understanding of the status of Christ given in its formula of one Person and two natures has its counterpart in the ecclesial assistance given to our understanding of the role of Christ by its characterization of the "threefold office of Christ": prophet, priest, and king.[46] The *munus triplex* is given sharpest articulation by Calvin, but is employed in catechetical and dogmatic literature across the spectrum of Protestant thought, and appears in Roman Catholic and Eastern Orthodox theology as well, before and after the Reformers. This delineation of the work done by the divine-human Person reflects biblical data earlier discussed and has in turn been a factor in its identification. As such it is a refinement of the canonical picture of Jesus as *teacher and preacher of the kingdom, sacrifice for the sins of the world* and *victor over evil and death.*

The Gospels tell the story of Jesus. A large part of their account is occupied with the Good News of his ministry. And at the center of that is his preaching of the coming kingdom with self-understanding and signs that assume and manifest that message. We have seen that one influential critical reconstruction of the New Testament data portrays Christ as the eschatological prophet. Long before this, interpreters of the threefold work saw the same accounts as the chief expression of Christ's prophetic office. In it he points to the inbreaking of the divine purpose anticipated by the Old Testament "type," Isaiah, Jeremiah, Amos, Hosea. The prophet reveals what is and is to be, forthtells and foretells, bringing the radical claims of God's coming Future to bear on the present. Fur-

46. John Calvin, *Institutes of the Christian Religion,* trans. Henry Beveridge (Grand Rapids: Eerdmans, 1957), 425-32. See also W. A. Visser't Hooft, *The Kingship of Christ* (New York: Harper & Brothers, 1948).

ther, the prophet practiced what is preached, embodying in attitude and behavior the vision portrayed. And the meeting of vision with a resisting human reality brings the stoning of the prophet. Jesus fits the picture. In its characterization of Jesus Christ the prophet, a tradition helps to organize the rich materials of the canon in a way that brings out its decisive features. It also lays the groundwork for later developments of the prophetic image that show the relationship of the claims of the Future to the social, economic, and political injustices of the present.

Interpreters of the threefold office also point to another focal point within the Gospels and a refrain beyond in the entire New Testament, integral to the Good News of Jesus' work: the cross. They read its significance with the help of another type, the priest. As blood was shed on the altar and sins forgiven, so Jesus made oblation to God, as sacrificer but also as the sacrifice itself, making an offering for the sins of the world. As the prophet brought the command, the priest brought the gift. Yet the prophet reveals as well the further side of the imperative in the indicatives of the divine *Agape.* So too the suffering of the one who is priest and victim carries with it the claim on the forgiven sinner to "take up the cross," as well as receive the gift of mercy.

At the heart of the priestly work is the question posed by the developing narrative: What is to be done about our No! to the invitation of the holy God? The answer given on Golgotha is an act of God in the act of priest Jesus, the "blood of God" shed in Christ's sacrifice on the cross. Here the love of God receives the punishment that the holiness of God requires. So for the eye of faith the crossbar becomes the open arms of suffering love.[47]

How can we know these things are so? That the coming of the rule of God pointed to by the prophet is assured, and the sacrifice of the priest vindicated? How else than by a finalizing work of all that goes before: the Easter victory. The resurrection of Jesus from the dead is a royal work in which the foes of God that made their final assault on the Purpose of God are defeated. Sin, evil, and the last enemy—death—meet their match in the world's now undisputed Ruler. King Jesus ascends to reign in this time between the times of Easter and eschaton. This aspect of the Good News of Christ's good work is captured by the interpreters of the threefold office in the royal figure of Hebrew history: the liberator of the people from their enemies, the leader in times of stable governance.

47. Fackre, *CS,* 141-46.

Like the other offices, this one has a focal point in the life of Christ, the resurrection, but the royal work decisively revealed and achieved there is present in his Galilean life and ministry and his death on Calvary as well. The offices, though distinct, interact with and interfuse each other, as the New Testament descriptions indicate.

The fullness of Christ's redemptive role becomes clearer in the lens provided by the ecclesial formulation of the threefold office. Perhaps it is because it not only stays close to the canonical witness, but as the "doing" aspect of Christological content it reflects the narrative character of the gospel, a vivid portrayal of the central story within the greater overarching tale.

Modern Themes: Liberation and Reconciliation

The effect of the world on the church's enlargements of Christological meaning can be seen in the previous ecclesial frameworks of the Person and Work. In the first case, both foes and friends in the environment leave their mark. Gnostic religious impulses and Greek philosophical schools prompt the kind of distinctions made between the developing orthodox Christology and competing worldviews. At the same time, the church borrows selectively from the universe of discourse provided by this setting in stating its own case, as in the language of substance philosophy found in its credos. With the Reformers' use of the threefold schema, it is more difficult to show the exact linkages to extra-ecclesial culture, except in the obvious allusion to royalty. The turn toward biblical figures, however, is negative evidence of the world's impact, the Reformers' determination to set Christ against culture. One way to do it is to avoid the "worldly" categories they believed had corrupted the church they were seeking to reform. Hence the return to the code language of Scripture rather than cultural terms shows the impact of the world on theology.

We choose our last example of ecclesial enrichment of Christological content to demonstrate more clearly how human experience does affect the church's understandings of Christ, and can do it in an illuminating way. One could argue that the modern period, predictably, would show the hand of the world. In mind here is not the familiar accusation that the church was taken captive by the anthrocentricity of the Enlightenment, but that the effects on culture of an advancing science and technology magnified the impact of human decisions and interactions for good or ill. This includes not only what human beings are capable of doing to and for one another to hurt or heal, but the knowledge of what might be done in the future. It is no accident that moral experience became so formative in Christian thinking and teaching, with its influential mentors in the period of ascendancy, Kant in the overall rationale, and Marx in the systemic aspects of moral interaction.

As the stakes were raised higher and higher in the twentieth century, the twin issues of justice and peace came increasingly to the fore. And within ecclesial interpretations of Jesus Christ, corresponding accents on liberation and reconciliation took on a higher and higher profile. For some circles the conditions of both injustice and war have become so dominant, self-awareness by the affected constituencies so sharp, and conceptualities in culture addressed to them so influential that the content of Christ is exclusively identified in terms of human liberation or reconciliation. How to honor the place, and even the foreground place, of human peril and promise in the interpretation of the gospel to our times, yet not fall prey to the tempting accommodations and reductionisms, is a major challenge to contemporary Christian theology, and a leading concern in this systematics. The force of the issue comes home in the present discussion.

The experiential cum ecclesial contributions to our understanding of the biblical Christ, and its problems too, are illustrated by the Craigville experience chronicled in the Introduction. Here in a church known for its effort to include context in any reading of the biblical text—the search for "relevance"—the issues come clear, and a way of creative church/world encounter with Scripture takes place.

The first Colloquy took a Barmen-like position toward the culture-Christianity it saw in its church, manifest in adaptation to the middle-class environment of many of its congregations or the anti–middle-class activism of its bureaucracies. Sharpest criticism of the Craigville letter from Colloquy I came from exponents of one or another form of liberation theology who saw the confessional turn as a retreat from the justice and peace agenda of the church, documented for them by a hermeneutics of suspicion in the analysis of who was on hand and what was said. Determined to have its concerns heard for what they were, not against but within the framework of continuing commitment to justice and vigorous participation in the peace movement, the sponsors of the succeeding Colloquy invited the critics to be on hand and shape the Craigville process itself. The very issue around which the controversy swirled was addressed in the second Colloquy, the question of theological authority.

The dynamics described in the Introduction illustrate the difficulty of partisans in this highly pluralist setting hearing alternative perspectives. Yet the participatory process, including the spaces left for unpredictability, produced some surprises. The proponents of liberation theology most critical of the first Colloquy, organized for vigorous protest within the second, did so throughout. Further, they were well represented—possibly the majority—on the drafting committee. However, the Witness statement surprised everyone, as important elements of liberation methodology were incorporated, specifically feminist insights. They resulted in a deepening of the biblical, evangelical (gospel), and Christological aspects of authority. The strong interactionist paragraph insisted on the presence of "lived experience" in encounter with Scripture and tradition, in both descriptive and normative ways. Both the taint of self-interest, of concern to the suspicionist hermeneutics, and the validity of contextual engagement with Scripture, contributions of a liberationist perspective as well as other, found a voice. In addition, an effort was made to change left-hemisphere modes of expression to those in which affect emerged more significantly, as in use of metaphor and story. So too images used to express the authority of Christ and the Bible were fresh ones, or old ones interpreted in fresh ways: matrix, lens, prism, light. Stress was laid on solidarity with the victim and sufferer and participation in the struggle for justice and peace.

But the primacy of Scripture was maintained, with Christ as its interpretive center, and the content of Christ was established by the biblical data, not by an ideology forced upon it. The lived experience of newer constituencies provided an angle of vision on that data that opened up Christological and biblical meanings otherwise muted or missed.

HERMENEUTICS AS NARRATIVE

Craigville's dynamisms tell us more about the interpretive process than how the content of Christ takes form. They show something of the way in which hermeneutics not only employs a narrative component (gospel), but is *itself* a story. In hermeneutical narratology meaning comes in struggle and surprise, reaching its destination by the interaction of various principals moving through tension to resolution. How can Bible, church, and world so interrelate as to bring faithful teaching to be? And, plot within plot, how do the four senses engage one another in the pilgrimage toward meaning and significance?

Here we focus on the story within the full Story, the internal hermeneutical venture with its quest for meaning. In the next chapter, the contextual sense will find its place alongside the common, critical, and canonical, significance joined to meaning. As the work of disclosing the canonical sense of a text unfolds in relation to the common and critical data, the drama of textualization moves to its climax in the search for this sense. The plot lines can be charted in the following way:

world	world	world	
↓	↓	↓	
church	church	church	
↓	↓	↓	
Bible	Bible	Bible	
↓	↓	↓	
common	critical	canonical	= meaning

We have observed that at each stage of the meaning, the three fundamental elements of authority—Bible, church, and world—have made their presence felt. The many gifts brought by the members of the Body, shaped by their varied human experiences, enter into the understanding of the common sense of the text, its *esse.* Yet it is the common sense of the biblical text that is the source of this ecclesial resource and worldly setting. Scripture therefore remains the origin and standard.

So too with respect to the critical sense, the three companions interact. In this case the church is represented by its critical communities, reason's scholarly ranks, the prophetic company of conscience, sufferers who feel the wrong use of Scripture as a weapon wielded against them. Yet again the critical sense is the critical sense of an orienting text, not a construct out of its own wisdom. And the canonical sense with its Christological center and gospel substance is also shaped by the world-formed church in its diversity, a configuration itself always accountable to what is there in the givens of the canon. Thus along the main plot line the hermeneutical narrative proceeds, building from the being through the well-being to the full being of Authorial intention. Internal hermeneutics yields the meaning of a text. The story is not over until its personal and social significance become clear. To the final stage of the drama we now turn.

CHAPTER IV

The Context of Authority

Every pastor faces the hard questions of context in the weekly sermon. Will the people hear the Word? How can this text find its way into the life-world of those who listen? These matters are unavoidable—not only in the pulpit once a week, and in its worship habitat, but in the daily rounds of pastoral ministry. Where moral judgments are made, counsel is given, church policy is formed, action is taken in the community and beyond, and of course on the formal occasions of teaching the faith, basic doctrinal decisions are constant. And with them comes the challenge to "translate" the gospel in terms understandable to the people to whom it is addressed. Only the Holy Spirit can, finally, make this connection, but not without the medium chosen for that work by the vulnerable and historical God, in this case, the earthen vessel of pastoral practice. The care of this vessel means faithfulness to the ways of *contextualization* as well as textualization.

Already we have faced some of the questions in a preliminary fashion in our attention to the text, its common, critical, and canonical senses. Context, there and here, means the presence of "the world" in our dealings with Scripture. The "setting" is there formatively in the varied influences on the Christian community's contributions to the understanding of the text, as well as in our own personal confrontation with it. Its power is felt at the birth of the text itself in the who, when, where, and how of its circumstances, matters to which the historical-literary critic seeks entrance. Now we give the worldly context sustained attention. And we do so with normative intent: What makes a text come alive for me in personal context? For us in social context?

As we investigate the contemporary livingness of the text we shall move back and forth across the line between biblical exegesis and doctrinal exposition. Since the issue of contextualization is to the foreground of systematic theology today, we draw upon that discussion in our inquiry into biblical hermeneutics. But the hermeneutical issues of Scripture are themselves the vestibule of systematics. So what is done now passes easily into the larger question of theological authority. The Bible, church, world, and text-context of hermeneutics is in microcosm the Bible, church, world, and text-context of systematics.

A biblical text reaches its destination when it is appropriated in context. The contextualization of texts is warranted by a doctrine of revelation. The truth God discloses in and through Scripture is *truth for all* that becomes by its Author's intention *truth for us* in cultural context and *truth for me* in personal context. "Illumination" is the contextual gift given by the Holy Spirit at this point in a journey of God's Self-disclosure.

Historical/cultural/social illumination is its *noetic* aspect, giving knowledge of God's purposes through the text for a particular situation. Personal/existential illumination is the *fiducial* gift of the Spirit, for it brings faith to be through the text in a particular situation, either "convicting" (a personal import given an otherwise acknowledged truth) or "converting" (accepting as truth something not formerly accepted).

Contextualization so understood assumes the distinction between a textualization that is "truth for all" and the contextualization of "truth for us/me." We introduce major confusions when we do not recognize the particularities of each. This distinction underlies our division between internal and external hermeneutics, the former entailing the search for the *meaning* of a text in its common, critical, and canonical senses, the latter involving the quest for its *significance* in its contextual (social and personal) sense. We must argue the case further and will do so here, with historical, contemporary, and constructive references.

The issue of biblical contextualization, and thus external hermeneutics, has ancient and modern antecedents. The process begins within the Bible itself. Thus in the Hebrew Scriptures an eighth-century prophet's vision of justice and peace (Isa. 11:3-4) is resituated by a Babylonian seer pointing to the hope for a community in exile (Isa. 40:2, 3, 11), and again by a postexilic visionary who dreams of an Israel that will bring to the whole world "good tidings to the poor" and "liberty to the captives" (Isa. 61:1), all together constituting an encompassing Isaianic tradition. (Interestingly, all three are in the three-year ecumenical lectionary cycle.) Again, the citation of the Old Testament in the New Testament represents the *recontextualization* of texts as well as tradition, read now in the light of the Christological situation. And as the community of Christ moved beyond its own originating locale into other cultures it reenvironed its traditions accordingly, as in the appropriation of Hellenistic categories in the Johannine writings.

The issues that contextualization pose took early form in the controversies between the exegetical schools of Alexandria and Antioch. Eager to find a point of contact with the culture of its day, including its philosophical self-interpretations, the Alexandrian exegetes sought to open texts up to larger significances, giving impetus to the later tradition of the fourfold meaning of Scripture. Here too we can discern traces of the social and personal distinction we shall make, a contextualization focused on intellectual cum cultural significance of Scripture, leaning more toward its mystical and thus personal significance. Meanwhile Antiochan scholars showed a restlessness with these extensions of textual meaning, calling for a return to the literal sense, verifiable by the tools of inquiry then available, a textualization that at the very least controls contextual adventures and at most questions their very legitimacy.[1]

A significant new turn in the development of the question came with the rise of radical historical consciousness in the nineteenth century, and its subsequent exfoliation and applications in the twentieth. Given the novelties in history and the varieties in culture, how can—or, more fundamentally, *can*—an ancient document that is the creature of its time and place have meaning for readers who are the citizens of a very different time and place? How can—*can*—we get into their context, or out of ours? These puzzling questions were compounded by a "critical" version of historical consciousness that viewed ideas as not only the creatures of historical particularity but also the weapons used by its masters to maintain themselves in power and to keep others in thrall to it. Thus the Scripture in its genesis and subsequent use is seen to have been an instrument of oppression and the opiate of the masses who

1. R. P. C. Hanson, "Biblical Exegesis in the Early Church," *Cambridge History of the Bible,* vol. 1 (Cambridge: Cambridge Univ. Press, 1970), 412-52, and R. M. Grant, *The Bible in the Church* (New York: Macmillan, 1958), 63-81; Walter M. Dunnett, *The Interpretation of Scripture: An Introduction to Hermeneutics* (Nashville: Thomas Nelson, 1984), 69-70.

should be overthrowing the oppressors and wresting their weapons from them.

While both historical consciousness in general and its critical subset have themselves been used in turn as weapons in the battle against biblical authority, there is no reason to reject either as usable tools in biblical hermeneutics. Historical awareness is an outworking of the assumption of human finitude, a premise integral to the Christian doctrine of creation. We are all creatures rooted in biological and cultural soils, living now in time and not in eternity. As such, our thought is perspectivally shaped, and always short of the realm of Light in even its most inclusive formulations. The hermeneutics of suspicion that looks for the power agendas of texts and their interpreters, regularly cloaked in piety, is also consonant with the Christian doctrine of the fall, which sees the will-to-power in all human ventures and is particularly sensitive to the self-righteousness that smokescreens its self-interest. How these insights are used as instruments in the hermeneutical venture, rather than as full-scale ideologies that take charge of it, is the challenge we have already sought to address and to which we now return.

We will consider several responses to the issues posed by contextualization and then move to an alternative view. The first is a traditionalist reply, the appeal for a return to textualization and a rejection of contextuality. Its most vocal current exponent in Protestantism is a hard-line position: "What the Bible says, God says." And that is the plain meaning of the text, preserved in all respects from error. The appearance of this position in its most polemical form among today's political fundamentalists is replete with ironies. The neofundamentalist's interpretation of Scripture regularly entails two hermeneutical moves. What purports to be the plain meaning of key texts is one that is first contexted in the political agenda of the New Right, and, second, contexted in the ecclesial tradition of the modern movement of North American fundamentalism. The absence of critical awareness of contextuality, either descriptive or normative, and the reduction of the ecclesial framework covertly employed seriously impairs biblical exegesis, and therefore undercuts biblical authority. The final irony is that political fundamentalism is, in this regard, one of the best contemporary illustrations of "secular humanism."[2]

2. For an analysis of the evidence of secular humanism in the new Christian Right see Gabriel Fackre, *The Religious Right and Christian Faith* (Grand Rapids: Eerdmans, 1982).

Another version of the traditionalist response is a parallel appeal for a return to the text, but this time the text is the church, or the teaching office of the church, rather than the biblical text. The sense that the modern context so threatens to overwhelm the stable points of textualization contributes to a rush toward the tangibilities of authority. The small but significant flow of conservative evangelicals into the Roman Catholic Church is a sign of the insecurities of the time. (A very traditionalist construal of that church goes with this move, one that is not shared by many Roman Catholics.) The rise within post–Vatican II Roman Catholicism of an ecclesial neofundamentalism, "ultraconservatism," is a part of this movement, too.

Modern contextualist theologies respond very differently. They embrace contextuality, using it as the grounds for restating the meaning of biblical authority. We discussed scenarios of world-oriented authority in Chapter One and mention again several of them in this external hermeneutical investigation. Many forms of contemporary liberation theology espouse a contextual hermeneutic that asserts that the key to biblical texts is given only within the framework of a critical consciousness of oppression and liberation. The meaning of the Bible is found in a network of texts and themes read in the context of the oppression/liberation problematic, a refrain set forth in Luke 4:17-21, Jesus' call to proclaim good news to the poor and release to the captives. Minimally, this means that one cannot understand the Bible unless it is read with the eyes of the poor or the captive, or in solidarity with them. Maximally, it means interpreting Scripture in terms of social theory that explains their plight and formulates a way out of it, as in Marxist analysis of the historical dialectic with its current protagonists, the proletariat and the bourgeoisie.

A wider contextuality moves to philosophical conceptuality rather than socioeconomic theory to discern biblical meaning. Thus process philosophy seeks to contextualize Christian texts in the world of modernity shaped by scientific method and evolutionary modes of thought. Employing categories that befit the move from a substance to a process world, it finds in Jesus' life and teaching the "creative transformation" that moves the universe toward the good. And in the portrayal of the God of Jesus it discovers a primordial divine nature that envisions the possibilities for all actual occasions, inviting them toward novelty cum mutuality, and a consequent nature that takes feelingly into itself and preserves all that has come to be. Thus the conceptual framework that rises from and speaks to the modern world provides the principle of the selection and interpretation of biblical texts.

Both liberation and process contextualizations assume by the way they work that the Bible does have a thread of meaning that is recoverable as intended, and the recovery operation is achievable by the hermeneutical key the designated act of contextualization provides. Other contextual views have less confidence in bridging the historical gap. One such view looks more to the world of art and literature than to socioeconomic or philosophical perspectives for its categories of contextualization. The text of Scripture as an art form is seen as having a life of its own—not some discursive "meaning" intended by its writer but the "meaningfulness" perceived in the text by the reader who meets it at a level below the subject-object relation. What does this text "say to me," how does it "confront me," what decision does it "wrest from me," what aspects of reality does it "disclose to me"? Thus the transfer of meaning from ever-new contexts gives a personal meaningfulness that enriches and transforms. Biblical texts are polyvalent, open to a variety of significances as is appropriate to a pluralistic world. Ventures from the "new hermeneutic" to many forms of narrative, metaphorical, and symbolist theology move in this direction, as do some varieties of liberation theology and pluralist theology for whom the particularities of the Christian text have become oppressive.

All forms of contextual theology bring an important witness to external hermeneutics. The God of Scripture is the historical One ever and again contexting the divine purpose in dealings with particular peoples, definitively in the incarnation of the Word in Jesus Christ. God comes to us today in a way commensurate with who God is and what God has done in these decisive deeds. Texts come home in contexts, which are both social and personal, noetic and fiducial, as is testified to by the kinds of contextualization just reviewed.

The major flaw in exclusively contextual theologies is the fusion and therefore the confusion of the meaning and the significance of a biblical text. The liberation and process contextualizations are legitimate efforts in seeking the significance of Scripture for important contemporary social contexts. But the *significance* of the Bible for these settings has swallowed up their *meaning* for all settings. Liberation perspectives enlarge our understanding of Scripture as a whole as well as critical threads of teaching in it, and correct oppressive readings of Scripture. They do not replace the total meaning of the Bible or exhaust the meaning of any single text. The Scripture read according to the common, critical, and canonical senses developed in our discussion of internal hermeneutics (chap. 3) entails meanings that go beyond the problematic identified by the various liberation theologies and the contextual construals that grow out of a very particular and historically conditioned response to that problematic. The same thing is true for a process reading of biblical texts, illuminating when it is offered as a venture drawing out the significance of Scripture for a particular ethos in the culture of modernity, but obscurantist when claiming to constitute the meaning of Scripture. What is lost in both of these moves to fuse meaning with significance is the *freedom of the text* to hold accountable all our efforts in contextualization. Without this freedom and distance, our legitimate efforts to indigenize are tempted to take charge of Scripture, using it for our own ends. Textualization as the intended meaning for all in every context is the teacher and critic of contextualization, as well as a student learning from it.

These same things must be said as well for the claims to personal contextualization represented by the noncognitive experiments in external hermeneutics. While Scripture must finally be *pro me,* its personal significance cannot dissolve its universal meaning. Whatever is claimed as constituting personal significance for me must cohere with textual meaning construed in its common, critical, and canonical senses. Scripture is *not* a picnic in which authors bring the words and readers the meaning.[3] In the case of both personal and social significances, "truth for all" is the trajectory along which "truth for us" and "truth for me" finds its way.

Postcontextual Perspectives

A cluster of new perceptions has begun to challenge a reductionist reading of context determined by an ideology of historical consciousness. It appears in diverse settings and disciplines: biblical scholarship, missiology, systematic theology, ethics, and the history

3. Contra Northrop Frye: "It has been said of Boehme that his books are like a picnic to which the author brings the words and the reader the meaning. The remark may have been intended as a sneer at Boehme, but it is an exact description of all works of literary art" (Frye, quoted in E. D. Hirsch, Jr., *Validity in Interpretation* [New Haven: Yale Univ. Press, 1967], 1).

of doctrine. While there is no uniform framework, there is a common challenge to assumptions about the nature of texts and the character of the hermeneutics. We note some of these developments, ones that have influenced this work.

In biblical studies, the canonical approach, especially as articulated by Brevard Childs, raises questions about historical-critical orthodoxies and points in a new direction. As earlier noted, this approach points to the hand of canonical editors, working from the oral tradition through literary distillation to final form as they ordered the Testaments and their materials theologically. This canonical editing has sought to render Scripture available to the faith community of the future, providing enduring parameters and themes of Christian identity, rather than speaking only to the historical context in which texts first emerged and to which they then spoke. One therefore cannot understand texts only, or even essentially, in terms of the context investigated by the standard methods of historical-critical study, but must explore them in terms of a canon criticism and theological scrutiny that seeks these unities and continuities.

George Lindbeck, working in systematic theology, especially in his encounter with ecumenical questions and interreligious issues, has written the important book *The Nature of Doctrine.* Lindbeck questions the "experiential-expressive" model that "interprets doctrines as noninformative and nondiscursive symbols of inner feelings and attitudes, or existential orientations."[4] He also considers inadequate the "propositional" model, which holds that doctrines "function as informative propositions or truth claims about objective reality."[5] He offers in their place a "cultural-linguistic" view where "a comprehensive scheme or story [is] used to structure all dimensions of existence. . . . One learns how to feel, act, and think in conformity with a religious tradition that is far richer and more subtle than can be explicitly articulated. . . ."[6] This total scheme and ethos living and growing provides identity and unity over time. He believes that this third model of doctrine can incoporate "both variable and invariable aspects" to which the other perspectives point, avoiding the too-fluid subjectivism of the first and the too-rigid objectivism of the second. Doctrine therefore has a transcon-

4. George Lindbeck, *The Nature of Doctrine* (Philadelphia: Fortress Press, 1984), 16.

5. Ibid.

6. Ibid., 35.

texuality in its function as a rule of discourse or regulative principle of theological inquiry.[7]

In *Constructing Local Theologies* Robert Schreiter strikes a similar note in seeking the meaning of Christian tradition in a "grammar" and "language system" of the community that continues through, illumines, and is illumined by its contextual journey. With extensive knowledge of cultural anthropology and missionary history and theory, Schreiter seeks to bring together in a fresh way the necessary elements of contextualization. On the one hand, he is aware both of the historical fact and theological necessity of "inculturation." "All theologies have contexts, interests, relationships of power, special concerns—and to pretend that this is not the case is to be blind."[8] Further, for Christological reasons, in entering a culture the church must be attentive to the Wisdom (Christ) already at work in it, incorporating the concerns, sensitivities, and insights entailed in the "local theology" right for that context. On the other hand, contextualization stands in relation to a wider and longer "tradition" of the church that functions to "test, affirm and challenge" it.[9] In the church, as in all human community, tradition contributes three things: It furnishes resources for identity; it is a communication system providing cohesion and continuity in the community; it offers resources for introducing innovative aspects into a community.[10] Within the tradition of the church there are "loci of orthodoxy (however construed: Scriptures, creeds, councils, confessions, magisterium) [that] represent a grammar, mediating competence and performance."[11] Competence is the faith out of which every Christian lives, wise and simple, and performance is the varied articulations of faith including theological ventures. With regard to the latter in its work of theological contextualization,

7. The greatest weakness of Lindbeck's theory that doctrines are "communally authoritative rules of discourse, attitude in action," (ibid., 18) is its unclarity about the relation to objective reality. In a searching review of Lindbeck's book, Avery Dulles makes this point from a Roman Catholic perspective: "For me, the church's claim to impose a doctrine in the name of revelation implies a claim of conformity to the real order, rather than a mere claim or a power to regulate language" (Dulles, "Observations on George Lindbeck, *The Nature of Doctrine,*" unpublished paper delivered at the Divinity School, Yale Univ., Sept. 14, 1984).

8. Robert J. Schreiter, *Constructing Local Theologies* (Maryknoll, N.Y.: Orbis Books, 1985), 4.

9. Ibid., 103.

10. Ibid., 105.

11. Ibid., 115.

tradition cum loci of orthodoxy serves a delimiting function, setting "boundaries of belief, but does not attempt to describe all combinations within the boundaries."[12]

Schreiter has striven to bring what we call here the source and resource of authority into dynamic relation with their setting, with an accountability to the former that is not often heard in contextual theory, but yet one stated more dialectically than the normativity of Scripture and tradition set forth in traditional views.

A group of evangelicals with strong mission interests have agonized over the authority of the Bible and the seriousness of context. Included in this number are Third World evangelicals determined to maintain the primacy of Scripture while relating it to the struggle for justice as well as personal evangelization, among them René Padilla, Orlando Costas, and Guillermo Cook.[13] With strong commitments to this kind of social and personal contextualization and extensive knowledge of linguistic and cross-cultural issues faced in missionary situations, Charles Kraft has produced a charter for an "ethnolinguistic interpretation" of Scripture in *Christianity in Culture.*[14] The extensiveness and complexity of his categories (thirteen basic perspective models, each with two to five subcategories, with thirteen factors influencing the advocacy of change, etc.) are both illuminating and intimidating. However, we risk a brief summary of some points that link Kraft and other evangelicals with the concern to respect both a descriptive and a normative contextuality while rejecting the ideology of contextual*ism.*

Kraft holds that both ends of engagement with Scripture—the text and its receptor—are "culture-specific." He criticizes "plain meaning" advocates for ignoring the influence of their own historical location, and for not probing critically the original culture of the text. At the same time he challenges the critic who presumes "objectively" to recover the original meaning with scholarly apparatus. That meaning emerged in "down-to-earth" situations and therefore is more accessible to ordinary folk who share them, and requires immersion in the receptor culture for seeing new import in those same texts. While insisting on this kind of contextuality,

12. Ibid., 116.

13. See C. René Padilla, *Mission Between the Times* (Grand Rapids: Eerdmans, 1985); Orlando Costas, *Christ Outside the Gate* (Maryknoll, N.Y.: Orbis Books, 1982) and *The Integrity of Mission* (San Francisco: Harper & Row, 1979); Guillermo Cook, *The Expectation of the Poor* (Maryknoll, N.Y.: Orbis Books, 1985).

14. Charles H. Kraft, *Christianity in Culture* (Maryknoll, N.Y.: Orbis Books, 1984).

he also holds that the text is the "tether," "yardstick," and "set radius" for all acts of subsequent contextualization.[15] It is so as "an inspired collection of classic cases"[16] that invite a "dynamic equivalence" translation process undertaken by a partnership of ordinary people, fully involved in the life of their culture, with critical scholars who work with the text and the context, helping us to know their context and the processes of communication in and among cultures.[17] In this encounter the biblical message comes alive for the receptor. Part of that aliveness is a distillation of a "general principle" embedded in the particularity of enculturated texts that is recoverable cross-culturally. And part of it is the application of it in a different way in the fresh context.[18] Beyond the intensely contexted texts of Scripture from which general principles can be recovered is the "basic ideal" level, in which supracultural assertions related to "a pancultural human commonality" are to be found ("Love the Lord your God with all your heart," Matt. 22:37).[19] And here "the plain meaning principle is often adequate for interpreting information presented at this deeper level of abstraction."[20] Thus Kraft and a contextually oriented group of evangelicals insist upon the importance of what we are calling here the Authorially intended meaning of a biblical text, and also a critical awareness of the cultural conditioning of original writing, but not at the cost of textual authority in its recoverable transcultural principles or supracultural assertions.[21]

The concern for continuity and identity in these kindred ventures is reminiscent of the return to the text by Reformation exegetes. The medieval practice of the fourfold interpretation of Scripture, for all its potentialities, produced results not unlike contextualization ideologies that dissolve textual meaning. We can learn from this tendency in understanding the possible traps in our own journey into context. The social and personal contextualization required by external hermeneutics carries forward the tro-

15. Ibid., 146, 37, 397-98.

16. Ibid., 398, 194-215.

17. Ibid., 143-46.

18. Ibid., 133-34, 141-43.

19. Ibid., 142.

20. Ibid., 139.

21. The studies and commentary of Max Stackhouse on contextuality are also part of this new concern for transcontextuality: see Max Stackhouse, *Apologia: Contextualization, Globalization and Mission in Theological Education* (Grand Rapids: Eerdmans, 1988).

pological (moral) and anagogical (mystical) impulses of earlier exegesis, and with them the dangers of an allegorization that loses touch with textual intention. We must undertake the pilgrimage from text to context with great care, striving to respect the identity of the biblical meaning and attending to the continuities that must persist in, and the transformative power it must have on, the act of contextual significance.

The Place of the Church

Crucial to the maintenance of textual integrity (identity and continuity) is the bridge factor between source and setting. That connector of Word and world is the church. Too seldom is its descriptive and normative presence acknowledged in the discussion of hermeneutics. The issue is often posed as the relationship of the two poles, text and context, and the hermeneutical circulation from one to the other. However, ecclesial reality functions, whether we recognize it or not, as a communal context within cultural context that both shapes the way in which one reads biblical texts *and* influences the manner in which one perceives the cultural context. We have seen already, in our examination of the common, critical, and canonical senses of Scripture, how ecclesiality works. As earlier stated (and later to be developed), it is right that this should be so, on the grounds of a doctrine of revelation in which the interpretive role of the Christian community is affirmed as a "resource" in understanding both the text and context (illumination). The church does not determine either text or context, on the grounds of the same doctrine of revelation. On the one hand, Scripture, as the prophetic-apostolic testimony (inspiration) to the center and substance, is the source of knowledge about divine reality and purpose. On the other, the world of general human experience beyond the church is graced sufficiently to enable it to go forward in the human narrative (impartation), for all its stumbling and falling. As such it is capable of insight into its own condition on the basis of this general revelation. The church, therefore, is a *textual* community that brings Scripture to bear on the discernment of the nature of the context. And it is a *contextual* community that carries the world's self-interpretations into conversation with the text.

While the common Christic grace in creation legitimates the hearing of the world's understanding of its own agenda, the damage done by the fall to its capacity to see (even itself) aright establishes a more dialectical relation between the textual community and contextual self-understandings than is often allowed for. Thus we cannot follow Tillich in his appropriation of a culture's literary, psychological, sociological, artistic, and philosophical self-interpretation as formulating "the question" of an age to which "the Christian answer" is addressed. While there is evidence of Tillich's own ecclesial tradition (e.g., Lutheran elements) at work in the choice of the sources and categories he employs in cultural interpretation (a fact that renders the question-answer method of correlation too simplistic), the most serious problem is his uncritical use of cultural diagnoses that have not been appraised by a textual community for the effect they might have on the construal of the text itself and, subsequently, on the text's contextualization. The evidence of this can be seen in how "the medium" identified by Tillich with the instruments of cultural self-interpretation so impacts "the message" that the latter's purported content bears a striking resemblance to the premises of the former.[22] Here is the problem that drives Barth to question all contextualization. But his plea for a return to the text eliminates, in turn, the text's own testimony to a revelatory grace that moves in a wider arc, and conceals the function of cultural categories in his own view. We seek yet another alternative in honoring the role of the textual/contextual community of faith.

Both *how* and *what* it brings to the text-context encounter are crucial to the ecclesial community's role. Its way (the "how") must be catholic. Here again we meet the importance of an ecumenical reading of textual meaning. Thus the commonsense reading of a biblical text is not the discovery by solitary persons of plain meaning, but the collegial discernment of textual intention. Ordinary people in the Body of Christ in all their heterogeneity together weave this tapestry of meaning. So too the contribution of the scholar, representing yet another constituency, makes for its well-being. And the heritage of the Christian community, its fathers and mothers, enters the conversation. This inclusive community, across both time and space, is at work in clarification of *context* as well as text. It employs its charter, the Bible, in asking what question or questions are being posed by the context to which the text can

22. Paul Tillich, *Systematic Theology,* vol. 1 (Chicago: Univ. of Chicago Press, 1951), 34-68 and *passim.* An analysis of Tillich's view of revelation and authority will appear in Vol. 3 of this series. On the relation of the perennial human questions to primal myths see Paul Ricoeur, *The Symbolism of Evil,* trans. Emerson Buchanan (New York: Harper & Row, 1967), *passim*.

speak, and what idiom is provided by the context in which that same text can speak. It has recourse to the same catholicity sought out in the construal of textual meaning, looking to the perception of ordinary people as well as the arts and intellectual disciplines of a given time and place. To the extent that it is such an inclusive perspective, the ecclesial community will be fruitful in its contextualization and faithful in its textualization.

To believe in inclusivity of perspective does not preclude historical moments of exclusivity. Hermeneutics as narrative means drama and tension on the journey. To assure the recognition of truth denied or obscured, its advocates may have to stand alone or in a critical minority—so a Martin Luther or Martin Luther King, Jr. Time along the narrative line supports the ecumenical vision, the church catholic learning from its critics, and there are special moments in the history for the perception of this inclusivity itself.

The content ("what") the community brings to the process also contributes to the maintenance of identity and continuity at both the textual and contextual poles. This content is the theological lore of the community, the "tradition" in its universal sense. The church's inclusive tradition is its understanding to date of the tradition at the Scripture's core—Christ and the gospel—those things that can be shown to be believed always, everywhere by everyone (Vincent of Lerins) within the ecumenical community. It rises out of the *sensus fidelium* becoming the *consensus fidelium* touching the center and substance of Christian faith.[23]

Various advocates of the historicism so formative of the mind of modernity question the existence of such a body of belief. All claims to locate it are seen to be only the limited and finally imperial assertions of partial perspectives and the weapons of vested interests in their oppression of marginalized groups. Others are quite convinced that there is such a common framework of faith but hold it to be the possession of their own segment of the universal church, to which all others must come for its acquisition.

History itself appears to be overtaking both of these orthodoxies.

23. On the Roman Catholic discussion of *sensus fidelium* see the following: Yves M.-J. Congar, "The sensus fidelium in the Fathers," in *Lay People in the Church* (Westminster, Md.: Newman, 1957), 441-43 and *Tradition and Traditions* (New York: Macmillan, 1966), 314-38; John Henry Newman, *On Consulting the Faithful in Matters of Doctrine* (rpt., New York: Sheed & Ward, 1962); Jean M. R. Tillard, "Sensus Fidelium," *One in Christ* 11 (1975): 2-29.

Ecumenical developments of a *doctrinal* sort are risking communal judgments regarding basic Christian teaching. Within the World Council of Churches the document *Baptism, Eucharist and Ministry,* for all its shortcomings, is evidence of a movement out from behind old fortifications. More so is the WCC's long-term venture, "Toward a Common Expression of the Apostolic Faith Today." And on parallel tracks are *The COCU Consensus* and sundry agreements reached in bilateral conversations, especially the remarkable convergences in Roman Catholic–Lutheran dialogue on justification by faith and in Lutheran-Reformed discussions on the sacraments and ministry. The Craigville colloquy process is a laboratory for these dynamics. What is present in the recent ecumenical moves, and anticipated in earlier experiments in united churches around the world and in the ecumenical movement, is an insight of which both relativist and traditionalist positions are devoid. It is an acknowledgment of the truth in perspectivalism that the perception of core teaching is always conditioned by finitude and sin. But rather than either abandoning the search for truth or striking back by making imperial claims for an ignored perspective, it holds that approximations of truth are possible through a catholicity of perspective. Thus the diversity within the Body is welcomed as key to the hermeneutical project.

To believe that a catholic approach can approximate truth does not entail the claim to finality. Time occasions yet other perspectives. And all these taken together do not yet constitute the eschatological finale when we shall know as we are now known by the all-seeing Eye.

Inclusivity has its political underside. The presence of a variety of advocates struggling toward definition introduces a process of checks and balances. As such, the will to power that functions in theological partisans as much as in any other pursuit (perhaps more so given the materials of ultimacy with which theology works, and hence the occupational hazard or "theological rabies") is moderated, and its destructive consequences reduced by countervailing constituencies. While catholicity is a vision brought to be out of the eschatological promise of the gospel, it also corresponds to reality. The end of all things is present as the purpose of creation forming it toward that future, incarnate in the flesh of Jesus, and present in the Body of Christ that grows out of that event. Christians have every right to believe that the life together that God *is, manifests,* and *wills* for the world undergirds our small ventures in theological work together, even in the sobering realities of political give and take.

Ecclesial Contextualization: A Case

We will here examine briefly the "how" and the "what" as they might function in an act of ecclesial contextualization. A situation presents itself in which political tyranny denies elemental freedoms, and economic oppression "grinds the faces of the poor" (Isa. 3:15, KJV). What does the Christian community bring to the contextualization of biblical texts on the nature and mission of the church in that situation?

Contextualization here requires immersion in the life and issues of the setting. From within that act of "presence,"[24] the community reaches out to its brothers and sisters, engaging all those in the present context who will to be together in the quest for response. And it invites the dead also to be at its council table, its "mothers and fathers," the community that has gone before it in struggling with the identity and purpose of the church. It gathers the wisdom from these vertical and horizontal communities, honoring in particular any catholicity of tradition that has emerged among them. At the center of this conversation is its charter, in its encompassing canonical sense, as well as the particular text it engages.

Into the dialogue on what the church is and must be in this context will enter a variety of viewpoints. The pressure to define itself in such a situation, and in similar ones, is by no means new. Avery Dulles has pinpointed "models" of the church that have emerged over time in a variety of contexts: herald, servant, sacrament, mystical communion, institution. Depending on the circumstances in both the church and the culture, one or the other has indeed taken form as a response to cultural contexts. The church has challenged the culture, taking the side of the oppressed as servant church. It has withdrawn from culture to preserve its identity and vision in sacramental or communal life together. It has proclaimed its identity and vision to its members and urged them

24. On "Christian presence" see Fackre, "Ministry of Presence," in the *Dictionary of Pastoral Care and Counseling,* ed. Rodney Hunter, H. Newton Malony, et al. (Nashville: Abingdon Press, 1987).

to live out these mandates as individuals in culture, as herald church. It has acceded to the way things are conforming to culture as institutional church.

Measuring these partisan viewpoints against the canonical paradigm of the church's nature and mission found in the stories of its origin in Acts (chaps. 2–4), it comes as no surprise that warrants are to be found for the servant model in the diaconal care of the poor and disabled and the confrontation with the day's power systems (2:45; 3:6-7; 4:3, 8-13); the herald model in the kerygmatic stance of Peter (2:14-40; 3:12-26); the sacramental model in the acts of *leitourgia* in bread, wine, and water (2:41-42); and the mystical communion model in the *koinonia* of a sharing, supporting community (2:42, 46-47). There is no evidence of the model of the church as institution, which suggests that at this point Dulles's scheme may be mixing normative features with a descriptive category. To the extent they are structured already, the four mentioned here are incipiently institutional. And they have not yet settled comfortably into the culture in the sense of negative institutionalization.

What is striking about the scriptural portraiture of the four signs of the Spirit so noted is their integration in the life of the primitive community. They are not separate models but interrelated parts of a common Body. As such they reflect the unity of these "marks of the church" in the very person of Christ. His Body on earth continues his own kerygmatic, diaconal, koinonial, and liturgical life and work.[25] The inclusiveness of the canonically construed Pentecostal community points toward the way in which subsequent Christian communities must understand themselves in their varying contexts.

The major statement of the nature of the church that comes from the period of the (relatively) undivided church carries forward the inclusive vision of the Pentecostal community. In the Nicene formulation the church in which we believe is "one, holy, catholic and apostolic." Whatever else these words mean, they also bear a striking resemblance to the gifts given to the church on its birthday. A church that is one has the life together of koinonia. A church that is holy is set apart and claimed for diaconal servanthood. A church that is apostolic preserves and preaches the apostolic kerygma. A church that is catholic in the sense presupposed by Nicea is bound

25. For a discussion of this interrelationship see Fackre, *CS*, 159-63.

together by its eucharistic liturgy. These are the marks of the church universal, definitive of its nature and mission.[26]

The ecclesial contextualizer brings these visions and perceptions while reading the variety of biblical texts in the setting of cultural tyranny and oppression. In such a context the claims of the texts of servanthood forcefully come to the fore. The servant church must care for the disenfranchised and confront the powers and principalities, even as did the early church. The lame at the gate are ministered to (Acts 3:1-8). The oppressive structures of power are challenged (4:1-22). A price is paid for challenging the status quo (4:2-3, 18-21). Without this compassionate and confrontative action ecclesial contextualization would be a mockery of Scripture and tradition. But is that the end of the matter? Not if the bridging work of ecclesial contextualization goes on. The church of inclusive definition cannot be reduced to those who have caught the vision of servanthood to human political and economic need. If it is, then a sect is born, one that separates itself from the rest of the Body, indeed claims to alone *be* the Body (1 Cor. 12:19). For that moment in time, in that social context, it is charged with special responsibility, to alert the whole Body to the *kairos* and the foreground Word to be heard in it. Yet there are other parts to the Body, other movements to be made, other needs to be addressed, other accents of the Word to be honored. Those who witness to the heraldic, liturgical, and communal gifts of the Spirit here must give their testimony. That witness is *not* made when these gifts are themselves employed *only* to serve the political and economic agenda discerned by the servant church. They do it when that bonding *is* insisted upon, but at the same time the freedom to range across a wider horizon of divine intention and human need is maintained. Other gift-ministries within the Body may be needed to remind the church of the issue of *universal sin,* the sin in the champions of justice as well as in its foes; the issue of *death* that brings an end to just as well as unjust societies and persons; the *error* that infects the good as well as the evil. The contextualizing church that stewards the gospel in catholicity will resist the flight from the frontier of servanthood those partial to other marks will encourage and refuse as well the reduction of the nature and mission of the church to the single issue the servant model advocates. In exegesis this means the determination to avoid an exclusivist "canon within the canon" fixed upon a thread of texts hospitable to advocacy groups.

26. Ibid., 163-71.

It means a willingness to read the foreground texts that "speak to the situation" of political tyranny and economic injustice in the light of the whole canon, and, in particular, the canonical vision of Christ and the gospel that witness to the manifold nature and interrelated catholicity of the Body of Christ.

The most painful custodianship of this vision comes when the context does not seem to permit the very servant role demanded of the church then and there: a totalitarian society that denies the Christian community ways of response. In such contexts a "survival" ecclesiology may be the only option, as in black churches in a radically racist society that protect human dignity by an intense piety and life together. Eastern Orthodox liturgical life together under the constraints of a Marxist society, Anabaptist conventicles in the face of drastic cultural antipathy—a *disciplina arcani,* "confessing church"/"waiting church" in situations that imperil the existence of the church itself. In these cases the way of servanthood may be, paradoxically, the otherwise bashful roles of herald, sacrament, or conventicular community.

Ecclesial contextualization does its work well when it brings the wisdom of the Body to bear on text and context, drawing on the multiple gifts Christ gives to the people of God who compose it.

A CONTEXTUAL PERSPECTIVE

The act of contextualization always entails an organizing principle. The manifold data of a given time and place are interpreted according to some framework. It may be unconscious or conscious, a wide-ranging assumption (secularity), a developed philosophical system (Neoplatonism), a socioeconomic theory (Marxism), a psychological construct (Jungianism), an artistic sensibility or conceptuality (new literary criticism), or an eclectic assortment of some or all of these or other frameworks. Where the ecclesial community is faithful to its textual as well as contextual commitments and plays its role in the contexting process the biblical text will inform the categories employed as well as provide the content for the journey from Word to world. We shall develop here in more detail the "perspective" to which brief reference was earlier made.

As Tillich has noted, the church's responses to the social context have focused at one time or another on salvation from sin (Reformation), mortality (patristic period), ignorance (Greek-influenced epochs), or suffering (nineteenth-century social reform).[27] Indeed, in one form or another the human problematic in Christian perspective appears to be sin and guilt, transiency and mortality, evil/devil/suffering, and error/ignorance. These issues manifest themselves in four major types of atonement theory that have emerged in the history of the church.[28] What God saves from and for—the doctrine of at-one-ment that presupposes an understanding of alienation—is a central clue to Christianity's historic interpretation of contextual issues. Thus one atonement tradition concentrates on Christ the Galilean teacher and example who reveals the truth that saves from ignorance and error. Another directs attention to Calvary where the forgiveness of sin is made possible by the sacrificial work of Christ. Another stream of interpretation looks to the resurrection for the victory won over the evil that brought crucifixion. Still another turns to Bethlehem and incarnation itself as the union of eternity with time that overcomes our mortality. While one or the other comes to the fore in a particular context, all four soteriological themes are held together in a central doctrinal tradition reflecting the New Testament's multiple metaphors and motifs of Christ's work. So in Volume 1 the threefold office of Christ is used as an inclusive framework for interpreting the doctrine of atonement, one in which the incarnate Word (eternity in time) exercises prophetic (truth overcoming error), priestly (forgiveness of sin), and royal (liberation from evil) roles.[29]

We begin our articulation of a perspective by recognizing this well-honed instrument of discernment, learning from its employment by the ecumenical community today, weighing the culture's self-interpretations in the light of it, and listening to the questions posed by the people with whom we serve and with whom we live and work. To the extent we are present with and attuned to the context our perspective will not only be *for* our time and place but *from* it.[30]

Quickly the question comes, "Where are the boundaries of social context?" How do you tell a context when you see one? Is it nation? Region? Society? Culture? Era? Race? Class? Sex? Condition? Parish? The whole world as parish? Answers to these bewildering

27. Paul Tillich, *Systematic Theology,* 1:48-49.

28. Fackre, *CS,* 123-35.

29. Ibid., 135-53.

30. For comments on this distinction see Colin E. Gunton, *Yesterday and Today: A Study of Continuities in Christology* (Grand Rapids: Eerdmans, 1983), 49-51.

questions are helped along by lessons from earlier ecclesial contextualizations. The fourfold understanding of contextual problematic—sin, suffering, error, death—suggests that, at least at one level, an encompassing reply is appropriate. Where one or another was thought to be the question—however limited it, in fact, proved to be—these are the boundaries of context. We are much more aware since the Enlightenment of the contingency of what we think of as "the world." Nevertheless, the partisans of historical relativity are the most eager to remind us of the worldwide range of historical relativity. So too are those who advocate a class, race, sex, age, or condition key to contextuality. These categories are offered as universal explanations, and are not confined to a here or there, or even a now or then.

We shall take a clue from the ecclesial tradition in which time, rather than space, seems to be formative of context, a ripe time, a "pregnant moment," a *kairos* that calls forth a contextual Word from the community of faith, appropriately so for a narrative gospel.[31] Let that Word also be for "the world." But whether it is a global contextualization, or a more restricted one, the judgment is a risk of faith and not an unquestioned assumption. The knowledge of cultural particularity will sober us about such claims. So will realism about the imperial pretensions of power cultures and centers of cultural power. Nevertheless, commonalities of threat and possibility, and the interaction that modern technology has brought to all cultures, suggest that some contextualization might reflect that universality. Only the testing of a venture in contextualization will demonstrate the validity of the proposal.

The world of the late twentieth century to which this systematics is addressed is one in which human suffering comes to the foreground. The science and technology that have decisively shaped this epoch have not only made it possible to think of a bonding of cultures that constitutes them as a common "world"; they have also raised sky-high the human stakes. The promise of living better—the survival of multitudes who before had died of starvation and disease, the attainment of minimal physical and mental securities for multitudes who never before could think beyond survival, the relative comfort of multitudes who might come to expect now as not before both "bread *and* roses"[32]—is implicit in new technol-

31. On *kairos*, see Paul Tillich, *The Protestant Era*, trans. James Luther Adams (Chicago: Univ. of Chicago Press, 1949), 32-51.

32. A slogan from the mid-century labor union movement.

ogies and their application. At the same time, the peril is there as well, often more visible than the promise. Thus the power to bring a nuclear winter becomes more likely. So too, the effects of injustice mount with the concentration of the instruments of new possibility gathered into the hands of those who control the technologies. These same powers in the communication sphere disseminate an awareness of the disparities to those who suffer from them.

Experiencing both the promise and the peril more keenly, and a heightening awareness of their dynamics through access to new media, the disinherited and the threatened make their voices heard and presence known with greater and greater insistence. As the twin forms of suffering come to greater consciousness—injustice and war, or, in larger terms, bondage and alienation—so too appear more forcefully their commensurate metaphors of hope—"justice and peace" or "liberation and reconciliation." While the idiom for such a time which commands wide attention comes from one sector, others who name it differently and focus on their particular issues—"pro-life," "the battle for the mind," "peace of heart"—bear witness to their own forms of suffering and hope.

Certainly the other great human questions—sin, death, and error—are there in the perceptions and analyses of a generation wrestling with agony and expectation. Yet they are consistently taken up into the framework employed, rather than understood in their own terms. Sin is the malevolence of the oppressor and warmaker, the perversion of the enemy in the battle for the mind and soul. Death is what is dealt out to us by the moguls of power and the warmongers, or those pro-murder rather than pro-life. Error is what afflicts the foe. The universalizing features are erased—my/our sin, my/our death and death-dealing, my/our error and ignorance. Likewise the universality of suffering is muted in the sharp juxtaposition of my agony and your oppression. Thus the Manichaean (and Zoroastrian) temptation that attends every genuine grasp of the facts of human anguish and wrongdoing: Here is the good kingdom and there is the "evil empire"; here are the forces of light and there are the battalions of night. As we sharpen the perspective that accepts suffering and hope as the broad context in which the biblical text is to be interpreted, we shall strive to maintain the integrity of the universal questions of sin, death, and error and the scriptural responses to them within, but not reduced to, the contextual framework employed. And we shall try to show how just that integrity in fact illumines more profoundly both the context and our response to it—an encounter with suffering that knows the sin in the champions of justice and peace as well as in its foes, a death that hangs over all our achievements of justice and peace, an error that persists in our causes and conclusions. With these comes hope that speaks also of the forgiveness of sin, the resurrection of the dead, and a revelation to be known and seen through our common night.

Suffering and Hope in Twentieth-Century Theologies

What we meet in the closing decades of the twentieth century as "the human prospect" has been long germinating in cultures shaped by the science and technology that have brought us to this point. A case can be made that twentieth-century theologies, initially in the West then beyond that as these forces did their universalizing work, reflect the movement forward of the tandem themes of suffering and hope. For example, in the second decade of the century a developing technology was harnessed to war making on a world scale with a horrifying result. In its wake emerged theological movements that responded variously to theodicy, the "problem of evil," the suffering question posed in its profoundest way in the theological tradition. How can an all-good and all-powerful God countenance such misery? In the midst of both the anguish and the agonizing question emerged a challenge to the traditional doctrine of divine impassibility and a postwar exploration of "the suffering of God" in British and German theology.[33] Significantly, following World War II and the dropping of the atomic bomb on Hiroshima and Nagasaki, a similar reflection on "the pain of God" became part of Japanese theology.[34] And in that war, the events that led up to it and the questions that grew out of it touching the fate of six million Jews, the fact of Holocaust, pressed the issue of theodicy to its limits. The profound wrestling with this question in the thought of Abraham Heschel (once again the "suffering of God"), Emil Fackenheim, and Elie Wiesel, other Jewish theologians, and all Jewish believers underscores the primacy of this issue in our time, as well as points to resources in the Judeo-Christian tradition for response to it. Taking up both the Holocaust question and the kind of response anticipated earlier in accents on the divine vulnerability Jürgen Moltmann speaks of "the crucified God" and did so significantly first in the decade of the seventies when the more hope-

33. Examined in J. K. Mozley, *The Impassibility of God* (Cambridge: Cambridge Univ. Press, 1926).

34. Kazoh Kitamori, *Theology of the Pain of God* (Richmond: John Knox Press, 1965).

filled momentum of the sixties (including his own "theology of hope") had to face the stubborn realities with which all visionary movements must contend. The same struggle to hold together suffering and hope in the historical context of these decades came to be seen in the thought of E. Schillebeeckx. His encyclopedic work in Christology has as its organizing principle this theme as embodied in the text he brings forward as key to his project: "That you may not grieve as others do who have no hope" (1 Thess. 4:13).[35] Archbishop Desmond Tutu has from within the same caldron, given powerful and precise definition to the universal question of our time in his *Hope and Suffering.*[36]

From among those who have suffered so much in this century has risen another theological reaction, one different from those heretofore described with their confrontation of suffering with a transcendent hope of one sort or another. Thus Richard Rubenstein announces not the suffering but the *death* of God. In this high rhetoric, paralleling Christian versions of the same, a secular theodicy answers the problem of suffering. Honesty demands that we cease to believe in God. No such trust in a good and almighty deity can stand before the withering fires of Holocaust. The acceleration of the processes of secularity after World War I were not, as such, the result of the increasingly empirical mindset of a culture of science and technology. In this history, the problem of evil, not the problem of evidence, seems to be the decisive factor in the loss of faith. While the death of God theology (also the death of code morality and the death of church ecclesiology that accompanied it in the nineteen sixties)[37] expressed the issue flamboyantly and finally only transiently, the secularization process in theology has been a constant in this century. It manifests itself in those movements that justify religious loyalties by their efficacy in dealing with the fact and/or the cause of human suffering. This is true not only about the naturalisms and humanisms with their tenuous connections to religious traditions, and the modernisms and pragmatisms that ground whatever is held to be transcendently true in moral

35. Edward Schillebeeckx, *Jesus: An Experiment in Christology,* trans. Hubert Hoskins (New York: Seabury Press, 1979). So on the dedication page: "Dedicated to all my readers—known and unknown—and especially Bernard Cardinal Alfrink 'That you may not grieve as others do who have no hope' (I Thess. 4:13)."

36. Desmond Tutu, *Hope and Suffering,* comp. Mothobi Mutloatse, ed. John Webster (Grand Rapids: Eerdmans, 1984).

37. For the linkage of these three phenomena see Fackre, *Humiliation and Celebration* (New York: Sheed and Ward, 1969), *passim*.

results, but also about the pietisms and fundamentalisms whose warrants are to be found ultimately in the *secular* payoffs, the assuagements of suffering, personal or political.[38] The moral productivity of faith, of course, has a long history, and, rightly conceived, belongs to the nature of Christian faith. However, the reduction of faith to its moral significance, always resisted in the Christian tradition in the struggle against works-righteousness, Pelagianism, etc., has taken an increasingly higher profile since Kant, a fact not unrelated to the developments in science and technology that have set us on our present course. The appearance of Feuerbach, Marx, Nietzsche, and Freud signaled things to come. The morality of suffering *coram Deo* took center stage.

Yet another reaction from within a suffering people is a clue to a larger theological direction. When the wrongness of things is so clear—when bad things happen to good people—but one is not able to reject outright the God of one's heritage, then the *kind* of God thought to be there in the face of misery must be changed. Yes, with Heschel, a suffering God, but can we be so sure of rescuing so much meaning from misery? We can make no such implicit or explicit claims for a good resolution. God is finite not infinite, powerful but not all-powerful, able to be defeated, never all-victorious. God does the best God can under the most trying of circumstances, and that is enough for those who can trust such a companion. This Fellow-Sufferer who understands comes to meet us earlier in the century in the process philosophy of Whitehead and then later in his process theology heirs. So too arrives the limited God who must fight the surd of evil in the universe in Brightman and the personalist tradition. The working piety of many in the congregations of the West may well be of this order, not ready to give up on transcendence, but sobered by its apparent defeats in our personal and social histories. The ecumenical appeal of Kushner seems to bear this out.[39]

Setting its face against the rejections, qualifications, or dialectical interpretations of divine transcendence, an "in spite of" response to human suffering in the twentieth century has spoken its own different word. Here the very worst of circumstances invites the boldest of assertions. In Karl Barth's letter to Christians in Great

38. As argued in the programmatic essay for *Humiliation and Celebration*, "The Issues of Transcendence in the New Theology, the New Morality, and the New Forms," in *New Theology 4*, ed. Martin E. Marty and Dean Pierman (New York: Macmillan, 1967), 178-94.

39. Harold Kushner, *When Bad Things Happen to Good People* (New York: Schocken Books, 1981).

Britain at the height of the Nazi peril can be heard this ringing note:

> The world in which we live is the place where Jesus Christ rose from the dead. . . . It is on this world in its entirety that God has set His mark. . . . He has exalted the name of Jesus above every name, "that in the name of Jesus every knee should bow, of things in heaven and things on earth and things under the earth" (Phil. 2:10). Since this is true, the world in which we live is not some sinister wilderness where fate or chance holds sway or where all sorts of "principalities and powers" run riot unrestrained and range about unchecked. Since this is true, the world has not been given up to the devil or to man that they may make of it some vast "Insanity Fair." . . . The Kingly rule of Christ extends not merely over the Church as the congregation of the faithful but, regardless whether men believe it or not, over the whole of the universe in all its heights and depths; and it also confronts and overrules with sovereign dignity the principalities and powers and evil spirits of this world. . . . For Jesus Christ, according to the teaching of the whole New Testament, has already borne away sin and destroyed death. So also has He already (Col. 2:15) completely disarmed those "principalities and powers" and made a spectacle of them in His own triumph in order finally to tread them down under His feet on the day of His coming again (I Cor. 15:15). It is only as shadows without real substance and power that they can still beset us. We Christians, of all men, have no right whatsoever to fear and respect them or to resign ourselves to the fact that they are spreading throughout the world as though they knew neither bounds nor lord. We should be slighting the resurrection of Jesus Christ and denying His reign on the right hand of the Father, if we forget that the world in which we live is already consecrated, and if we did not, for Christ's sake, come to grips spiritedly and resolutely with these evil spirits.[40]

Whatever else the theology of Barth means, viewed in the setting of the four perennial human quandaries, it surely can be understood as an address to the question of suffering and hope. Barth knows of the suffering of God, the absence of God, the weakness of God but the dominant note is the *triumph* of God.[41] That

40. Karl Barth, *A Letter to Great Britain from Switzerland* (London: Sheldon Press, 1941), 10-11.

41. So an early Barth: "Knowledge of God is not an escape into the safe heights of pure ideas, but an entry into the need of the present world, sharing in its suffering, its activity and its hope." Quoted in Eberhard Busch, *Karl Barth: His*

Barth can speak about triumph through suffering, absence, and weakness, thereby taking account of other accents—albeit organized around his controlling vision—and can find a place as well for sin-forgiveness (as in his "neo-orthodoxy"), error-truth (as in his "theology of revelation"), and death-life (as a theology "supernaturalist" and "eschatological") is a measure of the greatness of his work. Yet this catholicity is sensitive to the whole range of scriptural witness, and ecclesial concern is woven into an Easter tapestry seen in the light that comes from the divine majesty, framed by Calvin, signed by Barth.[42]

In striking parallel to Barthian thought, touching both the large contextual issue and the answering accent in faith, is the Lundensian theology, especially that of Gustav Aulén. *Christus Victor!*[43] Here a Lutheran tradition found a word to speak before the Nazi juggernaut. It can be no accident that Aulén rediscovered the "conflict and victory" motif in atonement in the agonizing decade of Hitler's advances, the first hints of Holocaust, the church's travail. For Aulén, contexted biblical text has to learn from the Christ who contests the powers and principalities that inflict their final pain on Good Friday, a Christ who rises to rule over them on resurrection morning. So appears the dramatic "motif" and conflict and victory model, the royal leader who has won the day for us and empowers us to struggle against foes that have already met their fate.

We can hear these same notes in one way or another in the mid-century developing ecumenical theology, especially in the World Council of Churches and its predecessor movements. The concluding statements of the first assembly in 1948 on "Man's Disorder and God's Design" and of the second assembly on "Christ, the Hope of the World" strike this chord.[44] Formative here were not only Bar-

Life from Letters and Autobiographical Texts, trans. John Bowden (Philadelphia: Fortress Press, 1976), 100. See also Barth, "Hope," in *Evangelical Theology: An Introduction* (Grand Rapids: Eerdmans, 1979), 144-56.

42. See H. G. Berkouwer, *The Triumph of Grace in the Theology of Karl Barth,* 2d ed. (Grand Rapids: Eerdmans, 1956).

43. Gustav Aulén, *Christus Victor!,* trans. Eric H. Wahlstrom (Philadelphia: Fortress Press, 1960), *passim.* The parallel is shown by Donald Bloesch in *Jesus Is Victor!* (Nashville: Abingdon Press, 1976).

44. See "Message," First Assembly of the Council of Churches in *Man's Disorder and God's Design* (New York: Harper & Brothers, 1949), 229-33. The message reflects the refrain in the commission reports also appearing in this volume; "The Message," Second Assembly of the World Council of Churches in *The Evanston Report: The Second Assembly of the World Council of Churches* (New York: Harper & Brothers, 1955), 1-3 and *passim* in reports of the sections.

thian and Lundensian influences but also the complex of ideas described variously as "biblical theology," "acts of God theology," "*heilsgeschichte,*" etc. the thought of Reinhold Niebuhr, the resurrection strains within Eastern Orthodoxy, broadly evangelical accents, especially from mission frontiers in Third World countries, and the special stamp left by ecumenical leadership itself such as Visser't Hooft, Newbigin, and the Anglican heirs of Archbishop Temple.

The "in spite of" theodicy continued in subsequent decades but took a different turn. Imperatives came up alongside the indicatives and even began to edge in front of them. The possibilities rather than the impossibilities drew the eye of faith, reflecting horizons that the culture itself seemed to open up. So too the perception of non-Western cultures entered, not so preoccupied with the anxieties and dreads of war-weary westerners, made aware of disparities and manifest injustices, influenced by conceptualities that held out the possibility, indeed the certainty, that things could be different for them. The turn to the imperatives came in the humanization accents of the sixties, grounded here in faith, not a simple secularization, with some roots in Bonhoeffer, some of the dreams of a Martin Luther King, Jr., some of the vision of a John XXIII. In spite of the magnitude of the problem, there is a way through the suffering. This faith is grounded in the God of hope. And hope mobilizes. Thus a theology of hope-in-action rose in the "in spite of" community. King himself gave it significant formulation. Jürgen Moltmann (with a picture of King giving his "I have a dream" speech on his study wall) gave it European theological voice and precise theological formulation.[45] Pannenberg with interests more epistemological (*revelation* as history) moved along similar lines in a theology of the future, with its portent in the resurrection.[46]

Hope and humanization took yet another step and another turn in the liberation theologies that have emerged among the disinherited of every kind—class, nation, race, sex, age, condition. The metaphor itself, compared to "humanization," suggests a sharpening of the issues and a deepening of their conflictual nature. The indictment of an enemy is forceful, the mandates are urgent. But

45. Moltmann comments on the visual impact of King's witness in *The Church in the Power of the Spirit,* trans. Margaret Kohl (New York: Harper & Row, 1977), 286.

46. Pannenberg, *Jesus: God and Man,* trans. Lewis Wilkins and Duane A. Priebe (Philadelphia: Westminster Press, 1968), 53-114.

the indicatives are there along with the imperatives. With the indictment comes the assurance that there *is* judgment that awaits the oppressor, backed by the One who is in solidarity with the sufferer. With the urging to action, first and foremost directed to the disinherited themselves, comes the assurance that there *is* hope beyond suffering, warranted by the God of history who will bring the mighty from their seats and exalt those of low estate . . . in spite of what we see now to be the case.[47] It seems to be a long way from Barth to Third World, black, and feminist liberation theologies, many of which excoriate him along with other western, white, middle-class, male, triumphalist doctrine-makers. But those we have mentioned and their kin, along with this most recent constituency, all have put to the fore in their own way the regnant issue of suffering and hope. And a trail can be traced within both the theological community and the larger culture that takes us from one to the other.

An important figure in the identification of the broad problematic of our time and place is Paul Tillich. He knew that whatever our disclaimers, those of Barth most of all, our theology cannot help but be and must be correlative. We speak out of and into our context. The science of the "method of correlation" is a self-awareness of our own perspectival limits; the art of it is discerning the nature of the time. Both science and art are needed to say the right word at the right time. In the view espoused here, Tillich did indeed rightly discern the signs of the times. He understood the *kairos* that stretched across the century and its cultures. Yet he expressed it in the postwar idiom of existentialism, the anxiety, alienation, and dread of a period or at least the literary and artistic interpreters of a period that had eyes essentially for the abyss. And he seemed to have less to say in his later writing about the prospects of social history, to which he gave attention in his earlier religious socialist phase, than about the agonies and ecstasies of the depth dimension. For all that, his own characterization of our era's question fits what we have called the suffering and hope problematic. More clearly than by a thousand definitions do we see this in the interpretation and use of literary and artistic symbols, whether they be the theodicial quandaries of Camus's *Plague* or Picasso's *Guernica*. Similarly,

47. For the assertion of these hopes in the face of the bleakest of circumstances see James Cone, *For My People: Black Theology in the Black Church* (Maryknoll, N.Y.: Orbis Books, 1984), 189-206 and *Speaking the Truth: Ecumenism, Liberation, and Black Theology* (Grand Rapids: Eerdmans, 1986), 4-34, 129-41.

Giotto's *St. Francis* was able to suggest a theonomy that shone through in another era, inviting us to consider what an ultimate hope might mean that pointed to the new Being beyond presently experienced nonbeing. Like Barth, his comprehensive theological mind sought to include the other human perplexities. But he did it by interpreting them wholly within his framework: sin as alienation, error as the conditioned before the unconditional, death as the nonbeing of meaning. The absorption of all questions into our question, the commensurate reading of our answer as "the Christian answer,"[48] and the route taken from the first to the second by a cultural construal of "the medium" that finds its way finally into "the message" puts us on notice to Barth's concern about the whole method of correlation, and thus contextualization itself.

But we do not have to take the way of Barth to honor the concern of Barth, the captivity of the meaning of the text to the perceived significance of the text. Contextuality is part of the Author's intention, one neither to be swallowed up by textuality (Barth) nor in turn to dissolve it (Tillich). Their life together is the task we set for ourselves in this hermeneutics, with the sober recognition of how difficult it is to maintain the integrity of each and the partnership of both, for all our good intentions.

Narrative Perspective

Our contextual angle of vision on Scripture begins with the question: Is there hope for overcoming the personal and social suffering we know and experience in this time and place? In posing the question, and putting it the way we have, the "doing" dimension of human experience moves to the foreground, before our categories of "thinking" and "feeling." A thinking perspective might read this as a "Kantian" approach to faith, locating it in an intellectual tradition, indeed a western one, showing how quickly we absorb data into our own interpretive frameworks. However, if the technological forces have been as formative of our problematic as earlier contended, then Kantianism itself is a child of our era, a philosophical response to deeper cultural currents, subsequently influential in its own way but not determinative of either the analysis or the issue or the proposals addressed to it. The moral claim rises from the exigencies of the situation itself, the peril and possibilities of life,

48. Paul J. Tillich, "The World Situation," in *The Christian Answer,* ed. H. P. Van Dusen (New York: Scribner's, 1945), 1-44.

accelerated by the new instruments of this weal or woe. This judgment assumes that the capacity to know that the situation constitutes peril and possibility, and to will to do something about it, is accessible to human beings (a doctrine of general revelation that recognizes a sullied but not destroyed image of God in us). Further, from both this "reason" and from "faith," it discerns the influence in our moral sensibility of a far deeper interpretive stream, that of the world-affirming Judeo-Christian tradition, one which accounts in part for the rise of science-technology in this culture and our "doing" response to it.[49]

The way we state the problem, as well as the problem itself, has repercussions in the kind of perspective developed. Suffering is social and of this time and place, as well as personal and universal. As such, institutions in historical process and locus are integral to the problematic. The period's refrain, "justice and peace," presupposes systemic concerns and solutions. That means social, political, and economic metaphors and motifs are appropriate elements in forming perspective. In the refining of language for translating faith into this setting, as in identifying the cultural question, *what* metaphors and motifs are chosen and *how* they are used must always be under the scrutiny of the Christian tradition that employs them. Translation keys tend to take on a life of their own shaped by the context from which they come and can seriously skew the faith they seek to communicate. With the foregoing in mind we lift up *liberation* and *reconciliation* as perspectival symbols and themes with their counterparts *bondage* and *alienation*. Both, linguistically and conceptually, have a history in Scripture and tradition. Each identifies one of the twin systemic issues of our time, justice and peace. Both are associated with concerns with which the ecumenical Christian community today identifies, however ambiguous the movements that employ the language. Each is susceptible of interpretation that includes but goes beyond the political, social, and economic habitat in which they regularly are found. Already this multivalence is found in much Christian discourse. Liberation is deliverance from political, economic, and social oppressors. As we move from the social contextuality (where it functions predominantly) across the ecclesial bridge to biblical textuality, we soon discover that it also includes liberation from sin, death, and error. These latter understandings will affect how we in turn construe

49. Alfred North Whitehead, *Science and the Modern World* (New York: Macmillan, 1925).

political, social, and economic justice. Reconciliation is nations beating swords into plowshares in a world threatened by nuclear destruction, devastated by our technological assault on it, and nature in harmony with itself. By ecclesial route to Scripture it is the reconciliation with God of self, societies, and cosmos, a peace that the world cannot either give or take away.

Thus liberation from the state of bondage and reconciliation that overcomes alienation are motifs that express the suffering and hope marking our epoch. They are terms that are at home in both context and text, ways to express the dynamism of the world in which we live that afford translation keys for the communication of the gospel. That translation, as we shall shortly see, entails a *transformation* of their cultural meaning in which both the limitations and distortions of their cultural usage are challenged.

In company with these organizing motifs are metaphors that have currency in our time and place. The visual and visionary aspects of hope are put forward in the figure of *vision* (not to replace but to complement the verbal-auditory symbol so prominent in the tradition, Word), and *reality* in counterpoint.[50] And its *light* keeps company with *night.* Thus vision and reality, light and night are ways of expressing the hope of liberation and reconciliation in the midst of the suffering of bondage and alienation.

The idiom used to characterize our historical context is tension-filled, earthy, human, future-oriented. Plot, people, places, tension, movement, resolution—these are the ingredients of *narrative* which provide their overarching framework. (Since we have dwelt already on the importance of story in this systematics we will not repeat the particulars.) Thus narrative is the *perspective* that takes shape within the worldly context in which we interpret the text. It speaks to the *problematic* of suffering and hope in the *motifs* of liberation and reconciliation and the *metaphors* of vision and light. The contextual perspective is treated in the *mode* that has characterized the textual inquiry as well, catholicity of participation by the many parts of Christ's body in every aspect of the theological task.

Before taking up the contextualization process we need to remind ourselves of the traps that await the pilgrim along this way. Each of the terms and concepts we are using has its own life, its own constituencies, and its own ideologies. How easy to be enamored of them and, chameleonlike, blend into the scene. How often the communication of those eager to context the faith has become

50. Cf. Margaret Ruth Miles, *Image as Insight* (Boston: Beacon Press, 1985).

accommodation to culture! Narrative theology can become fixation on storytelling with no accountability to the Christian Story, liberation and peace theologies can allow the categories of liberation and peace movements to determine the content of their message, the metaphor of vision can replace the claims of the Word, the images of light and night can become harnessed to a Manichaean dualism, political and theological inclusivity can become the slogan of a New Age religion of holism. In all these cases the text is dissolved into the context, the world drowns out the Word. Contextual helps are always just that, instruments to communicate something other than themselves, the evangelical text, the gospel of Jesus Christ.

MODELS OF CONTEXTUALIZATION

In the mode of catholicity, we now hear out various ways to bring the text into relationship with the context. We shall call them translation, transition, traduction, transformation, trajection. In them we meet again some of the same protagonists introduced in the review of options in authority and in the opening section of this chapter. Now they appear as models of contextualization, seen through their theories of indigenizing the gospel.

In appropriating insights from each perspective we are, of course, drawing on the resource role of the church. The Christian community is the bridge across the traffic flow of text to context and back again. It counts heavily here. In the practical work of the pastor it means the local congregation and any group within its life that engages directly or indirectly in the search for the meaning and significance of a text. But the ties that bind the pastor to the Christian community extend far beyond that. They are found in the paraparochial and supraparochial settings of influence and interpretation. Such may be a pastor's study group on the lectionary or other noncongregational settings in which the pastor has regular or occasional concourse. This also may include life together in the ecclesial family, a larger network of denominational, interdenominational, and ecumenical ties, from seminary formation through national agencies and actions to grassroot movements.

Translation

"Translation" is the general metaphor we are using for the external hermeneutical task. Here we examine it as a particular model of contextualization. The meaning of the word is not as self-evident as it is often treated when used for theological purposes. In fact, some roundly criticize the term and concept.[51] Three major kinds of literary translation provide guidelines for hermeneutical translation.

Translation can be done in a *literal* fashion, in which no deviation is made from the original linguistic structures. The words used in one language are replicated in the second, the sentence order and grammar of one faithfully reflected in the other. Critics of this mode argue that the meaning may, in fact, be lost in this rigid crossover, since words in one language do not have a necessary equivalency of meaning in another. Further, the sentence order in one may require a different sequence in another to be faithful to the intended meaning of the original. Hence a second kind of translation, identified sometimes as *dynamic equivalence,* which allows a modest latitude and gives a place to the translator's judgment in the arrangement of word order and introduction of new terms. A third form of translation allows even greater freedom from the original, encouraging a more aggressive role for the translator. In this case, the transition from one context to another is sought by way of *paraphrase.* Some translators employ all three of these modes, working often with dynamic equivalence but allowing for both the literal and the paraphrastic.

The range of approaches to the text-context question is parallel to these three modes of translation. Those for whom the transition from text to context requires wariness about the corruption of the text seek to import the text without alteration into the new clime. Contextualization is exact contouring to the original. Here theological translation is virtually the activity of finding synonyms. "Christ the Lord" becomes "Christ the sovereign." Indeed, the logic of this kind of transposition would be to retain the original textual language on the grounds that there is no equivalence to the inspired words of the text. Communication in a new setting would entail the repetition of the code language of the original. In its most radical form, this can be found in Islamic traditions that forbid the translation of the Koran from the Arabic original.

Another kind of translation effort is similar to dynamic equivalence. It retains a determined faithfulness to the intention and structure of the original but at the same time it desires to clarify

51. David H. Kelsey, *The Uses of Scripture in Recent Theology* (Philadelphia: Fortress Press, 1975), 122-59, 185-92.

the intention of the text by finding equivalence in the new context, one not thwarted by slavish repetition. This contextualization takes the translator beyond the particularities of the text to search for their conceptual equivalence in the new setting. Faith is stated in the new idiom, one that is responsible to the original intention. Christ as Lord might well become in a new setting Christ as "servant leader," with the assumptions of his special regency not conveyed by a literal crossover of terms but stated in language that strives to capture the intention of the original with a different idiom. The translator's role is enlarged here but always within the constraints of textual intention, the communication of Lordship as the "King who reigns from the cross."

A third method of translation appears when the text is read even more extensively than the foregoing in the light of the new context. As in a literary paraphrase, the translator's formulation predominates and the textual contours recede much further. The intention of the text is still assumed to be the orientation point for the translation, but the translator's freedom and the function of the context take on major proportions. In theological paraphrastics, cultural categories, intellectual systems, and contextual sensibilities become the key to translation. Christ as Lord then becomes Christ as "archetype," "creative transformation," "liberator."

The hermeneutical approach used in this systematics falls largely in the dynamic equivalence category, although neither the literal nor the paraphrastic are totally excluded, and are used when occasions suggest their appropriateness.

Transition and Traduction

The translation model of contextualization comes in large part from a spatial setting in which an existing piece of writing in one culture is carried into the language of another, even though the former can be an ancient document. Another kind of contextualization has a more temporal referent. Here the issue is: How is what is said in an earlier time understood in our own? How is the chasm created by history bridged? We have already considered some of the implications of this in our discussion of the critical sense of the text, but return to the subject briefly to identify the contextual models entailed as "transition" and "traduction."

Exponents of a traditional view are suspicious of the too-easy solutions of moving from one setting to another associated with translation advocates. They believe the literal approach is precritical in its lack of historical consciousness, assuming equivalence of concepts and the magical transfer of the same from one culture to another. With respect to dynamic equivalence, many transitionalists question the appropriateness of the language analogy to contextualization. It may work with living languages and cultures in which equivalencies may be determinable, but is inappropriate in the contextualization of historical documents where the original setting is not easily accessible. What transition requires with regard to biblical texts is first the hard slogging work of finding out "what it meant" in the obscurities of its past.

While the search for what it meant is common among transitionalists, the hopes for success in that venture and what is done with the results vary. Some join the dynamic equivalentists and believe it possible to make a connection from the ancient to the modern context. Hence the venture of "hermeneutics" as it is conceived in some quarters as distinguished from the "exegesis" that does the digging for what it meant with historical-critical tools. Others point to the contextual relativity of the digger as well as the dug, asserting that the practice of recovering what it meant is itself so influenced by the circumstances of the investigator that one cannot rely upon the results without a determined self-critical awareness of, and provision for, these factors. Yet others are skeptical about the results of either of these critical pursuits and return to the texts with other eyes, ones that lead them to strategies kindred to the paraphrastic approach in translation. That is, the text becomes the occasion for our own creativity or interests. In the former instance, it is often treated in a symbolist fashion as evocative of sensibilities otherwise untouched, or expressive of realities otherwise inaccessible. In the latter case, the text is seen as a warrant for the political, social, economic, or philosophical program of the interpreter.

Overlapping some of these positions is the traductionist view, a variant of the critical consciousness earlier discussed in which "whose it is" rather than "what it meant" is the uppermost issue. Both the original text and the present interpreters are scrutinized for the ways in which interest shapes the end product. What is written then and interpreted now is not taken at its face value but judged to be self-serving of the power concerns of text and contexter. As the criticism of "ideology" here is part of a larger theory of oppression in which ideas used for or against the oppressed are inextricable from material interest, the appropriation of text in context is considered do-able and legitimate to the extent that the text serves the interest of the oppressed. In their endeavor to contextualize, therefore, traductionists may join some transitionalists and paraphrastic translationists in accenting the framework of the interpreter.

As we have sought to find a place for critical inquiry in the textualization process, so we do here in the contextual movement. In external hermeneutics, the role of critical scholarship is affirmed in establishing the "well-being" of significance. And it means the place of critical inquiry in forming an opinion on the nature of the context. It also entails a self-critical spirit about vested interest in the contextual process, one which requires much more than an act of intellectual honesty. That "more" is the presence of the community in which diverse interests are represented that afford checks and balances to private agendas, providing an enlarged perspective for our parochial vantage points. Catholicity is the hermeneutical corrective to partial and self-serving interests and includes the presence and witness of those with other interests, but is not delimited or defined by any ideology imported into the hermeneutical process.

While the community in its fullness is a corrective to a too-narrowly conceived transitional or traductional model, it is the text itself that must challenge the reductionist tendencies of each. These tendencies appear when the transition model reduces the meaning of a text to its critical component only, ignoring the common and canonical features, or when the meaning of the text is absorbed into its significance by either transition or traduction views. A larger view of the contextualization process is necessary in which one maintains textual integrity, as in the dynamic equivalence translation model, but does so more critically with the self-awareness of these approaches and within the broadness and diversity of the community befitting a catholic translation.

Transformation

In the foregoing discussion we have portrayed the text as the object of scrutiny by the wise and the simple, the elusive target of the translator, the wax nose of the traducer. While we have argued that there is hope for this object to emerge with clarity and luster in both external and internal hermeneutics, we have not yet spoken about its most forceful presence. As the Word of God, the text is a living reality; it is a Subject taking initiative as well as an object of our investigation. In this role the text is not passive material to be carried into and adapted to the context, but an active agent transforming the context into which it speaks. Thus the text in its own right challenges the context, as well as being the object of contextualization.

One of Karl Barth's contributions to our understanding of biblical authority lies here. He reminded a generation of the initiative and independence of the text, the occasion of God's own address to us. These human words by the power of the Spirit become the Word. At God's initiative the Word happens in our midst. It convicts and convinces. It is the *personal contextualization* of Scripture, speaking its special word to our condition. And it changes us. Barth is not alone in this conception of Scripture, of course. In their own ways, the traditions of "internal testimony of the Holy Spirit" associated with John Calvin and his heirs, the devotional encounter with Scripture in pieties and spiritualities, ancient and modern, the "subjectivity" accents of Kierkegaard from which Barth himself learned so much, down to the "word events" of the new hermeneutic, the disclosive and transformative accents of symbolist and narrative theologies, the integrity and power of the text itself have asserted themselves. In this role, the text speaks. Personal contextualization is not something we are in charge of. Talk of translation, appropriation, and textualization in such a moment can only appear to be a move to silence the Word by our loud chatter.

We seek to honor the integrity of the text and its power to transform here, but do it differently from those who view this as the sole relationship of text to context, or who employ too exclusively an actualist framework for construing this integrity and initiative. There is "a time to keep silence, and a time to speak" (Eccles. 3:7). Our story of scriptural engagement has many chapters. There is occasion in this narrative for the careful weighing of the layers of tradition with the scales of scholarship; there is a time for bringing this learning to fresh settings and a place for the struggle to find their significance in them. There is a moment in which God brings our weighing and our contexting to a halt in order to say a Word to us. Or, more accurately, given the Spirit's full range of working its due, God speaks a Word to us through the active use of objective hermeneutical disciplines, and speaks to us again in the time of receptivity when all our discursive tools are laid aside. Here something and Someone over which and whom we have no control enters our field of vision and our range of hearing. A Word and Vision happen to us, shaking our foundations, altering our horizons.

In describing such events of address and new envisioning, the language of affect comes to the fore. Neoorthodoxy employed the dramatic and militant imagery of encounter, confrontation, shaking, inbreaking, eruption, and disruption. More recently, those who see contexts as art forms have put forward the softer accents of disclosure, insight, and imagination. One tends toward symbols of sound and the other toward symbols of sight. Both enrich our understanding of how texts transform. Yet standing alone, an affective view of textual initiative drifts into the mists of "meaningfulness": subjectivity becomes subjectivism; actualization becomes actualism; imagination becomes imaginationism. When a text comes alive under the power of the Spirit and does a transforming work, it is *through* not around the objective truth claims made by that text. The text is evocative in its cognitive role, not without it or by the reduction of cognition to affective evocation. Thus the assault made by an earlier neoorthodoxy and the complaints heard more recently from a symbolist view of Scripture against propositional interpretations are partly misplaced. Misgivings about propositional*ism* are to the point, for biblical truth is not to be compared simplistically to the assertions dissected in the classrooms of logic. Biblical assertions, whatever their genre, do make truth claims of an objective sort, affirmations about the nature of reality to which the proper answer is "yes" or "no." They correspond or conform to something or someone in time or beyond it. We should more properly think of these propositions as they come to us in the stream of biblical commitment as *affirmations,* since they reach us at the level of deep affect and make a personal claim upon us—*my* yes or *your* no.

Trajection

The text has a Word to address to us on its own, the context receding from view, except as recipient of what is new. However, there is a bolder role for context, one that changes our perception of the text itself. When we speak in this manner we approach the dangers of acculturation to which Barth's transformative view is so alert. This is a proper warning. Context does not control text. However, as this judgment is grounded in a doctrine of revelation, another revelatory assumption makes it possible to conceive of the human context not simply as a threat to the hermeneutical project. Even a fallen creation is carried forward by the triune God who does not give up on it. Neither must we. In the Great Narrative the continuing human context performs a function in the interpretation of Scripture. That function is *catalysis.* Context educes from the text dimensions of its meaning over the course of God's narrative action.

We have already attended to one catalytic function in the discussion of translation. A given time and place calls forth interpretation of the text that sounds and looks different from those of earlier epochs or other locales. A text talks in the idiom and engages the issue of that setting as indicated. The necessity for every new translation has been wrongly read by some as giving us each time the meaning of the text for that time, so that the text becomes an ever-changing scene of transpositions.[52] This is inadequate on two counts: (1) There is a core text that persists throughout the changing horizon of interpretation by which translation is always measured; (2) translation can mean, on occasion, also (not always) what we shall call *trajection.*

Trajection is the development of the inner meaning of the text: drawing out the text's implications, educing its intended meaning. This intentionality refers, as earlier noted, not to the human author but to the purpose of God in the scriptural words. This developing insight into the intention of the divine Author is its *sensus plenior.* The fuller sense of the meaning is in continuity with the original trajectory. As such it is a development along this line, coherent with it and extending it into a new setting.[53]

A raised consciousness about the dignity of women in cultures sensitized by feminist movements can illustrate the phenomenon of trajection as it impacts the interpretation of key texts. Thus in Galatians 3:28 the intended meaning that in Christ there is no male or female is deepened and moved beyond its former limited construal. Before God, by the norm of Jesus Christ, there is equality and partnership. However, Paul and his hearers so verticalized the interpretation of this verse in its earliest cultural context that its horizontal import received only minimal outworking: the widow was given special dignity, female children were assigned higher status than in the surrounding culture, some women attained leadership posts, the husband-wife relationship reached toward mutuality. However, wives were still viewed in subsidiary roles in the conjugal bond, women were silenced then and in subsequent

52. Maurice Wiles, *The Remaking of Christian Doctrine* (London: SCM Press, 1974), 7ff.

53. Raymond Brown's careful study is *The Sensus Plenior of Sacred Scripture* (Baltimore: St. Mary's Univ., 1955).

Christian history, and subservience was assumed to be their place in much of Christendom. A deepened understanding of the implication of the vision of Galatians 3:28 waited centuries to emerge. Such a time, as seen in narrative perspective, was a struggle for the divine intention expressed in the original text to be seen for what it was. The journey was not unlike the other implications of that text regarding the "slave" and "free." Because God works by the way of the cross—in vulnerability over time by the persuasions of the truth—there is a narrative struggle and not a fiat victory.

In these developments the providence of God provides stimuli from outside the church to draw out the buried import of its charter. Forces at work in the wider culture, in both cases, pressed the Christian community to examine its texts in a new light. Of course the influence of the text itself in that culture is an indirect factor in the culture's own facilitating judgments. We are not concerned to argue this point here, or to locate the specific streams of influence in the Renaissance and Enlightenment or in the liberation movements of our day on the enlarged grasp of the meaning of social justice. Whatever the particulars, it has been the impact of cultural forces that enabled the process of trajection to go forward. Their catalytic role with regard to the Galatians text (and its analogues in the teaching of Jesus and the prophets and elsewhere) opened a new understanding. Truth latent was rendered patent. That culture should have this impact on our understanding of Christ is related to the work of Christ in culture, an assumption of the underlying doctrine of revelation. Indeed there is the parallel between the development of doctrine and the trajection of biblical texts.

NARRATIVE HERMENEUTICS: CONTEXTUAL SIGNIFICANCE

The hermeneutical story moves toward its climax. What does the Bible signify *for us* in our time and place, and for you and me personally in our own situation? The personal and social contextualization discussed here take the step from *meaning* to *significance.* We reach the resolution stage of this narrative hermeneutics through the employment of a translation model of contextualization, enlarged and enriched by the perspectives of transition, traduction, transformation, and trajection. Contextualization must be critical, catholic, and evangelical. Thus we seek the dynamic equivalents of textual meaning in a new context, using critical analysis of that context as well as the original text, viewing both from within the manifold of the community's life and learning and according to the transforming gospel substance and central Word.

The same tributaries are present in contextualization as in textualization—Bible, church, world—but in reverse order.

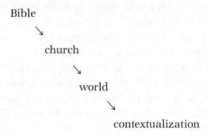

Bible
↘
church
↘
world
↘
contextualization

Using critical tools and consciousness we strive to identify the ruling characteristics of our historical setting. We do that not in solitary rumination or intellectual abstraction but in thought that rises out of personal engagement with the formative processes of our time. This involvement takes place within the company of believers in turn immersed in the issues and idiom of context. Thus the world is experienced and interpreted through the eyes of the church and in reference to its Center. From this interaction the contextual perspective of narrative with its motifs and metaphors—liberation and reconciliation, vision and reality, light and night—has taken shape.

As the contextual flow approaches the hermeneutical stream its categories are in relation to the textual direction.

contextual
↘
common → critical → canonical = meaning = significance

When we read the text from within the context, we do so with the light from Scripture focused by its Center and substance. Joining the narrative momentum, they are given definitive biblical orientation. Transformation takes the context with it toward the Author's intention in the particularity of personal and social situation.

The identity of the context is not erased by this encounter. While the direction is always forward, according to the meaning trajectory, it must pass through the courseway of significance made from the confluence of tributary and river. The text does its work in partnership with the context, not in the dissolution of it.

Our linear figures—journey, story, stream—have allowed us to portray the insights of translation, traduction, and transformation models. We can also incorporate the contribution of the trajection model. With it, significance not only refers to how a text can come alive for a time and place and in a particular person but also can indicate how what is learned there can find a permanent place in the meaning range of the text. Significance enters the meaning stream in its own right, extending its trajectory into the future. That is, something learned about the text in a new context not only has *application* for that setting but *implication* for all settings. What is implicit in the text is rendered explicit by the catalytic action of that special environment, releasing it for use by all others who come after. Significance thereby sometimes, though not always, contributes to the growth of meaning. So the well-known words of Pastor Robinson are best understood: "Ever new light and truth shall break forth from God's holy Word." Similarly, in the related field of doctrine, theological timeliness can be to the development of doctrine as contextual significance is to the trajectory of textual meaning.

In these chapters on internal and external hermeneutics we have traced a theory of biblical interpretation. But, as suggested by the last parallel between the trajectory of the text and the development of doctrine, more than that has taken place. Systematic theology is biblical hermeneutics writ large. The interpretive processes applicable to a text *of* Scripture are the same ones that function in the teaching task that grows out of it. Theology is done not only with a text of Scripture but with the text *as* Scripture. The question of authority presents itself in microcosm in hermeneutics and in macrocosm in systematics.

The purpose of the next chapter is to show how the concept of authority works in the practice of biblical hermeneutics. There, as we relate the principles of interpretation to the task of exegesis, the hermeneutical journey becomes very real. To show in similar concrete fashion how authority works in the practice of systematics can only take place in theological reflection on Christian doctrine, the work to be undertaken in the remaining volumes of *The Christian Story*. However, in Chapter 6 we will summarize the themes that have emerged in the hermeneutical and exegetical forays and suggest their implications for systematics.

CHAPTER V

Authority and Exegesis

The most revealing test of the pastor's concept of scriptural authority comes in dealing with the text of the Sunday sermon. Hermeneutical principles go to work immediately whether or not one is aware of them. We enter this laboratory, therefore, to show how the theory of interpretation set forth in the previous two chapters functions.

To stay close to the homiletical setting with its characteristic "text" we focus on a single verse of Scripture. Our exercise therefore is "exegesis," the application to a specific biblical passage of the principles of interpretation. In the concept of authority being developed here the principles emerged in the following areas: (1) The distinction between internal and external hermeneutics and its commensurate quest for both meaning and significance, and the four senses of Scripture: common, critical, canonical, and contextual; (2) the place of Bible, church, and world in an overarching theory of authority (source, resource, and setting; center, substance, guide, aid, and perspective). Each wrestle with a text includes all these issues and many of these elements in one or another constellation. The challenge is to bring them to critical self-awareness. That is the role of a systematic inquiry into hermeneutics.

At various stages of preparation for this textual test, I attempted to be faithful to my own contextual requirement, the encounter of the text within an inclusive community of believers, as that community is immersed in the issues and idiom of its own time and place. That meant four occasions of lesser or greater length when this text was examined in the company of mission-oriented clergy and laity in a self-conscious attempt to consider the hermeneutical tools employed.[1] Beyond that, the doctrinal implications of the text were developed for both ecumenical and evangelical audiences in an article and in a programmatic essay in a volume of perspectives on biblical authority.[2] Learnings found their way into the subsequent exegesis, as well as into the overall understanding of biblical authority.

Becoming very clear in the preparatory work was the impact of both ecclesial and cultural settings on the way in which the text was read, whatever method was espoused or whatever sense on Scripture came into focus. The most rigorous efforts to locate the critical sense, as well as the loudest protestations of faithfulness to common sense all showed the marks of social and theological location. The importance given to catholicity of perspective grew in proportion to the evidence of parochial influences. Discernment of the riches of the text is in direct relationship to the depth and width of ecclesial vision.

The preparatory work also was humbling with regard to the raggedness of the understanding process. This confirmed the importance of a narrative approach. Claims to "mastery" of a text are out of order. Every time one seems to "have it," a fresh angle appears, a new slant offers another insight, an unforeseen horizon opens up, a correction of previous ideas is made, and so on. Exegesis is journeying, full of fits and starts, turnings and returnings. The Story goes forward with suspense and surprises. Only at the end shall we see as we are seen, know as we are known.

Yet, if so much depends on right understanding, how can we be in such a state of uncertainty? If the Word is for the hearing so that in it we may know the truth that saves, how can we speak of exegesis as ambiguous and unfinished? Here again narrative hermeneutics sheds light. We *are* on the way, the Story *is* unfolding. If the inquiry is faithful to the text, catholic and committed, the trajectory can be revised but not reversed. This is no unfocused process or hopeless and planless meandering. The text, rightly read,

1. The groups included a weekly theological tabletalk exchange in which each clergy present examined his or her own exegesis and the principles used in interpreting this particular text; a seminar of M.Div. and Ph.D. students with the same exercise and self-examination of hermeneutical principles; a group of laity in a Boston congregation; a group of clergy in the Boston area.

2. Fackre, "The Use of the Bible in My Work in Systematics," in Robert Johnston, ed., *The Use of the Bible in Theology* (Atlanta: John Knox Press, 1985), 200-226.

puts us on the way toward the truth. Sound exegesis is a matter of being on course in the company of travelers who know the road.

The text we will exegete is John 14:6, selected because it takes us quickly into a nest of hermeneutical questions. With its Christological subject matter it puts us at the "center" of the "substance." The particularist claims it makes force the issues of pluralism and press the question of hope, demanding thereby both personal and social contextualization. The Johannine genre with its symbolic language and manifestly theological purpose makes us look for all the help we can get from critical and canonical readings. So we begin the trek.

COMMON SENSE

During a supper held near in time to the feast of Passover, after washing the disciples' feet and counseling the way of servanthood (John 13:4-18, 34-35) and an exchange with his betrayer (13:18-30), Jesus begins to speak with his disciples about his departure to God. This prompts Simon Peter's profession of loyalty and anxious queries, "Where are you going? Why cannot I follow you?" (13:36-37). Jesus replies, "Let not your hearts be troubled . . ." (14:1), and assures them that "a place" is readied, one to which they know the way. The place is "my Father's house" with its many rooms (14:2). A puzzled Thomas exclaims: "Lord, we do not know where you are going; how can we know the way?" (14:5). Our text is Jesus' response: "I am the way, and the truth, and the life; no one comes to the Father, but by me" (14:6).

Philip persists with the same line of questioning: "Lord, show us the Father, and we shall be satisfied" (14:8). Jesus replies in the visual imagery in which the request was put, "He who has seen me has seen the Father" (14:9), and stresses the unity of the Father and the Son in various ways through the rest of an exchange that continues through the seventeenth chapter (14:11, 13, 20, 24, 28, 31; 15:1-11, 16, 23, 26; 16:3, 5, 10, 15, 23-24, 26-28; 17:1-26), one anticipated in the section before (13:1, 3, 31-32; 14:1-2). Interspersed are the urging to the life of love that befits a disciple (14:21-24; 15:4-25) and the promise of the power and wisdom of the Spirit (14:25-26; 15:26-27; 16:7-15) given especially to face tribulations to come (14:18, 27-30; 15:6-7; 16:1-11, 20-24).

A close reading of the common sense of the text locates it in concentric circles of literary meaning. So we have positioned John

14:6 in the immediate exchange with Thomas as that is part of the larger supper conversation with its actions and actors. This dialogue leads to and away from the focal passage, providing expositions of it or ancillary comments that shed light upon it. Beyond the sentence itself with its paragraph, chapter, and five-chapter conversation unit are the remaining sections of the book with the events and interpretations that lead toward and away from it. Of significance also is the prologue (John 1:1-18) that an ordinary reader can see introduces the book, and a less clearly defined but nonetheless discernible interpretative section (chap. 21) that concludes it. Within the sentence are key words whose meaning must be available—I, way, life, truth, Father—at an entry level of linguistic convention, and capable of being grasped when read within the literary units described.

The ordinary sense of the text is inseparable from the pivotal word "way." In common speech it can mean either a path to a goal or the manner in which one proceeds (on a path) toward a goal. The former has an objective ring: there it is, something made for you to travel on. The latter has a subjective resonance: what am I supposed to do to get on to it, or on with it? The drift of the disciples' questions is toward the latter. You say you have a place prepared for us, your "Father's house." What do I do to get to this house, or how do I get to see "the Father"?[3] Jesus seems to turn things around. The way, for him, is less the manner and more the route—not "do this," but "here am I." The word about the route tells us first and foremost how it is made, who made it, indeed who it *is*. After we get the indicative straight, then comes the imperative. This

3. An inclusive hermeneutics entails a commitment to inclusive language. Throughout this work that rule has been observed with respect to language for humanity and deity when the words involved are mine. (When quotations are taken from standard translations of Scripture or other works the given usage is followed.) One exception to the practice has been made in crucial formulas or language for God with ecumenical implications, as in the traditional trinitarian language for the three Persons. Therefore in exegeting a text such as this one the traditional name "Father" for deity is used in both quotation and interpretation. Of course the word "God" itself can be understood to be of masculine gender, and a consistent commitment to depatriarchalizing religious language appears to require use of the balancing "Goddess" or the neologism God/ess. However, "God" is, in biblical faith, the name of the deity, not a description to be altered at will. Goddess language therefore is rejected. See my article, "God," in the *Dictionary of Religious Education*, ed. Kendig and Iris Cully (San Francisco: Harper & Row, forthcoming).

is the way you must come to God and why you must "know me" to know God. The finding of "the way" brings with it the consequences, "the truth," and "the life."

This reading is confirmed by the stress in surrounding portions of the supper conversation on the unity of Jesus with God, and the "I am" accents, refrains found through the whole of the book. When the text is read against the background of the prologue to the gospel, the matter is further sharpened: "the way" is the way God made into the world when "the Word became flesh" (1:14), the center of a divine drama that began in eternity, moved to creation, then to the contest of light with night, then to law and prophet and then to Christ. To return to the figure of the text, the Son is the way to the Father's house. The home is co-owned. "I and the Father are one" (10:30).

When we view "the way" as the pivotal word in the sentence, and read it as the route of God into the death and night of the world's resistance, then the fruits of this action are the natural sequel. The way brings light to night and life to death. The glory that is God and God's to give is in Christ. And "the glory which thou hast given me I have given to them" (17:22)—they can share in the light and life. The way, therefore, gives the light, enabling those who see it to know what the world does not know. To see Christ the light is to know the unknown God, to know "he who has seen me has seen the Father" (14:9). Knowing makes a difference, and the difference is life. The promise of life in Christ in 14:6 echoes the whole Johannine witness. "God so loved the world that he gave his only Son, that whoever believes in him should not perish but have eternal life" (3:16). Such a life begins now not later, and continues forever. Life with God, wherever found, is evidenced by life with others. Such a life is in Christ and flows out of that union, being therefore a life of love of the brothers and sisters and a life of servanthood (13:4-16, 34-35; 15:12-17). And the life that is not part of "Christ the life" is on the way to death and night (3:11, 21-30).

The common sense of the text that takes shape in these various observations has developed from a close reading that observes the rules of grammar and logic, linguistic convention, and the literary unities. I arrived at the judgments involved in this first step in exegesis informed implicitly and explicitly by the perceptions of other members in the community of common sense, the four groups in which the text was studied, and a study of classical ("precritical") commentary (Augustine, the Greek fathers, Luther, Calvin).[4] Elements discovered that have a high profile are: (1) The way as the route from and to the Father, which is Jesus Christ; (2) the unity of Jesus Christ with God as befits the relation of an only Son to the Father; (3) our access as only through the One who leads to the Father's house and is therefore of God; (4) the consequences of our bonding with Christ in God, which are in the gifts of truth and life, given by the One who as the Way alone can give these gifts; (5) the failure to find and follow the Way issues in the night of untruth and the destruction of death.

CRITICAL SENSE

The critical interpretation of John 14:6 means the use of a range of rationally sharpened tools of inquiry available to communities of special skill. As noted earlier, these include the knowledge of the text in its original language, resources in word study, archaeology, information about authorship and circumstances surrounding its creation and transmission as these are illumined by the disciplines

4. Martin Luther, *Luther's Works,* vol. 24, ed. Jaroslav Pelikan and Daniel Poellot (St. Louis: Concordia Publishing House, 1961), esp. 31-54; John Calvin, *Calvin's Commentaries: The Gospel According to St. John, 11–21,* trans. T. H. L. Parker, ed. David W. Torrance and Thomas F. Torrance (Grand Rapids: Eerdmans, 1961), esp. 73-92; St. Augustine, *Sermons on the Liturgical Season,* trans. Sr. Mary Sarah Muldowney, in *The Fathers of the Church* (New York: Fathers of the Church, 1959), esp. 7-9, 21-22, 27-34, 407-8; idem., "Sermon 346: On Life's Pilgrimage," *Commentary on the Lord's Sermon on the Mount with Seventeen Related Sermons,* trans. Dennis J. Kavanaugh, in *The Fathers of the Church* (New York: Fathers of the Church, 1951), 301-5; idem., *"Christian Instruction, Prologue and Book, Book I," The Writings of St. Augustine,* vol. 4, trans. John J. Gavigan in *The Fathers of the Church* (New York: CIMA Publishing, 1947), 19-60; St. John Chrysostom, *Commenataries on St. John the Apostle and Evangelist: Homilies 48-88,* trans. Sr. Thomas Aquinas Goggin (New York: Fathers of the Church, 1960), esp. 281-91; Clement of Alexandria, "The Miscellanies," in *The Writings of Clement of Alexandria,* vol. 2, trans. William Wilson, *The Ante-Nicean Christian Library* (Edinburgh: T. & T. Clark, 1972), 229-32; Origen, "Origen contra Celsum, Books II-VIII," in *The Writings of Origen,* vol. 2, trans. Frederick Crombie (Edinburgh: T. & T. Clark, 1872), 408-12, 500-504; Ambrose, *St. Ambrose: Selected Works and Letters,* trans. H. De Romestin, E. De Romestin, and H. T. F. Duckworth, *Nicean and Post-Nicean Fathers,* 2d ser. (New York: Christian Literature Co., 1986), 111, 145, 208, 211, 219, 223, 267, 275; Gregory of Nyssa, *Gregory of Nyssa: Dogmatic Treatises, etc.,* trans. William Moore and Henry A. Wilson (New York: Christian Literature Company, 1893), 105, 108, 117, 364.

of history, cultural anthropology, sociology, and psychology, skills of literary analysis, etc. In, but often beyond, these is the critical perspective that asks the questions of power and interest in the creation and reception of the text, as these questions are posed by either scholarship or those who find themselves the victims of economic, political, and social power, especially as Scripture is used by vested interests of oppression. Critical inquiry of the formal kind will make use of representative resources available to the pastor such as Kittel's *Theological Dictionary of the New Testament, The Interpreter's Dictionary of the Bible,* commentaries on John in various series *(The Interpreter's Bible, The Anchor Bible, Hermeneia, Jerome Bible Commentary, The Expositor's Bible Commentary, The Broadman Bible Commentary),* studies of the Gospel of John or aspects of it (Brown, Schnackenburg, Bultmann, Barrett, Dodd, Cullmann, Miranda, Meeks, Perkins, J. A. T. Robinson, J. M. Robinson, Kysar, Culpepper, Hoskyns, Howard, Hort, Fuller, Martyn, Sanders, Childs).[5] In addition, a wider sweep of resources will be

5. C.K. Barrett, *The Gospel According to St. John: An Introduction with Commentary and Notes on the Greek Text* (Philadelphia: Westminster Press, 1978); Raymond Brown, *The Community of the Beloved Disciple* (New York: Paulist Press, 1979); idem., *The Gospel According to John: Introduction, Translation and Notes,* 2 vols., Anchor Bible (Garden City, N.Y.: Doubleday, 1966, 1970); Rudolf Karl Bultmann, *The Gospel of John: A Commentary,* trans. G.R. Beasley-Murray (Oxford: Blackwell, 1971); Brevard Childs, *The New Testament as Canon: An Introduction* (London: SCM Press, 1984); Oscar Cullmann, *The Johannine Circle,* trans. John Bowden (Philadelphia: Westminster Press, 1976); R. Alan Culpepper, *The Anatomy of the Fourth Gospel: A Study in Literary Design* (Philadelphia: Fortress Press, 1983); C. H. Dodd, *The Interpretation of the Fourth Gospel* (Cambridge: Cambridge Univ. Press, 1953); Reginald Fuller, *The Foundations of New Testament Christology* (New York: Scribner's, 1965); Ernst Haenchen, *A Commentary on the Gospel of John,* trans. Robert Funk, ed. Robert Funk and Ulrich Busse, vols. 1-2, *Hermeneia—A Critical and Historical Commentary on the Bible* (Philadelphia: Fortress, 1984); F. J. Hort, *The Way, the Truth and the Life* (London, 1887); Edwyn Hoskyns, *The Fourth Gospel,* ed. Francis Noel Davey (London: Faber & Faber, 1940); Robert Kysar, *The Fourth Evangelist and His Gospel: An Examination of Contemporary Scholarship* (Minneapolis: Augsburg, 1975); idem., *John's Story of Jesus* (Philadelphia: Fortress Press, 1984); James Louis Martyn, *History and Theology in the Fourth Gospel,* 2d rev. ed. (Nashville: Abingdon Press, 1979); James Louis Martyn, *The Gospel of John in Christian History: Essays for Interpreters* (New York: Paulist Press, 1979); Wayne A. Meeks, *The Prophet-King: Moses Traditions and the Johannine Christology* (Leiden: E. J. Brill, 1967); Pheme Perkins, *The Gospel According to St. John* (Chicago: Franciscan Herald Press, 1978); J. A. T. Robinson, *The Human Face of God* (Philadelphia: Westminster Press, 1973); Joseph Newbold Sanders, *A Commentary on the Gospel According to St. John,* ed.

brought into play that do not deal with this text as such, but raise either directly or indirectly the questions of critical consciousness about the use of Scripture as a weapon of oppression or an instrument of distortion, as in feminist critical consciousness (Fiorenza, Ruether, Russell) or social-cultural critical consciousness (Gottwald, Knitter).[6]

Critical studies have shown that John is divided into two main sections, chapters 1:19 through 12:50 or the "book of signs" and chapters 13 through 20:29, the "book of glory" (or "exaltation") with its farewell addresses and passion and resurrection narratives, and the famous prologue of 1:1-18, concluding remarks in 20:30-31, and an epilogue in chapter 21. Further, critical study has shown that interpretation of John, long understood to present a record of Jesus different from that of the Synoptics, has rearranged chronology and organized content according to pronounced theological interest replete with symbols. Using internal and external evidence, critics have challenged the traditional identification of the authorship of the beloved disciple, John the son of Zebedee; traced a history of traditions within the book; and identified redactions associated recently with a canonical shaping of its final form. A hypothesis receiving considerable attention is the formative role of a Johannine community's period of struggles (Martyn)—early, middle, and late—with the expulsion of Christians from the synagogue in the middle of the eighties being most influential. Yet the particular turn given the text by historical circumstances must be held together with evidences of a canonical hand that has shaped the material toward an audience beyond its immediacies and thus sent on its way as the overall "Gospel" that it is. Here the purposes set forth in the prologue and epilogue are key, as is the summary statement at the close of the second book (20:30-31).

Against this general critical background, we turn to the specifics

and completed by B.A. Mastin (London: Black, 1968); Rudolf Schnackenburg, *The Gospel According to St. John,* trans. Cecily Hastings et al. (New York: Seabury Press, 1980); Bruce Vauter, "The Gospel According to John," in *The Jerome Bible Commentary,* vol. 2, ed. Raymond E. Brown, Joseph A. Fitzmeyer, and Roland E. Murphy (Englewood Cliffs, N.J.: Prentice-Hall, 1968), 414-66.

6. As in the discussion of Fiorenza, Ruether, and Russell in the contextual section of Chapter 1. On sociological and cultural critical consciousness see Norman Gottwald, *The Tribes of Yahweh: A Sociology of the Religion of Liberated Israel, 1250–105* B.C. (Maryknoll, N.Y.: Orbis Books, 1979) and *The Hebrew Bible—A Socio-Literary Interpretation* (Philadelphia: Fortress Press, 1985).

of 14:6 set within the farewell conversation and monologues. Brown, De La Potterie, and Michaelis are persuasive in their arguments for *hodos* as the primary predicate, and *aletheia* and *zoe* as epexegetical. Brown has shown that "way" is to be read in the light of its usage in Hebrew Scriptures (as in the parallels in Ps. 86:11), in turn influenced by the absolutist claims of the Qumran tradition, rather than determined by Mandean and Hermetic sources. "Way," like other figures used for Israel—"temple," "vine," "sheepfold"—is here borrowed and applied to Christ.

In developing the interrelationship of way, truth, and life, De La Potterie is convincing in his connection of the Hebrew usage with Christ by comparing it to God's making of a way through the desert. Hence the linkage with Isaiah 40:3: "In the wilderness prepare the way of the LORD, make straight in the desert a highway for our God." Christ is the way, the route, made for (by) God into and through our desolation. Thus, with Schnackenburg, truth and life are manifestations of the way. We have truth and life because Christ has made the way to the Father's house where gifts are given. Brown seems to imply these interrelations, especially in his insistence that the person of Christ, and not his role as teacher, is being asserted. But his preoccupation with Christ as revealer gives the matter a decidedly subjectivist turn that contests the ontological emphasis: the point of the person is to disclose the truth and thus find the way. While Brown rightly stresses "the mission" of Jesus to avoid dissolving the text into speculative "metaphysics," Jesus' mission of bringing the truth is based on *God's* mission in and as Jesus. The revelation is of a reconciliation accomplished; what is seen is what is done in the incarnation.

A canon-critical reading—the evidence of canonical editorial work in a book of the Bible as it bears on the understanding of a text in that book—clarifies this textual intention with the help of the prologue and epilogue. The mission of God is the divine way into the world (1:1-14) that brings with it light and life. And again in the closing remarks, the action of God in Jesus as "the Christ" evokes the "believing" that in turn gives "life" (20:30-31). The subjective is dependent on the objective, not the other way around. The "way" metaphor from the desert scene in Isaiah is specifically associated with Christ in 1:23. There Christ is portrayed as "the LORD" of Isaiah 40:3 whose way is being prepared by the prophet John.

A study of the history of usage of *hodos* adds further perspective to the historical- and canon-critical observations. The term has been employed in the twofold commonsense fashion identified earlier as a route and path, or the manner of executing a task or reaching a goal. In theological contexts, it appears as what God or the gods do, or what we must do. Thus we meet the objective and subjective options turned up in a commonsense reading. The text's declaration, critically read, that the person is the way, features the divine action and thus puts the objective route meaning to the fore, with the "coming to the Father" along that path in life-giving belief in this truth being the response. Also illuminating in word usage is the *ego emi* pattern that recurs throughout John and is also found here. John's elevation of the person of Christ in this recurrent and auspicious self-declaration converges with the astounding claims within the passage—and more so when linked with the divine "I AM WHO I AM" reading of the burning bush incident (Exod. 3:14).

If the immediate historical circumstances of this text are the encounter of the Johannine community with the *birkat ha-minim,* the ban on deviators in the synagogue who are marked as such by confessing Jesus as Messiah, then the sharpness of the statement is understandable. The self-definition processes within Judaism and its exclusionary act are met with a self-affirmation and exclusivity in kind. The particularism is retained in the canonical bequest, but it is situated in a larger environment, both within John—"and I have *other* sheep, that are not of this fold" (10:16), and beyond that, in the New Testament all the references to the wider arc of the divine action. While we confine our remarks here to the *canon-critical* reading, the appropriation of the text in its full meaning and truth in its *canonical sense* will return us to the consideration of the more extensive scriptural habitat and its theological importance.

Literary-critical investigation casts yet more light on the well-being of our understanding. Already we have indicated some of its features, as historical criticism merges into these matters. Indeed "literary criticism" itself has an encompassing sense—the critical investigation of texts—inclusive of authorship, milieu, and the traditioning process. Following the handbook of Hayes and Holladay, we confine it however to "the world of the text," with its questions of composition, structure, and mood. However, it is hard to see much distinction between these and many of the concerns of grammatical criticism, the genre features of form criticism insofar as they are separable from "life situation," and the literary form aspects of source tradition and redaction criticism. Within literary criticism are longitudinal variations as well as latitudinal comings and goings. And older literary inquiry is being overtaken by a "new literary criticism," structuralism, and canon criticism. We draw on these literary insights wherever we can find them with respect to the Book of John in its entirety and this text in particular.

Clement of Alexandria put a label on what has become the standard introductory judgment about John, calling it a "spiritual Gospel." Like the Synoptics it is a Gospel, Good News of things that happen, not a theological tractate. Unlike the Synoptics the narrative is so self-consciously colored by theological interpretation (of course the others are shaped by the same kerygmatic impulse) that narration flows regularly into interpretation, and that of a highly symbolical, mystical, and allusive kind. As a work of imagination, chronology takes its bearings more from thematic purpose than historical data ordering. The events cited are the occasion for long ruminative monologues and conversations. Their refrain is Christological identification and self-definition as represented by the recurrence of the "I am" formula. Unlike the Synoptics, it has no parables, although the cryptic flow of symbols has its evocative power. Narrative with symbols that reach the deep places (archetypal) cannot help but leave its mark.

The syntax is simple, as sentences tend to be devoid of subordinate clauses, suggesting to some commentators "a Semitic mind." The kind of symbols chosen, with their Torah background—temple, vine, bread, water, light, way—underscores the polemic and apologetic aspects of the writing, Christ in each case replacing the charter and limited horizon of the forebears. However, "the Jews" appears to be also a theological construct of alternative readings of the human condition, giving the work a larger and longer didactic meaning, one supported by the juxtaposition of light and darkness with its Gnostic and wider cultural associations.

The structure of the book, referred to earlier, is sometimes also organized as prologue (1:1-18); book of signs (1:19–12:50); farewell addresses (13–17); passion (18–19); resurrection (20); epilogue (20). A case has been made that a collection of miracle stories furnish the occasion for the various interpretive discourses. The latter may have originally been homilies on these narratives. Many have thought that earlier passion and resurrection traditions provide the material for the evangelist or redactor. An active editorial hand seems to be at work throughout, furnishing commentary on events, filling in historical data, and providing a connection to overall themes. Included in its figural style is the exploitation of ambiguity for the purposes of bringing out new truth, as in the suggestive comparison of Jesus' death with the destruction of the Temple (2:19) and the use of irony (the King—the crucified) (19:19-22).

Canon-critical scholarship has found warrants for its position in its investigation of literary form. John's Christological argument is actively related to Old Testament elements in the developing Christian canon, including not only the specific citations of texts but also the use of the wisdom category in the prologue, appropriation in the book of signs of Israel's symbols—temple, living waters, bread, etc.—for Jesus, and the witness of Abraham, Moses, and Isaiah as well as John the Baptist to the One who has come. Its thesis that Scripture is formed toward its future use as a standard of Christian identity is supported by the mood of assurance in the farewell addresses that the Spirit's presence continues, in the resurrection section of the availability of Christ to those who have not seen him, and in the epilogue the establishment of instruments of the continuing life of Christ and the Spirit through the pastoral office, the feeding (with eucharistic import) and the trustworthiness of the things written down.

John 14:6 is an exemplification of many of these literary characteristics. Here in a farewell address is a crescendo of images, with their juxtaposition to Torah, but beyond that to any other way, truth, and life that makes ultimate claims. In the text the theological intent of the whole book is sharply stated, its Christological point becoming a burning point. As we find ourselves inside the story, the puzzlements of the disciples are our quandaries too. We, like them, are jolted into an either-or choice. And in our wandering we too hear the assurances of a way home.

A novice in newer forms of literary analysis suspects that a structuralist view holds promise with its suggested diagramming of "actantial" constants (arrival-departure, conjunction and disjunction, domination and submission, etc.) and other aspects of "deep structure." These sets and other binary opposites (life/death, good/bad) appear to be at work here. However, as the *Handbook of Biblical Criticism* notes, "as it relates to Biblical exegesis, the approach is still in its infancy and much remains to be answered."[7] We reserve judgment on how polar categories and their relation to the structures of the mind illumine the text in question.

With guidance from the "new literary criticism," attention to

7. See "Structuralism" in Soulen, ed., *Handbook of Biblical Criticism* (Atlanta: John Knox Press, 1981), 184.

linguistic meaning from within the world of the text makes its contribution. We allude briefly to some possibilities in style and construction of argument here and return to some of its metaphors in a later feminist reading. The supper discourses appear to be disjointed, with Jesus and the disciples talking past each other. Yet these jars and jolts for the disciples and the reader function like many Synoptic parables, opening us to self-examination and new insight. Peter's professions of loyalty are countered with predictions of faithlessness known to the reader (13:36-38). Confessions about the way are answered by the self-evident (14:5-6). Assumptions that the chosen will "get it" are followed by simple observations that they don't (14:7). Comforting words not to be troubled, and assurances that the disciples will not be left desolate (14:1, 18) are combined with announcements of betrayal (13:21-30), radical demand (13:34-35), and denial of access to where Jesus is going (13:33). Here is the separation of a family, a child from the parent, yet their mystical joining ultimately (14:1-4) but also even now (14:23). And that coming of the divine One appears to be at the same time Son, Father, and the Counselor (chaps. 13–17, *passim*). Not only are these the materials for the paradoxes and mystery of classical doctrine—soteriological, Christological, trinitarian—but the literary evocation of sensibilities otherwise unawakened.

The earlier reference to ecclesial disputes and the mark such social influences leave on a text takes us now to the possibilities in a critically construed John 14:6 that is conscious of self-interest factors. Thus Paul Knitter reasons that the drastic assertions of special status made by the early Christians are natural defense mechanisms of a community marginal to the ancient world, beset by competing religions with high visibility, and in dispute with a sister faith about a common heritage.[8] He views the assertive claims that Christ is the only Lord and Savior as "survival language," bolstering the church's self-esteem. Combining the hermeneutics of suspicion with a literary-critical judgment allows Knitter to appropriate the language for what he believes it to be, the poetry of faith, the metaphor of commitment, not the metaphysics of objective truth. Taking it from a polemical context that asserted the latter to our own time of pluralism in the former mode removes the exclusivist self-definition and relativizes ancient Christian truth claims.[9] John

8. Paul F. Knitter, *No Other Name?* (Maryknoll, N.Y.: Orbis Books, 1985), 184.
9. Ibid., 184-86.

14:6 provides as pointed a challenge to this demythologizing as can be found in the Christian canon.

Other forms of critical consciousness can read the text as promoting the interests of a special class, sex, or ethnicity. A rising tide of "urban Christians" or lower-middle-class believers may use the rhetoric of faith to forward their interests. On the other hand, the disenfranchised and marginal of ancient society may put forth exclusive claims to bolster their self-identity. Again, feminist critics can show the assertion of a male figure as God's only victorious way into the world and our salvation as dependent on profession of faith in "him" to be the reflection of a patriarchal power system, one that makes the Christian religion hostage to misogyny. Also, voices from other cultures can point to the particularism of a revelation in Jesus the Jew, and argue that this is an unhealthy ethnocentrism that has to be met by finding equivalent disclosures and deliverances through other cultures or religion-cultural complexes.[10]

Sometimes a suspicionist critical consciousness can be combined with historical- and literary-critical moves to appropriate the text from within a community of protest. Thus a feminist reading of either kind might see in 14:6 the submerged but no less powerful presence of female imagery. The "life" figure and the organic imagery—"in me"—that runs throughout, including the separation that underlies the supper conversation—the cutting of the umbilical cord—is attached to male figures, father and son.[11] Jesus as the giver of life, as the one whose veritable womb bears those "in him," and from whom umbilical separation is forecast, is a parent figure in all these relationships. As he is clearly not the Father, what parent is left? The strong medieval "Jesus as mother" tradition supplies an answer taken up by some streams of feminism.[12] Indeed the Word that comes upon the Christ to be is through the Counselor, the Holy Spirit who tradition has from time to time identified with feminine gender.[13] This Word of Wisdom very naturally carries a message of consolation in desolation, joy in time of trouble, associated with the comforting maternal presence.

With the use of these various instruments of criticism—elementary linguistic and grammatical study, historical-literary investi-

10. Choen-Seng Song, *Third Eye Theology* (Maryknoll, N.Y.: Orbis Books, 1979).

11. I am indebted to Dr. Rosamund Rosenmeier for this insight.

12. Caroline Walker Bynum, *Jesus as Mother* (Berkeley and Los Angeles: Univ. of California Press, 1982).

13. Letty Russell, ed., *The Liberating Word* (Philadelphia: Westminster Press, 1976), 93-94.

gations, ideological-critical analysis—the probe of John 14:6 is carried out with greater precision. The patient does not suffer death under the knife as is alleged by those who fear the work of the critical surgeon. At least that is so if the work is carried out deftly, and within the limits of professional expertise. As in any healing process, matters of life and death are settled by a gestalt of factors, including the mysterious working of the body's own powers of replenishment and God's good grace. The well-being, not the being, of the body—physical or textual—is the province of the trained critical eye and instrument.

Making a distinction between the genuinely professional use of criticism and its unprofessional exploitation with regard to this textual inquiry entails the following:

1. Theological dismissal of the Johannine testimony because it is apostolic interpretation and therefore not what it purports to be in its record of events or the words it puts in Jesus' mouth is an active theological interpretation itself not demanded by the responsible use of critical tools. A high doctrine of revelation is consonant with this kind of critical judgment. Apostolic inspiration can take place in the act of literary interpretation in a biblical text, and is not tied to either a recovery of the *ipsissima verba* of the historical Jesus or the accuracy of the words reported by a first-century kerygma-oriented portraiture.

2. The influence of cultural factors and literary dynamics and the impact of other religions on textual material do not destroy the validity of the truth communicated by a text so shaped. The historical God of biblical faith lives in this medium and works with this material and would be another kind of deity if this were not the case. The fundamental words—*Logos, hodos, aletheia, zoe*—are appropriated and transformed by their new hermeneutical locale, Jesus Christ. Circumstances of the humblest sort are employed and transmuted, a Johannine community with its internal and external feuds, a ragged oral and written transmission process, etc.

3. The earthiness of the textual process includes the mixed motives, limitations, and pretensions of the human organs of textualization. God uses these "base things of the world" to accomplish the divine purposes. Thus the possibility (not yet solidly established) that sociological and psychological survival factors were at work in the means through which the particularist claims of the Gospel does not preclude their truth. The theo-logic of earthen vessels as well as the logic of the genetic fallacy discount this allegation. And the maleness of Jesus can be understood as the medium appropriate

to a historical God working through the contextuality of a patriarchal environment. But at the same time, the assumptions of patriarchy are challenged at their root by the vulnerability of the male figure Jesus, contesting male ideologies of invulnerability so omnipresent in human history. Again, the offensiveness of the saving action of God in Jesus the Jew unalterably marks biblical faith as a historical religion, one that takes time and place with a seriousness that no simplistic and finally ahistorical universalism can do. At the same time the character and direction of this prophet, priest, and king of Israel are radically universal.

Whether or not these rationales for ambiguities perceived in the text are persuasive, the principle stands: For a faith that views the world as finite and fallen, and believes the action of God to be in a Person incarnate in this kind of a setting, the disclosure of truth will be in a fashion commensurate with who God is and how God works. These things are true contra the ideology sometimes associated with the hermeneutics of suspicion which holds that because dubious motivation is exposed, the validity of faith is undercut, that the ontological claim of particularity has to be given up, and the text construed only as a community's symbolic self-identification or as a weapon in the warfare against a perceived oppressor. On the other hand, when the hermeneutics of suspicion opens up vistas of textual meaning long obscured by a docetic reading (the humanity of Jesus lost) or the hegemony of an oppressor (as in the feminist recovery of the life, womb, and parental imagery in chap. 14), the critical function that makes for the well-being of textual meaning is an important contribution to exegesis.

CANONICAL SENSE

The canonical sense of John 14:6 brings the *plene esse* and *vere esse* of its meaning. In this final phase of *textual* exegesis we can call upon a wealth of resources from the Christian community. Canonical interpretation of John 14:6 invites into the discussion theological clarifications of Christ and the gospel long discussed in the history of the Christian church.

Jesus Christ is the path God makes through the wilderness to us so we can come this way of the Son to the Father's house, receiving in the coming, as in the arriving, eternal light and life. In one fashion or another the Christian canon echoes these themes wherever witness is made to who Jesus is and what Jesus does. With respect to the focal predicate, "way," the New Testament titles for Jesus point to the kind of way he provided—the Messiah, Son of God, Son of man, Savior, Lord, Teacher, Shepherd, Master, Servant, Lamb of God, Priest of God, Prophet, King, Pioneer, Victim, Victor, Redeemer. Implicit in the titles and explicit in many threads of interpretation of them is the work this person has done to open the way. The pathfinding labor depends on the kind of wilderness perceived. Is it the desert of our *sin and guilt?* Then God gives in Jesus a sacrificial Lamb and a Priest to atone, a Savior from sin, a receiver of judgment, a Redeemer of our debt. Is it the threatening land of evil powers that brings us *suffering?* Then the road through misery is open to the freedom of the future by the Pioneer and Messiah. Is the desolation that awaits us *death?* Then Jesus is the King who triumphs over this night on Easter morning, the Lord of life. Is the forbidding terrain one of *error and ignorance?* Then Christ the Prophet points to the horizon light, the Teacher gives us knowledge of the truth, therein illumining the path of God. And all the metaphors are mobile, for Jesus is Savior from death as well as sin, Redeemer from the powers as well as from personal guilt, the Messiah who brings the forgiveness of sin, the Lord who reigns over the kingdom of death, the Teacher of the mercy of God as well as the love of the neighbor. And in each act of way-making, the same mobility and paradox are apparent. At one time to the fore is a Jesus who is one of us, "Son of man," and another the Christ who is of God, the "Son of God." Here is the enigma of *Jesus,* the *Christ,* the way to God and the way from God, a person both human and divine, the one Jesus Christ. So too the way of the Way, the vulnerability and weakness of the Servant, yet the invulnerability and strength of the Master, the mystery of the power of powerlessness.

Inseparable from the astounding claims for the person and work of Christ as the way made through the wilderness are the benefits to the world of God's path-making. Again the assertion in the text that Christ is the truth and the life as well as the Way, the truth and life by virtue of the Way, is a refrain wherever these consequences are spoken of in the canon. Throughout the New Testament, Christ is Revealer of the truth, the Prophet who speaks the word from God, the veritable Word of God. Our knowledge of the truth of Christ is consistently linked in the Christian canon to the life given by him on the path made by him: "For I am not ashamed of the gospel: it is the power of God for salvation to every one who has faith, to the Jew first and also to the Greek" (Rom. 1:16). Faith is knowledge of the gospel and the assent of the illumined mind to it.

The canon also puts before us numerous reminders that knowledge of and belief in the things of Christ are not, *as such,* saving. "The devils believe and tremble" (James 2:19). When *notitia* and *assensus,* belief of the mind and assent of the will, are joined to *fiducia,* the trust of the heart, then faith, when graced, is what it is intended to be, saving faith. But this capstone of the work of salvation in us cannot be stressed to the exclusion of the foundational canonical testimony to the life that comes with the light, the *necessary, but not sufficient* presence of disclosure with personal deliverance. Hence the cruciality of *belief* and *assent* as well as trust. Vast issues of evangelization, pluralism, the relation of Christian faith to other religions and people of good conscience are all at stake here, matters to which we shall return in the contextualization of this text. An understanding of the fullness of this text's meaning, as illumined by its canonical setting, is crucial for the struggle with these questions.

In the internal hermeneutical interpretation of this text, the trails of canonical investigation reinforce the particularism of its assertions. The route God makes into and through the world is Jesus Christ. Our way to God and the treasures to be found in God's house are accessible only in Jesus Christ. But a canonical setting is a rigorous monitor of exegesis. Are these corroborating and clarifying texts of Christological particularity the *only* relevant canonical context for this text? No. The Christian canon includes the Old Testament. Further, both Old and New Testaments testify to significant evidence of life and light that does not have any reference to Jesus Christ. And there is evidence as well of ways of God in the world that appear to be devoid of any Christological focus. Justice cannot be done to the full meaning of this text, its canonical reading, until we take into account these assertions of universality.

The presence of the Hebrew Scriptures within the Christian canon means that the decisive way God has made into the world in Jesus Christ must be read in the light of the way of God with Israel. We are dealing with a drama that unfolds in major acts that precede and form whatever takes place in both the Person and Work of Jesus Christ. Once again, the narrative character of the gospel makes its impact felt. The struggle with Marcionism and its elimination of crucial Hebrew chapters of the Story was an early canonical contest. Further, in this long stretch of God's dealing with the world, recorded and interpreted in the Old Testament, going well beyond the small segment of time and place in which God engages a particular people, issues of the universal range of the divine way and consequences for life and light are brought into view. In the Old Testament as in the New, of course, the focus is on the particular deeds of God, but their horizon is universal history. This horizon provides a necessary perspective on the particularity of the New Testament, one also assumed as circumference to its Christological center.

The most embracing Old Testament category for interpreting the universal way, truth, and life of God with the world, one that connects with the formative Old Testament motif of particular covenants with Abraham and Moses, is the universal covenant with Noah. "Then God said to Noah and to his sons with him, 'Behold, I establish my covenant with you . . . and with every living creature that is with you. . . . This is the sign of the covenant which I make between me and you and every living creature that is with you, for all future generations: I set my bow in the cloud, and it shall be a sign of the covenant" (Gen. 9:8-10, 12-13). God's promise is accompanied with expectations of faithfulness to the light given by the bow in the sky, and the gift of new life given after the death-dealing flood. Faithfulness to the immediate covenant injunction requires fruitfulness, the care of the earth and the honoring of the dignity of humans made in the divine image, the latter expressed in the prohibition of shedding of human blood or the eating of flesh of animals with blood (Gen. 9:1-7). And pressed home in all these things is the remembering of the God of the covenant, even as Yahweh will see the rainbow and remember the promise (Gen. 9:8-17). In this covenant, God keeps the promise made to all creation to continue to be with it through thick and thin, not to let the world's rebellious ways deter these salutary actions and their beneficial issue.

Throughout the Old Testament, God supports life in the world, as in the regularities of nature alluded to in the covenantal moment (Gen. 9:11). The soil brings forth fruit in season, the sun rises and the rain falls, lease on life is given to a multitude of God's creatures (Pss. 19:1-6; 65:9-13). Again God watches over humankind, setting "the solitary in families," setting families in communities, making the nations to cover the earth (Pss. 8; 9; 68:6). For this universal plenitude humankind continues to be steward. The Noachic pledge maintains the light in creation given to see the way forward in this custodianship, even in its flickering state. God's promise will not permit sin to put the light out as long as the Story goes forward.

Here is the rudimentary knowledge of God that invites grateful response. As the way of God proceeds in a fallen world, that elusive presence cannot escape notice even through the veil of sin. Discernible as well is the way of good into which all human beings are called. Proverbs, Job, Ecclesiastes, and portions of the Psalms all presuppose some knowledge of the conduct God wills all the world to have. The wisdom to seek wisdom rather than gold and silver, to speak forthrightly and not deceitfully, to foreswear pride and arrogance, to be honest and not steal, to care for and not belittle one's neighbor, to share one's substance with those in need, to work and avoid sloth, to aid the poor and seek justice for the needy, to live in faithfulness to one's spouse, look after one's children and honor one's progenitors, to avoid violence and live peaceably, to anger slowly and forgive readily, to be fair and just—these are the things of wisdom that make and keep life human (Proverbs, *passim*). When human beings ignore these elemental expectations they suffer the consequences, as when Amos declares the judgment of God upon "the transgressions of Damascus, Gaza . . . Edom . . . the Ammonites . . . Moab . . ." (Amos 1–2). They are the universal laws of life together. Sometimes described as "natural law" or "moral law," rabbinic tradition more accurately calls them "the Noachian precepts." This is the code of conduct to which all humans are accountable, referred to in minimalist terms as early as A.D. 120 by Chanina ben Gamaliel, who already assumes its existence.[14]

The ways of God with Israel and the world at large, and the truth and life shed abroad in them, are themes taken up through the New Testament canon. We have already noted how the content of Christ is influenced by the Old Testament and the gospel substance includes the chapters of creation through covenant recorded primarily in the Hebrew Scriptures; we will return soon to these things as they bear on this text. Their special significance here lies in the fact that no understanding of the singularities of way, truth, and life can ignore the larger particularity of Israel and the universalities of God's actions, gifts, and call to responsibility among and to those beyond the stream of "holy history." The recognition of this fact in the Old Testament portion of the Christian canon is explicitly continued in a thread of commentary that must be included in any canonical reading of John 14:6.

14. C. H. Dodd, "Natural Law in the Bible," reprinted from *Theology* (May-June 1946): 7.

Universality Texts

Of special importance is material in which specific references are made to the universal way of God and its consequences in such much-discussed passages as Romans 1:19-20; 2:14-15; Acts 14:17; 17:22-28; John 1:9. Also of great importance are many texts that do not state these universal themes as such, but clearly imply them. We shall examine both kinds of evidence.

The two passages in Romans have been long in dispute as whole theologies are at stake in their interpretation. To make them say something fundamentally different than the witness given by evidences of universality just adduced would do violence to their canonical sense. The ambiguity of God's way and will to which they allude cannot be dissolved by a Christomonistic reinterpretation. But we must deal with an intertextual ambiguity as well, for they could be read as themselves in conflict, the first chapter suggesting that the capacity to discern the way and will of God is destroyed by sin—"They became futile in their thinking and their senseless minds were darkened" (Rom. 1:21), and the second seeming to say that not only is the capacity to know God not lost by sin but the Gentiles "who have not the law do by nature what the law requires" (Rom. 2:14). Still more perplexing is the suggestion that the capacity to do what the law requires is of sufficient merit to make them "the doers of the law who will be justified" (Rom. 2:13). How can this be, in the very Pauline charter of justification by faith alone that repudiates any thought of salvation by the works of the law?

C. H. Dodd sheds some light on these puzzlements by stressing the importance of the audience for each of these passages.[15] The comments in chapter 1 have the Gentiles in mind, pointing to the evidence of the corruptions in their society as indicating the failure of response in them to the claims they know, and calling on the very conscience given them in creation, and maintained in the Noachic covenant, to recognize both their responsibility and their breach of it: "Therefore you have no excuse, O man, whoever you are . . ." (Rom. 2:1). In chapter 2, the same determination to call to responsibility is at work, this time addressed to Israel, the elect of God. Paul exposes his audience to judgment by comparing their own failures and faithlessness to Gentiles who respond "sufficiently," that is, sufficient to the response God requires for the hu-

15. Ibid., *passim*.

man venture to go forward. In both cases, one by denunciatory description and the other by denunciatory comparison, both judgment and call to responsibility are rendered. In the process, Paul assumes the knowability of the claims on them and some capacity to respond to them.

A vocal tradition in Christian interpretation takes the Gentile knowledge and performance a step further, asserting that a response is possible (by grace) in those outside the particular covenant stream (Abraham, Moses, Christ), a response that will win salvation, adducing Paul's own words in chapter 2 that God "will render to every man according to his works: to those who by patience in well-doing seek for glory and honor and immortality, he will give eternal life. . . . the doers of the law who will be justified" (Rom. 2:6-7, 13). Similar interpretations are in traditions that speak of "the just pagan" and in modern theories of "anonymous Christianity."[16] Such a judgment removes these texts from their immediate literary context as well as from Romans as a whole, the Pauline corpus, and the witness of the canon. Included in the interpretation of these aforementioned Romans texts must be: "None is righteous, no, not one; no one understands, no one seeks for God. All have turned aside, together they have gone wrong; no one does good, not even one. . . . all have sinned and fall short of the glory of God" (Rom. 3:10-12, 23). All this is just a few verses later. Thus Paul's allusion in chapter 2 to being justified by works and a patience in well doing that appears just before these assertions is to be seen as the *intention* of God in the world as it should be, not the *achievement* in the world as it in fact is. For those who do the law in that intended world and "seek for glory" (Rom. 2:7) there will be eternal life, but for those who fail in that intention and are "factious and do not obey the truth, but obey wickedness, there will be wrath and fury" (Rom. 2:8). And who will do the law as intended? "No one" (Rom. 3:10), for "all . . . fall short of the glory of God" (Rom. 3:23). We cannot forget Barth's searching exegesis of these texts. There are no warrants here for overturning *solus Christus, sola fide, sola gratia.* But neither are there reasons to

16. On "the just pagan," see the illuminating survey of views by Gordon Whatley, "The Uses of Hagiography: The Legend of Pope Gregory and the Emperor Trajan in the Middle Ages," *Viator* 15 (1984): 40-63. Karl Rahner's view on "anonymous Christianity" is found in *Foundations of Christian Faith,* trans. William V. Dych (New York: Seabury Press, 1978), 311-21. See also Karl Rahner, *Theological Investigations,* vol. 5, trans. Karl-H. Kruger (Baltimore: Helicon Press, 1966), 115-34.

forget the lessons of the canon on universality. There is a Noachic way God has with creation with its commensurate light and life. Dodd's modest observations correct Barth's overstated exegesis: "There is sufficient knowledge of God available to ensure (human) responsibility and sufficient practice of the law of God among pagans."[17] Dodd's "sufficiency" goes too far, on the other hand, in the direction of anonymous Christianity, but more about that later. Narratively considered, sufficiency means a way-making that gives enough light and life for the story to proceed toward its intended outcome. This light and life along the way is not the same as salvation by grace through faith, and the relationship of the one to the other must become clearer in the exegesis of John 14:6. The decisiveness of Christ as the way of God into the world must be related to the other ways of God, and the truth and salvation of the former defined vis-à-vis the light and life of the latter. Similarly, we need to clarify the particularity of the way of God with Israel and the particularity of the way of God in Christ, with their own associated disclosures and deliverances.

Paul launches immediately upon just this issue in the fourth chapter of Romans as he links justification by faith in Christ with Abraham's justification by faith in God (Rom. 4:1-25). Abraham is the veritable "father of faith," who saw the light and was given life without knowing Christ after the flesh. We shall follow this thread further, including its implication both for today's children of Abraham and also for those who do not know Christ "after the flesh."

The other explicit texts on the way of God outside the Way carry along the theme of the Romans passages. Relevant here is Paul's remark at Lystra that God "did not leave himself without witness" in doing "good [giving] you from heaven rains and fruitful seasons, satisfying your hearts with food and gladness" (Acts 14:17). And at the Areopagus Paul acknowledges an intuition of the true One in the altar to the unknown God that shows evidence of the intimations God leaves so that they might "feel after him and find him" (Acts 17:27), including a citation from the poet Epimenides with its sense that "In him we live and move and have our being" (Acts 17:28). (Also an approving word for Menander's epigram "Bad company ruins good morals"—1 Cor. 15:33.) So too the casting of the lines of covenant back behind Noah to Adam, with the light given to each one, a light that still "enlightens each man coming

17. Dodd, "Natural Law in the Bible," 8.

into the world," a light that shines even in the night of sin, for "the darkness has not overcome it" (John 1, *passim*). Here in the Johannine prologue are some of the Christological links that unite all the ways of God in the world, for the Word is the One through whom all things are made, who gives the light that enlightens each one whose light *is* "the light of men," the Word that is the source of the law given to Moses (Rom. 1:17), who "became flesh and dwelt among us" in Jesus Christ in the fullness of grace and truth. Here is an introductory key to the themes of way and truth, light and life throughout John, illuminating John 14:6. We draw on its resources in exploring the unity of universality and particularity.

Another stream of New Testament witness to the larger covenant with all creation is found in appeals to Christians to live so as not to bring the faith into disrepute before the Gentiles. Such admonition assumes the Gentiles' capacity to judge by their own lights what that behavior would be. "Maintain good conduct among the Gentiles, so that in case they speak against you as wrongdoers, they may see your good deeds and glorify God on the day of visitation" (1 Pet. 2:12). So also Paul in Romans 12:17 says, "Repay no one evil for evil, but take thought for what is noble in the sight of all," assuming understanding not only by Christians but universally. Again Paul presupposes some understanding among all peoples of the right ordering of society in his discourse on the state (Rom. 13:1-6), with the power to know right from wrong and administer it fairly vested in those who govern.

In the record of Jesus' teaching, the same kind of universal awareness of standards of right and wrong is regularly assumed. The parable, for example, draws on a sense in wider culture of relationships that make and keep life human. So too Jesus' teaching on marriage (Mark 10:1-9; Matt. 19:1-9) appeals to an ordering in creation known to all since the beginning. With Christ, as with Paul, is the reminder that what is done will reflect on what is said, for the world can recognize authenticity: "You will know them by their fruits" (Matt. 7:16). And again, "let your light so shine before men, that they may see your good works and give glory to your Father who is in heaven" (Matt. 5:16). The explicit statement in Matthew 7:11 that acknowledges that fact of the fall and its crippling effects can yet go on to say, "If you then, who are evil, know how to give good gifts to your children, how much more . . ." (Matt. 7:11).

We have reviewed a set of texts in both Old and New Testaments that are necessary for understanding the full meaning of John 14:6, as that richness can come to us through a canonical reading of Scripture. Yet to be shown is its specific impact on the interpretation. To that we now turn as we draw on the theological themes of substance and center. Because of their inextricability touching this particular Christological text we shall treat them together.

The Gospel of Christ and the Text

We are to read John 14:6 in the light of, and within the limits of, the gospel of Jesus Christ to which the Christian canon testifies. And as a summary Christological and evangelical statement of it, the text itself contributes to the formation of our understanding of the narrative of faith and its turning point. We live with this dialectic in every gospel text, and especially so here. Thus we are dealing now with the gospel in its full range as the Good News of God's deeds of holy love that bring the world to be, continue with us in the face of our spurning of the divine invitation to life together, the bonding of a people in a deepening move to reconcile, entering our midst decisively to achieve that purpose against the worst of the world's resistance, sharing the benefits of the reconciliation achieved in the deliverance of persons and communities from sin, evil, and death, and bringing the Great Story to a close with the consummation of all things, disclosing these deeds and deliverances in general and special revelation. How are we to interpret the way, truth, and life that Jesus is and brings in their canonical gospel sense? That sense must do justice to the kind of texts just examined, and help to shape our understanding of it in the points about which John 14:6 speaks, as well as illumine the themes in the overarching narrative on which it bears. Given the *only* claims of the Johannine text, the *not only* features of the canonical witness come quickly to the foreground. Thus what appears to be both *a scandal of particularity* and *a scandal of universality* must be brought together.[18]

A bridge from John 14:6 out to the wider canonical "not only" themes is the Johannine prologue. The first eighteen verses of the book not only supply an introduction to a construal of the special images in this particular text and throughout the book, but the plot line of the Christian narrative found in it takes into account both the ante-Christ particularities and the universalities of the divine working to which the whole canon points. They show us how the

18. The thesis of my article "The Scandals of Particularity and Universality," *Mid-Stream* 12 (Jan. 1983): 32-52.

deeds, disclosures, and deliverances of the gospel Story can be related to the way, the truth, and the life of John 14:6.

In the gospel, in the prologue, and in the text, Jesus Christ is the decisive path God makes *into* the world to reconcile the alienated, to liberate those in bondage. But this way is kindred to all the other ways of God *with* the world, the way of intimacy in the covenant with Israel and the way of universality in the covenant with humankind in Adam and Noah. The commonality lies in the particularity of Jesus Christ. The one who is enfleshed in the Galilean carpenter is the eternal Word. That Word, one with God and therefore God, is inseparable from the work of creation, for "all things were made through him, and without him was not anything made that was made" (John 1:3). This Word is, in fact, the source of whatever light and life there is in the world since its making (1:4, 9, 10), and no amount of darkness has been able to put out the light and no amount of destruction has been able to extinguish the life (1:5, 10). This same Word, as in the Old Testament synonym "word of the Lord" for "law" (*Torah* with its qualities of *chesed* and *emeth* ("grace" and "truth") is the source of the "law given through Moses" (1:17), establishing Christ as a presence in the covenant particularity of Israel. Yet both the universalities and particularities of these ways and this truth and life move forward to the center of the Story where the Word enters directly to contest and overcome the world's resistance. "And the Word became flesh and dwelt among us" (1:14). Here is the uniting proximity that is "*full* of grace and truth" (1:14), the abundance that can come only with presence, the "*fulness* . . . we all received, grace *upon* grace" (1:16). The Word is the medium of the divine way in all creation. The same Word is there in giving special gifts to Israel, the gracious and truthful law and its prophetic lineage culminating in the "man sent from God, whose name was John" (1:6). Yet before the event in which the Light blazes in our midst, in which "we have beheld his glory, glory as the only Son from the Father" (1:14), other graces and truths can be seen only in their anticipatory roles in the drama, as "the law . . . given through Moses" compared to "grace and truth . . . through Jesus Christ" (14:17), as a prophetic pointer who "was not the light, but came to bear witness to the light" (1:7). And those who see the light will have the life. "To all who received him, who believed in his name, he gave power to become children of God; who were born, not of blood nor of the will of the flesh nor of the will of man, but of God" (1:12-13). As children in Christ, they know their way home (14:2).

The prologue gives us the story, or much of it, and its own version of it. The Johannine communities and their redactor speak out of the issue of Jewish-Christian interrelationships in the closing decades of the first century, in the rhetoric of mystical encounter and the excitement of fresh discovery before which other realities pale, and with strong noetic concerns. But the canonical hand as well as the content of the introduction take us with these things to the larger landscape of a particular cum universal gospel. With its help we return to situate the text in that wider context. In making that passage, however, we shall draw on other related canonical material.

Jesus Christ is the Way made by God to God for us. This Person is the path to the Father's place. This Way is the only way: "No one comes to the Father, but by me" (John 14:6). But the journey begins well before the opening of this Way. The world travels toward it (Jesus Christ incarnate) on trails hewn through long-standing forests. God has made these paths possible, too. They are the ways of divine working in all creation and its focusing particularity in Israel. They are not *the* Way, which awaits the final stage of the journey, but they lead toward it. The covenant with Noah assures passageway ahead for all humankind, wandering though its course may be. The covenants with Abraham and Moses begin a straight route whose promise is fulfilled in the connecting Way to the hoped-for destination.

The light that comes from the Way God makes in Christ illuminates all the paths that lead toward it. In it we recognize what they are, God's own ways with the world. But the light of Christ shows them to be *Christ's* ways. In his light we see his other ways in the world. And as the Way brings truth and life so these ways, as his, also bring truth and life. These ways anticipate and are tributary to the Way. They have truth and life commensurate with their location on the map, their stage of the journey, their time in the narrative. Here is grace and truth in Noachic and Mosaic covenants that lead toward the personal presence of the divine Glory and thus the fullness of grace and truth.

The light imagery of John enables us to view retrospectively the work of Christ in all the world, from the vantage point of the incarnation of the divine Glory. The pathway figure in John, on the other hand, makes passible a *retroactive,* as well as retrospective, interpretation. The opening of the way to God's house at this crucial point in the pilgrimage changes the character of all that has gone before. Because this final leg of the journey as the Way reaches its destination, it establishes all the foregoing quests as *more* than quests. They are now changed in their very nature, the Way making them part of a road going somewhere. However winding and incomplete their progress, they are elements in a movement that reaches its goal. The last phase of the journey on the path to the Place does reach home, making all of the journey prior to it worth the taking. Thus this final segment that reaches the Father alters the very nature of the connecting trails, establishing them retroactively as *of* the Way. This retroaction makes the retrospection possible, allowing us to see it in the light of Christ as belonging to him.

The insight that Pannenberg has brought to Christology is enriched by the imagery of John. The future does change the past.[19] The path made by Christ transforms ways that have gone beforehand into a trajectory assured of its goal. Indeed, putting together spatial with temporal imagery, we might portray the triune God as proceeding from the Father's house by way of the Son's path in the power of the Spirit to constitute the very gospel narrative from its beginning.

What is the nature of the truth and life that are Christ's to give and to show on the larger landscape and longer journey? What are the gifts of the Word along its many ways in the world? The testimonies of the canon are there to the knowledge of God given in the damaged but not destroyed image, sustained by the grace of the Noachic covenant, and in the patterns of nature and processes of history in which the divine ways and counsels are manifest to the eyes of a common humanity. Read in the gospel light through the lens of this text, whatsoever things are of good report come from the graces of a universal Christ. The world is sustained in the Story by this wisdom available to humanity, one that makes its life livable toward the future God has in store for it.

Wisdom, of course, is worthless if it is not taken to heart and lived out in conduct. Because grace is *power in* as well as *favor toward* us, the common Christic grace in creation has its effects. The seeds of the *Logos spermatikos* bear fruit. God gives the gift of doing and being, as well as that of seeing and knowing, something of the good, the true, and the beautiful. There are those within the Noachic covenant who are armed in the struggle with

19. Wolfhart Pannenberg, *Jesus: God and Man,* trans. Lewis Wilkins and Duane A. Priebe (Philadelphia: Westminster Press, 1968), 135-38.

covetousness, malice, envy, gossip, slander, the hating of God, insolence, haughtiness, boastfulness, the invention of evil, malignancy, murder, strife, disobedience, foolishness, faithlessness, heartlessness, ruthlessness. So Paul's counsel to the people of Moses would suggest about some of the people of Noah (Rom. 2:14), even while he lashes out against the latter when they breach the law of life.

The presence and power of Christ in a world that does not know him is given classic expression in the parable of the sheep and the goats. Those who meet him on judgment day are told that they kept company with a hidden Christ. "I was hungry and you gave me food, I was thirsty and you gave me drink, I was a stranger and you welcomed me, I was naked and you clothed me, I was sick and you visited me, I was in prison and you came to me" (Matt. 25:35-36). Not knowing the Christ with whom they had to do, they did not know the wisdom of compassion and yet were empowered to follow its counsels. Those who did not follow suffered the consequences. In this passage the way of Christ is an incognito way, one taken in solidarity with sufferers. Its New Testament angle of vision means that the way of God in the world is the way of Christ, that this way of Christ is disclosed by Christ himself, and that it includes both the truth and the life that are inextricable from the Way.

Too much or too little can be made of this oft-discussed passage. It can be used as a warrant for anonymous Christianity in which the act of mercy itself is considered salvific for those who did not know the revealed Christ. It can also be interpreted as a parable of and for the Christian community alone, presupposing the knowledge of Christ in the hearers, though not their knowledge of him in the doing of the deeds of mercy. In the latter case, the text has no bearing on issues of universal grace. Each of these interpretations seems right in one respect but wrong in another. The first correctly asserts the presence of Christ incognito in acts of love and sees a relationship of this to salvation. But it wrongly suggests that personal salvation is based on works (albeit graced works) and can be had without explicit faith in Christ. In both cases the great canonical refrains are ignored. The second helps us to see that this is indeed a conversation between Christ and believers. However, it is an *eschatological* one in which the respondents know they stand before Christ at this moment of judgment, and do so as those who have acknowledged him. They are portrayed as reviewing from this eschatological reference point a life that had gone before them in which they did not know him as such.

As the singular Way is different from the ways, so too are the unique Truth and Life to be distinguished from the knowledge and salvation available in the ways of God outside the incarnation. The truth of Christ given in the Word enfleshed is the disclosure about Christ and the gospel that can be known only at the center of the Story. This is "special revelation" at its climactic point given to us in the apostolic testimony to the Person and Work of Christ. It is the Word about God which we need that is not heard in a world that has shut its ears to it, a Vision to be seen that eyes blinded by sin cannot perceive. Like the path that must take a new turn and move to a new stage to reach its destination, so the Word uttered along its way that goes unheeded must be sounded directly into the world, be present in it, rather than shouted at it. Jesus Christ is the only Way and Word to be had to know the Truth. But as the path is a way through the wilderness, allowing us to be on our road toward God's destination, so the Word of truth that is given on the circuitous trail does a purposeful work. This worldly Word encourages us in our pilgrimage and saves us from the perils of the wilderness. The Word here makes the travel do-able. Therefore God has not left our journey without some witness, some signposts of the goal, some words of direction and warnings of misstep that make the way negotiable. As this is the way toward the turn in the road that leads home, it is Christ's path.

Following the little light and attending to the Word that is on this wandering path gives us life. The rules of the road, the law of this wilderness land contiguous to the promised land constitute the codes of making and keeping life human. To feed the hungry, heal the sick, welcome the stranger, visit the prisoner, do justice, and make peace is to do the things that keep the human story moving forward. They make the journey viable. So too do the pursuit of wisdom and the love of beauty. And the honor given to God in the intimations in and beyond these things of good report is the highest humanizing. The suffering that comes from and constitutes hunger, sickness, estrangement, imprisonment, injustice, violence and war, ignorance and error, ugliness and ungodliness is opposed to the willing and acting in mercy, justice, peace, truthfulness, loveliness, and saintliness. We are, therein, *saved* from evil and suffering by the grace of Christ, active in the hearts and deeds of love to neighbor, nature, and God. *Salvation,* understood canonically (as Cruden's *Concordance* indicates), includes salvation from misery and destruction as well as from sin and guilt.[20] The "life" that Christ brings through those who minister to him is the life free from hunger, sickness, injustice, war, ugliness, despair. These things are not to be excluded from the gifts given by the One who came "to give life and give it more abundantly" (John 10:10). Christ made the path for it, gives the light on it and the life in it!

Life as deliverance from misery willed by God to fulfill the divine purpose of wholeness is a refrain throughout the entire Bible. Ronald Sider has traced it in Old and New Testaments, providing a canonical context for reading a crucial dimension of the meaning of the life. We draw on his investigation found in *Cry Justice!*[21]

Exod. 3:7-10; 6:2-9; 20:1-3, 13, 15, 17; 22:25-27; 23:6-8, 10.
Lev. 5:7-11; 12:6-8; 14:1-22; 19:9-18, 32-36; 23:22; 25:8-17, 35-55.
Deut. 1:16-17; 8:1-20; 10:17-19; 15:1-11; 16:18-20; 23:19-20; 24:10-11, 17-22; 25:13-16; 26:1-11; 27:19; 32:4.
1 Sam. 2:8.
1 Sam. 11:1-4, 6, 14-15; 12:1-7.
1 Kings 21:1-19.
Neh. 10:31.
Job 5:11-16; 22:5-9; 24:1-12, 19-22; 29:1-17.
Pss. 9:7-12, 18; 10:2-4, 15-18; 12:5; 15:1-5; 35:19; 37:22-26; 41:1-2; 68:5-6; 69:30-33; 72:1-4, 12-14; 82:1-5; 89:14; 94:1-15, 20-23; 96:10-13; 103:6-7; 109:30-31; 113:5-9; 140:12; 146:1-10.
Prov. 14:21, 31; 15:25; 16:11-12; 17:5; 19:17; 21:13; 22:9, 16, 22-23; 23:10-11; 28:3, 8, 27; 29:4-7, 14, 26; 31:8-9.
Eccles. 4:1.
Isa. 1:10-17, 21-26; 3:13-25; 5:8-13, 15-16, 22-24; 9:6-7; 10:13-19; 11:1-4; 25:6-8; 26:5-6; 29:17-21; 32:1-3, 6-8, 15-17; 33:14-16; 42:1-7; 58:1-10; 61:1.
Jer. 7:1-15; 12:1-2, 5, 7; 22:1-5, 11-12.
Lam. 3:34-46.
Ezek. 18:5-9; 22:1-3, 6-12, 15-16, 23-31; 45:9-10.
Amos 2:6-8; 4:1-3; 5:6-15, 21-24; 6:4-7; 7:10-17; 8:4-8.
Mic. 2:1-10; 3:1-4, 9-12; 4:1-4; 6:6-8, 9-15.
Hab. 2:5-12.
Zeph. 3:1

20. Alexander Cruden, *Complete Concordance of the Bible* (London: Lutterworth Press, 1977), 560.

21. Ronald J. Sider, *Cry Justice! The Bible on Hunger and Poverty* (New York: Paulist Press, 1980), *passim*.

Zech. 7:8-10; 8:14-17.
Mal. 3:5
Matt. 5:17-20; 6:1-4, 11, 24-33; 7:12; 10:42; 12:1-8, 15-21; 19:16-30; 23:23; 25:31-46.
Mark 8:1; 10:41-45.
Luke 1:46-55; 3:7-11; 4:16-21; 6:20-25; 7:18-23; 11:42; 12:32-34; 14:12-23; 16:19-31; 19:1-10; 20:45-47.
John 2:13-16; 13:1-17, 34-35.
Acts 2:41-47; 4:32-37; 6:1-7; 9:36-41; 11:27-30; 20:32-35.
Eph. 4:28.
1 Tim. 4:4-7.
James 2:1-9, 14-17; 5:1-6.
1 John 3:11-18; 4:7-12.
Rev. 7:13-17; 21:4-5, 22-27.

Interpreted Christologically, the physical, social, and historical wholeness mandated and given in these passages is by the grace of the Savior, the eternal Word of Shalom, "the Life of the world."[22]

The Word of life along this way, so precious and so necessary, is not the last Word or the final life. It gives bread for the journey and breath for the strides along the way. But we do not live by bread alone, but by every Word that proceeds from the mouth of God (Matt. 4:4). Nor do we live by the breath of the human pilgrimage but by the breath of the Spirit that comes from the mouth that speaks the Word. Deliverance from suffering and the winding path through desolate places gives the *rudiments* of life. There is another deliverance that comes with knowledge of the crucial turn in the road and the Way found there to the Father's house. Here are given the *fundaments* of life. So the Johannine testimony that "God so loved the world that he gave his only Son, that whoever believes in him should not perish but have eternal life" (John 3:16).

While the life of love, the love that makes human life livable along every path, is itself eternal—"love never ends" (1 Cor. 13:8)—those who live it on the universal paths are not thereby granted eternity. Why not? Because our living of it is rudimentary, enough to make life livable in this world but *not* the complete love intended for the kingdom. That perfect love by which we finally measure all our broken efforts is the love of God manifest in the life of Jesus. By that standard "none is righteous, no, not one. . . . since all have sinned and fall short of the glory of God" (Rom. 3:10, 23). For that

22. The theme of the Vancouver Assembly of the World Council of Churches.

reason, "no human being will be justified . . . by works of the law" (Rom. 3:20). There is no way to God's house by this route. Christ must take us on the final leg of our travel, making a special way with its particular truth and fundamental life. The life in question is the life of a sinner without merit being declared righteous by God's gracious favor. The eternal life given herein comes by knowledge of the Person and Work of Christ, and trust in what has been done for us in that being and doing. His life, death, and resurrection offer us the life of lasting reconciliation with God and thus with our neighbor and with nature in the reign of God. Participation in everlasting life comes by faith alone. "He who through faith is righteous shall live" (Rom. 1:17). This faith by grace brings us to the Father's house by the path of Christ.

The life Christ gives on the path Christ makes comes through the truth Christ proclaims. The life of faith then depends on knowing the gospel. "So faith comes from what is heard, and what is heard comes by the preaching of Christ" (Rom. 10:17). Again and again and again, we hear of the benefits of God's path-making work in the Person of Christ for those who "believe," "have faith," "repent," "follow," "obey," "draw near," "receive in meekness," "hear" and "are baptized," "abide in him," "hear" and "do good works"—in short, "keep . . . the faith in Jesus." The gifts given with the grace that makes such a "good confession" possible are described in many and various ways: the forgiveness of sin, mercy, redemption, justification, regeneration, sanctification, blessedness, renewal in the Spirit, expiation, righteousness, peace with God, fellowship with the Father and the Son, fellowship with one another, participation in the Body of Christ, eternal glory with Christ, being healed, being cleansed from unrighteousness, partaking of the divine nature, purification, abiding in Christ, dying and rising again with Christ. The giving of these gifts is inseparable from faith in Jesus Christ. "There is salvation in no one else, for there is no other name under heaven given among men by which we must be saved" (Acts 4:12).

And how do we know about this name? Those whom Christ has made as his Body (Peter in this case) "will declare to you a message by which you will be saved, you and all your household" (Acts 11:14). Let everyone around know the truth, and in knowing it be saved. "God our Savior . . . desires all men to be saved and to come to the knowledge of the truth" (1 Tim. 2:3-4). Salvation for you and for me, touching the fundaments of personal life with God here and hereafter in the reign of God, comes only by faithful response to the gospel proclaimed by the Body of Christ. This universal judgment of the New Testament canon is a hard saying, a stone of stumbling in a pluralistic world.

In the contextual section to come we shall examine the alternative readings of and responses to this—hard sayings against the backdrop of modern pluralism and secularity. Here we note that the special offense to modernity lies in the *life* claims of the New Testament: the ultimate wholeness, health, rightness, fulfilling of the self is only available by a personal act of faith in Jesus Christ. There can be no compromise on this for those who espouse Scripture as source of the gospel truth. Yet in the exegesis of this text, and in the larger question of the New Testament witness to salvation, not everything has so far been said by a traditionalist perspective that must be said. The position of imperial singularity professing loyalty to the offensive particularity, in fact, qualifies the hard saying in its own way by obscuring the "scandal of universality" we must see in conjunction with the scandal of particularity.

We have already indicated one aspect of the second scandal in the canonical Word on the encompassing aspect of "life." Salvation as life in its rudiments is a gift given by the universal Christ present incognito wherever human life is made and kept human and the earth is ennobled. Here we are saved by grace through love from the evil and suffering that militates against the divine purpose. This is the *penultimate* salvation that Christ makes possible along the wandering ways of the world. It is bread for the journey of all pilgrims in every time and place who choose to go forward. Christ delivers from poverty, sickness, injustice, violence, and despair wherever love reaches out to those in need. As the favor and power of the Savior who moves the world toward its purposed end, this common grace is both Christic and salvific. We cannot compartmentalize it as a grace of creation different from the grace of redemption, or as the creative work of the first Person separated from the redemptive work of the second. There is distinction but not separation. The distinction has to do with the timing and placing of the grace in the Great Narrative. Grace before and beyond the particular action of God with Israel and in Christ moves the drama toward its denouement in this stream of events. It is no less Christic and salvific touching the needs appropriate to these times and places, delivering humanity from the obstacles on its path, and making the passage inviting in goodness and truth, beauty and piety.

There is a second aspect of the universality of life that we must hold in dialectical tension with the canonical testimony to its particularity. As the apocalyptic expectations in the primitive communities began to wane, and the churches prepared for a longer "time between the times" of Easter and eschaton, an awareness grew of the stretches of humanity not reached by the offer of life through faith in Christ. While evangelistically energizing—the preaching of the gospel to all the world became linked with the very coming of the end (Mark 13:10)—the apostolic community asked itself about the destiny of those who had not heard the truth and therefore could not know the way and have the life. At the edges of the Johannine communities' own assertions of particularity are indications of its answer. There *are* those who do not know the Name or belong to the community of Jesus who shall have life. These are the "other sheep, that are not of this fold" (John 10:16). But they too shall come to know Christ and belong to the fold: "I must bring them also, and they will heed my voice. So there shall be one flock, one shepherd" (John 10:16). But when will this voice of the shepherd be heard by those not now in the sheepfold? In a key passage that brings together truth and life, time and eternity, the Johannine Christ declares,

> Truly, truly, I say to you, the hour is coming, and now is, when the dead will hear the voice of the Son of God, and those who hear will live. For as the Father has life in himself, so he has granted the Son also to have life in himself, and has given him authority to execute judgment, because he is the Son of Man. Do not marvel at this; for the hour is coming when all who are in the tombs will hear his voice and come forth, those who have done good, to the resurrection of life, and those who have done evil, to the resurrection of judgment. (John 5:25-29)

Here in John is the evidence of an *eschatological evangel.* For "the other sheep," the Word will speak, the shepherd's voice will sound. And "those who hear will live" (5:25). Those who "heed my voice" (10:16) will join the flock of their shepherd. Those who now and in the future have a graced and faithful hearing of the shepherd's voice and therefore do "good" will be given the "resurrection of life," and those who fail to hear and heed and therefore do "evil" must face "the resurrection of judgment" (5:29).

This theme of eschatological encounter is taken up in other late New Testament writings that consider the destiny of those who had not heard the Word through the Body of Christ on earth. The most widely discussed passages of this sort are in the first letter of Peter (3:18-20; 4:5-6). In these verses are cryptic references to Christ who "also died for sins once for all . . . and preached to the spirits in prison" (3:18-19), and "preached even to the dead" (4:6). While a figurative interpretation is a possibility, with "those in prison" or "dead" referring to a spiritual condition, that construal does not cohere with the specific reference in this passage to those living during Noah's time, presumably dead, to whom Christ preached upon his own descent at death to the place of the dead (3:20). The allusion to Noah is interesting in the light of the Noachic covenant discussed earlier. Do these passages mean that all those who during the time of "God's patience" (3:20), when Noah was saved and the world was preserved on its way toward a future reconciliation, all those who did and did not know of the Reconciler await that Word and will hear it from the eschatological voice of Christ? Not a few of the early Fathers who faced more of the lengthening timeline of Christian narrative concluded that this was the case. An authoritative expression of this belief appeared, in fact, in the Apostles' Creed: Christ's descent into "Hades," the place of the dead.[23]

Another text that contributes to this postmortem theme in canonical teaching on life makes specific reference to the descent. Drawing on the height and depth metaphors of the Psalms, Ephesians 4:8-10 declares, "Therefore it is said, 'When he ascended on high he led a host of captives, and he gave gifts to men,' " with its parenthetic question and observation "(In saying, 'He ascended,' what does it mean but that he had also descended into the lower parts of the earth? He who descended is he who also ascended far above all the heavens, that he might fill all things.)." While in the context of the discussion of the visible Body of Christ on earth, the passage as a whole is about the inclusive range of God's love "above all and through all and in all" (Eph. 4:6), and the manifoldness of the Body of Christ with its many gifts and ministries (Eph. 4:4-6). The descent of Christ into *hades* is also to reach the last and the least of those who are to hear the Word.

Assumed in the eschatological proclamation of the gospel is the possibility of a fundamental decision for Christ after death, an idea

23. See Pannenberg's discussion of this in *Jesus: God and Man,* 271-74. See also the illuminating comments of George Lindbeck, *The Nature of Doctrine* (Philadelphia: Fortress Press, 1984), 56-63. For an extended discussion of the subject see Thomas P. Field, "The Andover Theory of Future Probation," *The Andover Review* 7 (May 1887): 461-75, and Egbert H. Smith, "Probation after Death," *The Homiletic Review* 11 (April 1886): 281-91. For contrary opinion in the period of heated nineteenth-century discussion see William Love, *Future Probation Examined* (New York: Funk & Wagnalls, 1888).

that standard views of salvation find difficult to accept. Many evangelicals believe that it weakens the evangelism mandate. The Roman Catholic tradition, even in its more recent thinking about "the final decision," and earlier in its purgatorial teaching, stops short of an eschatological view because it permits no postmortem remission of mortal sin. Our destiny is determined by our time on earth. Church tradition is our resource in exploring the biblical source and we must listen carefully to these critics, especially when they resist any volatilizing of the historical nature of the Christian religion. However, the scriptural source keeps calling us to reexamine our inherited tradition. Does this strand of texts suggest something new on our horizon? With different eyes formed from a canonical reading in pluralist times we begin to look at the New Testament faith possibility of this witness. Does the comment in Revelation that the gates of heaven remain open ("the gates shall never be shut by day," 21:25) support this interpretation? And although baptism for the dead seems to be an impenetrable text in the light of a canonical reading, does it not imply that the status of the dead before God is not inalterable (1 Cor. 15:29)?

Periods in church history when the horizons of the Christian community were widened by new cultural facts forced a rethinking of accepted exegesis and inherited doctrine. Concerning the salvation associated with faith in Christ alone, the patristic period and the missionary centuries sharply posed questions of soteriological particularity and universality. The Fathers' proposals on the proclamation of Christ to those who did not know him after the flesh came in one such period. Another was the nineteenth-century overseas mission movement. Andover Seminary, founded in the time and place of this ferment of mission, experienced an early form of "plural shock." In their cross-cultural exposure on the mission fields of the Pacific, Asia, and Africa, the graduates were made aware of the vast numbers who had not and would not hear the gospel. They were helped along in this raised awareness by converts in these fields who asked the same questions about beloved ancestors who had died before hearing the Word. Proponents of the late-nineteenth-century "Andover theory" read many of the texts we have just mentioned as validating an eschatological option for those who had not been confronted in this life with Christ. They, too, had a chance for knowing the truth and thus having the life, a theory of "second probation." Similar thoughts were already in the air in the continental theologies of Martensen, Dorner, Van Ossterzee and Julius Muller, and their North American counterparts in the Mercersburg theology, with the same position taken in British commentaries by Plumte and Alford.

An interesting parallel experience with plural shock seems to have come not from the mission field as such but from the heightened awareness of infant mortality that appeared with broadening communication and grasp of the wider perimeters of human life on this planet. Thus Princeton theologians Charles Hodge and Benjamin Warfield "solved" the theologically troubling problem of millions of children who die in infancy in a way befitting their predestinarian assumptions, which did not require occasions for choice before Christ for salvation. They declared that *all* such progeny are saved by "the unconditional decree of God."[24]

We count these sometimes idiosyncratic proposals to be important experiments in biblical interpretation that had to wait upon the unfolding of new times and places in God's continuing narrative for them to appear. The Fathers and the missionaries searched the Scriptures for answers in their new contexts, answers that had not been available to them before. As we ask the contextual questions of John 14:6 we deal with them again, but this time with the resources they provide for a better understanding of the source. With their help we part company with the imperial option in this second respect as well. Because Christ is really Life, death has no hold on him. His ministry cannot be constrained by our "no trespassing" signs. The Body of Christ that speaks the Word and brings life to those who feed on it by faith can be a *glorified* Body as well as a Body on earth. The Body that ascends to rule can descend to seek. "If I ascend to heaven, thou art there! If I make my bed in Sheol, thou art there!" (Ps. 139:8). As this Body beckons to all humans in this world, so too it reaches the uttermost parts of the world to come. Herein is the wideness of Christ's mercy and the length of loving pursuit. Christ is the hound of heaven that will follow the hind to the end. Here is the particularity of life offered only by faith in Jesus Christ, but one that must be seen in its universal scope, a merciful Word that goes out to all and to the end. Once again we are involved in the surprising twists and turns of the Story of an implacable Love.

The gospel narrative in both the large and small print of its canonical reading gives us an understanding of the "only/not only"

24. Charles Hodge, *Systematic Theology,* vol. 1 (New York: Charles Scribner and Co., 1872), 26-27.

paradox at its center. Christ is both scandalously particular and offensively universal. Each of the three predicates of John 14:6—way, truth, and life—has its particular and universal dimensions. In the discussion of contextualization to follow, we shall chart the differences between our view here and other contemporary responses to pluralism that struggle with the same question. Three opinions on this matter that bear directly on the question of eschatological option deserve our attention at this point.

It is a short step from the view that Christ preaches the gospel of life to the dead who have not known it to the conclusion that all so addressed will accept it. "Universalism" of this sort has looked at some of the textual evidence to which we have referred and drawn the conclusion that the love of God is such that no one will be turned away, the preaching of Christ so compelling that no one can refuse. Yet this claim to know the outcome of the encounter in each case—here and hereafter—eliminates the surprises that go with a Story not yet over. The canonical testimony to the majestic freedom of the Author to complete the tale and to the risky freedom of the participants to take up their own place in it is not given sufficient due in the rigid blueprints of universalism. With the eye of faith we do know the storyline and where it is going. And because its promise is that God "shall be all in all" and that "every knee should bow . . . and every tongue confess that Jesus Christ is Lord" (Phil. 2:10-11), we have a right to hope for a universal "yes." So Barth's wise words, spoken with his characteristic stress on the divine freedom.[25] A universal*ism* that appends itself to biblical universality is not warranted from Scripture. The universal reconciliation *(apokatastasis)* can be here only a modest *article of hope,* not an article of firm faith.

A second judgment on the eschatological evangel poses a hard question. Does not the belief that Christ preaches to the dead undercut evangelization? If all have a chance in a realm to come, then why bother with spreading the gospel right now? The thread of New Testament teaching on eschatological invitation does not affect the sense of urgency in the Johannine, Petrine, and Pauline writings in which it appears, not the canonical editors who included it. But perhaps the implications suggested by evangelical critics of this developing theme have yet to be faced. The issue must be joined at a prior point, the legitimacy of the inference drawn.

25. Karl Barth, *CD* IV/3, 477-78.

This criticism that an eschatological option precludes evangelization is questionable on theological, psychological, and logical grounds.

The sense of urgency about the evangel rises out of a graced Word in the believer who has personally experienced, as well as cognitively understood, the "Good News." Grace is power to warm the heart as well as favor to change the mind. It convicts as well as convinces. The finding of "a pearl of great price" brings a cry of joy and the will to invite others to share in the discovery (Matt. 13:46). The psychology of evangelism lies in the theology of grace. The will to share the gospel comes, first and foremost, from inner conviction not from outer argument. One does not coolly calculate the cost-benefit ratio of believing and then decide to proclaim the faith. "Woe to me if I do not preach the Gospel!" (1 Cor. 9:16).

Since our minds as well as our hearts are active in the love of God (Luke 10:27), we cannot help asking, at some point, the question that the doubters of the eschatological option put to us. While it will not prevent the evangelical impulse to share the gospel with all who do not know it, it can weaken the impulse. But more important than these practical considerations, the love of God with the mind *requires* us to face the hard questions of theological logic. In this case: If the implacable Christ ultimately confronts all in eternity, why is there a mandate to share the News in time? The answer comes in the Johannine writing that has posed these issues so sharply for us: "He who believes in the Son *has* eternal life" (John 3:36). Through the gospel eternal life begins for us in the *here and now.* Saving grace is given, with all its benefits—love, joy, peace, patience, kindness, goodness, faithfulness, gentleness, self-control (Gal. 5:22; John 14:27)—in time. To pass through our sojourn in time without this grace and these gifts is to be on the world's way without yet finding the path to our final destination. While that way in the world *is* livable, and the Way *may yet be* found in the life to come, how could we not want for the wanderer the eternal life offered here and now? A life without faith is an impoverished life, one without the fullness of the gifts St. Paul enumerates. The logical as well as the psychological rationale for sharing the faith is grounded in the theology of grace, its offer and power both now and then.

A third view in range of, and in conversation with, a postmortem evangelical choice is the proposal within Roman Catholic theology of a "final decision," especially as developed by Ladislaus Boros and Edmund Fortmann.[26] Christ's encounter with all those who have not known him or made a responsible choice for or against him comes at the time of death itself. In a luminous moment on the boundary of life and death, an occasion is offered in which Christ communicates the truth, and the choice for or against him is made. Often associated with this idea is a confidence in a hidden grace that works strongly enough during life to empower the conscience of those outside of the revelation of Christ to know and to do the truth given universally, in which case the final decision is the confirmation and strengthening of graced choices already established. The location of the final decision here rather than after death, or at the final reckoning before Christ, is related to the continuing influence of a doctrine of purgatory that precludes the changing of our relationship to God after death for those in mortal sin, as well as the long-standing assertion of the decisiveness of options offered in this world for human destiny. Also influential is a last rites tradition and deathbed spirituality in Roman Catholicism in which the time of life/death crossing is focal. While we have stressed the crucial role of the church and its traditions in the interpretation of Scripture and in the formation of doctrine, we have also, on the one hand, pressed beyond the confines of any one part of the Christian community for the witness constitutive of it, a catholicity of community, and on the other hand, have held all tradition under the authority of Scripture. In this case that means the great Roman Catholic tradition of last rites, its teaching on purgatory, and its exposition of final decision have to be taken with great seriousness. In this respect it does support the Christological encounter themes expounded here, and also the mystical character of it in the realm of death, albeit on its borders in final decision. The universality of the constituency of this church brings it into contact with the multitudes in many cultures that are outside the church and remain unreached by the gospel. In this respect it experiences the same plural shock that the missionary movements in

26. See E.J. Fortmann, *Everlasting Life after Death* (New York: Alba House, 1976), 71-156; Ladislaus Boros, *The Mystery of Death* (New York: Herder & Herder, 1965), *passim;* and Karl Rahner, *On the Theology of Death,* trans. Charles H. Hickey (New York: Herder & Herder, 1961), 71-74. On this subject see George Lindbeck's review of positions in "Fides ex auditu" and "The Salvation of Non-Christians: Contemporary Catholic and Protestant Positions," in V. Vajta, ed., *The Gospel and the Ambiguity of the Church* (Philadelphia: Fortress Press, 1974), 91-123.

Protestantism confront, forcing upon it, as upon the missionaries, insistent questions of universality and particularity. Its teaching of final decision, like that of eschatological accountability, is an effort to be faithful to the Christological center but to place particularity within a more universal scope. In this regard the theory of final decision holds that heritage and horizon together more faithfully than other experiments in universality within Roman Catholic thought that abandon one or another aspect of particularity, as in options ranging from anonymous Christianity to a post-Christological "theocentric" interpretation of the way, truth, and life.[27]

In the final analysis, the absence of an ecumenical catholicity in both the spirituality and theology of death do no yet qualify the ecclesial insights here discussed for an ecumenical systematics. But more decisive than that is the authority of Scripture to which every ecclesial judgment must be accountable, the church serving as resource to the biblical source of Christian teaching. On these latter grounds there does not appear to be any textual evidence of a moment at death of final Christological decision. The suggested threads of texts on the eschatological option we have traced weigh more heavily than an ecclesiastical theory as such, especially when joined by the lengthy tradition of the undivided church concerning the descent of Christ into the place of the dead, located within the creed itself and in almost all subsequent usage of it. Further, we must also challenge the confirmatory nature of the final decision held by many. Here the final decision is interpreted as the acknowledgment of the One who in principle has already graciously saved the doer of good works responding to the universal stirring of conscience, therefore relating this view to the long-standing Roman Catholic exegesis of Matthew 25. When the text is read canonically, especially in light of the fall's incapacitation of conscience to know and to do the ultimate will of God, and against the background of the singular action of Christ in making a way through this wilderness to the household of God, then the final encounter with Christ must be more than a formal legitimation of an informal salvation already accomplished. That "more" is its evangelical character: Jesus Christ preaches the Good News wherever that takes place, in this world through the Body of Christ on earth or in the place of the dead through his glorified humanity. The final decision is a real finality and a real decision. It is an eschatological Word spoken in

27. On the latter, see Knitter, *No Other Name,* 145-231.

our last place of abode as a last option with its ultimate consequences.

In passing we note the occurrence of a view found in Protestant theology, often in otherwise very traditional Protestant theology, similar to both the confirmatory version of final decision and the idea of anonymous Christianity. Like them, this position holds that those who have not heard of Christ are judged by God according to the degree of light given to them. Thus salvation comes in "uncovenanted mercies" by response to the general revelation given to the broken but not destroyed image of God and in the traces of divine intention in those depths and in nature and history. Those outside the knowledge of ultimate truth in Christ are not left "without a witness." To whom the much is given, from them much will accordingly be expected. To whom the little is given, proportionately less will be expected (Luke 12:48).[28] When espoused by some orthodox Protestantism there are various ironies here. Gone is the Reformation insistence on the radical nature of the fall, for assumed is both the capacity to understand enough and to will well enough to be saved, however much these things are qualified. That means questioning justification by grace through faith alone; salvation is by good works (graced), done in response to the prompting of conscience. Introduced as well (as in theories of anonymous Christianity) is the unavoidable conclusion that not knowing the truth in Christ is more favorable to salvation than knowing it, since the "little" expected from the light of conscience is less demanding than the knowledge of Christ that, becoming known, carries with it the "much" that is to be expected. Sharing the gospel is, in this sense, bad news to those who hear it, for it adds a burden to their lives formerly judged by a lesser light. Also missing here when a larger option is described as the result of "uncovenanted mercies" is the biblical teaching that the universal revelation cum salvation of this sort also comes under a covenant, the covenant of Noah.

The impulse to universality in all these views is a sound one, but must find theological expression in a way coherent with the Christological and evangelical particularities of Scripture, and within a canonical reading of them. There is no "mind of the church" yet on this mystery of particularity and universality. We offer the proposal discussed as a way toward it.

28. Note the interesting line of thought in Matthew Henry, "Faith in Christ Inferred from Faith in God," in *The Miscellaneous Works* (London, 1830), 785-86.

Eternal Life and Abraham's Heirs

The promise of eternal life to those with faith in Christ poses sharply yet one more issue, the ultimate destiny of believing Jews. While this question is regularly placed within the discussion of the relation of Christianity to world religions, a canonical and narrative interpretation of the gospel cannot do so. The Story of God moves redemptively through the history of Israel, setting it in a qualitatively different relationship to the incarnation from other people and places. The Christian canon with its Hebrew Scriptures as Old Testament puts it on the line of particularity itself, and as such distinguishes all our conversation about Israel from the themes of universality with which we have been dealing. Yet what kind of a particularity can this be, touching salvation by grace through explicit faith in Christ, if Israel before Christ did not know this truth, at the time of Christ largely rejected it, and subsequently became separated from it? Paul deeply felt this agonizing dilemma and set the terms of it in his letter to the Romans both in its early discussion of Abraham as the father of faith, and in chapters 9–11. We turn to his struggle in this letter, taking our lead from it, and situating the exploration of it in the present inquiry about eschatological options. Doing so, we will touch on numerous related questions, past and present: anti-Semitism, evangelization, the State of Israel, the Holocaust, Jewish-Christian relations. We can only begin to examine these questions here, and only by way of the soteriological question at hand, but we shall return to them throughout this systematics.

We must forthrightly face the implications of the salvific particularity in John 14:6, a meeting distasteful to any Christian who has agonized over the Holocaust or has honestly faced the still virulent anti-Semitism in the closing decades of this century. Has not the claim of Christian particularity contributed to and even caused these horrors? Have not those who have spoken most ardently of salvation by Christ alone and by faith alone often been the worst offenders—from Luther's diatribes against the Jews to the subsequent evangelical climate in Germany in which the seeds of Holocaust hate grew? This meeting is distasteful too for those who have frequently found themselves allied with those of Jewish lineage and faith in struggles for justice and peace, because Judaism's faithfulness to the vision of the reign of God often puts to shame those of us who bear the name of the one who preached this kingdom. The plight of the Jews, Christian sins of omission and commission toward them, and the prophetic witness of the Jews together are enough to silence the offensive particularities of the evangel in many parts of the church, either making exception to the evangelical claims in their case, or relativizing the entire gospel message.[29] With these accommodations also goes the authority of Scripture, whose clear testimony to the stone of stumbling has been the burden of this exegesis. Once again, we seek to learn from the issues posed by context, rather than allow the context to determine the meaning of or dispose of the text. Thus the Holocaust and all of the associated questions of Jewish-Christian relationship does put the textual inquiry into a new light. In this respect we anticipate the succeeding discussion of the contextualization of the text, especially the enlarged meaning of the text that a new setting may draw out. Our active consideration of the eschatological evangel is one example of enriched meaning that comes through contextual significance. So too is our present initial examination of the destiny of the heirs of Abraham after the flesh that explores a fresh line of interpretation in continuity with the tradition, but past its present stopping place.

Paul sets us on the trail of it. He cites Genesis 15:6 approvingly, "Abraham believed God, and it was reckoned to him as righteousness" (Rom. 4:3). This is no passing allusion used to strengthen the case of justification from the past. In a long disquisition in which he exegetes this Scripture, Paul argues that Abraham is the "father" of faith (4:1-25). He thereby shows that the way of salvation has already been by faith and not works. By making his case for faith and against works, he also speaks to our question at hand. The one who begins the particular covenant with Israel, and presumably all those who continue in Israel in covenant faithfulness (cf. Heb. 11 for those as well as their predecessors Abel, Enoch, and Noah), the one on whom David pronounced the blessing of God "apart from works" (4:6), and all other descendants so blessed by forgiveness received, demonstrate the way of God with a sinful world. Paul, of course, is building a case against limiting salvation to the circumcised and the practitioners of the law, and for his message of salvation by grace through faith in Christ. But in the process he

29. Rosemary Radford Ruether, *Faith and Fratricide* (New York: Seabury Press, 1974) and *To Change the World* (New York: Crossroad, 1981), 31-43; Paul Van Buren, *Discerning the Way: A Theology of the Jewish-Christian Reality* (New York: Seabury Press, 1980) and *A Theology of Jewish-Christian Reality*, part 2: *A Christian Theology of the People Israel* (New York: Seabury Press, 1983).

has equated the consequences of grace through faith in Christ with grace through an Abrahamic faith that knew of no Christ after the flesh. On this basis two parallel traditions grew in the church about the salvation of those in the covenant of God with Israel. A patristic and medieval view held that the faithful but non-Christological piety of our Hebrew forebears assured them of a salvation that waited upon their acknowledgment of its source. In Christ's descent into the place of the dead in the time between crucifixion and resurrection he gave this knowledge to the fathers and mothers of Israel who received it "unto salvation." This interpretation was formative of the inclusion of the descent into hades as part of the creed. Another view, associated with the Reformation and its stress upon election and divine initiative, did not require an act of eschatological disclosure and assent, but declared instead that the benefits of Christ were automatically transferred after they were won by Christ to all faithful Hebrews preceding Christ. They were saved by Christ, therefore, retroactively. However conceived, church theology in all cases sought to follow the exegetical implications of Paul's Abrahamic testimony (and other New Testament witness): true faith in Israel from Abraham to incarnation is, before God, Christological. We shall try to learn from this tradition, and already have indicated some of its effects in the earlier discussion of the retroactivity of Christ's work.

Paul returns to the subject of the destiny of Israel in the famous soteriological struggle of Romans 9–11. In it comes the "existential" question: What about the present Jews who *do* know Jesus Christ but do *not* confess him with the present faith that Paul believes continues Abraham's act of proleptic faith? Well, for one, not all of the descendants of Abraham reject Jesus, for Paul along with others constitute a "remnant" (11:1-6). For another, it would seem that by the hardening of their hearts, the mission of the gospel to the rest of the world was set in motion: "Through their trespass salvation has come to the Gentiles" (11:11). Perhaps the gift of salvation given to the latter will make the former jealous "and thus save some of them" (11:14).

But is the "rejection" of Jesus by most of Israel and its sad consequences the last word? Paul ruminates: "If their failure means riches for the Gentiles, how much more will their full inclusion mean!" (11:12). And inclusion there *will* be: when the right time comes, "all Israel will be saved" (11:26). As it says in Scripture, "The Deliverer will come from Zion, he will banish ungodliness from Jacob'; 'and this will be my covenant with them when I take away their sins'" (11:26-27). It is in the nature of the promise given to them and the process begun in them: "If the dough offered as first fruits is holy, so is the whole lump; and if the root is holy, so are the branches" (11:16). Put another way, God will not spurn the faithfulness of Abraham and the forebears. Their descendants will be taken up into the life of faith even though right now "they are enemies of God . . . ; as regards election they are beloved for the sake of their forefathers" (11:28). This is so because "the gifts and call of God are irrevocable" (11:29). That means they too are destined, somehow, some day, some way, for life with God. Their function in the providence of God to make possible mercy to others will work so that they too "may receive mercy" (11:32). In the unfathomable mind of God, good things happen to bad people, ourselves most of all; our rejection of the promise of God, wherever found—including Israel's of Christ—is turned to redemptive purposes. Theirs is, and ours is. "How unsearchable are his judgments and how inscrutable his ways!" (11:33).

The Christian *memory* of and *hope* for Israel as set forth in the extended Pauline reflection distinguishes the relationship Christ has with Israel from the relationship of Christ to all other religions and people of conscience. As grafted into Israel's tree, their past is ours, and soteriologically their forebear is our forebear in faith. But their branches, which were broken off, "*will be* grafted in" (11:23). Of course, humanly speaking, there is a big "if": "if they do not persist in their unbelief" (11:23). But finally, puny human resistance is nothing to God, for the election, the gift, is "irrevocable," the momentum is irresistible, "so all Israel *will* be saved" (11:26). In hyperbole or not, this is a grand claim. Like all sharing of the faith, let it go on with the Jews as with Gentiles, but in a different framework, this time with a confidence that in God's calendar the promise of God to deliver will be kept. Could it be that the eschatological evangel that we have been examining is the logical time for such ingathering? The Book of Revelation gives a figural witness to that form of hope (Rev. 7), one that invites the predictable speculations of apocalyptic fundamentalists and the evangelistic strategies and Near Eastern policies of the political fundamentalists.[30] Finally, Scripture cannot satisfy this political and apocalyptic curiosity, for

30. The study of same by Grace Halsell is *Prophecy and Politics: Militant Evangelists on the Road to Nuclear War* (Westport, Conn.: Lawrence Hill & Co., 1986).

it gives no timetable, only the assurance of the favor of God on this people, B.C. and A.D.

Grace is power as well as favor. The prophetic witness the people of Israel continue to bring to human issues is the fruit that comes from a living branch. Is this a sign God has left that there is in this people much more than a religion of works? Are these works of mercy and justice the evidence of an implicit faith that in God's timeline will someday be rendered explicit? With the record of hate and hostility by those that bear the name of Christ toward the Jews, can they ever really hear the Word of Christ from us? Perhaps only an eschatological gospel, from Christ alone, free of the deeds that have made our words unhearable, can render the response of faith explicit. Yet the Christian is reminded ever and again by the lives and witness of Jewish people that the shalom toward which Christ points and which he is, is witnessed to regularly by those who stand in the company of the prophets.

That Israel is part of this special stream of continuing as well as ancient grace and power is a fact that radically challenges slanderous portrayals of this people that have emerged from time to time in Christian history. Can these assaults on the Jews have come from Christian shame over our own lackluster commitment to the prophetic aspects of shalom they have continued to espouse? The people of Israel are our promised sisters and brothers, progeny in the flesh of Abraham and promised to be in the faith of the Abraham who is the father of all of those destined to believe. Christians honor, proleptically, this common family not by ignoring the particularities of the way, truth, and life short of the time of final shalom, but by being allies with Israel where there are theological, textual, and moral commonalities, and being in solidarity with them before the anti-Jewish attacks that are mounted when hate seeks its scapegoats.

Portrayal of the Path

A summary of our exegetical cum systematic reflection on the Way and the world's ways, knowing the truth and receiving the life, Israel and Christ, the narrative journey, the gospel offered in time and beyond it might be portrayed something like the illustration on page 302:

The world's way from Adam and Noah is a wandering one, kept open by the good God to make life livable toward the future. In the path made from God's house in and by Christ, the world's path is rendered more than it had been by Christ, and therefore also

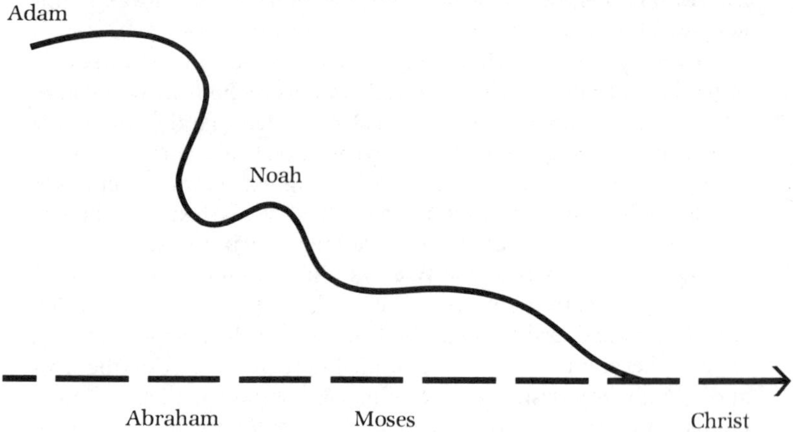

becomes Christ's path. Those on it can find their way by making the sharp turn onto the last leg of the journey.

This path had its own origin in the straight way God made through the wilderness in the call of father Abraham, the gift of exodus from Egypt, and the claim of the Mosaic covenant. The life made toward Christ, the connection made by the path of Christ, has continuities that differ from the way of the world. No sharp turn, but for all that, a new road, one that comes in Christ from the house of God to fulfill the promise of the covenant with Israel; that road too is Christ's road, full of a grace that will be received and a truth that will be known.

When that turn toward the truth will be made and the ultimate life lived for those that travel on the winding road of the world or on the straight way of Israel is a timetable not so easily visualized on a two-dimensional map. But that too is part of understanding the meaning of this key text. We leave its portrayal to better imaginations.

In this internal hermeneutical exercise, which has taken us time and again from exegesis to systematics, we have been on a search for the meaning of a text using common, critical, and canonical methods. These methods have shown us the meaning of John 14:6, that Jesus Christ is the one way God makes into the world to connect it to its destination, bringing us across this path to the home of God where the final truth and life can alone be found. Christ is the only way by which those who know and trust him have final access to truth and life. Here is the scandal of particularity. In making the path from the house of the Father by way of the Son, all the wandering trail of the world sustained in its movement forward by the same God is possessed by Christ, transformed by Christ, making it a way with universal truth and life necessary for its own project. The same Christ who gives strength for this journey, unknown as such by the traveler, comes in the end as the Known. So too the path of Christ continues and completes the way of God with Israel, with its assurance of graced faith now and in the not yet for those who hear and believe and do. Here is the scandal of universality.

CONTEXTUAL SENSE

In the final stage of narrative hermeneutics the interpreter brings the text into contemporary context. What is the *significance* of its *meaning*? How does the meaning of a text that persists over time and place become significant for *this* time and place? Significance is meaning for *us* in cultural context and for *you* and for *me* in personal setting. The confusion of meaning with significance, the reduction of meaning to significance or significance to meaning, the temptations to shortcut the hermeneutical process are always with us and have been noted in the options of the interpretations earlier examined. We seek here to recognize the importance of the difference by distinguishing external from internal hermeneutics, the task of finding the contextual sense from that of inquiry into the common, critical, and canonical senses. Exegesis requires a touchstone, a meaning from which the move to significance proceeds and to which it must always return.

While there is distinction and sequentiality to textualization and contextualization, it should be clear from our exegetical work so far that there is unity and concomitance as well. In each of the three senses investigated so far the "world" has made its mark as a setting that has influenced the ecclesial resource through whose eyes we have read the biblical source. In the inquiry after the canonical sense of the text, for example, the questions of particularity and universality posed by a contemporary culture of pluralism have been active. The circularity within narrative linearity regularly makes its presence felt. The difference is that *the world* is the conscious entry point for exegesis in the contextualizing process, focusing the discussion accordingly. Along with the difference in foci, the integrity in each sense, and the referentiality of contextualization to textualization, is this interaction and interrelationship.

Social Contextualization

When we bring the contextual perspective of this systematics to John 14:6 we seem to be confronted with a textual answer given to an unasked contextual question. The text tells us of a way made by God to God in which the knowledge of this truth of God brings life with God. Yet the context cries out for a word of hope in a world of human suffering, vision in the face of historical frustration, liberation from economic, political, social, and psychological powers that enslave, reconciliation rather than the alienations of persons and nations, humans and our earthly habitat. The world asks for a way home to its own house, yet the Word speaks of the way home to the Father's house. Our questions of immanence are met with the answer of transcendence. The puzzlement of Jesus' disciples is matched, therefore, by that of our modern interlocutors. How can what is uppermost in our minds be linked to the assertion of this text, which appears to have something else on its own mind? It is no accident that José Miranda's liberation hermeneutics, which takes the Gospel of John as its field of interpretation, exegetes numerous passages within it but skips this one.[31] John 14:6 does not appear to speak to us where we are in this time and place.

To frame the contextual issue in the way we have done just now is to introduce covertly a theory of contextualization with its special correlative and idiomatic assumptions: that contextualization is the correlation of cultural question with the answer given by the biblical "message," one done in culturally familiar idiom. Here we have presupposed the translation and transition models. However, contextualization may also be *transformation* in which the cultural questions are challenged because they fail to ask the right question, and therefore cannot hear the answer given by the gospel. We shall see how this, in fact, is the case in John 14:6 in its transformative aspect, constituting as it does an offense to modern sensibility. But there are translation as well as transformation aspects to this text, which speak in the idiom and to the issues of our time and place and afford a way in which the challenges of context themselves make themselves heard.

Modern technology, in raising the stakes of human peril and possibility, bringing suffering and hope, vision and reality into high profile and the immanent issues to the fore, has had its effect as well on world religions in general and Christianity in particular,

31. José Porfirio Miranda, *Being and the Messiah,* trans. John Eagleson (Maryknoll, N.Y.: Orbis Books, 1977).

given its proximity in the West to the technological forces. With the dramatic increase in powers of communication and transportation has come the raised awareness of other religious options and worldviews, both around the world and in our own personal life-world. Technological advances have also released us from the power of inherited traditions and accordingly given mobility to our ultimate commitments. Processes of pluralization have in turn contributed to the secularization process that technology's promise and danger have encouraged. The "ultimate questions" that seem to preoccupy traditional religion appear much less compelling when the variety of options is spread before us, when the civility that a pluralistic society requires softens their aggressive claims and thus relegates their religious choices to a private sphere. This, together with the pressing nature of penultimate questions accelerated by technological power, makes up the context for hearing the Johannine text.

Because pluralization is inextricable from secularization, and with it our horizon of suffering and hope, this text of high particularity cannot help but speak to that issue and its "only" and "not only" features. The contextual move, according to our procedure, entails listening to the text from within the Christian community, and thus participation in the contextual conversation going on within it about these matters of only and not only.

Pluralism, indeed "plural shock," has produced various responses in the Christian conversation as well as beyond it that attempt to find their way through the issues posed by the apparent particularism of traditional Christian belief. As preparation for our exegetical task we enter the theological debates on the uniqueness of Christ vis-à-vis other religions and other worldviews by way of a typology that organizes the options in terms of the claims of particularity in John 14:6, the singular way, truth, and life in Christ. Using the language of Barth we shall identify "way" as the deed of *reconciliation,* "truth" as the disclosure of *revelation,* and "life" as the deliverance of *redemption.*[32]

32. The following typology is reproduced from my essay, "The Scandals of Particularity and Universality," *Mid-Stream,* 22 (Jan. 1983): 34-43. John Poulton in the preparatory materials for the Vancouver Assembly of the World Council of Churches employs the typology from earlier mimeographed materials. See John Poulton, *The Feast of Life* (Geneva: World Council of Churches, 1982), 69-71. S. Mark Heim makes creative use of this framework in *Is Christ the Only Way? Christian Faith in a Pluralistic World* (Valley Forge, Pa.: Judson Press, 1985), 111-27.

Parallel Pluralism

We begin our typology on the left end of the spectrum with the response that shows the most marked effects of plural shock. This does not mean that the proponents do not have strong loyalties to Jesus Christ. They do. But they seek to join them to an affirmation of the legitimacy of other points of view. Parallel pluralism comes in at least three forms.

A familiar version of this type with a history that dates in the West at least from the Enlightenment holds that there is in every valid ultimate commitment a "common core." For example, eighteenth-century Deism asserted that below the level of particular religious accretions is a reasonable central belief in "God, virtue, and immortality." A variation on the theme of commonality locates the essence in religious experience rather than in a set of shared ideas. The experience of the holy, the sacred, absolute dependence, ultimate concern, etc., is believed to lie underneath the richness and variety of its expressions in explicit religious traditions or cultural phenomena. Or again, the moral, rather than the religious or rational, may be viewed as the defining factor. Each religious tradition or moral passion manifests virtues that make and keep life livable.

The best-known exponents of parallel pluralism today are not very interested in the Enlightenment quest for a common factor, at least in its deist form. Influenced by movements characteristic of modernity—historicism, existentialism, Marxism, language analysis, sociology of knowledge—they formulate this option accordingly. A familiar expression of this kind of legitimated pluralism is a "confessional" view. Because we are formed by our historical context, and because faith by definition entails personal commitment—descriptive and normative considerations—Christian faith must therefore be *for me.* Faith is both where I stand and where I choose to stand. Since authentic faith is so engaged, it does not allow me to rise above this rootage and commitment in order to make spectator judgments as to the truth or falsity of other religious claims. In principle, others are granted the equivalent right to confess that their faith is true for them. Religious claims are confessional, not discursive, personal truth for the individual, not impersonal truth for all.[33]

33. As formulated by Donald G. Dawe: "The pattern of new being encoded in 'the name of Jesus' is one that is encountered in many religious traditions. Christians identify it and celebrate it because of what they know through Jesus Christ.

A variation on this confessional theme makes use of amatory analogies to argue its case. As a lover swears allegiance to the beloved, so the believer uses a similar rhetoric of absolutes: "You are the most wonderful person in the world." This is understood, of course, in a "poetic" rather than a literal sense. The profession of commitment in religion is a testimony of personal meaningfulness rather than a statement of metaphysical fact.[34] In a larger sense, it is a "blik," the value orientation of the confessor.

Another manifestation of this type is an ethnic view of the relation of Christian faith to other options. Here it is assumed that Christianity as it has been received by us today is so shaped by the host culture that it cannot make transcultural claims. At the present time ethnic theologies have chosen to rework this enculturated tradition selectively, owning their Christian inheritance in terms of a truth that transcends earlier captive formulations. For example, Exodus provides an important paradigm for liberation theologies. However, there are signs of another more radical movement of parallel pluralism. Choen-Seng Song argues for a paradigm within Asian experience equivalent to the Exodus event in the received tradition.[35] Here is a form of ethnic pluralism in which the biblical paradigm is itself relativized in the quest for ethnic particularity.

In each of these expressions of parallel pluralism, all three of the constitutive factors of Christian faith are extended beyond the bounds of their own history. Reconciliation as the objective source of salvation is found in a basic determinant below the surface of particular allegiances, in core experiences, visions, or commitments. Revelation, as truth worth knowing, is not confined to Christian faith but is available in different guises. And redemption as the effective presence of the salvific—from temporal peace to eternal rest—is not limited to Christianity but accessible in religions of equivalent power.

Christian interpreters of pluralism in religiously heterogenous

Other traditions live out of this power of new being in accordance with the names by which they encounter and participate in ultimate reality" (Dawe, "Christian Faith in a Religiously Plural World," in Donald G. Dawe and John B. Carman, *Christian Faith in a Religiously Plural World* [Maryknoll, N.Y.: Orbis Books, 1978], 31). See the astute comments on this position made by the Jewish theologian Eugene Borowitz, ibid., 59-68.

34. On theological love language see Krister Stendahl, "Notes for Three Biblical Studies," in Gerald H. Anderson and Thomas F. Stransky, eds. *Christ's Lordship and Religious Pluralism* (Maryknoll, N.Y.: Orbis Books, 1981), 13-15.

35. Choen-Seng Song, *Third-Eye Theology*.

societies find this kind of parallelism attractive. Its charity provides the framework for civil relationships among diverse populations. As nations and cultures grow more interconnected, and as the peril to all is increased by the destructive capacities of each, the irenicism of "you do your thing and I'll do mine" becomes increasingly popular.

Synthetic Pluralism

If the previous type declares, "*To* each his own," this one announces, "*From* each his own." Synthetic pluralism sees the differences in religion not as mutually legitimate articulations whose variety is their genius, but rather as fragments of a potential unity. An identifying mark of synthetic pluralism is the assertion that religions are in fact different and not variations on a common theme, nor of equal legitimacy. Individual religions or communities of religion have distinctive features. (E.g., the contrast between the historical religions of the Near East and the ahistorical religions of the Far East.) These distinctions carry with them both strengths and weaknesses. Therefore it is to the benefit of all to share their strengths and thereby reduce or eliminate their weaknesses.

Sociological factors contribute to the difference between types one and two. The first model makes its home easily in culturally static situations, or in a majority Christian ethos. The latter option is influenced by a conservative impulse to retain the Christian commitment for oneself, but in a pluralistic situation to declare for the theological parity of other claims. The first type is more apt to arise as an a priori notion consequent upon initial plural shock. The second type is often the result of an a posteriori knowledge of the details of other religious options. Data are at hand to provide warrants for the synthetic proposal and enthusiasm for it develops out of a socially dynamic situation in which religious mobility is either actual or potential. Further, a minority Christian ethos is a more hospitable setting for the appearance and progress of this type.

In its most ambitious form, this view would merge Christian faith with other religions in a new world faith. More accurately, it would take those features of Christianity conceived to be its best contribution and fuse them with the superior contributions of other religions. Baha'i is a tribute to the zeal for a synthetic pluralism that seeks to transcend all particularities. In more modest expressions within the Christian tradition the model occurs as a hope to be achieved by interreligious dialogue, one that puts itself on the path to unity while acknowledging that the present stage requires of the participants a location short of that vision. John Hick's efforts to "deparochialize" Christianity in the search for a "global theology" is an example of this type.[36] In yet another form, that of a bilateral syncretism, Christian motifs are incorporated into a larger view made possible by a subsequent revelation, as in Mormonism or Unificationism.

In synthetic pluralism we have an interesting configuration of the three traditional Christian claims. Insofar as each high religion has something to contribute to the ultimate synthesis, all are participants in the root action of what we have called reconciliation. As in type one, no individual religion can lay claim to that matrix. But, in contrast, only as the pieces fit together at the goal point of unity is the salvific event consummated. Thus reconciliation is yet to be, although it is present in foretaste as the incompleteness of each religion bespeaks the larger unity for which it was made.

Revelation is forthrightly partial in this view. Only as the wisdom of each is joined together can true insight be gained.

Redemption is both present and absent. Redemption in the sense of vertical salvation, the self's standing before God, is possible in all high religions. But redemption in terms of historical healing—personal, social, ecological, political, etc.—is restricted in the present state of our divisions. In our fragmented condition we cannot reap the benefits of other religious traditions, although by random efforts and intellectual or spiritual synthesis we can anticipate that ultimate unity.

Degree Pluralism

As in model two this next view declares that Jesus is different. But in contrast to it there is no denial of the definitiveness of Christ, no need to supplement Christian truth from another source. Christ is distinctively different and exhaustively so. He is the full expression of reconciliation, revelation, and redemption.

This decisiveness does not, however, exclude others from access to what ultimately matters. Christ is different indeed, but different

36. For various sorties see John Hick, *The Center of Christianity* (New York: Harper & Row, 1968); idem., *God and the Universe of Faiths*, rev. ed. (Glasgow: Collins, 1977); idem., ed., *The Myth of God Incarnate* (Philadelphia: Westminster Press, 1977); idem., *Death and Eternal Life* (New York: Harper & Row, 1976). A variation of the theme of global theology is set forth by Wilfred Cantwell Smith in *Toward a World Theology* (Philadelphia: Westminster Press, 1981); John Hick and Brian Hebblethwaite, eds., *Christianity and Other Religions* (Philadelphia, Fortress Press, 1980).

in *degree.* Christ and the faith we have in him is the supreme expression of what is available everywhere. He is the highest manifestation of the divine work that ranges far beyond any one embodiment, a Mt. Everest in a chain of lower peaks. Yet in this place, especially in the character and teaching of the historical figure of Jesus, we have a clear view of the ultimate truth and a powerful incentive to ascend the spiritual heights.

Translating this model into our three categories, we can say that: (1) All share in the divine revelation. That is, all high religions, holy movements, and good human beings discern some of the truth, usually understood as the love of neighbor and the love of God. Yet Christ gives us the clearest window into that ultimate truth. (2) All have access, in principle, to redemption. God does not exclude any human beings from the divine gifts, however conceived. (And one can think of them either in terms of the fit and good life in this world or an unending life in the world to come, life for and with humans or before and with God, or both.) In Christ and the religion that rises from him, there is the greatest resource for obtaining life abundant and/or unending. (3) Reconciliation, as in the two previous options, is not associated with the particulars of the given religion. The "way" the benefits of religion are effected is anterior to any historical event or persons. The sources of salvation are the divine presence and process themselves. On the current theological scene it is "process theology" that gives one of the clearest articulations of this model. The Christology developed by Norman Pittenger in his well-known work, *The Word Incarnate,* is representative of degree pluralism in process form.[37]

Centripetal Singularity

We cross an important line in the move to this fourth type, as suggested by the rubric "singularity." Jesus Christ—who he was

37. W. Norman Pittenger, *The Word Incarnate* (New York: Harper & Brothers, 1959). Process theologian John Cobb's response to pluralism is a unique blend of models two and three. He attempts to hold together a deep personal "faithfulness to Christ" with total openness to the correction of historic Christian teaching by other religions. For his hopes for the "Buddhization of Christianity" see his papers "Can a Christian Be a Buddhist Too?" and "Can a Buddhist Be a Christian Too?" at the 1979 Claremont Conference on "Heidegger, Mahayana Buddhism and Whitehead: Perspectives on Interfaith Dialogue." The latter is published in *Japanese Religions,* 11 (Sept. 1980): 35-55. Suggestive formulations are found in his 1981 Harvard address, "The Meaning of Pluralism for Christian Self-Understanding," and his earlier thought appears in *Christ in a Pluralistic Age* (Philadelphia: Westminster Press, 1975).

and what he did in our history—is not only different and distinctive, but also determinative. Through this figure and the events that surround him God makes possible whatever benefits are to be had by the world. He is the singular Way God works to bring salvation.

Yet we are not to understand this determinative singularity in the sense of traditional Christianity ("no salvation outside the church," or "no salvation outside the faith"). While God acts in a unique way to accomplish the divine purpose, the benefits of that singularity are everywhere available. Thus we have here an effort to maintain both the particularity and the universality of the Christian claim.

This view makes its home currently in segments of the Roman Catholic community, and is traceable to the thought of Karl Rahner. Our description of this model as "centripetal" is based on some of the specifics of Rahner's thought and also on the Catholic ethos out of which the position rises.

Jesus Christ "manifests" and renders "irreversible" the saving purposes of God.[38] Christian decisiveness is related, in the first instance, to the disclosure of the divine grace at one point in time in an unequaled manner. Here is found the fullness of "categorical" revelation, the purest form of the self-interpretation of a universal "transcendental" revelation. This kind of finality is kindred to that of degree pluralism, a distinctiveness of disclosure by virtue of its completeness, one prepared to acknowledge the partial and incomplete disclosures available in other religions, movements, or people of good conscience.

The theme of irreversibility, however, is Rahner's unique contribution to the issue at hand and a key to the type itself. In Jesus Christ, the "absolute Savior," God is so present in the unity of deity and perfected humanity that the goal of universal grace is assured. Drawing on such traditional formulas as *"intuitu meritorum Christi,"* the Aristotelian notion of final cause, the Teilhardian motif of the Omega Point, and the theme of "searching memory," Rahner sketches a picture of Christ drawing all the compass points of grace

38. The Christological cum pluralist themes run in one form or another through much of Karl Rahner's writings. Key passages on particularity and universality include: Karl Rahner, *Theological Investigations,* vol. 5, trans. Karl H. Kruger (Baltimore: Helicon Press, 1966), 97-134; idem., *Theological Investigations,* vol. 17, trans. Margaret Kohl (New York: Crossroads, 1981), 24-50; idem., *Foundations of Christian Faith: An Introduction to the Idea of Christianity,* trans. William V. Dych (New York: Seabury Press, 1978), 138-321.

to himself. Thus the redemption and revelation available universally is made possible by the absolute mystery radiating its power through the absolute Savior. The latent possibilities in human beings are rendered salvific by Christ, even retroactively (thus resolving the question of the availability of salvation before the appearance of Christ, a nagging problem for Rahner). What is good in all religions, movements, and persons so graced is drawn intrinsically toward fulfillment in the Christian religion by the agency of Jesus Christ.

The image called up by this line of thought (especially as we compare it with the next type growing out of the Protestant ethos as represented by Karl Barth) is that of a Catholic Mass with the worshipers proceeding to the altar, drawn by Christ the Host. Thus the soft metaphor of centripetal action best expresses this model of Christ at the determinative center of history drawing the world to himself. We should understand Rahner's widely discussed idea of anonymous Christianity in this context. The transcendental thirst for absolute mystery is "elevated" by a universal grace. As such it makes available "unthematically" the benefits of grace through the incognito Christ and thus is fruitful of faith, hope, and love. All who respond aright to this omnipresent Christic grace before or outside of the knowledge of the historical event, Jesus Christ, are to be recognized as anonymous Christians.

In this sophisticated Christology sensitive to the questions raised by plural shock, we have a reconception of reconciliation, revelation, and redemption in the following way: Reconciliation is the bringing together of God and the world by a historical action in the life, death, and resurrection of Jesus Christ. By the powers emanating from this determinative event the universal potential for *revelation* and *redemption* is made operative. As such, *redemption* can be found in principle throughout all humanity (always through some social expression, indeed, for the historically conscious Rahner), based on the more or less inchoate revelatory disclosure. However, the highest expression of revelation comes in the event of Jesus Christ as conveyed to us in the thematized interpretations of the church. And the redemption available in the church by virtue of the certainty of this revelation and the Christological centrality of God's action is richer in potential reality, but does not exclude life and truth found elsewhere.

These themes have been elaborated in various ways by such Roman Catholic interpreters as Merton and Panikkar, engaged as they have been in interreligious search or dialogue, and are put forth in more radical fashion by Paul Knitter, who fuses elements of model one with this Rahnerian option.[39]

Centrifugal Singularity

If Karl Rahner has shaped the centripetal model, Karl Barth has formed the centrifugal one. The former reflects Roman Catholic sensibilities and the latter shows evidences of its Protestant setting. As the picture of Christ at the altar drawing the worshiper forward suggests the centripetal view, so the image of the preacher declaring the Word from the pulpit to the hearers fits the centrifugal model.

In contrast to the first three views and in company with the fourth, centrifugal singularity asserts the determinative nature of God's act in Jesus Christ. What happened here in him has transformed the world. In his life, death, and resurrection the powers of evil and death have been defeated, sin and guilt have been conquered, and a new age has been born.[40]

The definitive and determinative deed in Jesus Christ has its consequences for all the world, as in the previous model. But there is a significant difference in how this is conceived and the effects it is seen to have. The centrifugal model views the relationship of Christ to the world as an explosive entry into a land with an assault upon its occupying forces. Whatever happens to alter enemy terrain must take place through this one invasion beachhead. Indeed, to continue this appropriate military figure, the capital is thereby taken and the land is saved from its usurpers.

Two theological points underlie these militant metaphors. On the one hand, the total captivity of the world is assumed, and on the other its liberation can come about only by action from beyond, through a single point of entry made by that Liberator. Initiation and action are extrinsic to the inhospitable terrain, driving outward

39. Raimundo Panikkar, *The Trinity and the Religious Experience of Man* (Maryknoll, N.Y.: Orbis Books, 1973); idem., *The Intrareligious Dialogue* (New York: Paulist Press, 1978); Thomas Merton, *The Asian Journal,* ed. N. Burton, P. Hart, and L. Laughlin (New York: New Directions, 1973); idem., *Zen and the Flying Birds of Appetity* (New York: New Directions, 1978); Paul Knitter, "Jesus-Budda-Krishna: Still Present?" *Journal of Ecumenical Studies* 16 (Fall 1979): 650-71; idem., "Christianity as Religion: True and Absolute? A Roman Catholic Perspective," *Concilium* 136 (1980): 12-21.

40. Barth, *CD* IV/1, 2, 3. On the subject of redemption/life see the probing work of Waldron Scott, *Karl Barth's Theology of Mission* (Downers Grove, Ill.: InterVarsity Press, 1978).

from the entry point to shatter and transform this fallen world. This is different from the centripetality of the fourth model, which also works from the same Christological center point but differs in two ways. (1) It assumes a more hospitable territory with at least underground forces ready to link up with the liberating armies. Or in a more appropriate and less military figure, a welcome home is given to a long absent lover. A searching readiness ("transcendentality") is already there for the One who is to come, and who is as such, in intrinsic relationship to his home (in contrast to rebellion and resistance). (2) The fourth model draws on and out this latency, giving it luster, direction, and finally fulfillment in Christ who beckons all into his embrace. This idea is different from the view that the sole resources of the Other move extrinsically to overcome an implacable foe.

Whatever the difference in direction and interaction between models four and five, the centrifugal view has, in its own way, as unconventional a concept of the relation of the Christian faith to other religions as its partner in singularity. Because of a similar stress upon the universal consequences of God's reconciling act in Christ, the relationship of all human beings to God is altered by the particular event; as all are in Christ, they die with him and rise with him, and thus enjoy a new status. What this means for the question of personal salvation of those outside the historical Christ, universalism, etc., we shall now examine under our three motifs.

In the centrifugal mode, *reconciliation* between the world and God is won through the singular action of God in Christ. Given the hostility of the world to the divine purposes, centrifugality refers also to revelation. There are no lines leading from the world to Christ; all the light comes from this center point. Barth's long struggle against "natural theology" lies behind this insistence on the Word enfleshed as the sole disclosure point for ultimate truth. Yet on the third theme, as we have interpreted it, particularity opens out into a striking universality. That is, because the consequences of God's unique act in Christ are so radical, every human being becomes a "virtual brother in Christ." Those called into the church are charged with the "vocation" of telling others that they enjoy this new status and what it entails.

Does this mean that all are saved, as in conventional universalism? Barth himself says "No." His commitment to the freedom of God is such that he will not prescribe for the sovereign majestic One what the individual destinies of human beings shall be. But

Barth believes we have a right to hope for universal restoration.[41] Whatever we conclude about Barth on that point, it is clear that personal redemption is not tied to our response of faith to the proclamation of the church; mission is the mandate of vocation for the believer, not the bearer of salvation to the unbeliever.

Developed out of the fifth type, especially as it stresses the theme of divine majesty and mystery, is a version of centrifugal singularity that maintains an intentional silence about the consistency of ultimate redemption and rejection, especially as it touches those who have not heard the Word nor had the opportunity for a responsible act of faith.[42] In this view there may even be a properly self-critical assurance of salvation for the Christian believer, but an eschatological agnosticism about the nonknowers of Jesus Christ. It is the business of the believer to thank God for what is known and given, and to share it with others in determined evangelization. What we know then is the offer of salvation, and not only the imperative of vocation. But one must at the same time observe a proper modesty about God's ultimate plans for those who have not heard.

Imperial Singularity

Our sixth type is a familiar traditionalist view. The race is fallen. While we may see traces of the divine purpose in a darkened world, not enough is knowable by our natural light to see aright, nor is our enslaved will capable of choosing aright, hence the alienation of the world from its Maker. God acted in Jesus Christ to open the eyes of the blind and to reconcile the alienated. In him is the one Way chosen to remove the barrier to divine fellowship. Only in response to him is found the one true and eternal life (however conceived—through faith alone, through faith and love, through sacraments of the church). To tell of this way, to share this light, and to invite to this life constitute the mission of the church. Not to see the light or have life is to be consigned to eternal darkness and death. The zeal for this model is rooted in the conviction that the messengers of reconciliation are therefore bearers of revelation and redemption.

41. Barth, *CD* IV/3, 477-78.

42. For a profound wrestling with these questions from a perspective that brings together themes from Karl Barth with a ministry in Indian and ecumenical contexts see the writings of Lesslie Newbigin, especially the typology and constructive alternatives in "The Gospel among the Religions," in *The Open Secret* (Grand Rapids: Eerdmans, 1978), 181-214.

Qualifications are made occasionally around the edges of this main set of convictions. Some declare that Israel before Christ is given opportunity for eternal life without knowing Christ, either proleptically drawing on the benefits of his work, or eschatologically confronted by him. Some in traditions that stress divine election declare for God's right to choose any outside the biblical covenants (Socrates, Gandhi) and/or the certainty that all unable to make their own decision (viz., infant death) are automatically saved by Christ's benefits. Others allow for the possibility of special revelation to those outside Christ on the grounds of the freedom of God. Others speak marginally about the uncovenanted mercies of God at work in the responses to the small light given in the conscience. But we cannot finally integrate these latter views into the structure of this model because of its assumption that a will in bondage cannot induce a faithful response to whatever light is shown. (If it did, it would be salvation by works.)

With our text as principle of organization we have listened to the roundtable discussion going on in the church about the question of the particular and universal. What can we learn from these various positions that might contribute to a catholic hermeneutics?

Contextualization and Contemporary Theology

In responding to these points of view in the community conversation on particularity and universality we return to the contemporary problematic and our perspective on it: the narrative of suffering and hope, liberation and reconciliation, vision and reality. On the face of it, the "religious question" posed by pluralism seems very different from the "secular question" associated with these particular themes and images. The upwelling of religious issues in the seventies appears to put in question the secularization theories of the sixties.[43] Indeed, the two kinds of contextual analysis have lived in awkward relationship ever since.

We discussed earlier a sociological link in the growing pluralism and sense of multiple life options that places religious profession increasingly in the private sphere, lowers its visibility, and reduces its claims. We note here an important theological connection. The *nature* of the religious question is influenced by the secularization process. Suffering and its correlate hope come to the fore in cultures

43. E.g., Andrew M. Greeley, *Unsecular Man* (New York: Schocken Books, 1972).

of historical peril or promise, and thus the questions of guilt, ignorance, and individual mortality recede. To the extent that it is given attention or credence by the culture, religion is cast in the role of giving hope in time of misery. Well, what else would religion be for? The answer is that it has been "for" other things at other times and in other places. And in its own intrinsic reality, the gospel is for other things as well: the forgiveness of sin before the judgment of God, everlasting life with God in the world to come, knowledge rather than error in our understanding of God. And most fundamentally God is not "for" the sake of any human project, however worthy, but is to be loved and served for God's own sake.[44] The functional view of faith and its rationale as a help to the human prospect are so deeply ingrained in our psyches that it is difficult to think of it as otherwise.

A history of modern theology could be written in terms of the outworking of the suffering-hope question. Such a reading would illuminate the particularity/universality issue under discussion.

A variety of modern theologies in their standard interpretations—liberation, hope, secular, process—are united in their focus on issues of immanence and their address to the making of human life more livable. They represent different theories of the nature of human suffering and the way to hope, and the function of religious belief in that venture forward. They also all tend to be activist theologies, holding that change for the better is possible, that our efforts can make a difference, that God supports and gives this momentum toward the reign of God, rule of God, kingdom of God. Late-twentieth-century theologies of this kind have their antecedents in the Enlightenment theologies that gave precedence to the doing and thinking tasks that enrich the human enterprise.

Another stream of theology can also be interpreted as addressing the human plight and promise. In contrast to the former one that believes historical change possible, this cluster of viewpoints and their allied pieties does not hold out such hope for external improvement, but interprets faith as a way of coping with human suffering. The neomystical, New Age, therapeutic, self-help, self-esteem versions of Christian belief that have appeared in the seventies and eighties are popular expressions of religion cum suffering/hope. Understandable also is the appeal of the religions of the Far East, especially Hinduism and Buddhism and their permuta-

44. Fackre, *Humiliation and Celebration* (New York: Sheed and Ward, 1969), 140-49.

tions, found both in the wider culture and in Christian adaptations, as these are religions for which suffering is *the* problematic. So too the recovery of prayer, "spirituality," and piety is not unrelated to the search for methods of coping with the heightened fact and perception of human suffering. The modern versions of receptivity/adaptivity religion also have their predecessors in nineteenth-century Romantic forebears and its experientialist and spiritualist streams. In this tradition, past and present, suffering is met and hope is given to the extent that the self can find ways of living with and triumphing over the cares of the world and the ills of the flesh. Thus its proponents seek to "accept the things that cannot be changed" (that acceptance entails, of course, self-change while history "out there" is left largely as it is), rather than believing as the first option does that they must "change the things that can be changed."[45]

The common assumption of these two streams of theology is that God is a "very present help in time of trouble," whether that help be in changing circumstances or in self-help. However, suffering may seem to be so intractable that the conviction about the helping deity begins to weaken. So enters theodicy, the "problem of evil." In making its entrance in cultures at this critical point, theodicies tend to loosen the grip of a simple functionalism, open suffering outward to the other perennial questions of death, guilt, and ignorance, and upward toward transcendent issues in their own right. Who *is* this God who appears not to be a sure helper in time of affliction? Who is God in God's own right? The giver of the affliction? One too weak to come to our aid? The ultimate if not the penultimate righter of wrongs? Is suffering because of our sin? Is suffering real or only due to our ignorance? So comes the struggle with suffering at the transcendent as well as immanent level, awareness of which is given in the universal intimation of the presence of One with whom we have to do. So too appear the standard solutions to the problem of evil that focus on one or another element in the theodicy equation: the love of God is removed with an insistence on the power of God as the cause of the reality of evil; the power of God is canceled and replaced by a loving but limited

45. The phrase is from Reinhold Niebuhr's well-known prayer, "Oh, God, give us serenity to accept what cannot be changed, courage to change what should be changed, and wisdom to distinguish the one from the other," in June Bingham, *Courage to Change: An Introduction to the Life and Thought of Reinhold Niebuhr* (New York: Scribner's, 1961), title page.

deity who contests the reality of evil; the reality of evil is eliminated with the retention of an all-loving and all-powerful God. Treatments of theodicy in our time tend to be those that have an anthropocentric turn, showing how the answer supports human need or reconceives transcendence in a humanizing way. Thus the concept of the God who is limited as we are, who understands what we suffer occurs regularly in popular and scholarly discussion.

Those who experience suffering most deeply are less prone to conceive of God as a simple help or settle for a humanized theodicy. Against the background of the Holocaust, Jewish theodicy often evidences the most profound wrestling with the problem. Elie Weisel will not fit deity into a manageable schema, recovering instead elements of an ancient tradition that in the face of massive suffering accuse and argue with God. Emil Fachkenheim does the same, questioning the goodness of God. Abraham Heschel refuses to soften the fact of suffering, instead pressing it into the very being of God. Richard Rubenstein concludes from the outrages of unjust suffering to the death of God. Most forms of Jewish theodicy continue a determined resistance to suffering in spite of the theological puzzles, shaped as it is by the prophetic consciousness.

Similar wrestling with the theological dimension of suffering and its more sober assessment of God's relationship to it has gone on in Christian theology when the depths of travail have been experienced. As noted earlier, "Suffering God" theologies found their voice during and after the First World War, a time in which technology was applied to the means of destruction on a scale hitherto unknown in the world's history. In German and British theology a strong theopaschite note was sounded. Suffering means the passability, the passion and agony of God. In Japanese Christian theology after the Second World War, against the backdrop of Hiroshima and Nagasaki, a theology of the pain of God appeared. As the suffering of that war, including the Holocaust event within it, took hold on the Christian mind, especially among those burdened with their own country's role in inflicting massive pain, the theology of the suffering God took form. Georgia Harkness's early sensitivity to "the agony of God" was followed by Jürgen Moltmann's searching thought on "the crucified God," taking hold in an era of the frustration of raised expectations, dashed seventies' hopes for the sixties' visions for a more human world. With an eye for the forces of negativity in both history and nature, Paul Schilling has brought together the threads of Christian thought about divine and human suffering, although casting them essentially in the tradition of a limited deity. The sharp reaction to suffering and God's relation to it found in Rubenstein is echoed in the Protestant death of God theologies of the 1960s, influenced as much by theodicy as by the secularization theories associated with it. The prophetic determination of most Jewish theodicy to keep on fighting suffering in spite of the toll it takes and the theological questions it raises is paralleled in Christian theodicy by those forms of political and liberation theology that speak of the solidarity of God with the poor working in and with them toward hope.

The enigma of massive historical suffering occasioned by the abuse of modern technology in a world made and ruled by God pushes many in this culture to the breaking point of faith. Atheism has always been a response to suffering, as in the early formulation of the problem of evil itself. Twentieth-century horrors have increased its attractiveness as a worldview. Its power can be seen in literary and philosophical existentialism—Sartre, Camus, Heidegger—and their counterparts in the growth of religious doubt and withdrawal from the church in European countries ravaged by war and among workers experiencing industrial dehumanization. The intellectual secularization process in the modern world is advanced as much by the theological questions posed by technological devastation as by the creative powers technology puts into the hands of humanity that thereby take away the need for a "god of the gaps."

A very different response to twentieth-century war, hunger, poverty, oppression, social disorganization, and economic collapse in a world *coram Deo* took place in the rise of so-called neoorthodoxy. While significant differences exist among those described by this term, the major figures in the movement do share basic responses to the theodicy question. The theologies of Barth, Brunner, and Reinhold Niebuhr all took form in conscious relationship to the twentieth-century social maelstroms—war, economic injustices, and the rise of totalitarianism. All found in the "strange new world of the Bible," or its beliefs, an orientation point for interpreting the meaning of God in the confusions and destructions of the modern world. (Barth's counsel to hold the Bible in one hand and the daily newspaper in the other represents this neoorthodox dialectic.) And all, to one degree or another, pointed to the imperial will that lay behind the century's debacles, the state of human rebellion against the divine purpose. Thus the problem of *suffering* could not be faced without at the same time confronting the problem of *sin.* This confrontation is not to be in the manner of Job's false counselors with their direct correlation of personal sin with personal suffering. Rather, the sin in every human heart woven into the collectivities and empowered by the technologies of the modern world inflicted on the weak of that world is the travail of these times. Blaming God, rejecting the reality of God, using God as a justification for causing evil, accommodating to the reality of evil, fleeing from engagement with evil to a private god—all these moves are manifestations of the sin that occasions the suffering of others. The gospel calls us to face the bad news of our own sin as well as the bad news of human suffering, and then we shall understand that there is Good News of the forgiveness of sin as well as Good News about the overcoming of misery.

Neoorthodoxies of this sort never lost their prophetic concern with the hurt and the helpless, for their interpretation of misery came out of their own involvement in the struggles for justice and peace, and always included the twin problematic of human suffering and human sin. We can see this duality in the ecumenical theologies of the forties and fifties, especially in the circles of the World Council of Churches. At work in them were the applicability of the doctrine of sin to social issues, under the influence of Niebuhrian thought and the *Christus Victor* themes of Karl Barth, Gustav Aulén, and others. We turn briefly to the latter and speculate on the connections that may exist between an emphasis on the victorious rule of Christ over the powers and principalities and the question of epochal suffering.

The *Christus Victor* theme claims the "secular" arena for Christ, and changes our perception of the forces that appear to be ruling there. It construes them as vanquished foes rather than as ultimate threats, and thus empowers resistance to them and a life of serenity in the face of defeats experienced. In its social and systemic reading of the forces at work in the world, it warrants social and systemic action by the church and fresh thinking about the ministry of institutions.

As both human possibility and threat increased in the twentieth century, the neoorthodoxies that had originally stressed the sin/forgiveness Word of Christ the Priest increasingly accented the evil/victory notes of "Christ the King." The triumph of grace in Karl Barth became more and more the divine power over evil than the divine mercy for the sinner, the regency of Christ over the powers and principalities that "for a time" run riot in this world. Visser 't Hooft's restatement of the kingship of Christ, with influences from Barth and Calvin, opened a way into the World Council of Churches' postwar discussions of "Man's Disorder and God's Design" and "Christ the Hope of the World." It was a short step from that to Moltmann's "theology of hope" with its stress upon the theology of resurrection, and even the subsequent emphasis on Christ the liberator, especially in the writings of James Cone, who shows the influence of both Barth and Gustav Aulén. The Lundensian theology earlier read Luther in the light of *Christus Victor* themes and did so against totalitarian forces in a way similar to Barth's employment of the Reformed emphasis on divine sovereignty. These same motifs are formative in this present work, and have been so in thought over the years leading to it.

As *hope* moved to the foreground in response to the growing fact and awareness of suffering, *faith* withdrew more and more to the background, and with it the awareness of sin. Or faith was reconceived as warrant for hope with its biblical precedent, the "assurance of things hoped for" (Heb. 11:1). The suffering of God that was spoken of in conjunction with the victory of God had less and less to do with the suffering of God on the cross *for* the sins of the world and more and more as the solidarity of God *with* the sufferers of the world. Christian teaching around these profound accents on the suffering of God and the liberation wrought by God in Christ came more and more to be associated with the human struggle against suffering. The God of crucifixion and resurrection who is to be confronted in God's own right and for God's own sake—accountable *coram Deo,* sinful *coram Deo,* forgiven *coram Deo*—not as an instrument to our own ends, even the worthiest of them, becomes the helper of humans in their need.

Several very different reactions to this anthropocentric turn are worth noting. One of them is the response of Dietrich Bonhoeffer. He knew firsthand the facts of political suffering and the struggle against the powers and principalities, was deeply influenced by Barth, and can be seen as a barometer of the *Christus Victor* theme and its effects. Was he more Barthian than Barth in his exposition of the secular meaning of the gospel? His attack on the "god of the gaps," his refusal to use even a "helpful" doctrine such as *Christus Victor* as a word hurled at the foe or even a support to the sufferer (no "positivism of revelation" can be understood to mean that this kind of bold proclamation is theologically inappropriate as well as incapable of being heard by a secular world) had to do with the rejection of any functional construal of doctrine. God is to be loved for God's own sake. That means a hidden life with God in the *disciplina arcani* in which all Christian belief, even the most orthodox, is held to be true, not because it makes us better for the struggle, but simply because it *is* true. God is to be loved in this way of trust and obedience, let the consequences be what they may—joy and peace or sorrow and strife. Because this God with whom we have to do in our age suffers for our sin and in our pain, our portion is to be where God is and where God goes, and thus "to participate in the sufferings of God in the world." We are called to be in solidarity with sinners and sufferers, and speak and act the way God does in that terrain, in our incognito as God is in the divine incognito. With the sinner and the sufferer we are secular as God is secular, giving not the arcane Word but the human word.

The rise of evangelicalism in the last half of the present century in the West and around the world can be read as a reaction to the anthropocentric tendencies in modern theology and piety. Evangelicalism as the personal intensification of the formal and material principles of the Reformation—the authority of Scripture and justification by faith—appears to be a faith that seeks to know and love God for God's own sake, professing loyalty to the Word regardless of human consequences, and confronting squarely the fact of sin in each self, as exposed by the light and fire of divine holiness and received in the grateful obedience of the forgiven sinner. In those sectors of the movement that are sensitive to the plight of human suffering as well as sin, and lift up the Good News of salvation from evil as well as guilt, the possibilities of faithfulness to the significance and meaning of Scripture, its contextualization and textualization, are strong. However, large sections of the evangelical movement carry the strong accent on personal appropriation to the point of recommending peace with God because it brings "peace of mind," or proposing a right relationship with God because it produces results in "successful living," including the crassest sort of commercial benefits as well as personally therapeutic dividends. On the other hand, activist evangelicalism, discovering the social mandates, becomes more and more absorbed in the political agenda, and faith becomes fused with and judged by its contribution to causes on the political right or left.

Eucharistic theologies as well as evangelical ones, developing in the present anthropocentric context, also represent potential counterscenarios. Grateful worship to the God who has delivered the world from sin and communion with the One whose body and blood broken then and now for us is a context in which the love of God for God's own purposes rather than human ones readily thrives. Here too one cannot forget the problematic of sin and its response in the divine mercy as one remembers the sacrifice on Calvary and receives its reality in the elements shared. Transcendence is met on its own terms in this innermost sanctuary of the whole Christian worship. Yet here also one can separate the cross from the resurrection, and see the eucharist as a celebration of the divine bounties that fill our needs, spiritual and physical, and as an occasion for professing our commitment to one another and to the life of service and sacrifice. And in popular piety, worship in general as well as holy communion can be justified as the periodic "fill up" at the weekly spiritual pump so that we may live more abundantly in the world.

The loss of the sense of sin and forgiveness in wide sections of Christian theology and practice today, including its weakening in evangelical and eucharistic theologies that strive to honor the verticality of Christian faith, is a tragic accompaniment of an otherwise necessary response to the context in which we now live. That these theologies do take with utter seriousness the ministry of hope in and to human suffering is a right Word that must be heard and done. Our challenge here to the accommodation of faith to culture does not carry with it a scorn for the necessary addressing of it. The transformation model of contextualization needs the translation model. In our time of unprecedented suffering and the raised awareness of it the church must be more than ever in solidarity with the weak and speak passionately a gospel of hope. Christ is deeply present in the places of suffering, leaving there signs of hope and pressing ever toward the reign of hope, calling us to be with him there. The triune God wills the world to find its way through the wilderness and makes life along that path livable, gracefully sustaining justice and mercy, truth, peace, and joy. Further, the divine vulnerability is such in Christian faith that God is willing even to be *used* for human purposes that accord with the divine ends.[46]

The sensibility to human suffering, the construal of God as the bringer of the reign of justice and peace, the ever-present divine Help in self and society, the mandates to love the neighbor, the message of hope for today and tomorrow—these are the dominant notes in Christian preaching and teaching today. In one way or another—some crudely, some in sophisticated fashion—all stress salvation as *deliverance* from the ills of the flesh and the cares of the world. This is a *right* response to the context in which we live. Let this note be sounded in a way faithful to the scriptural witness,

46. Fackre, *Humiliation and Celebration*, 123-39.

to the prophet who pointed to shalom and called the oppressor to account, to the One who preached Good News to the poor and healed the sick, and to the apostle who cared for the widow and orphan and distributed to each according to their need. But when it is sounded as the *only* note on the biblical scale, when the fact of suffering *obscures* the fact of sin, when the call to hope *silences* the call to faith, and the Good News of redemption from evil and reconciliation *makes no room* for the Good News of the forgiveness of sin and reconciliation with God, then a serious distortion of the gospel has taken place.

Irony attends the reduction of the gospel to hope in suffering without faith in forgiveness. Because human issues are interrelated and the gospel is whole, the missing note of sin-forgiveness has its effect on the possibility of hope in the face of suffering. Astute observers of human behavior report that an awareness of sin in matters social and personal is not unrelated to hope and healing in just those places. A knowledge of the persistence of the self-serving impulse in political and social theory and practice makes society more livable as systems of checks and balances are introduced to set bounds to the imperial tendencies of our self-will, and change agents are freed of illusions that bring self-righteous fury or despair. Personal as well as social life is healthier to the extent that the self acknowledges its own will to power and has methods to deal with it or disciplines to restrain it. To ignore the reality of sin is to invite suffering, individual and collective.

That humanity can know its own problem is sin as well as suffering is due to the universal revelation that illumines even our fallen world. This is the light given to make our circuitous way through the wilderness. Yet the sin we know and the life discernible by this light do not reach the depth of the fallen human condition, which can be exposed only by the incarnational Light and renewed by the atoning Life. The invitation to this Light and Life has no appeal for the fructification of life in the world, indeed they seem to be only an added burden. To love and serve God for God's own sake and to suffer as Christ suffered? Who needs it when it is all we can do to cope without own suffering! Give us hope, not a cross! Yet there can be no Easter without a Good Friday in this faith.

THE SOCIAL SIGNIFICANCE OF JOHN 14:6

The significance of this text will carry its meaning into the context of pluralism and its implications in a world wrestling with the question of suffering and hope. The quest for significance goes on here by way of a narrative perspective that uses the motifs of liberation and reconciliation, the metaphors of vision and light, and is carried out in the mode of catholicity. We can describe the external hermeneutical journey so understood in the following way.

Our internal hermeneutical inquiry has sought to show that the way of the world is joined to the Way of Christ. As the last leg that gives access to God's house, the Way alters the wandering path of the world, assuring it of its destination. The link that brings the traveler home makes it possible to speak of even the earlier winding route as also Christ's path. The way belongs to the Way, the world belongs to Christ.

The world's way in our time is the way of suffering. Its technologically increased capacities for good or ill, and its technologically heightened awarenesses of good or ill, relentlessly confront us with it. As we know suffering, so too is this One "acquainted with grief" (Isa. 53:3). His Way is the path of the cross. In his full humanity "in every respect" (Heb. 2:17) he shared the pain and sorrow the world knows. And as deity inextricable from this humanity, Christ is the God of sorrows as well as "the man of sorrows," in solidarity with us then and now. The suffering of the world on the way is the suffering of the Son, the Way, the "crucified God." And the path of the cross is a *chosen* Way into the world, emptied of the prerogatives of eternity, assuming our vulnerability. "Taking the form of a servant, being born in the likeness of men. And being found in human form he humbled himself and became obedient unto death, even death on a cross" (Phil. 2:7-8).

The kind of suffering that is the Way of Christ is the pain that comes from the world's enmity. "He was despised and rejected by men" (Isa. 53:3). In the way of the cross he experiences the hate and hurt of the powers and principalities of this world. He felt the attack of the systems of power and privilege, political, religious, military, social. As the God-Man who lives now among us, Christ even yet keeps company with the despised, rejected, oppressed. He is present in and with the hungry, the thirsty, the naked, the sick, the prisoner (Matt. 25:35, 40). What they receive from their oppressors, Christ receives, and what they know, he knows.

The Way of Christ in the world then and now is not passivity. The Way gives light in the night and brings life out of death. The path of the cross leads to the empty tomb on resurrection morning. To make light and to give life is to bring hope. Jesus Christ is the hope of the world. What does this mean for people today who suffer and hope?

The eye of faith opened to see the Easter radiance looks at the world differently. Because the world belongs to Christ, it has always been sustained in its sorrow by a hope given to it through that hidden Presence. Wherever humans refuse to accept the suffering inflicted upon them as their fate, wherever the rejected do not accept rejection as their lot, wherever the oppressed "resist the powers of evil," there Christ is present. The glimmers of this light of hope have been given on the world's wandering path, sufficient to carry the travelers forward. Enough bread has been given for the journey, so that life may be sustained on the world's way. The light has been seen in the broken but not destroyed mirror of the divine Light, the "image of God" sustained in every human being. The truth of hope is seen in the rhythm of nature and the lessons of personal and social history for those with wisdom to perceive them. Hope comes with special power in the world's religions whose sensitivity to the Source and End of our pilgrimage, beyond the wisdom of the world, empower multitudes to make their way in hope through the world. This light of hope wherever found comes from Christ, "the true light that enlightens" everyone (John 1:9), one that the worst darkness of suffering "has not overcome" (John 1:5).

The life as well as the light, or the light that *is* life (John 1:4) is given along the world's way whenever hope mobilizes humans to liberate from bondage and reconcile the alienated. Where humans struggle against hunger, their own or others', where they contest bondage, their own or others', where they make for peace among themselves or for the world, the powers of life contest the powers of death. Where these things are so, there is Christ. He came "that they may have life, and have it abundantly" (John 10:10). Because he is the giver of life, there Christ is working in "all things . . . made through him" for "in him was life" (John 1:3-4). Wherever action toward hope happens, Christ is to be found. In our time, those whose hope strengthens them for secular struggles against human misery, and for life, receive it from the One who is Life. And where religious vision empowers for the causes of justice and peace, the God of hope is to be praised.

The Way of Christ is suffering, its truth is hope, its life is the acts of liberation and reconciliation in and toward hope. For the followers of the Way, the path is well marked. The Christian believer is called to take up the cross and follow the Way (Matt. 16:24). To deny the self and keep company with Christ is to "participate in the sufferings of God in the world" (Bonhoeffer). To suffer *in hope,* to take the cross toward the Easter horizon, is to struggle for signs of the life of justice and peace that are made possible by Christ the Light and Life present in the world. Not to so suffer and serve, but rather to pass by with no sight for the victim (Luke 10:29-37), is to be on the wrong road, to lose the Way.

Discerning the social significance of John 14:6 entails the situation of the text in the setting of our time and place. We begin the contextualization therefore by relating those aspects of the text's meaning arrived at by common, critical, and canonical interpretation to the themes of suffering and hope. Thus the features that have to do with the universal Christ present in the human experiences emerge and the question posed insistently by our epoch comes initially to the fore. Contextualization as translation requires equivalencies in the world of the text and the context. They are warranted by the revelatory universals that surfaced in the quest for textual meaning. These allowed us to honor truth and light to be found on the world's way and the claim of Christians to participate in them and to be open to the Christic grace in both secular circumstances and movements and other religious traditions. The three pluralism models earlier discussed and the universal themes in the two models of singularity witness to the importance of this aspect of contextualization.

For all the continuities between the source and the setting that make "translation" possible, there is a fundamental discontinuity that makes "transformation" necessary. The next step in contextualization therefore is to show how John 14:6 questions the adequacy of the culture's formulation of the question of suffering, and the legitimacy of its reasons for hope. Yet this challenge to the sufficiency of human experience's questions and answers is not a thunderbolt hurled from beyond. It is the reinforcement of a doubt that arises from within the world, itself communicated in a way the world understands. That is, the culture's unasked question of sin is, in principle, as accessible to universal human experience as is suffering. And the biblical Word of faith addressed to the problem of sin can be heard in a narrative translation that is connected with human experience. Thus, we make our way to the scandal of particularity in John 14:6 on the path of the scandal of universality.

Those who suffer and struggle for justice and peace must ultimately face the limits of their capacity to achieve their goals. Toughmindedness about the prospects for liberation and reconciliation in this world will know the ambiguity of the things accomplished and the shadows over the things hoped for. The most radical honesty—honesty about the self's own role in things achieved and hoped for—is able to grasp the self-will at work in the most righteous declamations and action. Those most determined to pursue the path forward discover that the way wanders. They know there must be another way.

When the biblical Word meets this searching and self-doubt, it shatters whatever illusions about self and society remain. The bad news that our finest dreams cannot be realized on our terms or our terrain is mercilessly driven home. So also is the worse news that we the righteous in our self-righteousness are the chief enemies of our own ends. But we can stand to hear the very worst just because it comes to us joined to *Good News.* There is a Way *beyond* our wilderness way. It is not part of the world's path, but a Path made to it. This Way completes our way, assuring us that our hope is not a vain hope. Yet its completion is on its own terms, by God's power not ours, and on its own terrain, the kingdom that comes in God's time not ours. And its gift is not only a shalom that fulfills all our hopes for liberation from social, economic, and political bondage and the reconciliation of neighbors and nature, but also a liberation from our sin against God and our guilt before God, and thus a reconciliation with God.

God makes this Way into the world in Jesus Christ. It happened at a specific time and place. Events took a new turn. That is what makes it news. It is new, unique, never known before, a "scoop" of the first magnitude. This news story must include background material to put it in perspective. One must know the full depth of the problem to appreciate its radical claim that it is the ultimate Good News to be had. Hence the narrative of creation, fall, and covenant that give us the storyline that leads to the turn of events in Christ, and the new tack taken by time itself toward salvation and consummation. So an era of drama, struggle, suffering, and hope hears a Word spoken in the language of drama it understands. Yet it is not an echo of the tale already known but an utterly new Word, a radically different Story that transforms the meaning of our familiar narrative categories. The Word takes our "storied world," speaks its language, but turns it upside down.

To return to the specific assertions and imagery of our text, a story with its decisive turning point from conflict to resolution must speak the language of "only" and "once-happenedness." No one gets to God's house except by following the turn in this road. "I am the Way . . . and no one comes to the Father but by me." Narrative translates the scandal of particularity. But it cannot remove the final offense, especially so in the time of a captivating pluralism. The pluralist theologies so eager to mute this dissonant note in the gospel are ample witness to the attraction of a pluralist ideology. But scandal it is. And that is why the gospel is set against culture in a transformative contextualization. As humans, we know something of truth and life because our way in the world is not alien to the Way. Christ suffers with the sufferers, supports the world's hopes of justice and peace. But we cannot know from our world the Good News of a suffering that takes away the sin of the world. Finally, the One who has "borne our griefs and carried our sorrows;" "was wounded for our transgressions [and] was bruised for our iniquities; upon him was the chastisement that made us whole, and with his stripes we are healed" (Isa. 53:4-5). And we would not know of the suffering of Christ in our worldly suffering or the ultimate Hope but for the Easter overcoming that grounds all our penultimate hopes. This is the truth that we cannot know and the life we cannot have without being on the Way, being joined to Christ by faith and so following the path to the house of God. Here is a way that forces us to examine ourselves in our sin, turn from the old way, take up the cross, and follow Christ to our intended habitation. But his narrow and "hard" way is finally the way to life with God, and those who find it know the paradox of faith, that the burdens of it are "easy and the yoke light" (Matt. 11:30).

A scandal, yes, but not one that is against the divine justice and love that is God. A just and loving offense is one that will not deny the ultimate choice of this narrow way to anyone. And thus again the dialectic of universality with particularity manifests itself. Christ will make known the final way for each who have not heard this Word in the world, and that in God's good time and good place. The eschatological proclamation in the "not only" passages provides the intertextuality needed for a right reading of the "only" claims of John 14:6. We come only through Christ to the Father. Yet this Christ is the ascended Lord of heaven and earth who speaks the Word of knowledge and calls in a fashion commensurate with those addressed, through the Word of the Body of Christ on earth and through the Word of the glorified Christ in realms beyond it. Nothing can separate us from this love of Christ, "neither . . . things present, nor things to come" (Rom. 8:38). For this suffering from separation from God and for the hope of reconciliation, as well as for the suffering of this world and for hope in this world, did the Savior suffer and rise again. In all the richness of its significance for our time and place in its translation and transformation is Jesus Christ the way and the truth and the life.

Two other models of contextualization contribute to determining the social significance of John 14:6. A traductive significance is associated with the scandalous particularity. We must be ready to acknowledge a factor from within universal human experience at work in the formulations of particularity. The divine vulnerability is able to carry this treasure for us in an "earthen vessel." Thus the minority status of the Christian community, its patriarchal habitat, and the interests of class and condition among its marginalized followers who were "nobodies" in their social situation could have given impetus to the assertions of particularity. This kind of critical consciousness has yet to produce the "sociology of knowledge" evidence its theory requires. But there is no reason to reject the insights of traductive contextualization. Docetism long ago was exposed as a false Christological option, and so must be its epistemological counterpart. But an Ebionite epistemology is as much in error as a Docetic one. The humanity of textual claims does not exclude the Word active in them. The Way of particularity comes to us in the finitude of the human way. Traduction can be the vehicle of transformation.

The contribution of a trajective contextualization appears in the raised awareness in our time of Christ's participation in the social and systemic character of human suffering and hope. Latent in the prophetic tradition and thus in the Christian paradigm of Christ the prophet, and in the New Testament teaching concerning the powers and principalities, they have become patent in the liberation and peace theologies of our time when the structures of oppression and war have shown their full face. We can no longer speak and act as if the light that enlightens humanity is only a personal hope and life is only the making whole of individuals. Trajection means that the Way of Christ is linked with the way of social suffering and his presence is in systemic movements that bring "good news to the poor . . . proclaim release to the captives . . . set at liberty those who are oppressed" (Luke 4:18). Thus the social significance of a New Testament textual strand for a given time and place so enlarges our understanding that it becomes a permanent part of the meaning of these texts, and of our overall understanding as well of the Person and Work of Christ.

The contribution of trajective contextualization appears as well in the reference to an eschatological evangel in our exegesis. A canonical reading of John 14:6 points toward a possible development in both the understanding of this text and larger questions of Christological doctrine. In this case the context of pluralism has forced us to look more intently at the implications of Christ's encounter with the dead as suggested by a thread of texts and by earlier ecclesial reflection on the "descent into hell." The question raised by modern world-awareness, the recognition of multitudes who have not been reached by the gospel and will not be so reached, presses the church to draw out more actively the implications of an eschatological overture and consider giving it a doctrinal status. There is no "mind of the church" on this, being one of a variety of options alongside the responses we have canvassed. To the extent to which this view holds together the necessary affirmations of both particularity and universality better than the alternatives, it becomes a candidate for inclusion in the development of doctrine.

Also significant for contextual trajection is the assertion of universal grace in other religions and people of "good will." In one form or another—general revelation, natural theology, common grace, *Logos* Christology, the uncovenanted mercies of God, anonymous Christianity, the incognito Christ, etc., and their soteriological import—this theme is further along the path of developing doctrine than the eschatological option. However, both the latitudinarianism that accompanies it in one set of advocates (redemption for all who respond to the inner light) and the delimitations associated with it in another (these things being considered a grace of creation and not redemption and with Christological import) are inadequate. The Christological and soteriological nature of this universal grace must be part of developing doctrine, with faith in the revealed Christ not thereby denied, and salvation from evil by grace through love keeping company with salvation by grace through faith from sin.

THE PERSONAL SIGNIFICANCE OF JOHN 14:6

"Personal contextualization" is not an idea that comes naturally to those engrossed in text-context questions. Theological attention to contextualization has emerged in our time and place as a result of the historical consciousness that, on the one hand, requires ancient documents and teachings to be understood in their setting, and on the other seeks their relevance in new settings. "The individual" does not come to the fore in these conceptions of reality then and now. However, another point of view in Christian theology and faith stands as a reminder of the personal dimension of reality. An ecumenical hermeneutics will be taught by it. It finds expression in individually oriented traditions that are pious, existential, or mystical—Protestant, Roman Catholic, or Orthodox. The narrative of interpretation of John 14:6 does not reach its destination until it elicits a deep personal "Yes" from the interpreter.

Finally, the social contextualizers also must acknowledge this personal aspect of hermeneutics. Without a commitment by the interpreter to the issues of historical setting the most astute contextualization of the biblical text remains an intellectual exercise, as removed from reality as those who ignore the situational process itself. To contextualize a text personally is to take what has become significant *for us* in our collective reality, and render it significant *for me* in my personal reality. In this respect the journey of truth as well as meaning goes forward: the meaning of a text that is true *for all* becomes the social significance of a text true *for us* that now becomes true *for me.* The hermeneutical *pro me* entails both a convincing of the truth of the text when not heretofore so convinced and the conviction of its personal applicability when heretofore intellectually convinced but not convicted.

To conform to the language of hermeneutical process we have spoken of the act of rendering the text personally significant, just as previously we sought to discover the common, critical, canonical, and socially contextual senses. But in the act of personal contexting the subject and predicate are reversed. In the personal appropriation of the text, when the moment of personal truth arrives, the Word convinces and convicts, the interpreter is interpreted, becomes a hearer not the doer, does not act but is acted upon. Our effort, so much to the fore in the "search" and "quest" for meaning and significance, cannot finally achieve its end on its own. The Author is the final authority. God gives you and me the message that we are to hear in the biblical text. Those who have reminded us of the dynamism of interpretation here make their witness: the Scripture is an event in which its words become the Word only by divine initiative. This actualist understanding of a text in both its Barthian and Bultmannian variations has a long history in traditions of Christian piety and mysticism. In the language of Calvin, the personal reception of the truth and significance of the text is by the "internal testimony of the Holy Spirit." By introducing the *grounds* for the authority of the text—the work of the Holy Spirit—we have moved from the concept of authority to the doctrine of revelation that underlies it. While concept and doctrine are inseparable, as we have discovered at each step in the discussion of authority, they are distinguishable. The historic teaching on "illumination" is that aspect of the doctrine of revelation which we here meet in the hermeneutics of textual significance in its personal sense.

If all is of God in the personal Word that convinces and convicts, then is there no human action here, only a waiting upon the divine initiative? Here we confront the classic paradox of faith: "I worked harder than any of them, though it was not I but the grace of God which is with me" (1 Cor. 15:10). There is no polarization between our efforts and God's, and no synergism, we doing some and God doing the rest. "God does all and we do all." In the coming of grace to us, as in incarnation, human weakness is God's medium through which the divine purpose is accomplished. We are given to know this in the personal coming to the truth of Scripture, in the moment that the gift is given, so that the testimony may be to illumination by the Spirit, not by our own lights. But in retrospect we can see from this point that the many labors to discover the common, critical, canonical, and socially contextual sense are also empowered by the Spirit. All is of grace and none is without its medium in our strivings and stumblings.

Because God chooses the weak things of the world (1 Cor. 1:27) to accomplish the divine ends, so too here in the coming of personal signification we have work to do. For me to hear God's Word in the text, I must position myself where Scripture teaches us to stand. All the elements that enter the quest for meaning and social significance once again appear: attention to the Word with all resources brought to bear on that task in its fourfold challenge, immersion in the church as it encounters its charter, engagement through the church with the world into which God calls us. But there is a special location in the church and the world before the Word as it speaks *pro me.* The personal aspect of each, and each together, is the life of personal prayer and the life of personal witness in the world.

The testimony of the church is that Scripture's significance comes always in the atmosphere of prayer. Our speaking to God is the climate in which God speaks to us. Our communication is our openness to the divine communication. The prayer in and through which we can hope for the personal Word is a life of regular adoration, thanksgiving, confession, petition, intercession, and commitment. It is also a specific prayer for this text to be opened to us: "Speak to us (in it) the Word we need and let that Word abound in us until it has wrought in us your holy will." Prayer is not magic. God is not at our beck and call. Prayer is our act of grateful obedience in which we place ourselves where we are called to be, and where we have a right to hope for response. So we have been taught by the experience of the Christian community and by the promise of Christ. How that response comes and what that Word will be is only God's to give.

As the church has learned that the personal Word comes in the climate of prayer, so it has also been taught that the Word is heard in the midst of our work in the world. Involvement in the issues of the hour, participation in the places where Christ is present in the world's journey forward is to be present where the Word may be spoken to us. Again we do not control this sovereign Word, which will be uttered when God chooses to convince and convict. But we know the works of justice and mercy, truth and peace we must do to be where Christ promises to be, and we can hope that the history of hearing the Word in the church from within that cauldron of living and dying may continue in our own history.

We have rehearsed again some of the features of personal significance because the setting in which we live today as we listen to this particular text constitutes a special challenge to our personal contexting. The overwhelming mood of sociality in all talk of contextualization, linked with the nature of corporate peril and promise in the culture of the late twentieth century, together with our embarrassments about the personal import of Christological singularity, makes the personal significance of John 14:6 all the more in need of attention.

The way Christ has made to God is *for me.* Christ lived and died and rose again for my sins. To know that is so, and to accept it in faith, is not to perish in the wilderness but to find one's way home. To know the truth is to be free for life (John 8:32). For those who have not found this path, the personal Word spoken in this text is a very special kind of convincing. Here is *the* Truth claim, the acceptance of which is Life itself. Convincing, therefore, is *conversion,* the radical turn in the trail that puts our feet on the new Way. Seeing the sign to this turning and deciding that it is the wrong way is the mood of modernity. The sign gives offense to a pluralist and secular society. Yet we have to do here with the very Center of the Story and our relationship to it. To choose the Way is to refuse the conventional cultural wisdom, to choose not to be conformed to this world but to be "transformed by the renewal of your mind" (Rom. 12:2).

For those who are already on the Way but grow weary in the passage or stumble along it, the personal Word here is one of conviction given to a truth already known and assented to, which brings new vitality, life given to spent energies and faltering feet. The gospel truth becomes an existential truth, just as a first convincing becomes an evangelical truth. Therefore the personal appropriation of scandalous particularity can be either conversion or conviction.

Yet the richness of this passage entails its universality as well as its particularity. Here too is a personal Word that is spoken in a very different way, a pointing done in a different direction. The one who confesses Christ as the Way to all Truth and Life must own truth and life wherever they are found. That means following Christ out from the Way into the way he also makes through the wilderness where the world is sustained on its course by every act of justice and mercy, light and life. Not to follow this world's way is to desert the Way. To keep company with Christ in the world is to minister to him in the suffering humanity of our time and place, feeding the hungry, visiting the prisoner, clothing the naked, doing justice, making peace. Christ makes this way also to the Father's house and those who reach it will do so by following him.

To hear this Word in John 14:6 has very practical and personal consequences. It means seeking out the signs of Christ's presence in the world among the hungry, naked, poor, and imprisoned, and in those who minister to these last and least, being alongside them and serving them by sharing in the merciful struggle for justice against hunger, poverty, and the chains of oppression. It also means being in dialogue with those of other religions or of no religion who in their teaching and actions show a sense of the transcendent claim upon them for these concerns and acts, and an awareness of the content of truth that makes life livable. The pressure of the particularity in this text explodes outward, driving the believer to affirm and to practice its universality.

And its richness takes us another step into personal significance. To bend every effort to follow Christ on this path of service in the world, to obey the Samaritan "rule of the road," in solidarity with the sufferer, and self-abnegation for the neighbor in need, is to find soon enough something about ourselves. As Luther sought to follow the mandates of service and self-denial, so those in this time and place confront the law of righteousness in the maelstrom of human suffering in the public arena rather than in the disciplines and ministrations of the monastery. Here the law is our schoolmaster teaching us the ambiguity of our motives, the failure of our will to serve, the power of our own self-will and self-delusion. We do not keep company with Christ, but abandon him. In such a knowledge that comes from involvement in the struggles against suffering, the law becomes our teacher, our schoolmaster. We learn in its classroom that justification is only by grace received in faith. So we are drawn back again to the particularity in the passage just when we experience its universal claims. The life with Christ comes in the knowledge of Christ as the way to God's house, by grace received in faith. In Christ alone is the final light and life—for me. And because it is offered to me, the believer will want it for others. So rises the passion for mission in which the Story is told so that others may see and, seeing light, have life.

But for me and for them there is a Word of universal hope that saves from self-righteous satisfaction and the fury that so often accompanies a convinced particularity. Here is an expansive hope that will not let those who hear and believe gather this treasure to themselves and consign to the night the multitudes that do not hear, for our lack of saying or for saying it wrongly. Here the eschatological meeting with Christ keeps the particularity firm—only in the knowledge of truth in Christ is life in Christ—but situates it within the universal stretch of divine love that reaches out with the gospel to pilgrims wherever they are on their march toward the end. So I must learn charity as well as have urgency in the personal meeting with this text. And charity in both senses: for myself to confess Christ if not known and to be convinced of the confession when known, and for myself to share with others the Good News that leads to life.

CONCLUSION

We have sought in the preceding exegesis to provide a laboratory in which we can test a thesis about the authority and interpretation of Scripture. In it we have used various instruments necessary for such an inquiry: internal and external hermeneutics, common, critical, canonical, and contextual senses, the Christological center and the gospel substance as guides to meaning, transformative, translative, transitive, trajective, and traductive approaches to significance, both social and personal.

Speaking of the specifics of this inquiry in the language of narrative, we may say that the exegesis of John 14:6 is the story of a journey that begins with the commonsense reading of the text from within an inclusive church formed from a multiple-contexted world. This sense declares Christ to be the path to God with the treasures of truth and life given in God's house. The understanding of the text's meaning is enlarged by a critical sense that reinforces the centrality of the Way with its epexegetical truth and life, and shows the historical conditions for claims to particularity, and the literary structure and rhythm in which it is made. The full meaning of the text and its truths are disclosed when it is read within the canon as a whole, with the gospel substance and the Christological center as orientation points. Here emerges a meaning and truth that joins a latent universality to its patent particularity, indicating that the Way of Christ is joined to the world's Noachic way with its own truth and light appropriate to its anticipatory stage, and to Israel's path with its special preparatory truth and light. A canonical reading also requires the universality/particularity of an eschatological evangel to illumine the text's own double scandal. So the meaning presses toward the text's significance in the context of today's peril and promise with its raised awareness of multiple faith options and their relation to suffering and hope. So the translation of its universality into comradeship and dialogue with worldviews that strive to make and keep human life human. So too the transformation of the world's question by the Way's with its offensive particularity. And so again the projection toward a fuller meaning of the text in the understanding of a particularity/universality in and beyond time. The journey of exegesis ends when the interpreter hears the personal Word for invitation home and for the turning with Christ to the path that makes its way into the world of suffering and hope.

The pastor-in-the-writer exclaims at the close of this trek: This long and complex trail for the exegesis of one verse of Scripture! Is this what is expected of the preacher who must proclaim the Word each Sunday? Circuitous travel laden with much gear and many maps?

No. Our exegetical inquiry is not a model of weekly sermon preparation. The human circumstances of the preaching context are other than those of the teaching context. Similarly, the purpose of systematics is different from that of homiletics. One point made well to a hearer listening in the receptivity of a worshiping community means infinitely more to the life of faith than a classroom lecture on Christology mistransported to the sanctuary. Yet the pointed homily in the sanctuary cannot do without the systematic inquiry in the study. This exegesis is for that kind of environment, an exegesis cum systematics that follows inferences of the text into the larger theological arena. We shall summarize the connection between the two in the chapter that follows.

Another caution is in order with regard to the relation of exegesis to preaching. Hermeneutics is not homiletics! The art of preaching must take the results of the foundational work in interpretation and mold them into another form. The profoundest grasp of a text will go unheard if it does not find its way into the real life-world of the members of the congregation. This can be a lesson from hermeneutics itself: the meaning of a text requires the move into the significance of a text in the congregation's personal and social setting if it is to reach home. Some preaching, very well attuned, on the other hand, moves far too quickly to it, the text being taken captive by the context. Preaching must be both valid in meaning and vital in significance. The temptation to reductionism in preaching is the same as that in biblical hermeneutics, and yet again in theology. Authentic preaching, exegesis, and systematics all strive to be both faithful and fruitful.

The exposure of theological premises in the labor of exegesis is a contribution that systematic inquiry makes to the pastoral task. Whenever and however a pastor interprets a text, whether done with a minimal or even a nonexistent awareness of the methods of exegesis, some sort of hermeneutical framework is functioning. An uncritical commonsense approach may be at work, and that of a highly individualistic sort, or one exercised with selective ecclesial attention. Or commentary may be piled upon commentary with apparently sophisticated exegetical tools self-confidently wielded, but with no sense of contemporary social contextuality or personal significance. Or a text may be given such a Christological reinterpretation or harnessed so directly to a particular ecclesial construal of the gospel that its common and critical meanings and its contextual significance are left begging. Behind each of these functional hermeneutics may lie as well an unexamined concept of authority and an uncritical doctrine of revelation. If such a pastoral practice were studied self-critically over time, the Bible-believing evangelical might be surprised to discover the extent to which a worldly contextuality with narrow ecclesial credentials can in fact control exegesis. The critical interpreter might also be made aware of how much of the richness of the text discerned by other methods with the help of the rest of the Christian community is bypassed by a parochial "criticism," and how much self-criticism needs yet to be done. Our exercise in exegesis was calculated to bring to consciousness the variety of methods and assumptions that are *in fact* at work in the interpretation by anyone of any text, to force a look at their respective strengths and limitations, to urge a catholicity of interpretation, and to argue for priorities and purposes within the elements of theological authority. Such a venture does take us down the winding trails of systematics cum exegesis and requires us to be familiar with the maps and materials needed for this arduous pilgrimage.

As an exegesis is at the edge of systematics, we move across the line from one to the other in the final chapter. The hermeneutical moves made in the former reappear in the concept of theological authority found in the latter. And the doctrine of revelation presupposed in both the hermeneutics of Scripture and the systematics of church teaching is also at work. We now turn to a summary of the concept of authority that pervades this volume, along with some clues about the doctrine of revelation implied, a subject to be developed in the following volume.

CHAPTER VI

Authority and Systematics

Our review of options in authority uncovered the great variety of points of view within the Christian community, showing how common professions of allegiance to Scripture (or other standards) can be quite diverse because of differing frameworks of interpretation. A proposal for the interpretation of Scripture, the source of authority in this systematics, followed, with the investigation of internal and external hermeneutics and the application of its principles to exegesis. In the hermeneutical and exegetical inquiries we touched constantly on the larger question of theological authority. The interpretation of the scriptural source made regular use of ecclesial and experiential reference points. Hermeneutics cum exegesis furnished us therefore with a microcosm of the issues of theological authority. We shall now follow the lines established therein out beyond the biblical center to their larger implications for systematic theology. The pursuit of "the lines" from "the center" is more than metaphor. In accord with our perspectival union of the visual with the verbal, we shall attempt to portray in lines and circles the relationship of biblical hermeneutics to a concept of authority in theological systematics.

Exegesis

The practice of systematics (S) and exegesis (E) take place along the line of movement identified by the arrows of perspective. At point E the interpreter (I) enters the circle of Scripture, attending

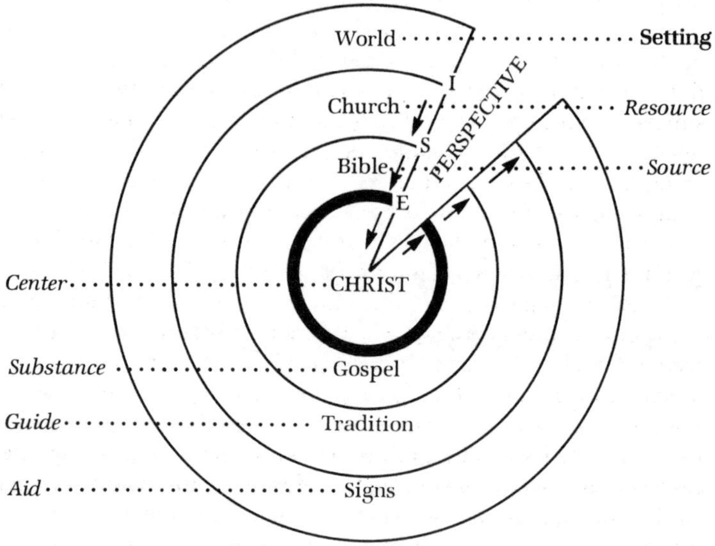

to a text within its canonical compass. We orient our work in it toward the gospel substance and the Christological center. Yet our point of entry to the canon and the text, and toward the substance and center, is established by the perspective that proceeds from the world through the church. We are of the world in the influences brought to bear by our personal and social setting on the reading of the text, and draw from the world critical tools for the investigation of the text. Our perspective is the situational angle of vision from which we view the text. The exegetical journey along its lines is further shaped by the resources of the community of faith with its tradition, inclusive in time and catholic in place. Special attention is given within this ecumenical reach to the worldly signs of suffering and hope that provide a hermeneutical locale for the interpreter and the community reading the text in perspectival context. Thus in the internal hermeneutical question for the meaning of John 14:6 in its common, critical, and canonical senses, we attend to "what it says," "what it meant," "how it works," "whose it is," and "what it meant to mean" as these are accessible to us in a worldly perspective enlarged and refined by ecclesial resources and oriented to the substance and center of Scripture.

The same act of interrelationship goes on as the exegetical task moves into its external hermeneutical phase, the reach for the contextual sense of John 14:6, its social and personal significance. The arrows now proceed from the source through the bridging work of the resource to the setting along the perspectival line. Here is the translation of the text in narrative idiom into the context of suffering and hope, according to the motifs of liberation and reconciliation. Yet the dynamics of the hermeneutical process will bring the translation itself under scrutiny. The turn toward the text entails the transformation of contextual questions by the text's own question. As a result, the fact of suffering is opened out toward the fact of sin, and the word of hope is joined by the word of faith. A responsible social contextualization may carry with it an enrichment of our understanding of the gospel substance, as in the trajection of church teaching further along the line of tradition, touching the issues of both particularity and universality raised by the Johannine text. The fruit of faithful personal contextualization is in the interior reality and individual commitment of the interpreter to the radical particularity and radical universality of Christ as the way, truth, and life. And so the journey continues, a "hermeneutical circulation" from setting through resource to source, source through resource to setting, yet always in relation to a "hermeneutical orientation" to the center.

Assembling these elements and their interrelationships, we come to a fuller definition of *exegesis.* Exegesis is the employment of hermeneutical principles for understanding the meaning and significance of a biblical text: the Scripture principle as source of authority read in the light of its substance, the gospel, and center, Jesus Christ, and interpreted in its common, critical, canonical, and contextual senses; the church principle as resource according to its guide, the tradition of the gospel; the world principle as setting with the signs of Christ as aid and perspective as aim.

Systematics

Systematics is the articulation of Christian belief "in the round" for the church in a given historical context. Like exegesis it looks for both the *meaning* and the *significance* of a text. But in this case the text is a teaching of the church rather than a passage of Scripture. Its meaning is the doctrine that emerges in catholic judgment, and its significance is the theological outworking of that meaning in contextual idiom and implication.

In our visualization we now locate the theological interpreter at the rim of the next concentric ring beyond the exegete. S is the task of teaching carried out in the church that is founded on and oriented by the trajectory of doctrine as tradition. This inner line of the teaching tradition parallels the biblical inner orb of the gospel. It is the church's effort over time to state and interrelate the essentials of Christian belief. As the ecclesial resource, ministerial to magisterial Scripture, the teaching tradition is always accountable to the gospel as discerned by faithful exegesis. Its unfinished nature, as corrigible and extendable, is suggested by the broken lines that continue the historical momentum. Doctrine develops. The theological interpreter therefore lives at this juncture of givenness and openness, and within its tension.

In the exposition of a Christian teaching—for example, the incarnation—the work of systematic theology begins with attention to its inherited doctrinal formulations and their interrelationship with other classical beliefs in the orb of tradition. The arrow of interpretation moves from there to the test points of the biblical source, as established by exegetical inquiry. This movement from systematics to exegesis, like the exegetical pilgrimage itself, is along a line of perspective that comes from the historical context of the interpreter, as it is received and in turn shaped by the Christian community. Self-awareness of social and personal context, the formative ecclesial factors, and an ecumenical expansion of these in both width and depth are necessary to the systematic venture. Thus a "critical sense" is at work in systematics in the clarification of doctrine, in both historical inquiry and "critical consciousness," similar in both respects to that employed in the exegetical task. Germane also is a "commonsense" interpretation garnered from the day-to-day work and witness of the church, and a "canonical sense" in the orienting role of tradition, the handed-on lore of community self-identification.

Again, in systematics as in exegesis there is hermeneutical transport of the text into context. "Theology" brings "doctrine" into conscious relationship to cultural setting. Systematic theology does its work with an eye on the full orb of tradition and according to carefully delineated perspectival principles. Thus in this systematics the church doctrine of the incarnation as warranted by its biblical source is translated as a chapter in the narrative of liberation and reconciliation with its vision of hope for a time of suffering. The Word spoken by the church into the world rises out of a solidarity with the *signs* of suffering and hope. Thus the systematic contextualization of Christian teaching seeks for the personal and social significance of the meaning of Christian doctrine.

Transformative as well as translative contextualization takes place in the authority structure and rhythms of systematics. Our seduction by too-easy equivalencies of doctrine and cultural categories is called into account by the movement of the hermeneutical arrow again toward the classical doctrinal statements, and then into the light of Scripture, both read collegially. So the world's questions are challenged by the Word's questions. The liberation of the sufferer from the tyranny of economic, political, and social oppression is deepened by the Word of liberation from the human sin that is its source, and by the work of mercy in Jesus Christ that is its salvation. So too the reconciliation of humans and nature, neighbors and nations is not divorced from the reconciliation of the self with God in an encompassing at-one-ment wrought by Jesus Christ.

In the process of indigenization, Christian belief is viewed from a new angle. In this fresh perspective we may uncover aspects of its formerly unseen meaning. In systematics, as in exegesis, enrichment in the understanding of the text can take place, in this case a development in doctrine. The solid line of the doctrinal trajectory moves a step further and the contextual model of "trajection" joins that of translation and transformation in the interpretive process. The appearance of a variety of perspectives around the orb of authority, therefore, does not constitute random points of entry to Christian texts but is part of a hermeneutical journey toward fuller understanding of those texts. The development of doctrine is of a piece with the Christian narrative itself.

Method

In this chapter we have taken the term *hermeneutics* out of its biblical habitat and used it in occasional reference to the systematic theological task. It does function in theological discussion in this way from time to time, as when "the hermeneutical circle" refers to the interaction between faith/doctrine and culture rather than only to the processes of literary interpretation, biblical or otherwise. However, to respect its literary habitat and to highlight the issue of biblical interpretation addressed in the preceding chapters, we confine the term to its exegetical precincts. The interpretive process in Christian theology, the hermeneutics of systematics, we shall refer to as "theological method," the descriptor that already has currency for this task (albeit with a life of its own that sometimes leads elsewhere).

Theological method, in general, is the manner in which a theological point of view interprets its materials. Method in Christian theology is the way in which Christian belief is explained. Method in systematic Christian theology is a set of stated principles of interpretation applied to the articulation of basic Christian doctrine. Method in this systematic theology is the application of the Scripture, church and world principles of authority, their elements and interrelationships, to the process of interpreting Christian doctrine. The method has been at work in the foregoing review of options in authority, the exposition of biblical authority and interpretation and its exegetical exercise, and in the portrayal of the factors and processes of theological authority. As we summarize the dynamics examined now under the rubric of theological method, the parallels in the exposition of method to the summary definition of exegesis will become immediately apparent.

Systematic theology is work done by a historically shaped Christian interpreter from within the Christian community of a given time and place with received doctrines of the Christian tradition constituting its *guide.* These doctrines are examined in the light of their biblical warrants as perceived through the lens shaped by the church and the culture in which it is situated. In this internal movement the Bible functions as *source* of doctrinal validity—the Scripture principle—the church as *resource*—the church principle—and the world as *setting*—the world principle. In the scrutiny by Scripture, a doctrine is located within the biblical *substance,* the gospel, and is measured by its final norm and biblical *center,* Jesus Christ, as each of these is read from within the church as resource and the world as setting.

Systematic theology aims to relate doctrine to historical context as well as to state it in accord with the biblical text. Its method requires an outward movement from biblical source to cultural setting along the line of *perspective.* Already perspective has functioned implicitly in the inward interpretive movement insofar as its selectivity has shaped the manner in which one views doctrine and biblical text. But in the centripetal phase of theological inquiry doctrine cum culture is held accountable to the biblical standard, its substance and center. That the biblical text is sufficiently free from its ecclesial and cultural context to challenge interpretation, contrary to regnant historicism, is a belief grounded in the doctrine of revelation that underlies this concept of authority and its related method. That the perspectival pilgrimage toward the setting, its centrifugal movement, has a claim upon the interpretation of the biblically tested doctrine is also grounded in the revelation presupposed in this method.

Interpretation entails a process of contextualization (an "external hermeneutics") in which the biblically validated doctrine is translated into situational idiom and issues according to a perspective related to the historical setting. The perspective is itself shaped by the resources of the Christian community and influenced by the biblical source, particularly with respect to the *signs* within the setting. These signs are places in the historical context in which the community of Christ perceives the hidden presence of Christ calling the interpreter to participate in and attend to these indicators of perspective. In this systematics, the perspective that seeks to be faithful to the source and resource and fruitful in the setting is *narrative,* one whose idiom is provided by the motifs of *liberation* and *reconciliation* (bondage and alienation), whose metaphors are *vision* and *light* (reality and night), whose issues are *suffering* and *hope.* The perspectival mode in which both the outward and inward interpretive movement is carried out is an *ecumenical* one.

REVELATION

Theological method presupposes a concept of authority. The concept in turn is based on a doctrine of revelation. At many points in the discussion of authority we exposed its revelatory foundations. The inseparability of the questions of authority and revelation make for much confusion in Christian theology. We have determinedly attempted to honor the integrity of each question, giving this volume over to the concept of authority in its own right. The original plan was to incorporate within it as Part II a complementary section on the doctrine of revelation. However, the detail required for the issue of authority was such that a Part II was deemed too cumbersome for a systematics designed for pastoral purposes. Volume 3, therefore, will be devoted to the distinguishable but inseparable theme of revelation. Nevertheless, we place at the close of this work a transitional section on the doctrinal underpinning of the concept of authority. In line with a theological perspective that finds a place for "vision" we employ a visual aid to suggest the elements in a doctrine of revelation and briefly indicate the meanings to be developed.

This preliminary diagram shows the presuppositional nature of the doctrine of revelation. Viewing the circles of authority in our earlier figure from another angle exposes their revelatory underside. The light of God shines through the lens of Christ as shaped by the aperture of the gospel in the Bible, transmitted through the church in the world to the eye of faith. The distance of each of these to the light shed on and in them, and the power of the Holy Spirit that shaped each of them, establishes their priorities and functions as source, resource, and setting. So too the light of the Holy Spirit opens the eye of faith for the *visio Dei.*

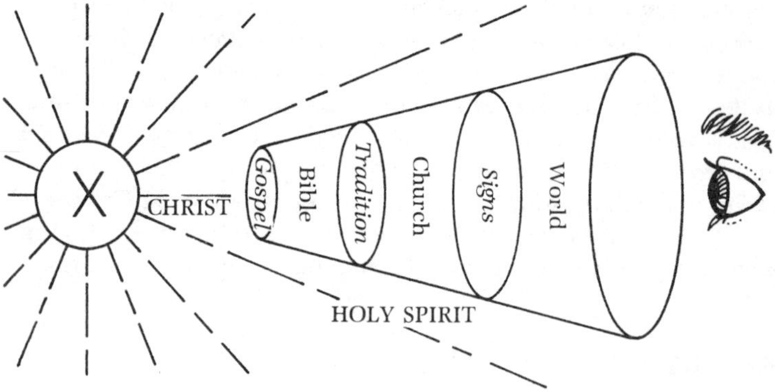

In the next portrayal a linear figure suggests the narrative character of revelation.

In this picture the narrative of revelation follows the course of the narrative of reconciliation. In creation the disclosure commensurate with the deed is the *impartation* of universal light given by God's *intention* in nature and to human nature. The fall is the night that descends on the light even as intention meets the world's rebellion. Yet a ray penetrates the shadowside of creation, as indicated by the broken light of universal revelation that continues. Its sustenance comes from the covenantal action of God, the next chapter of the narrative. Here a Noachic covenant brings providential light and life that makes the human journey forward possible. The Abraham-Moses covenant moves beyond the universal preservative covenant with creation. Election is an act of historical particularity, a special deliverance within the universal Providence signaled by the pillar of fire that leads Israel. With this unique deed comes the unique disclosure, the *prophetic* testimony of the Hebrew Scriptures

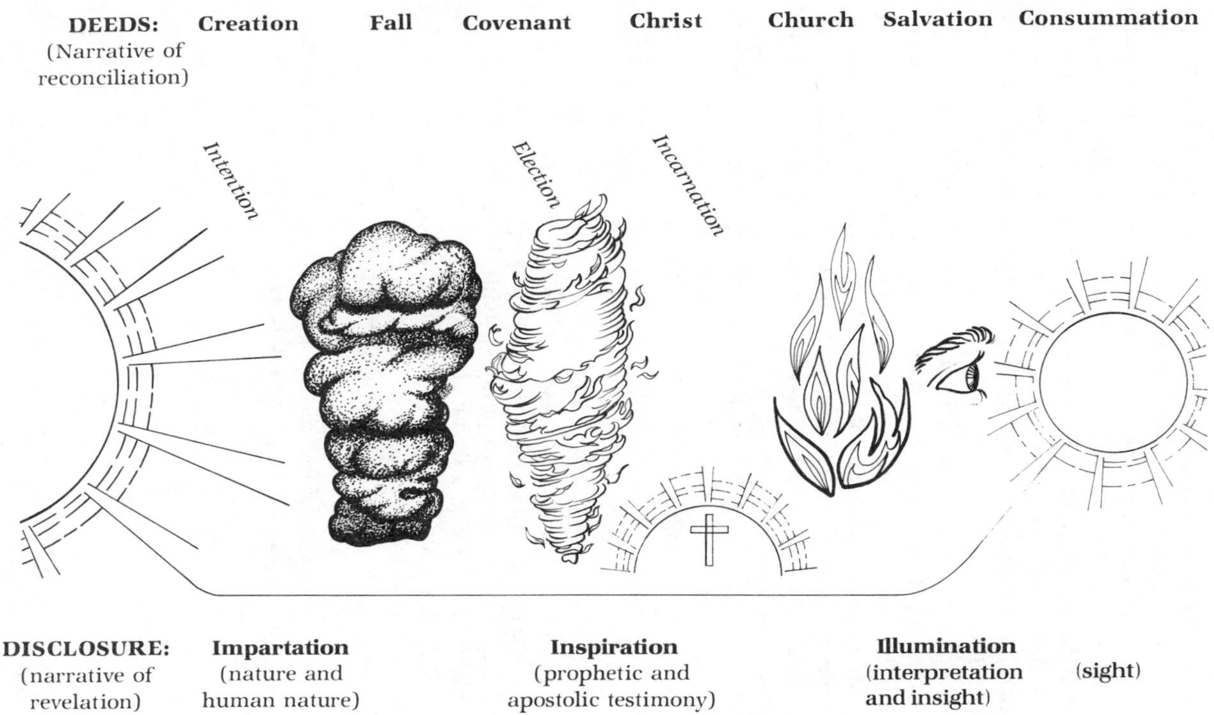
DEEDS:
(Narrative of reconciliation)
Creation
Fall
Covenant
Christ
Church
Salvation
Consummation
Intention
Election
Incarnation
DISCLOSURE:
(narrative of revelation)
Impartation
(nature and human nature)
Inspiration
(prophetic and apostolic testimony)
Illumination
(interpretation and insight)
(sight)

to election's meaning and direction. At the center of the story is the incarnational deed of redemption and light of revelation. The Person and Work of Jesus Christ liberate from sin, evil, and death and reconcile neighbor, nature, and God. The new age dawns. Its rising sun is Jesus Christ. Its "seers" are the *apostolic* community who bear witness to it, and join this new testimony to the writings of the Hebrew people in the Christian canon of New Testament and Old Testament. The power of the Holy Spirit in the seers of the pillar of fire and the horizon light constitute the *inspiration* of Scripture.

The story continues with the descending fires of the Holy Spirit on the day of Pentecost. That power brings the church to be and its light gives the gift of *illumination* to the Christian community. Illumination is commensurate with the catholicity and commitment of those who engage the prophetic apostolic testimony. Multiple perspective enlarges the periphery of vision. Involvement in the signs of *impartation*—the places of truth-seeking and life-giving—allow "ever new light to break from God's holy Word" in the continuing work of *interpretation.* Where illumination convinces a seeker of new truth or convicts a believer of an old one, personal as well as corporate light is given. This limited sight is a penultimate *visio Dei* of the *Visio Dei* (Eph. 3:4). This *insight* on the way looks toward the *sight* given only in the full Day of God.

Our figures and metaphors of revelation draw on the Scripture's own images and suggest ways of interpreting them in a pastoral theology for this time and place. As with the figural usage of the concept of authority, so with its employment in the doctrine of revelation: meaning must be sought in the metaphor, the discursive joined to the affective. The examination of the "truth of the symbol" that belongs with the evocations of "symbolic truth" are the work of systematic theology. In the volume that follows we shall investigate the structure of the doctrine of revelation to which we have alluded in this exposition of the authority of Scripture in the church for the world.

Scripture Index

SUBJECT INDEX

Subject Index

Subject Index